Intrusion Detection with Snort

Jack Koziol

Sams Publishing, 800 East 96th Street, Indianapolis, Indiana 46240

Intrusion Detection with Snort

Copyright © 2003 by Sams Publishing

All rights reserved. No part of this book shall be reproduced, stored in a retrieval system, or transmitted by any means, electronic, mechanical, photocopying, recording, or otherwise, without written permission from the publisher. No patent liability is assumed with respect to the use of the information contained herein. Although every precaution has been taken in the preparation of this book, the publisher and author assume no responsibility for errors or omissions. Nor is any liability assumed for damages resulting from the use of the information contained herein.

International Standard Book Number: 1-578-70281-X

Library of Congress Catalog Card Number: 2002110728

Printed in the United States of America

First Printing: May 2003

06 05 04 03   5 4 3

Trademarks

All terms mentioned in this book that are known to be trademarks or service marks have been appropriately capitalized. Sams Publishing cannot attest to the accuracy of this information. Use of a term in this book should not be regarded as affecting the validity of any trademark or service mark.

Warning and Disclaimer

Every effort has been made to make this book as complete and as accurate as possible, but no warranty or fitness is implied. The information provided is on an "as is" basis.

Bulk Sales

Sams Publishing offers excellent discounts on this book when ordered in quantity for bulk purchases or special sales. For more information, please contact:

U.S. Corporate and Government Sales
1-800-382-3419
corpsales@pearsontechgroup.com

For sales outside of the U.S., please contact:

International Sales
+1-317-428-3341
international@pearsontechgroup.com

Acquisitions Editors
Linda Bump
Jenny Watson

Development Editor
Mark Cierzniak

Managing Editor
Charlotte Clapp

Project Editor
George E. Nedeff

Copy Editor
Margo Catts

Indexer
Kelly Castell

Proofreader
Leslie Joseph

Technical Editors
Stephen Halligan
Bryce Alexander

Team Coordinator
Vanessa Evans

Multimedia Developer
Dan Scherf

Designer
Gary Adair

Page Layout
Julie Parks

For Paul Noeldner, who first aroused my interest in computing

Contents at a Glance

Table of Contents

About the Author

Jack Koziol is the Information Security Officer at a major Chicago-area financial institution, responsible for security enterprise-wide. Previously, he has held information security positions at an online health care company and a point-of-care Internet-based pharmacy. Jack has written for *Information Security* magazine, and released several whitepapers on intrusion detection. He teaches the CISSP and "Hack and Defend" courses.

Jack has architected, maintained, and managed Snort and other IDS technologies in large production environments since 1998. He has also written Snort signature sets designed for specific applications.

Acknowledgments

First and foremost I would like to thank my parents, Jeff and Arlene, for teaching me that "You can do anything you put your mind to" is more than a hollow cliché. I'd also like to thank my brother, Charlie, for inspiring me with his spirit of adventure.

I would also like to thank the folks at Pearson Education for providing me with the opportunity to work on this project, and for guiding me through some rough waters. I wish the best to my acquisitions editors Linda Bump, Jenny Watson, and Stacey Beheler, my development editors Lisa Thibault and Mark Cierzniak, and everyone else who worked diligently behind the scenes to make this book a reality.

The quality and factual consistency of this book would have suffered without the criticism and compliments of my technical editors, Steve Halligan and Bryce Alexander. These guys are tremendously knowledgeable and we are sure to hear great things from them in the future.

Much thanks indeed to the Snort team for developing the world's best IDS. Overwhelming thanks from myself and the community at large for releasing your hard work under the GPL and keeping true to the open source ideology.

Finally, I would like to thank all of the people who patiently waited for me to emerge from hibernation after six months of ignoring birthdays, social gatherings, and family events. In random order: the Koziols, the Beckers, the Spritzers, the Jacobsons, the Noeldners, the Golas, the Hoffmans, Ian Lange, DJ Carlon, Ryan Van Den Elzen, Darren Dalasta, Shawn Swenson, Matt Geesaman, Quasi, and of course, Dinesh.

Last but never least, thanks to Tracy Hoffman for putting up with me.

We Want to Hear from You!

As the reader of this book, *you* are our most important critic and commentator. We value your opinion and want to know what we're doing right, what we could do better, what areas you'd like to see us publish in, and any other words of wisdom you're willing to pass our way.

You can email or write me directly to let me know what you did or didn't like about this book—as well as what we can do to make our books stronger.

Please note that I cannot help you with technical problems related to the topic of this book, and that due to the high volume of mail I receive, I might not be able to reply to every message.

When you write, please be sure to include this book's title and author as well as your name and phone or email address. I will carefully review your comments and share them with the author and editors who worked on the book.

Email: networking@samspublishing.com
Mail: Mark Taber
         Associate Publisher
         Sams Publishing
         800 East 96th Street
         Indianapolis, IN 4624xvii0 USA

Reader Services

For more information about this book or others from Sams Publishing, visit our Web site at www.samspublishing.com. Type the ISBN (excluding hyphens) or the title of the book in the Search box to find the book you're looking for.

Introduction

MY GOAL IN WRITING *INTRUSION DETECTION WITH SNORT* has been to deliver the first comprehensive guide to using Snort in a real-world environment. Having worked in the field of intrusion detection in both small and large organizations, and having used a wide variety of intrusion detection technologies, I felt it was necessary to provide a book that covers one of the best kept secrets in the security industry—Snort.

Snort is often referred to as the security practitioner's Swiss army knife, and with good reason: Snort can be a practical solution for intrusion detection in a seemingly infinite amount of environments. Snort's flexibility, which has achieved a huge installation base worldwide (by some counts over 100,000 deployments), is also somewhat of a bear to manage. Snort is notoriously difficult to install, maintain, and use. The sheer number of settings, signatures, and associated applications that are required to work in concert with it can make the first-time Snort experience decidedly negative.

Frustrated users resort to costly and closed source IDSs, lose the ability to configure an IDS to suit specific needs, and give up on intrusion detection entirely, because the user lacks serious financial resources.

Like most open source applications, Snort's developers concentrate on adding new features, or fixing bugs rather than focus on the documentation. While there is definitely a large amount of documentation on Snort, it is often inadequate and assumes the reader has some prior experience with Snort or Intrusion Detection (usually as a profession). The goal of this book is to arm you with an arsenal of open source intrusion detection tools centered on Snort.

Snort makes an excellent Intrusion Detection System (IDS), but this is where it ends. It lacks an easy-to-use management GUI, has no method of sending alerts via pager or email, and presents a disorganized method of displaying alerting information. Snort's developers have concentrated on making it the best damn IDS possible, but left the rest for others to create. Fortunately there are hundreds if not thousands of ancillary applications, tools, and scripts to use with Snort. Finding the correct application, tool, or script and then getting it to work with Snort is increasingly difficult. In this book, I have done the legwork for you by covering the most popular and most effective ancillary applications used with Snort.

An alert management GUI, ACID, is covered in great detail. Two methods (swatch and syslog-ng) of generating real-time alerts are covered. Other signature management applications, such as IDS Policy Manager, will help you work with Snort. Finally, some advanced intrusion prevention tools, such as SnortSam, are covered in the final chapter.

This book would not be complete without a meticulous discussion of how Snort works from the inside out. Chapter 3, "Dissecting Snort," is dedicated to Snort's internal functions and sparsely documented components, such as the preprocessors that dictate how Snort behaves.

After you have developed strong working knowledge of how Snort works, I dedicated Chapter 4, "Planning for the Snort Installation," to guide you through difficult planning tasks that are often overlooked and that cause Snort deployment to fail. Important factors are taken into consideration, such as sensor placement and incident response procedure development. Chapter 5, "The Foundation—Hardware and Operating Systems," walks you through the Hardware and OS decisions, and describes a novel way of protecting sensors by modifying a simple Cat 5 cable.

The core of the book, Chapters 6 through 9, is a detailed installation and troubleshooting guide for deploying Snort in both the home-network and enterprise-class environments. Getting Snort to work in tiered topology that includes sensors, servers, and consoles is explained in detail. Installing Snort on a variety of platforms, including Windows and Linux, is covered as well.

At this point you will have a functioning open source IDS, but there are many activities that remain in order to have a truly effective IDS. A major thorn in the side of any IDS is false positives (also know as false alerts). When Snort is installed in its default configuration, it is likely to generate a veritable flood of false positives. The amount of false positives can cause the first-time Snort user to become insanely frustrated. Reducing the amount of false positives by tuning Snort is imperative, and is described in detail in Chapter 10, "Tuning and Reducing False Positives." Another important configuration task, getting Snort to send out alerts in real time, is covered in Chapter 11, "Real-Time Alerting."

Chapters 12 through 14 deal with more advanced issues, such as writing custom Snort signatures (termed *rules),* upgrading Snort, and using Snort as an Intrusion Prevention device. One of the greatest assets of Snort that separates it from closed source, commercial, IDSs is the ability to write super-granular rules. These custom-written rules can be used to monitor disallowed or malicious behavior specific to your organization, such as TFTP traffic heading out from your Web server to a suspicious IP address in a foreign country. The flexible and granular rules quasi-language is also a major factor in Snort's widespread acceptance (any knowledgeable person can write up rules and share them with the Snort community).

Finally, the two appendixes serve as a reference for the existing Snort rules and cover some of the most common installation and deployment issues.

When you walk away after reading this book, you will have created a bulletproof IDS that rivals and sometimes surpasses a multi-million dollar commercial IDS.

1

Intrusion Detection Primer

INTRUSION DETECTION SYSTEMS (IDSs) HAVE EVOLVED into a critical component in secure network architecture. Nonetheless, IDSs are a foreign concept to many security practitioners and systems administrators. This chapter offers a brief synopsis of intrusion detection, and illustrates why IDS is an important technology.

An *Intrusion Detection System* is any hardware, software, or combination of thereof that monitors a system or network of systems for malicious activity. An oft-cited analogy for Intrusion Detection Systems is that of a burglar alarm. With a burglar alarm, sensors are normally placed at common points of entry and exit. Logically, this strategy focuses on what it deems the weakest points in the structure and thus the most vulnerable to an intruder's attack. When protecting something of great value, you achieve more intensive monitoring with the use of sensitive sensors that can detect motion or even changes in temperature and air pressure. Data gathered from the sensors is subsequently delivered to an individual who then must determine the nature of the threat and act accordingly. IDSs operate with a similar imperative in the networked world. Sensors are placed at points of entry where attack is likely. The more valuable the information resource is, the more it is monitored with increasingly sensitive sensors. Just like a burglar alarm, IDSs remain dependent on a human operator to act on the data they collect.

An IDS is a critical component in a defense-in-depth information security strategy. *Defense in depth* is the method of protecting information resources with a series of over-lapping defensive mechanisms. The thought is that if one defense should somehow fail, others will be in line to thwart an attack.

A combination of hardened hosts, secured routers, correctly placed firewalls, and an entire host of additional equipment is required to provide defense in depth. An IDS permeates this network infrastructure and monitors it for misuse. Novices to Intrusion Detection sometimes make the false assumption that an IDS is a total security solution in itself. Think of it in terms of the burglar alarm: If you were to place a stack of gold coins on a busy city sidewalk and protect it with only an alarm, the gold would quickly vanish. A secured structure is needed in addition to the alarm. The same holds true for the IDS. A properly configured security infrastructure must be in place for the IDS to be effective.

Intrusion Detection Systems are the only means of detecting and responding to hostile attacks in a reasonable amount of time. IDSs allow for the complete monitoring of modern networks, giving an organization real-time insight into threats to information systems. Without an IDS, an organization could be repeatedly attacked and compromised without anyone realizing.

IDSs are a non-invasive technology. If properly configured, they cannot harm or disrupt business as usual. Other security technologies (like firewalls) can be single points of failure that add significant risk when implemented.

This chapter examines the different genres of IDS. Next is a cursory walk through a typical attack that some of the common categories of traffic generate. Finally, for the sake of objectivity, is a review of some of the problems with IDSs.

IDSs Come in Different Flavors

IDSs have matured to the point where there are essentially two types of IDSs: Network IDS (NIDS) and Host IDS (HIDS). Host IDS resides on one machine and monitors that specific machine for intrusion attempts. More popular is the Network IDS, which monitors traffic as it flows through a network en route to other hosts. One type is not better than the other; each is appropriate for specific situations.

Host-Based IDS

Host-based IDSs (HIDSs) monitor for attacks at the operating system, application, or kernel level. HIDSs have access to audit logs, error messages, service and application rights, and any resource available to the monitored host. Additionally, HIDSs can be application aware. They have knowledge about what normal application data looks like, and what abnormal data looks like. They can monitor application data as it is being decoded and manipulated by the actual application. The benefits that HIDSs enjoy stem from this privileged access to the host.

HIDSs are better able to determine whether an attack was successful. Malicious traffic looks remarkably similar to normal traffic, for this reason NIDSs are notorious for creating false alerts. On the other hand, HIDSs are more accurate at detecting genuine intrusions because they do not generate the same volume of false positives as a NIDS.

False Positives and False Negatives

When an alert is generated that is due to normal activity, it is termed a false positive. False positives are a major thorn in the side of the IDS analyst because they waste valuable time and resources. Tuning the IDS in a manner that reflects the network reduces false positives to a manageable level.

An IDS should have a healthy amount of false positives. If the IDS is not generating any false positives, it is likely that false negatives are occurring. A false negative is the inverse of a false positive; it is a situation where the IDS has missed a legitimate attack. It is preferable to have an IDS generating background noise due to false positives than to miss real attacks. For this reason, it is best to err on the side of caution and tune the IDS to set off some false positives to avert false negatives.

HIDSs leverage their privileged access to monitor specific components of a host that are not readily accessible to other systems. Specific components of operating systems, such as passwd files in Unix and the Registry in Windows, can be watched for misuse. There is too great a risk in making these types of components available to a NIDS to monitor.

HIDSs are in tune with the host they reside upon. They have deep knowledge that is available only to an IDS that actually resides on the same computer that is being monitored. Therefore, HIDSs can have specific knowledge about the host and the type of activity that is normal for it. Traffic sent to the host might appear perfectly normal to a NIDS, but be recognized by the HIDS as abnormal and malicious. For this reason, HIDSs can discover attacks that a NIDS would not be able to.

Host-based IDSs do have some significant disadvantages. Because they reside on the monitored host, they have a limited view of the entire network topology. HIDSs cannot detect an attack that is targeted for a host that doesn't have an HIDS installed. An attacker can compromise a machine that lacks an HIDS and then use legitimate access to a protected machine, and the HIDS would be none the wiser. To monitor for intrusion attempts, the HIDS has to be placed on every critical host. This becomes cost prohibitive as the number of hosts critical to the organization grows. Running IDSs at the host level also means that you need to have an HIDS version available for every operating system you need to protect. If you have obscure versions of operating systems at your organization or run legacy systems, you may not be able to provide the coverage even if your organization can afford it.

HIDSs that rely on audit logs and error messages are essentially detecting attacks after they have occurred, which can lead to all sorts of problems. Some attacks can compromise the host before data is written to a log, effectively disabling the HIDS. HIDSs rely on the host to facilitate communication to the intrusion analyst; therefore any attack that can disable the host outright goes unnoticed.

Network-Based IDS

Network IDSs (NIDSs) are placed in key areas of network infrastructure and monitor traffic as it flows to other hosts. Network based IDS has grown in popularity and outpaced the acceptance of HIDS. An IDS is more cost effective than an HIDS because it can protect a large swath of network infrastructure with one device. With NIDS, the intrusion analyst has a wide-angle view of what is happening in and around the network. Monitoring for specific hosts or attackers can be increased or decreased with relative ease.

A NIDS can be more secure and less prone to outages than an HIDS. The NIDS should be run on a single hardened host that supports only services related to intrusion detection, making it more difficult to disable. NIDSs lose the disadvantages of relying on the integrity and availability of the monitored host, and are subsequently less prone to unobserved outages.

By not relying on the security of the host, NIDSs are not as prone to evidence destruction as HIDSs. Because NIDSs capture data and store it on a different machine, an attacker cannot easily remove the evidence of an attack.

NIDSs do have some disadvantages inherent in their design. NIDSs must be extraordinarily proficient at sucking up large amounts of network traffic to remain effective. As network traffic increases exponentially over time, the NIDS must be able to grab all this traffic and interpret it in a timely manner. Currently, NIDSs must be carefully placed and tuned to avoid situations where packet loss can occur. This can often require placing several NIDSs downstream from a core router or switch.

NIDSs are also vulnerable to IDS evasion techniques. Hackers have discovered numerous methods for hiding malicious traffic in ways an NIDS cannot detect.

What is a "Hacker"?

The term "hacker" has become such an overused media buzz word that it has lost all meaning. No one really knows the true origin of the term. It is speculated that the original hackers were expert programmers who were employed to reduce the size of programs to fit into the limited core space of early computers. Generally these were the people who would know the system so well that they could write directly in machine code. Thus they were able to "hack" away at the code to improve it and make it fit into the core. Eventually the term was used to describe a person who attempted to reverse engineer a system—be it a car, a phone system, or computer network—to learn more about it. Hackers would make their own unsanctioned improvements and exploit a system to make it do things it was not intended to do. In the 70s these elements of the hacker culture became increasingly interested in the U.S. phone system. They figured out ways to exploit the system to make free calls, reroute phone calls, and sometimes create mischief. Everything changed when the *Washington Post* ran an article about these phone hackers. The long distance phone industry took steps to prosecute these wiley hackers. In turn, the act of hacking was branded as a disreputable act, and the public began an infatuation with hackers that has not ended to this day.

The information security and hacker communities have attempted to distinguish between persons involved with legal, ethical security research and people out to cause harm. The terms "ethical hacker," "penetration tester," "white hat," and "security researcher" are used interchangeably to refer to hackers interested in reverse engineering systems and discovering security flaws. The terms "malicious hacker," "cracker," and "black hat" are used to describe hackers attacking systems in an attempt to gain unauthorized access. There is also another term, "gray hat," which refers to those that ride the fence between security research and unauthorized hacking. A gray hat may hold a legitimate information security position at a reputable firm, but after business hours spends time attacking information systems from home.

In this book, the term "hacker" is chiefly used to describe persons attacking your network. Any further discussions over the correct use of this term or any other hacker term are avoided.

One such method takes advantage of the process that occurs when a network connection exceeds the maximum allowable size for a packet. When this situation occurs, the data is split up and sent in multiple packets. This is called *fragmentation*. When the host receives these fragmented packets, it must reassemble them to correctly interpret the data. Different operating systems reassemble the packets in different orders: Some start with the first packet and work forward, whereas others do the reverse. Reassembly order is insignificant if the fragments are consistent and do not overlap as expected. If the reassembly overlaps, the results will differ from each other, depending on the reassembly order. Choosing the correct reassembly order to detect a fragmentation attack can be problematic for NIDSs.

Another method of IDS evasion is far simpler. Because a NIDS captures traffic as it traverses a network, security measures intended to thwart eavesdropping can prevent a NIDS from doing its job. Encrypted traffic is often used to secure Web communication and is increasingly becoming the norm for delivering confidential information. Attackers can use this to their advantage by sending attacks in encrypted sessions, effectively hiding their exploit from the NIDS's watchful eye. Some NIDSs support features that decrypt traffic before the IDS engine interprets it, but this opens up a new vulnerability that some organizations may not be willing to accept.

A Mixed Approach

Both intrusion detection models can be an effective component of a defense in depth when properly configured and maintained. An important point to remember is that you don't have to choose one flavor of IDS exclusively. A NIDS has advantages that enable it to protect large portions of network infrastructure reasonably well. An HIDS offers fine-tuned protection for mission-critical hosts.

Most organizations start their foray into intrusion detection with an NIDS. After growing accustomed to intrusion detection they gradually place HIDSs on hosts that are critical to day-to-day operation. This methodology gives complete intrusion detection coverage for an organization.

Methods of Detecting Intrusions

IDSs have several methods of detecting intrusions at their disposal. Certain techniques are better suited to monitoring for different types of intrusions; IDSs are likely to employ more than one variety of detection.

Signature Detection

Signature detection identifies security events that attempt to use a system in a non-standard means. Known representations of intrusions are stored in the IDS and are then compared to system activity. When a known intrusion matches an aspect of system use, an alert is raised to the IDS analyst.

Known representations of intrusions are termed *signatures*. Signatures must be created to exactly match the characteristics of a specific intrusion and no other activity to avert false positives. In an NIDS, a specific signature is created that matches either the protocol elements or content of network traffic. When the NIDS detects traffic that matches the signature, an alert is crafted. The Large ICMP Packet Remote Denial of Service (DoS) attack for Internet Security System's BlackIce Defender is an easy-to-understand example.

BlackIce Defender is a common personal firewall for home and small business use. A security researcher found that sending an unusually large ICMP packet to a machine protected by BlackIce would cause that machine's remote host to crash. To detect attacks against BlackIce, a signature was created to trigger on any ICMP packet over 10,000 bytes. ICMP packets over this size are unusual in nature and this signature does not create an overwhelming number of false positives.

Signature detection is the most accurate technique of detecting known attacks. When a signature matches an intrusion, an alert is always generated. In addition, almost every type of malicious traffic can be identified by a unique signature. Therefore, most malicious traffic can be caught by an IDS using signature detection. There are certain categories of attacks that have proven elusive to signature detection, but they are a small minority and can be detected by other means.

Signature detection does have some limitations. Signature detection has no knowledge of the intention of activity that matches a signature; hence it triggers alerts even if the traffic is normal. Normal traffic often closely resembles suspicious traffic; hence NIDSs that use signature detection are likely to generate false positives.

Signature detection requires previous knowledge of an attack to generate an accurate signature. This fact makes an IDS that utilizes signature detection as its only means of monitoring blind to unknown attacks or attacks without a precise signature. In some cases, the modification of a single bit is enough to cause an IDS to miss an attack.

New attacks require new signatures, and the rising tide of vulnerabilities ensures that the signature bases will grow over time. Every packet must be compared to each signature for the IDS to detect intrusions. This can become computationally expensive as the amount of bandwidth increases. When the amount of bandwidth overwhelms the capabilities of the IDS, it causes the IDS to miss or drop packets. In this situation, false negatives are a distinct possibility.

Even with the issues with signature detection, IDSs that utilize it are the most prominent and reliable on the market today.

Anomaly Detection

Anomaly detection detects misuse by measuring a norm over time and then generating an alert when patterns differ from the norm. Anomaly detection comes in many different forms.

Anomaly detection can be used at the application level to monitor the activity of users. The anomaly detection IDS gathers a set of data from the system activity of the user. This baseline dataset is then deemed "normal use." If the user deviates from the normal use pattern, an alarm is raised. If a user had been logging into a system during business hours for a period of months, and then suddenly had a streak of logins at 3:00 a.m., the anomaly detection IDS would raise a flag.

Anomaly detection can be used to monitor for privilege escalation attacks. If a normal user account does not have privileged access to an important operating system file, such as the SAM file in Windows operating systems, but is seen to be accessing it readily, the IDS determines that potentially damaging activity has taken place and generates an alert.

An anomaly detection IDS is more adroit at catching sophisticated attackers. An attacker can replicate a signature matching IDS in a controlled environment. The attacker can test out potential intrusions and discover which ones the signature matching IDS will notice. With an anomaly detection IDS, however, the attacker cannot predetermine which intrusive activity will go unnoticed.

The key benefit of anomaly detection IDSs is that they do not rely on having previous knowledge of an attack. As long as the IDS can determine that the attack differs significantly from normal use, it can detect the attack.

Like signature detection, anomaly detection has some limitations as well. The training period presents a problem for this method of monitoring for malicious use. You must assume that the data collected in the baseline dataset is not malicious and is normal activity. If a user stole company secrets every night at 3:00 a.m. when the IDS was gathering baseline data, it would assume that this was normal behavior and never raise an alarm. In this respect, anomaly detection IDSs are prone to false negatives.

Anomaly detection can be prone to a relatively high degree of false positives. Suppose a particular type of traffic is rare, but non-malicious and normal. If this traffic was not captured when the IDS was generating baseline data, a false positive would be generated when the IDS encountered the traffic. This is a major problem, because over time network traffic is composed of significant amounts of randomly occurring rare data. This makes anomaly detection not as accurate and hence not as popular as signature detection.

Integrity Verification

Integrity verification is a simple but highly effective means of monitoring for intruders. It works by means of generating a checksum for every file on a system, and then periodically comparing that checksum to the original file to ensure a change has not occurred. If an unauthorized file change transpires, an alert is generated.

A large number of files on any system regularly change in the course of normal operation. The integrity verification IDS must be carefully tuned to avoid false positives. The checksums need to be reset when legitimate changes occur.

Integrity verification can be used to detect Web page defacements. Attackers often gain access to unpatched external facing Web servers and change the content the Web server displays. An integrity verification IDS could be deployed to create checksums and monitor specific Web page files. When the attacker changes the Web page's content, the checksum verification fails and the appropriate party is notified. The files on an external facing Web site should not change frequently enough to create a deluge of false positives. In addition, the IDS can be configured to automatically rollback the file to its unaltered state.

Integrity verification has some limitations as well. The primary disadvantage with integrity verification technology is that it requires access to sensitive files on the monitored host. This dictates that it be a strictly host-based IDS, meaning that it inherits all the inefficiencies and drawbacks of an HIDS. In addition, the checksums can be altered to match the adulterated original file, rendering the integrity verification IDS useless. Storing checksums on a dedicated, hardened server can reduce the risk of this occurring, but does not completely eliminate it.

Origin of Attacks

Threats to information resources come in a variety of forms. Security of information can be compromised by very simple means. An example is an insider who can walk off with backup tapes of confidential customer information. Although there are many threats to digital infrastructure, this section focuses on network-borne threats that an IDS is designed to monitor for.

Network-based threats can be separated into two categories: internal and external. Network security at most organizations can be compared to an egg: The hard outer shell is somewhat difficult to penetrate, but after the outer shell is breached, the inside is soft, gooey, and offers no protection. This castle-like defense of firewalls, DMZs, hardened hosts, and IDSs makes penetration external to the organization relatively tough. The inside is an entirely different story, with unencrypted confidential communication, hosts not properly maintained, and lax logical security controls that make an attack easy to perpetrate and even harder to detect. A common statistic is that almost 80% of successful attacks are internal.

Attack origins are important to the field of intrusion detection. You must know where attacks are initiating from to deploy intrusion monitoring in the most effective locations.

External Threats

One way of looking at the 80% statistic is that organizations are doing a pretty good job of protecting from external threats. It is likely that the vast majority of *attempted* attacks are orchestrated from the external side and not the internal. The overwhelming majority of these external attacks are unsuccessful, whereas most internal attacks are executed with some degree of success.

This is not to downplay the risks external to an organization. It takes only one small chink in the armor of an external defense to allow significant damage. A single remotely exploitable host, be it a router, firewall, mail server, or any other externally facing device, can cause serious harm. Although the compromised host may not be of great value itself, an attacker can leverage access to the host to penetrate deeper within the security layers. Attackers frequently utilize compromised externally facing hosts to access internal devices that have less stringent security controls.

External security is often overlooked at organizations that feel they are not visible public targets. Small- or medium-sized organizations make the mistake of thinking they are not important enough for a hacker to target them. Individuals often state that they do not have anything worth protecting on their home computer. The fact of the matter is that a good proportion of Internet-based attacks are not aimed at a specific target. A hacker frequently scans the Internet looking for hosts vulnerable to exploit code he or she has previously acquired or developed. In this case, the hacker is chiefly concerned with making use of a new exploit, instead of actively targeting a host. This grab-bag approach is no more likely to yield a major financial institution's ecommerce application than it is some unsuspecting home user's computer.

Responsible Internet Citizenry

You may think that you do not have data that is of interest to a hacker, and you may be right, but you do have something that they do want: an anonymous system from which they can launch attacks to hide their identities. Black hats routinely compromise a chain of systems to route attacks through. Additionally, they install remote attack tools to use your system to orchestrate denial of service attacks. Network security is not just about protecting your data; it is also about being a responsible Internet citizen.

Even if you are not concerned if your system is used to attack others, there are less altruistic reasons why you should be concerned. If your machine is used in a high-profile attack, you may have a hard time convincing law enforcement that you did not perpetrate the attack yourself. Remember, if you are smart enough to detect intrusions, it is likely you have the ability to commit them yourself. Additionally, there may come a day when persons who leave flagrantly insecure systems wide open on the Internet are sued for damages their systems cause in an attack. For these reasons, it is always a good idea to be a responsible Internet citizen and keep externally facing systems secured.

Internal Threats

Internal attacks represent the majority of successful attacks on network infrastructure. Internal attacks can be damaging and far more difficult to discover. One factor that aggravates the situation is company insiders having extensive working knowledge of security controls and ample time to plan an attack. Insiders can leverage the legitimate access they already possess to gain unauthorized additional access to systems.

Internal attacks are more difficult to detect than external attacks. This happens when organizations are not monitoring the inside as heavily as the outside. An internal attack may be the result of an employee gradually accumulating privileged access and information over a period of years or decades.

The internal infrastructure can also be unintentionally opened up to threats by uneducated or unsuspecting employees. Users can compromise internal security through the installation of firewall-defeating Peer to Peer (P2) file sharing and instant messenger applications. Some P2P applications are packaged with spyware or features that silently enable the sharing of the entire hard drive. Proxy-aware instant messengers, such as AOL Instant Messenger, can be used to slice through any open port on a corporate firewall. Modern viruses are bundled with numerous attack payloads that can open a system for the taking. Most non-technical users may be unaware that they are creating a gaping security hole by going about their daily activity.

An IDS on the internal side can be used to detect both intentional internal attacks and corporate policy violations. They can detect the signature of most P2P tools, inappropriate Internet usage, and instant messengers. This is in addition to the expected intrusion monitoring capability. These abilities make an internal IDS an extremely powerful security application.

The line between internal and external is increasingly blurred by corporate partnerships and the extranets that enable them. An attacker can hop from one extranet to another, making the source of an attack difficult to discern. As more and more internal security breaches are discovered, organizations will seek to increase internal security in the future.

Orchestrating an Attack

This section serves as a concise introduction to the genres of suspicious traffic you will encounter when using Snort. It is by no means an attempt to be all-inclusive or technically detailed. There are numerous resources, both in print and online, related to suspicious traffic analysis. If you have yet to develop intensive signature analysis expertise, this section will help you roughly understand the different genres of attack and their associated intent.

Several phases in orchestrating an attack (see Figure 1.1) are generic enough that they apply to most network-based attacks. Whether hackers are randomly searching for systems or targeting a specific company, they follow a tried-and-true methodology.

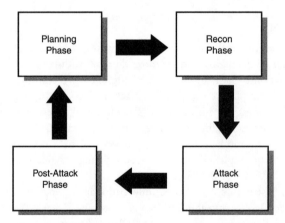

Figure 1.1   Phases of an attack

There is no scripted process hackers must follow; rather they exhibit this pattern because it is the most effective means of orchestrating an attack. If black hats find another more effective method of attacking your network, you can bet they will use it. Acquainting yourself with the methods of the enemy will help you detect the early warning signs of an impending attack and take action to impede it.

Planning Phase

Hackers often plan in advance for an attack on a system. Planning for an attack can take many different forms. The attacker often makes use of the system in its intended manner before making the attack. He may sign up for a brokerage account on an online trading system, or log onto a public FTP server. This type of publicly available legitimate access helps him define the scope and goals of the attack.

After the initial preparation is complete, the hacker decides on the scope of the attack. The attacker may have various goals, including

- Denial of service
- Escalation of legitimate privileges
- Unauthorized access
- Data manipulation

The motivation behind an attack often dictates which of these goals are chosen. A black hat that seeks only revenge or mischief may choose a denial of service attack. These types of attacks in isolation present very little in terms of real reward unless the hacker derives enjoyment from the frustration of others. Denial of service attacks can often be highly visible.

The Reconnaissance Phase

The attacker next gathers information or performs reconnaissance on your network. The attacker carries out a variety of different inquiries with the goal of pinpointing a specific method of attack. Reconnaissance in the networked world is carried out in a similar fashion in the physical world. A burglar may drive by her target, taking pictures and noting common points of entry and exit. She may research the target by accessing publicly available information, such as blueprints and vacation schedules. The burglar may even pose as the homeowner and call utility or burglar alarm companies to shut off service.

In the digital world, the goal of the black hat is to narrow down the field of thousands of possible exploits to a small number of vulnerabilities that are specific to the network to be exploited. The attacker attempts to make this reconnaissance as hard to notice as possible. Even so, there are many different means of reconnaissance, and some of them can be detected by an intrusion detection system.

Using Legitimate Public Data

Surprisingly enough, there are significant sources of publicly available information that can aid hackers in compromising your network. These data sources can be provided by a third party external to your network, making them hard to track. Black hats can also fool a resource on your network into giving up information that was intended to stay private. Some of the sources of information include

- Discussions in public forums
- Public information databases
- Public monitoring tools
- DNS zone transfer

Employees often participate in public forums on the Internet and discuss work-related topics that can aid an attacker in identifying targets. A systems admin could use a news-group to pose troubleshooting questions, which may reveal weaknesses in your network. To obtain accurate assistance, the sysadmin often has to describe the malfunctioning system in detail, including version numbers, IP addresses, and connectivity requirements. An attacker can easily find information by searching at sites such as groups.google.com for known employees or the business's domain name.

Black hats can also use information stored in public databases to gather information. Whois databases (such as www.arin.net) and spam tools (such as www.samspade.org) present an opportunity for identifying IP address ranges an organization uses. These tools can also be used to tell whether an organization is hosting applications in-house or if another company is responsible.

Public monitoring tools can be used to discover specific information pertaining to attack targets. You can use www.netcraft.com to identify the operating system and Web server running at a particular domain name. The Open Relay database at www.ordb.org can be used to discover whether a host is vulnerable to email relaying.

Another popular method of gathering public information is to take advantage of a misconfigured DNS server. A DNS server typically holds vital information about the hosts and relationship between hosts on your network. Attackers often attempt a DNS zone transfer to map out IP addresses and hostnames on your network.

Scanning for Vulnerabilities

After an attacker has used public data sources to gather information about your organization, she will attempt to discover vulnerabilities to exploit. The black hat can use a wide variety of scanning techniques to discover hosts.

Attackers can simply ping IP addresses to see whether a host is listening at that address. A good deal of hardened external network infrastructure is configured to not respond to ping requests, so this method is sometimes ineffective. The next option is to perform a TCP connect scan, which looks for open TCP ports to determine whether the IP address is active.

When the host is determined to exist at a chosen IP address, the attacker then searches for open ports with a full TCP and UDP scan. This scan details which ports have services listening on them. The most basic is a TCP connect scan. A TCP scan works by completing the TCP three-way handshake to determine whether a service is listening. The attacker sends a SYN packet to the host. If a SYN/ACK packet is received it is assumed that the port is open. If the attacker receives a RST/ACK packet, it can be safe-ly assumed that the particular TCP port on the host is inactive.

UDP scanning is somewhat different because of the connectionless orientation of the UDP protocol. No three-way handshake is established as with a TCP connection. When the scanner sends a UDP packet to a UDP port on a host that is not available, the host responds with an ICMP port unreachable reply. If no such answer is received, it can be deduced that the UDP port is active. A UDP scan can be less accurate than a TCP scan.

The port scan also records any banners advertising the services bound to them. A banner is the tidbit of information that a service displays, often prior to authentication. The following is an example of manually displaying a Telnet banner:

```
slash~> telnet banner.advertising.host.com
Trying 192.168.1.155 ...
Connected to banner.advertising.host.com.
Escape character is '^]'.

Linux Mandrake release 6.1 (Helios)
Kernel 2.2.13-4mdksmp on an i686
login:
```

This host is nice enough to tell us the OS, Linux flavor, kernel version, and the chipset. It would be trivial to nail down a specific Telnet exploit for this host. Another less precise method involves comparing open ports to a standard port list. Most services run on well-known standard ports, so the attacker can at least determine the service type by consulting a list. The combination of the port list and banners gives the attacker a pretty good idea of what type of services are available to exploit.

Secured hosts are often configured to not display banners and to run on nonstandard ports. In this case the attacker has to put forth extra effort to determine what is running at that particular port. The attacker would have to manually Telnet into the service and enter garbage commands in an attempt to make the service issue output that would give away its nature.

Most remote exploits are specific to a certain operating system. The attacker has to determine the operating system and version to use the correct exploit for the host. If service banners have not given away the operating system, an OS fingerprinting tool can be used. The tool attempts to identify the operating system by sending a variety of craft-ed packets that each operating system reacts to differently. One of these is a FIN probe. By sending a FIN packet, or any packet without an ACK or SYN flag, the tool can begin narrowing down what the remote operating system is. The correct, expected response from the operating system is to not respond to this unexpected packet. However, some IP stacks have been implemented incorrectly and respond with an RST. The FIN packet response is one of many crafted packets techniques that a tool can use to fingerprint an OS.

IDSs can easily detect traditional methods of scanning and probing for open ports. A TCP connect portscan covering several thousand ports in under a second sets off alerts on every brand of IDS. Experienced hackers therefore rarely attempt such brash and noisy reconnaissance. Better scanning methods designed to slip under the radar of an IDS have been developed.

These evasion attempts often use crafted packets similar in nature to the OS finger-printing method. Some scanners use what is known as a Xmas scan. It is termed a Xmas, or Christmas Tree scan, because all the TCP flags are enabled. With all the TCP flags enabled, the packet is "lit up like a Christmas Tree," hence the name. This type of scan proved elusive to most IDSs when it was introduced, and allowed attackers to portscan unnoticed.

Another effective method of disguising a portscan is to scan slowly over a period of hours or days. IDSs typically detect portscans by monitoring for a certain number of attempted port accesses in a set amount of time. If the attacker can scan slowly enough to fall below this threshold, the portscan goes unnoticed. Even a slow scan still attempts to connect to a large number of ports that are not normally used, so an anomaly detection IDS would still designate this as suspicious traffic. Another evasion method is to make the scan appear to originate from a variety of different sources. An attacker privy to a significant range of IP addresses can run each attempt through a different source address. This eludes IDSs that require a single source address to detect portscan attempts. These evasion techniques can be used in concert to evade an IDS, and are regularly employed by hackers.

For an attacker to successfully retrieve reconnaissance information, he must have access to the computer at the source IP address or an intermediate device. Information gathering attempts therefore rarely include spoofed source IP addresses.

Spoofing an IP Address

IP spoofing involves using a forged source IP address to create TCP/IP packets. On the Internet, only the destination IP address is used to route packets. As packets are forwarded throughout the Internet, routers ignore the source IP address. The source address is used only when the destination machine responds back to the source machine.

Forging the source IP address causes the responses to be misdirected to the spoofed source. If the source address is spoofed, a complete network connection can never be made with the attacking client. IP spoofing is an integral part of many network attacks that do not require a response to be effective.

A popular reconnaissance attack utilizes hundreds or thousands of spoofed addresses to hide a legitimate information gathering attempt. The spoofed addresses all attempt the same type of portscan as the black hat's legitimate IP address. The hope is that the real IP address will be difficult to pinpoint in the spoofed address flood. The attacker makes off with your system information while you are left trying to discern where the attack really came from.

Having the real IP address of the attacking host does not guarantee that the attacker is physically present at the source address. Hackers often use compromised boxes as sacrificial lambs to take care of their portscanning dirty work.

Nevertheless, when your IDS reports an increase in information gathering attempts, it is a good indication that your network is being actively targeted. In the wild, research has shown that reconnaissance is often the only warning sign of an impending attack.

The Attack Phase

After the initial planning and reconnaissance legwork is complete, the next logical step is to make use of gathered information and attack the network. The traffic generated from attacks can take many different forms. Everything from remote exploit code to suspicious normal traffic can signify an attempted attack that requires action.

Denial of Service

A *Denial of Service (DoS) attack* is any attack that disrupts the function of a system so that legitimate users can no longer access it. DoS attacks are possible on most network equipment, including routers, servers, firewalls, remote access machines, and almost every other network resource. A DoS attack can be specific to a service, such as in an FTP attack, or an entire machine. The types of DoS are diverse and wide ranging, but they can be separated into two distinct categories that relate to intrusion detection: resource depletion and malicious packet attacks.

Malicious packet DoS attacks work by sending abnormal traffic to a host to cause the service or the host itself to crash. Crafted packet DoS attacks occur when software is not properly coded to handle abnormal or unusual traffic. Often out-of-spec traffic can cause software to react unexpectedly and crash. Attackers can use crafted packet DoS attacks to bring down IDSs, even Snort. A specially crafted small ICMP packet with a size of 1 was found to cause Snort v.1.8.3 to core dump. This version of Snort did not properly define the minimum ICMP header size, which allowed for the DoS to occur.

In addition to out-of-spec traffic, malicious packets can contain payloads that cause a system to crash. A packet's payload is taken as input into a service. If the input is not properly checked, the application can be DoSed.

The Microsoft FTP DoS attack demonstrates the wide variety of DoS attacks available to black hats in the wild. The first step in the attack is to initiate a legitimate FTP connection. The attacker would then issue a command with a wildcard sequence (such as * or ?). Within the FTP Server, a function that processes wildcard sequences in FTP commands does not allocate sufficient memory when performing pattern matching. It is possible for the attacker's command containing a wildcard sequence to cause the FTP service to crash. This DoS, and the Snort ICMP DoS, are two examples of the many thousands of possible DoS attacks available.

The other way to deny service is via resource depletion. A resource depletion DoS attack functions by flooding a service with so much normal traffic that legitimate users cannot access the service. An attacker inundating a service with normal traffic can exhaust finite resources such as bandwidth, memory, and processor cycles. A classic memory resource exhaustion DoS is a SYN flood. A SYN flood takes advantage of the TCP three-way handshake. The handshake starts off with the client sending a TCP SYN packet. The host then sends a SYN ACK in response. The handshake is completed when the client responds with an ACK. If the host does not receive the returned ACK, the host sits idle and waits with the session open. Each open session consumes a certain amount of memory. If enough three-way handshakes are initiated, the host consumes all available memory waiting for ACKs. The traffic generated from a SYN flood is normal in appearance. Most servers are configured today to leave only a certain number of TCP connections open.

Another classic resource depletion attack is the Smurf attack. A Smurf attack works by taking advantage of open network broadcast addresses. A broadcast address forwards all packets on to every host on the destination subnet. Every host on the destination subnet responds to the source address listed in the traffic to the broadcast address. An attacker sends a stream of ICMP echo requests or pings to a broadcast address. This has the effect of amplifying a single ICMP echo request up to 250 times. In addition, the attacker spoofs the source address so that the target receives all the ICMP echo reply traffic. An attacker with a 128 Kb/s DSL Internet connection can conceivably create a 32 Mb/s Smurf flood.

DoS attacks commonly utilize spoofed IP addresses because the attack is successful even if the response is misdirected. The attacker requires no response, and in cases like the Smurf attack, wants at all costs to avoid a response. This can make DoS attacks difficult to defend from, and even harder to trace.

Remote Exploits

Remote exploits are the most high-profile means of gaining unauthorized access to a system. Exploits are attacks designed to take advantage of improperly coded software to compromise and take control of a vulnerable host.

Remote exploits can work in the same manner as the malicious payload traffic DoS attacks previously described. They take advantage of improperly checked input or configuration errors on the part of software engineers.

A common method of remotely exploiting a host is via a buffer overflow. Buffer overflows are perpetrated when an attacker inputs more data than a buffer (commonly an array) can handle. The data spills out into address space beyond the buffer. Often this simply causes the software to crash. When the input data is specially crafted, it can be executed in a way that causes the system to behave in a manner it was not intended to. This usually includes spawning a shell with root level access. A buffer overflow is made possible because modern computer architecture cannot distinguish between application code and input data.

The Apache chunked encoding exploit is a prime example of a remote buffer overflow exploit. When processing requests coded with the chunked encoding mechanism, Apache failed to calculate the required buffer sizes because of an improper interpretation of an unsigned integer value. Crackers used this buffer overflow to compromise Apache running on a variety of different platforms. The chunked exploit was the first remote exploit for Apache in over five years.

After most exploits are discovered, the vendor or open source team that developed the software usually releases a patch to correct the exposure within a few days. In a perfect world, this would render remote exploits ineffective. It is painfully obvious that this is not the case, because the majority of systems on the Internet have some degree of remote exploit vulnerability.

Remote exploits can come in many different forms that do not require a buffer over-flow condition. Hackers often find a method of causing an application to execute arbitrary commands or binary code on a system. The Unicode exploit for Microsoft's IIS makes use of a directory traversal exposure. The exploit enables a Unicode representation of a directory delimiter (/) to fool IIS into permitting a user to traverse out of the Web server's document root. The attacker can access any file on the Web server, including cmd.exe, which is used to run any DOS command. The following command lists the contents of the c:\ drive.

```
http://www.exposedhost.com/scripts/..%c0%af../winnt/system32/cmd.exe?/c+dir+c:\
```

The %c0%af is the Unicode representation of (/). The attacker can also use the cmd.exe command to establish a connection to a TFTP server and transfer files back and forth from the compromised box. The attacker can steal confidential information stored on the server, or execute malicious code on the box to leverage further access.

Remote exploits can also be found in Web application logic. Web applications that run dynamic code such as PHP, JSP, or ASP can be vulnerable if input is not properly checked. Web applications often use a token or a cookie to maintain state between the application and the user. This cookie can be used to authenticate the user to the application. Attackers have discovered methods of hijacking authentication cookies by fooling users into clicking on malicious hyperlinks. This class of attacks is called cross-site scripting (XSS). When the user clicks on a malicious XSS link, the cookie is transferred from the vulnerable host to a host controlled by the attacker. The attacker can then access the system with the credentials of the victim.

Another popular method of Web application hacking is SQL injection. Once again, if an application has not properly checked user input it can be vulnerable to SQL injection. SQL injection works by inserting SQL commands into user input fields. If specially crafted SQL is inserted, the attacker can modify the application's SQL logic to function in a manner that was not intended. An attacker can bypass a login script by terminating the SQL statement. The attacker can also utilize the SQL's privileged access to execute commands. On Microsoft's SQL Server, the attacker can run the xp_cmdshell command to execute arbitrary commands. This can include moving data via a TFTP server in a similar fashion as described above.

Trojans and Backdoors

By installing a backdoor or a Trojan, a hacker can bypass normal security controls and have privileged unauthorized access to a host. A backdoor can be deployed on a system in a variety of different ways. A malicious software engineer can add a backdoor into legitimate software code. Backdoors might be added for legitimate maintenance reasons in the software development life cycle, but later forgotten.

A Trojan or Trojan horse is slightly different, and is defined as software that is disguised as a benign application, much like the Trojan horse of Greco-Roman days. The term *Trojan* can also be used to describe a method of attacking a system. Remote control Trojans typically sit listening on a port like a genuine application. Through this open port, an attacker controls them remotely. Trojans can be used to perform any number of functions on the host. Some Trojans include portscanning and DoS features. Others can take screen and Webcam captures and send them back to the attacker. One hacking group runs a Web site that posts pictures of its victims' faces shot from a local Webcam at the moment they realize they have been Trojaned.

Trojans and backdoors have traditionally listened on a TCP or UDP port, making it easy for a security practitioner to portscan for Trojaned hosts. Recently, Trojans have evolved so they no longer need to listen on a TCP or UDP port. These new types of Trojans, such as SAdoor, listen for a specific sequence of events before processing commands. It may be a combination of predetermined source addresses, TCP header information, or false destination ports that do not match to a listening service. Trojans can employ some other clever tricks to disguise their presence. A popular Trojan, Back Orifice, encrypts communication between the Trojan and the attacker. Other Trojans make use of covert communication channels (such as ICMP). This new breed of Trojan requires an extra amount of diligence on the part of the IDS analyst.

Misuse of Legitimate Access

A black hat can misuse legitimate access or the access of unsuspecting others to execute an attack. An IDS plays an important role in discovering such accesses. It is often assumed that a person wishing to harm an organization must circumvent security controls. This is not true; there are ample opportunities for an attacker to harm a system by simply using legitimate access.

Attackers often attempt to gain unauthorized use of legitimate accounts by getting a hold of authentication information. The process can be as low tech as impersonating help desk personnel by phoning unsuspecting users and requesting their usernames and passwords. In some cases, this effort is not even necessary: a good proportion of devices come with default usernames and passwords. Often, these default usernames and passwords are not removed or changed after installation. Extensive lists of default passwords are readily available on the Internet for black hats to reference. The SQL Snake worm demonstrated the high number of systems installed with default passwords and connected to the Internet. The worm functioned by searching for Microsoft SQL Servers that had left the default root or SA password blank. In a matter of hours, the worm had infected tens of thousands of hosts on the Internet.

Attackers have more advanced methods of gathering authentication information. Attackers often use password cracking tools to automatically cycle through username and password combinations at high speed. This can be done by brute forcing every possible combination of characters, or by loading a dictionary file with common usernames and passwords. This type of password cracking activity is very noisy and relatively easy for an IDS to detect. Attackers also use tools to capture unencrypted authentication information as it is transmitted across a network. This can be detected after the fact if the attacker attempts to use valid authentication credentials for one host on another. It can also be detected by an anomaly detection IDS noticing unusual user behavior.

Even regular, normal traffic in suspicious or unusual situations can indicate a possible intrusion. If you suddenly notice TCP three-way handshakes completing on TCP ports 20 and 21 on a home Web server, but you know that you do not run an FTP server at home, it is safe to assume that something suspicious is going on.

Post-Attack Phase

After an attacker has successfully penetrated a host on your network, the further actions he will take for the most part follow no predictable pattern. This phase is where the attacker carries out his plan and makes use of information resources as he sees fit. Some of the different options available to the attacker at this point include the following:

- Covering tracks
- Penetrating deeper into network infrastructure
- Using the host to attack other networks
- Gathering, manipulating, or destroying data
- Handing over the host to a friend or hacker group
- Walking or running away

If the attacker is even somewhat skilled, he is likely to attempt to cover his tracks. There are several methods; most involve the removal of evidence and the replacement of system files with modified versions. The replaced versions of system files are designed to hide the presence of the intruder. On a Linux box, netstat would be modified to hide a Trojan listening on a particular port. Hackers can also cover their tracks by destroying system or security log files that would alert an administrator to their presence. Removing logs can also disable an HIDS that relies on them to detect malicious activity. There are automated scripts available that can perform all these actions with a single command. These scripts are commonly referred to as *rootkits*.

Externally facing servers in large network topologies usually contain very little in terms of useful data for the attacker. Application logic and data is usually stored in subsequent tiers separated by firewalls. The attacker may use the compromised host to cycle through the first three attack phases to penetrate deeper into the system infrastructure. Another possibility for the black hat is to make use of the host as an attack or scanning box. When skilled hackers want to penetrate a high-profile network, they often compromise a chain of hosts to hide their tracks.

The most obvious possibilities for the attacker are to gather, manipulate, or destroy data. The attacker may steal credit card numbers and then format the server. The cracker could subtract monies from a transactional database. The possibilities are endless.

Sometimes the attacker's motivation is solely to intrude into vulnerable hosts to see whether he can. Skilled hackers take pride in pulling off complicated hacks and do not desire to cause damage. He may turn the compromised system over to a friend to play with or to a hacker group he belongs to. The cracker may realize that he has gotten in over his head and attacked a highly visible host, such as the military's or major financial institution's host, and want to walk away from it praying he isn't later discovered.

The IDS Reality

Now that you have a pretty good idea of what IDSs do, the genres of IDS, and the traffic they can detect, it is important to remain firmly grounded in reality and examine what they lack.

When IDSs first arrived on the market, they were hailed as the silver bullet for network security. Customers thought they would throw in an IDS and walk away, never having to worry about network security again. Now the dust has settled and the hype has faded, and we have a clearer picture of what IDSs can do, and where they fall short.

IDSs Cannot Detect Every Attack

The slick salesman pushing the shiny new IDS on you may not tell you this, but even the most state-of-the-art signature and anomaly detection IDS cannot detect every attack. Both signature and anomaly detection IDSs have non-overlapping gaps in how they detect intrusions. Signature-based detection is unbeatable for known attacks, but has real trouble with unknown attacks. Anomaly detection technology has real difficulties establishing an accurate baseline to compare future activity to.

Even if the IDS industry were to somehow create an IDS that could detect every attack today, a hacker would surely up the ante and devise a new method of IDS evasion. For this reason, IDSs will always be playing catchup to creative hackers.

Intrusion Detection is Reactive

Every Intrusion Detection System is reactive in nature, meaning they can only detect intrusions. The IDS cannot, by itself, stop an intrusion from happening. It requires a carbon-based sack of water (a human) to interpret and act on alerts to prevent an intrusion.

Intrusion detection is still very much a human-centric application. An IDS is by no means an automated technology. Even the dream IDS that picks up on every possible attack would still require a person to take corrective action.

Deploying and Maintaining Is Difficult

An IDS is a very touchy application. A great deal of effort goes into tuning the IDS to ensure that false positives remain at a manageable level. When tuning for false positives, the analyst must take great care to avoid false negatives. This precarious balance, which can be achieved only by developing an intimate knowledge of monitored systems, makes running an IDS a difficult task. In addition, the IDS must be carefully placed within the network infrastructure if it is to have a chance of detecting possible intrusions.

An IDS requires the operator to have a wide skill set pertaining to many different operating systems, network protocols, and applications. To comprehend and avert an attack on a system the analyst must be an expert in the system itself. Not only must the analyst have solid IT skills, he must be dedicated enough to develop a special set of IDS skills to sit at the console. No matter what the brand of IDS, they all require an intelligent, sophisticated person to make the detection of intrusions possible.

These shortcomings are well known within the IDS community. There is considerable prestige in coming up with the next generation of IDS. The community is making strides to do more than detect intrusions. The open source community does have an inline intrusion prevention application; it functions by taking Snort signatures and dropping packets that match rules through the application. This application, Hogwash, is examined in Chapter 14, "Advanced Topics."

Summary

This chapter provided an introduction to the art of intrusion detection. An IDS is an important component in a defense in depth strategy for protecting information resources. Intrusion Detection Systems are analogous to burglar alarms in the physical world. They both monitor for intrusions and alert designated parties when suspicious activity is detected. IDSs are an important technology because they are the only tool that can monitor in real time for network intrusions.

IDSs come in two flavors: Host IDS (HIDS) and Network IDS (NIDS). HIDSs reside on the monitored host and have privileged access to sensitive files. HIDSs use this access to monitor for unusual activity. NIDSs reside within a network and protect large portions of infrastructure by capturing traffic intended for other hosts. Although both HIDSs and NIDSs have individual advantages and disadvantages, a total security solution includes both flavors of IDS.

Intrusion Detection Systems have three different techniques available for detecting intrusions: signature detection, anomaly detection, and integrity verification. Signature detection functions by recording unique malicious activity patterns into a signature. The signature is then compared to future activity; when a match occurs an alert is generated. Anomaly detection IDSs create a baseline of activity and establish it as the norm. When future activity differs from this norm, an alert is generated. Integrity verification creates checksums for important system files. At a defined time interval, the checksums are compared to current files. When a checksum does not match a file, an alert is generated.

Threats to modern networks can originate from two locations: internal to the organization or external. Most attempted external attacks are thwarted, whereas most internal attacks are successful. Internal attacks are more successful because company insiders have deep knowledge and legitimate access to systems. External attacks can be equally dangerous because external attackers need to find and leverage only a single security hole.

On the whole, network-based attacks follow a predictable pattern. Attackers execute an attack in the following phases: the planning phase, the reconnaissance phase, the attack phase, and finally the post-attack phase.

In the planning phase the attacker investigates the system via normal means. This helps the attacker define the scope of the attack.

In the reconnaissance phase the attacker utilizes legitimate public data and active scanning to identify possible weaknesses. Various public data sources, including discussions in public forums, public information databases, public monitoring tools, and DNS zone transfers can be utilized in gathering information on a target. The attacker also has methods for pinpointing specific attack points in a network, such as ping sweeps, TCP and UDP scans, remote OS fingerprinting, and banner grabbing. Hackers have developed advanced methods for eluding IDSs.

In the attack phase the information gathered in the reconnaissance phase is put to work. A specific attack strategy is narrowed down and the actual attack takes place. Some of the possible attacks include denial of service, remote exploits, backdoors and trojans, and misuse of legitimate access. Most attacks are made possible by coding errors that result in an attacker using software for something other than its intended purpose. Coding errors are usually related to failing to properly check input data to the software.

The post-attack phase is the least predictable of all of the attack phases. In post-attack, the hacker has a wide variety of options that are largely dictated by individual desires. The possibilities for the attacker include covering tracks, penetrating deeper into network infrastructure, using the host to attack other networks, gathering, manipulating or destroying data, handing over the host to a friend or hacker group, and walking or running away.

Even though IDS is a great technology for detecting malicious activity in a computer system, there is still significant room for improvement. An IDS cannot detect every possible attack, and most likely will never be able to. An IDS is still a very human-centric application that requires specialized training and in-depth knowledge. The IDS industry and the Snort community are making strides to rectify these IDS shortcomings.

2

Network Intrusion Detection with Snort

Snort has evolved from a simple network management tool to a world-class enterprise distributed intrusion detection system. Since its creation in 1998 to over half a million sensors installed worldwide, Snort has become by far the most widely deployed NIDS. Its author, Marty Roesch, originally designed Snort to be a personal tool to aid in network traffic analysis. Snort's original incarnation humbly decoded binary tcpdump data into a human-readable form. Never intending to release it to the public, Marty arbitrarily named it "Snort." It ended up being a quite catchy and memorable name.

Snort was released to the public, and evolved organically over the next few years. Snort has developed into the security practitioner's pocketknife. Snort is a tool that can be used for a variety of functions related to intrusion detection. Snort can be used as a sniffer, packet logger, or network intrusion detection system.

In sniffer mode, Snort functions by capturing traffic intended for other hosts on the same network. Sniffers take advantage of the shared nature of Ethernet networks. Ethernet networks were designed to utilize shared communication channels to reduce cost. Because computers share the same network infrastructure, it is possible for one computer to receive traffic that was intended for another.

On an Ethernet network, a computer sends packet information to all hosts on the same physical circuit. The packet header contains the address of the intended recipient, and only the machine with that address assigned to it is expected to accept the packet. Ethernet networks were obviously not designed with security in mind, as it is trivial to write a program to accept all packets. A network card configured to accept all packets regardless of what is contained in the packet header is said to be in *promiscuous mode*. An application that grabs all raw packets off the wire is termed a *sniffer*.

When Snort is run in sniffer mode, it displays the contents of every packet traversing the wire directly to your monitor. It can display packet headers as well as packet payloads.

In packet logger mode, Snort grabs packets in a similar sniffing fashion, but logs the gathered data instead of printing it to your screen.

Packets can be logged in ASCII text form or in binary tcpdump format. Tcpdump format is best suited for high bandwidth networks where performance could present an issue.

As expected, Snort can be run in Network Intrusion Detection (NIDS) mode. As with packet logger mode, Snort functions as a sniffer in NIDS mode and sucks packets as they travel down the wire.

Although NIDSs may seem sexy at first glance, they are really nothing more than souped-up sniffers. NIDS mode is similar to sniffer mode, in that it snatches up every packet it encounters, but the key difference is what NIDS mode does with the data. Rather than simply cope the data to a file or display it to a monitor, the Snort inspects each packet and determines whether it is benign or malicious in nature. Snort then sends alerts when it finds suspicious-looking traffic.

The primary focus of this book is Snort in NIDS mode. This is not to say the other functions of Snort are without value. The sniffing and packet-logging modes of Snort are excellent network analysis and forensic tools. They can furthermore provide value when used in concert with a full-blown intrusion detection system.

Snort's Specifications

Before getting into the details of how Snort functions as an IDS, it is worth the time to take a good look at the metrics of Snort and see whether it is suitable for your needs.

Requirements

Most high-performance applications require a specific set of supporting hardware and software. Because Snort uses a generic sniffing interface (libpcap) that has been ported to most operating systems, Snort can be run on a multitude of different platforms. Snort does not require expensive unique equipment to do its job; it runs on commercial off-the-shelf hardware. Snort is supported on the following architectures:

- i386
- Sparc
- Motorola 68000/Power PC
- Alpha

Snort is also compatible with almost every imaginable operating system. Some of the most popular operating systems Snort can be run on include the following:

- Linux
- OpenBSD
- FreeBSD

- Solaris
- HP-UX
- AIX
- Mac OS X
- Win32 (Win9x/NT/2000/XP)

Snort is coded in a proficient manner as well. Snort is efficient in terms of file size: The application itself takes up only a few megabytes of space. This makes low-resource installations of Snort possible on antiquated computers. An important fact to remember, though, is that this does not include the data that Snort produces. You could easily fill gigabytes depending on how Snort is tuned and the size of your network.

Bandwidth Considerations

Snort is remarkably fast, and is capable of monitoring every packet in a fully saturated 100Mb pipe with some skilled tuning. Snort begins to experience packet loss around the 200–300Mb level, and cannot be run at traffic levels higher than 500Mb. These statistics represent the outer limits of what Snort can accomplish in an ideal environment.

Very few organizations have more than a 100Mb connection coming in from a public network. Consequently, Snort stays effective for all but the most heavily used internet presences. Internal networks are another story: 100Mb traffic is seen quite often, but with careful planning you can find ways to accommodate this volume of traffic.

Snort Is an Open Source Application

In many respects, Snort functions like a typical open source project. Its original creator, Marty Roesch, is treated like a holy man within the community. It has a faithful following of developers that tirelessly toil to improve the application. There are reportedly over 200,000 installations worldwide, so even if the Snort install base is in reality only half that number, it is still as widely distributed as the closed source market leader (Internet Security Systems). Snort even has a few commercial ventures—Silicon Defense and Sourcefire—that provide value-added plug-and-play services for intrusion detection.

Snort: An Open Source Program

When a program is termed "open source," it means that the program's source code can be read, redistributed, and modified freely. Consequently, any programmer can legally add functionality to the program, fix bugs, and distribute it as desired. Open source does not require that programs be distributed for free, or prevent persons from charging for distribution, but the vast majority of open source software is distributed free of cost.

The inherent collaborative nature of open source programs allows them to grow and evolve rapidly. Because they are developed to meet the needs of individuals rather than corporate profit motives, open source programs are usually of a higher quality.

> Open source developers are under no market pressure to release unfinished, buggy code. Because open
> source programs bare their code for all to see, they are usually more secure than closed source programs.
> Thousands of eyes auditing code can discover security holes and bugs more readily than those of only a
> privileged few who have that access. Free from the need to establish and maintain market share, they can
> add in features that a closed source vendor would not. In the last five years, the open source movement has
> created an alternative for most major software applications.
>
> Open source programs flourish when an active thriving community supports them. There is usually a hard-
> core group of altruistic, dedicated developers that pump out the code. The group of core developers takes
> care of improving the software by adding features and fixing bugs. The virtual community surrounding an
> open source program is just as important as the developers. The community provides technical support for
> new users of the software and reports bugs back to the developers.

Snort signatures are written and released by the Snort community within hours of the announcement of a new security exposure. Because signatures are relatively easy to create, the Snort community can cook up an update, test it, and distribute it quickly. Some vendors can take days to create a signature and release it to the public. Because anyone in the community can create a signature, Snort has the largest and most comprehensive collection of attack signatures for any IDS.

So what does this mean for you? As a casual user of Snort, you get free software. Snort's source code is freely available, so you can modify and distribute it as you wish. It is also distributed free of cost, so you never have to pay for a thing. In addition, you get free expert technical support when you need it.

There are a few responsibilities that come with open source software. The first is to spread the word. If you enjoy the open source model for software development and distribution, educate your friends, co-workers, and managers. The second is to contribute what you can to the community. This doesn't necessarily mean money (although it's always nice); there are other ways to contribute. You can answer questions that new users have, provide documentation, submit bugs, or if you are up to it, contribute some time to help code. There is always room for another helping hand.

Detecting Suspicious Traffic via Signatures

The most effective means to date of detecting persons attempting to attack a system or network of systems is via signature-based detection. Signature-based detection is based on the premise that abnormal or malicious network traffic fits a distinct pattern, whereas normal or benign traffic does not. Because malicious traffic can be different in structure and content from all other normal traffic, it is possible to create an attack signature that matches it.

With Snort, a malicious traffic signature is used to create a rule that is loaded into Snort's detection engine. The detection engine is the primary component of Snort and is responsible for signature matching.

The easiest way to understand how Snort's detection engine functions is to take a look at how Snort handles rules. A Snort rule looks like this:

```
alert icmp $EXTERNAL_NET any -> $HOME_NET any
(msg:"ICMP PING NMAP"; dsize: 0; itype: 8;)
```

This might look somewhat intimidating at first glance, but if I translate this rule from Snortese to English for you, it will make more sense:

Generate an alert for ANY ICMP traffic that originates outside your network AND has an empty data payload AND has the ICMP type field set to 8.

Internet Control Message Protocol (ICMP) is the protocol most ping utilities use to discover whether a host at a particular IP address is up. It is also used by a utility called NMAP, a network discovery tool frequently used by black hats. In an effort to scan the widest amount of Internet address space in the shortest amount of time, black hats often configure NMAP to ping a host to make sure it is up before performing a more thorough scan. Remember, black hats are busy people; they don't want to waste valuable seconds scanning something that might not be there. The ICMP ping that NMAP uses has a specific signature; it sets the ICMP type field to 8 and has an empty data payload. This NMAP ping signature is different than a ping issued directly from a Windows or Unix operating system. Because NMAP has a unique-looking ping, we can create a rule that triggers whenever traffic matching this signature hits our network. Remember, Snort does not have to be running on the same computer as the one for which the traffic was intended; it only needs to be on the same network segment to sniff the traffic. Therefore, Snort can detect an NMAP ping intended for a number of protected hosts.

Detecting Suspicious Payloads

Snort signatures are not limited to packet header data; they can detect a malicious payload housed in a normal-looking packet. Take a look at this rule:

```
alert tcp $EXTERNAL_NET any -> $HOME_NET 139
(msg: "DOS SMBdie attack"; flags: A+; content:"|57724c65680042313342577a|";)
```

This rule states that an alert should be generated if any TCP traffic that contains "|57724c65680042313342577a|" in the payload is found to be headed from outside your network to a computer running the Server Message Block (SMB) service. The payload signifies a buffer overflow in the Windows protocol, which would crash the target host. Notice this rule triggers only when this payload is aimed at a computer running Netbios (TCP port 139) from the outside. The rule is made specific to Netbios sessions to reduce the possibility of a false alert. If this rule were not specific to your Web servers, a friend simply emailing you the rule would set off the alarm. The supposedly malicious content |57724c65680042313342577a|, would be included in the email content and match the rule. This is also one simple example of how Snort can be customized to your network.

Snort can capture a wide range of content types: everything from the latest P2P file-sharing tool signature to the content of a remote buffer overflow. Snort can be used to monitor and alert you to any type of packet payload your heart desires.

Detecting Specific Protocol Elements

For accuracy and performance reasons, Snort signatures can be specific to one element of a particular protocol. The following is an example of such a rule that is specific to HTTP content:

```
alert tcp $EXTERNAL_NET any -> $HTTP_SERVERS $HTTP_PORTS
(msg:"WEB-IIS ISAPI .ida attempt"; uricontent:".ida?";
nocase; dsize:>239; flags:A+;)
```

This rule states that any network traffic coming from the external network that is intended for your Web servers that has .ida? in the URL creates an alert. The .ida extension is a rarely used component of Microsoft's ISS Indexing Service. Most secured versions of IIS have the .ida extension completely removed. The .ida extension was found to have a serious remote buffer overflow that could result in remote control of the Web server. In addition, the exploit led to the hugely successful Code Red worm. There is very little legitimate use for an outside party to attempt to use Indexing Service via an .ida file, and there is a good possibility that the traffic with .ida in the URL is malicious. This type of rule is more efficient because it searches URL content only, instead of the entire payload.

Extending Coverage with Custom Rules

There are around 1,500 prewritten rules that come with Snort. Although this might seem to be extensive coverage, the rules supplied with Snort are intended to be generic for all networks. To do a stellar intrusion detection job, it is necessary to be able to create rules that are specific for your network. Modern networks use a mind-boggling array of platforms in a seemingly infinite number of unique configurations. Although generic rules provide some intrusion monitoring coverage, a higher degree of rule granularity is the most effective means of increasing coverage. Offering you the capability to write your own rules is a feature that is unique to Snort in the IDS marketplace. You can write your own rules in the fairly simple syntax you have already seen in the previous examples. Although it may look somewhat archaic at first glance, custom rule writing is actually pretty easy if you have solid knowledge of your network.

Suppose you were alerted to an abundance of suspicious reconnaissance traffic coming from a host in Eastern Europe. You know that your organization does not do business with anyone in that region of the world, and you have not granted permission for anyone to investigate your network remotely. If you know you are running an SSH server that holds important customer information, you may want to write a rule to alert you if the suspected host attempts to connect to it. Assuming the suspicious host is at 192.168.1.1, the following is a rule that logs access attempts to your SSH server:

```
alert tcp 192.168.1.1 any -> $HOME_NET 22
(msg: "suspicious host SSH traffic";)
```

The ability to write rules is invaluable to the IDS analyst, and, as you can see, Snort makes it pretty easy to do so. Rules can be written to match any traffic signature or payload. Rule writing is covered in greater detail in Chapter 12, "Basic Rule Writing."

Detecting Suspicious Traffic via Heuristics

As you can see, signature matching is a highly effective means for detecting suspect traffic. Unfortunately, signature matching is not 100% accurate. There are situations where traffic is harmful but has no distinguishable signature.

The Snort community developed the Statistical Packet Anomaly Detection Engine (SPADE) module to detect suspicious traffic that matches no signature. SPADE works by detecting bad traffic through heuristic pattern matching. SPADE observes network traffic and constructs a table that describes the normal traffic on your network. The table contains data about the types of packets and the source and destination addresses. After the table has reached a significant size, each packet that SPADE picks up is assigned a number based on the frequency in which it occurs in the table. Packets that are rare for your network are assigned a higher number, and when a configured threshold is reached, an alert is generated.

Suppose you want to use SPADE to protect a Web server. You deploy Snort with SPADE enabled on a network segment that leads out of the Internet. SPADE builds a table for incoming traffic—mostly TCP connections into ports 80 and 443. After the table is built, TCP requests on ports 80 and 443 are considered "normal traffic" and assigned low numbers. If an attacker were to probe the Web server looking for services on ports other than 80 and 443, SPADE would assign a high number to this traffic because it would be rare and unusual for this particular server. If enough attempts to unusual ports are made in a predefined threshold, SPADE generates an alert.

This is effective in detecting reconnaissance measures by hackers, who often probe ports slowly in an attempt to get lost in the background noise. SPADE is even smart enough to notice when a hacker is using multiple source addresses in an attempt to evade an IDS. Distributed Denial of Service (DDoS) attacks, where many compromised hosts flood a host with so many bogus requests that legitimate users cannot reach the server, are picked up by SPADE as well.

Gathering Intrusion Data

A powerful feature unique to Snort is related to its capability to gather data. Many commercial IDSs require the operator to specify in advance for which rules data should be kept. An intrusion analyst's work is often nebulous; having to predict what malicious hackers are going to throw at your network perimeter is next to impossible. The only solution is to save every payload that corresponds to suspicious traffic. Snort's creators realized this; hence Snort logs all payloads when possible.

Assessing Threats

The data contained in a payload is often a window into the mind of your attacker. To gauge a proper response to either a successful or attempted attack, it is imperative to determine the nature of your attacker. Payload data can help you determine whether an attack is being perpetrated by a human or not. The popularity and diversity of self-propagating worms can make this task difficult. Worms can contain sophisticated attack sequences that include a laundry list of exploits and the backdooring of the compromised host. This is often the same pattern that a human attacker would follow. If you have the capability to inspect payload data, you might be able to compare it to the worm's known behavior and ascertain what type of threat you have on your hands.

If it ends up that a human is behind the attack, you might be able to use payload data to determine the attacker's skill level. Determining whether you have a script kiddy or an überhacker to deal with is important in responding to the attack.

Script Kiddy

Script kiddy is a derogatory term used for a class of hackers that rely on previously written scripts to perform sophisticated attacks. They are looked down upon in hacker culture for being destructive and unskilled. Hackers that spend time researching and discovering vulnerabilities and are highly skilled in systems administration and coding are given more credibility. Script kiddies tend to be juvenile and more likely to do stupid things and get caught. This does not mean they are not dangerous; they often lash out randomly and attack you for no real reason. They have access to complex exploit scripts and easy-to-use point-and-click tools that simplify malicious hacking. A script kiddy can be identified by comparing the attack signatures to that of well-known tools. Often a script kiddy lacks the basic systems administration skills to make use of a newly compromised host.

Preprocessors

Snort's developers placed a high priority on creating a flexible, modular application that can adapt to the ever-changing ecology of network-based exploits. Snort has an extensible plug-in architecture that ensures that Snort will remain a proficient intrusion detection system. Snort has a class of plug-ins, known as *preprocessors*, that interact with data before the detection engine processes it. Preprocessors can be broken down into three functional groups: Data Normalization, Protocol Analysis, and Non-Signature-Matching Detection.

Data Normalization

New methods of attack and IDS evasion are constantly evolving that Snort's detection engine either does not detect or does not detect efficiently. Preprocessors are added to the Snort architecture to massage or normalize data so that the detection engine can properly interpret them. For example, the Fnord preprocessor written by Dragos Ruiu detects a clever IDS evasion technique borrowed from virus creators. In an effort to defeat an Antivirus's signature-matching engine, a virus's code randomly changes and mutates. This is known as a *polymorphic virus*.

The same technique has been applied to exploits; the shell code has been rendered polymorphic. The Fnord preprocessor can detect mutated *NO-OP sleds*, which are a series of no-operation instructions in machine code that are used to exploit a buffer overflow. The objective of a buffer overflow is to overwrite the commands in the processor's instruction pointer. = It is often difficult to tell exactly which memory address is the next step in the buffer, so the attacker will often use a trick known as a no-op sled. This is a string of machine code instructions that intentionally does nothing, so that when the buffer is overflowed, the next valid instruction will be a NO-OP-op. This keeps the programming from crashing and allows exploitation of the buffer overlfow As the processor steps through the no-op instructions it at some point reaches, and starts executing, the malicious code. The no-op sled is something that many IDSs identify easily, unless the sled is modified by polymorphic code each time it is used. Without the Fnord preprocessor, Snort would be blind to polymorphic shellcode.

Protocol Analysis

The detection engine has a short list of protocols that it can interpret. Others, including some protocols that are heavily used over public networks, it cannot cannot be interpret. This has lead to a class of protocol preprocessors that aid in detecting protocol abuses. An example is ASN1_decode, which detects inconsistencies in the Abstract Syntax Notation number One protocol. Higher-level protocols, such as SNMP, LDAP, and SSL, rely on ASN.1. A group of Swedish University researchers discovered hundreds of ASN.1 vulnerabilities for SNMP in mid-2002. Almost every SNMP-enabled device was affected by either a buffer overflow or denial-of-service (DoS) attack. This caused hundreds of vendors to release patches and created the first national security event in which the President of the U.S. was directly involved. A wide-scale attack never occurred, possibly due to the complexity of creating exploits from the vulnerability. The capability to detect misuse of the ASN.1 protocol is necessary to monitor for these types of attacks.

Non-Signature-Matching Detection

Some types of malicious traffic simply do not have a discernable signature. This class of preprocessor uses methods other that signature matching to catch suspicious traffic.

Harmless ICMP traffic is used to discover hosts on a public network. Normal TCP traffic can be used to discover open ports and the services bound to them. Traffic of this nature helps an attacker isolate a specific exploit and attack strategy that will be the most effective for the discovered host. These are called *reconnaissance attacks*, and are often the only warning sign that an attack is pending. Information gathering attempts can use out-of-spec traffic, but are usually not harmful in nature.

Normal traffic can be harmful, if it is coordinated in a flood of overwhelming traffic. DDoS attacks utilize a large number of compromised machines to flood a system with bogus requests, eating up enough bandwidth or CPU utilization that the system cannot respond to legitimate requests.

Preprocessors such as Portscan2 and Stream4 can discover this class of traffic and some of the evasive techniques that black hats employ to keep you from discovering it.

Alerting via Output Plug-ins

Snort's output plug-ins are the means Snort has to get intrusion data from the detection engine to you. Like its preprocessors, Snort's outputting functionality is modular and plugable. Different skill levels, network configurations, and personal preferences will dictate which outputting mechanism is right for you. Snort supports everything from a raw binary tcpdump output to various relational database outputs.

Snort's outputs are not intended to be human-readable. They are logged in various formats that make intrusion data readily accessible to other applications or tools. Outputting can be done in these formats:

- syslog
- tcpdump
- Text Logfile
- XML
- Relational database
- SNMP
- Snort Unified

This gives the user freedom of choice and saves the Snort team's time and energy. Rather than reinventing the wheel, the Snort team has left the presentation of data to previously written applications. Snort supports every major relational database platform, from MySQL to Oracle and even Microsoft's SQL Server.

Aggregating Data

Outputting to an industry standard format such as syslog lets you aggregate data from many disparate security devices. Most routers and firewalls support functionality to log to a syslog server. You can even import logs from other devices into the Snort database structure with logsnorter. It is convenient to have all logging- and intrusion-related information in one easily secured location. Aggregation via syslog is a simplified means of performing event correlation.

Event Correlation

In information security, *event correlation* is the act of associating occurrences of events as they happened at different devices on a system or across a range of systems. Event correlation is critically important to intrusion detection. Attackers rarely compromise a single host and walk away. Most attacks involve an attacker compromising a single host and then leveraging legitimate privileges to penetrate deeper within a protected network. Imagine a situation in which you have a compromised Web server, a sniffer installed on a Active Directory server, and your organization's confidential information posted on a Web site in Eastern Europe. Putting the pieces of the puzzle back together requires sifting through security alerts and logfiles for many different devices. Storing them in a central location makes this task much easier.

Logging with the Unified Format and Barnyard

Historically, the relational database output plug-in has been the limiting factor in how much bandwidth Snort could process. With a database plug-in enabled, Snort was capable of processing about 40% of the bandwidth compared to logging with the fastest method, a tcpdump file. Logging via a network rather than a local disk further exacerbated the problem. Snort's developers decided to outsource the database logging to a new application specifically designed for the task. Barnyard is the result of those efforts.

With Barnyard, Snort spools output data in the Snort Unified Format at the maximum speed it can write to disk. After an alert is written to disk, the Snort daemon is finished handling the alert and can concentrate on processing new packets. This frees up the resources that would have been used outputting to a database. The binary data is parsed by Barnyard into the various formats that are fed into database plug-ins attached to Barnyard. Barnyard runs as an entirely separate process that is independent of Snort. Alerts can now be posted to a database without impacting Snort's capability to capture traffic. If you plan on running Snort in a high-bandwidth environment, Barnyard is a necessary addition.

Alerting

Intrusion detection is not an automated process. It requires a human to receive the alerts and react to them in a timely fashion. As expected, getting real-time alerts out of Snort and to yourself can be configured in a multitude of different ways. The two primary means for alerting that will be covered in this book are real-time alerting with syslog and swatch, and the Analysis Console for Intrusion Databases (ACID).

Swatch is a simple but powerful tool. Swatch actively monitors a syslog file for preconfigured events and an alert when conditions are met. Alerts can be sent via pager gateway, email, or even an audible alarm.

ACID is a Web application that reads intrusion data stored in a database and presents it in browser. ACID presents Snort data in a human-friendly format and includes functionality to do complex searches. Complex searches can be created with over 30 different criteria to pinpoint events occurring in a vast sea of intrusion data. This level of accuracy is necessary to quickly identify and trim false positives.

ACID can group alerts into logically functional categories, and matches links to various common vulnerabilities and exposures (CVE) on the Internet. CVE is a standardized classification of vulnerabilities and exposures, and a great resource for identifying and understanding attacks. ACID can distinguish multiple installations of Snort from each other, and process data from other security devices. This makes ACID another option for event correlation through aggregation.

ACID includes a charting component that is used to create statistics and graphs. Although this might seem somewhat frivolous, it can actually be useful to chart how the threat to your organization changes over time. You can use them to demonstrate the value of the IDS as threats decrease over time. If they increase, you can ask for more funding to combat them. Either way, charting helps you deal with pointy-haired management types.

Prioritizing Alerts

An IDS needs to be able to categorize and prioritize alerts in an organized fashion. Not all alerts deserve the same attention and scrutiny. A simple ping is no cause for immediate alarm, but a remote exploit attempt against an unpatched server is. Alerting in the IDS market comes in three flavors:

- No prioritization
- Hard-coded prioritization
- Customizable prioritization

No Prioritization

In this system, all alerts have the same priority. This makes sorting by severity an impossibility. You have to wade through pages of alerts to find critical ones. With all alerts classified at the same priority level, notification becomes insanely frustrating. Any automatic emergency notification mechanism is rendered useless. How do you decide what is important enough to page you in the middle of the night? You can't be paged for every ping, and you can't miss a serious remote exploit. At the end of the day, not prioritizing alerts leaves the IDS analyst frustrated and ultimately disinterested in intrusion monitoring.

Hard-coded Prioritization

This is marginally better than no prioritization. Here the vendor has decided for you which alerts are important and which are not. Usually they are categorized as High, Medium, and Low. Although this does allow you to sort and filter out less important alerts, a "one size fits all" approach to alerting is inadequate. Take, for example, a particularly nasty Apache Web server alert, categorized as a high risk by the vendor. You would be notified of this alert (possibly by pager or cell phone), even if you did not run Apache at your organization.

Customizable Prioritization

The preferred way to group alerting data is by user-defined priorities. Modern networks are modular and therefore unique, so customizable prioritization of alerts is a necessity. Alerts can be sorted based on your priorities, so you can be alerted to what you feel is important. Having more than three severity levels for alerts is desirable.

Snort supports customizable prioritization of alerts. Snort comes with 32 predefined alert categories. The severity level of each of the categories can be modified at will. You can also add as many custom alert categories as required. Like signatures, alert classification is done via simple rules. A sample alert classification for Trojan traffic follows:

```
config classification: trojan-activity, A Network Trojan was detected, 1
```

This classification is for any genre of detected Trojan activity, including Netbus, Back Orifice, and SubSeven. This rule grants the highest severity level when logging the alert, 1. If for some reason you were not concerned about Trojan traffic, you could downgrade the rule to a 2 or a 3 by changing the numerical identifier at the end of the rule. Any signature rule classified as `trojan-activity` would correspond to this classification rule. This is done with the classtype identifier in the signature rule. The SubSeven signature rule has `trojan-activity` specified for the classtype:

```
alert tcp $EXTERNAL_NET 27374 -> $HOME_NET any
(msg:"BACKDOOR subseven 22"; flags: A+; content: "|0d0a5b52504c5d3030320d0a|";
classtype:trojan-activity;)
```

Now imagine you were not as concerned with SubSeven activity, but wanted to keep all other Trojans at alert priority 1. This is easy to accomplish: You can override the classification rule with a priority identifier. The new rule then looks like this:

```
alert tcp $EXTERNAL_NET 27374 -> $HOME_NET any
(msg:"BACKDOOR subseven 22"; flags: A+;
content: "|0d0a5b52504c5d3030320d0a|"; priority:2;)
```

Most reasonable alert prioritizing requirements can be handled by these means. Alert prioritization would be of little use if alerts could not be delivered in a timely, organized manner. Snort again displays its remarkable flexibility by giving you the choice of 12 different alert outputting modules. Modules can be used to log intrusion data in everything from raw output to point-and-click GUIs. You aren't limited to singling out one alerting output method; you can pick and choose as many as necessary.

Distributed Snort Architecture

It would present a real problem if gigabytes of data had to be stored on the same physical box that Snort was running on. Fortunately, Snort uses an n-tier architecture. N-tier architectures are fairly common. Large applications are rarely handled by one application on one box; scalability and security are chief concerns with a single tier architecture. Snort is most typically installed in a 3-tier architecture, but is flexible enough to accommodate a single-tier (the hybrid sensor/server) to four tiers (departmental clusters).

First Tier—The Sensor Tier

The first tier, known as the *sensor tier*, is where network traffic passes to be monitored for intrusions. The sensor acts like a digital vacuum: It grabs packets and feeds data up to the second tier. The Snort application runs on the sensor; it is responsible for interpreting the nature of sniffed packets and passing on alerts. Sensors have to be placed on the same network segments to be monitored for intrusions, so security is a priority. The sensor should have only Snort and its supporting applications running on it and nothing else. This is necessary for both performance and security reasons. IDSs are juicy targets for hackers, and you don't want to have any applications running on your sensor that could potentially open up an exposure. Linux or BSD is the operating system of choice, again for stability and security reasons. Although there is a Win32 port of Snort, I strongly recommend using a flavor of the UNIX operating system for the sensor.

Snort 3-Tier Distributed Architecture

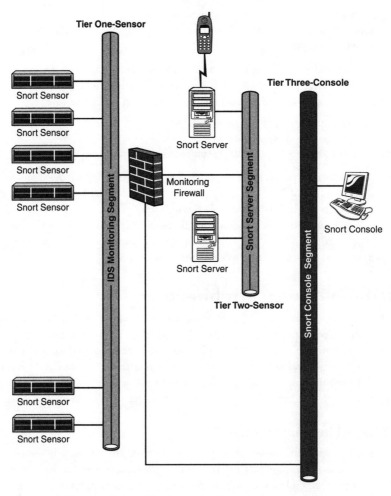

Figure 2.1   Snort 3-tier architecture.

The sensor has two network cards on it: one for the sniffing interface and one for the management interface. The idea is to keep all incoming sniffed packets with one interface, and all outgoing alerts with the other. The sniffing NIC does not have an IP address assigned to it and connects to the network segment to be monitored, so that traffic can flow in only one direction: from the monitored segment to the sensor. You do this by not binding an IP address to the interface, as you typically would for a network card. The card is then placed in promiscuous mode and therefore accepts all packets. This is called "operating in stealth mode," for obvious reasons. The primary rationale for doing this is for enhanced security. If an attacker can determine the IP address of the sensor, she can attack it like any other host on the network. Without an IP address, the worst she can do is cause a denial of service, either by overloading the sensor with data or discovering an exploit that causes the sensor to crash. This sounds bad, but it is better than having the intrusion detection system compromised and subsequently your protected internal network. The sensor can get away with not having an IP address because it accepts all packets on the segment regardless of the IP address in the packet header.

The management interface connects to a separate network segment than the sniffing interface. It has to have an IP address assigned to it so that it can communicate with the second tier. Alerting data is passed out of this interface up to the second tier. All control of the sensor is done through the management NIC. When you need to upgrade or patch the sensor, this interface is used. You also use the management NIC to tune Snort, by adding, subtracting, or modifying rules and preprocessors. In this design, the management network should protected from the outside world by a firewall. This design is good, but multiple physical or geographic locations can complicate this setup.

Second Tier—The Server Tier

The second tier, or the server tier, gathers alerting data from the sensors and presents the data in a human-readable form. The alerting data is fed from Snort into a relational database. Snort does not require a relational database; alerts can be logged via other means, such as syslog. The most practical way to get a grasp on a sizable amount of alerting data is to organize it in a relational database. Placing alerts into a database allows you to perform complex searches to better manage alerting information. It also allows other applications to present the data in an easy-to-work-with GUI. Snort supports many different databases; supported platforms include Oracle, Postgreql, and MySQL. Snort is also compatible with any ODBC-compliant database via unixODBC.

The server tier also supports a GUI that presents data in a human readable form. There are several GUIs available for Snort, including demarc, snortsnarf, snortdb, and the ACID. The server holds a lot of sensitive and confidential information, and protecting it is a priority. It is important to adhere to the principle of least privilege and install the minimum services necessary. Because you will be running a Web server in conjunction to serve up ACID, it is vitally important to keep up to date with the latest patches.

The Third Tier—The Analyst's Console

The third tier, or the *analyst's console*, is where data is presented. The only requirement for the console is a dedicated machine with an SSL-capable web browser installed. ACID works well with Internet Explorer, Mozilla, Netscape, and most other browsers. It is not as important to use UNIX-based machines for the console, so here you can get away with a Windows box. It is a good idea to make the console a dedicated machine, for both physical access control and to keep other applications from interfering with the Intrusion Detection System.

Securing Snort

Hardening your sensors, servers, and consoles and keeping up to date with patches will keep your intrusion data relatively secure while it rests on the tiers. It is equally important to secure the data while it is in transit. All the tiers of a Snort IDS utilize encrypted communication and strong authentication to identify a member of one tier to another. Stunnel can be used to encrypt alerting communication between the sensor and the server. The sensors use digital certificates and strong password authentication to authenticate to the server. The server allows only the sensors' IP addresses to connect to it. IP addresses are trivial to spoof, so RFC 1918 IP addresses are used. To spoof an IP address, an attacker would have to have access to a host on the IDS segment. The browser connects to the ACID Web server via SSL, and the pages are password- protected. The server allows only the browser's IP addresses to connect to it.

Shortcomings

Although Snort is a great application for intrusion detection, it does have its shortcomings. The good news is that the Snort community is working very hard to address a number of important issues, and is already on target for a few of them.

Flexibility Breeds Complexity

Snort is designed to be as flexible, customizable, and extensible as possible. This requires that Snort not be a turnkey, out-of-the-box solution. You can't pop in a CD and have Windows Installer do all the work for you. It is necessary to learn Snort plus other supporting applications to make Snort function.

Snort is also quite difficult to install correctly. There are several components that must be working in unison for the IDS to run smoothly. Little start-to-finish documentation on planning, installing, and maintaining Snort as an IDS is freely available. You have to go and buy a book or thumb through one over coffee at the local bookstore to figure it out.

Snort is dependent on libpcap to be portable to almost every OS. Libpcap is a great sniffing library, but it was never intended to acquire traffic beyond a saturated 100Mb pipe. Snort really starts to gasp for air above 100Mb megabits, even with Barnyard installed. A platform-specific sniffing library or even a hardware-specific library needs to be written to improve performance. The Snort team is making progress in this area with acquisition plugins that will be platform-specific replacements for libpcap.

Even though there are many advantages to open source software, there are some notable disadvantages. Some organizations do not permit the use of open source software for enterprise-class applications. They require a service-level agreement and a vendor that is on the hook to provide support. In the case of some organizations, such as financial institutions, a service-level agreement can be a regulatory requirement. Fortunately we now have two companies that provide support: SourceFire and Silicon Defense. However, companies still might have issues with using an unproven startup for an important application.

Problems with False Positives

Intrusion detection systems produce a deluge of data. IDSs are notorious for generating false positives. An IDS generates an alert for any traffic that matches a signature, and many legitimate applications create traffic that sets off alerts. Snort is primarily a signature-matching IDS, and consequently falls victim to the false positive quandary. There are some steps a Snort user can take to reduce the number of false positives. Some services are known to be likely false positive generators. DNS servers are often the culprit—take for example this UDP DoS rule:

```
alert udp $EXTERNAL_NET any -> $HOME_NET any
(msg:"MISC Large UDP Packet"; dsize: >4000;)
```

This rule posts an alert if a UDP packet is over 4,000 bytes in length. Large UDP and ICMP packets are unusual and suspicious in nature. They are suspect because hackers can flood a host with loads of large UDP packets to eat up all the host's available memory, effectively creating a DoS situation. Large ICMP traffic can also indicate the use of ICMP as a covert communications channel.

The Loki Trojan

The concept of the Loki Trojan is a new twist on an old idea. Using a covert channel to disguise or hide information has been around for thousands of years. Loki works by "hiding" information in the data portion of ICMP packets, creating a covert channel. ICMP traffic is usually not used to carry data; its primary legitimate purpose is for testing to determine whether a host is active at a specific IP address. For this reason, network admins often disregard the contents of ICMP_ECHO traffic, mistakenly assuming that it contains no payload data. Network devices are commonly configured to either pass, drop, or return echo requests, meaning that ICMP_ECHO traffic is rarely filtered.

The Loki Trojan works by appearing to be a normal application. After the Trojan is executed, it opens the covert ICMP_ECHO channel. Now any type of data communication is possible between the attacker and the compromised host by means of the covert ICMP tunnel. The attacker can now send commands to Loki to take control of the system. The attacker then uses Loki to remotely control the compromised machine via the covert ICMP_ECHO tunnel. When the attacker can control the remote host, any number of undesirable scenarios are possible, including the theft of sensitive information and using the host to attack other machines. If an IDS has not been deployed that can detect unusually large ICMP_ECHO traffic, Loki Trojans can be difficult to discover.

UDNS servers use UDP for name resolution, and sometimes randomly spit out a large UDP packet, so it is important to watch for false positivies.

- **Delete the UDP large packet rule**. This removes all false positives related to this rule, but creates a situation where you could miss a UDP DoS attack. This creates situations for more false negatives. For the IDS analyst, false negatives are much worse than false positives, so we want to avoid any situation that will create a false negative at all costs. *Note: This would be your only option if you were restricted to using vendor-supplied rules.*

- **Modify the UDP large packet rule**. You can inspect the traffic that creates the alert and try to find a threshold that the DNS server does not exceed. Typically this is somewhere around 8,000 bytes. This is a well-known threshold, and a witty hacker can still deny service to hosts without generating alerts.

- **Create a pass rule**. You can create a pass rule that is specific to your DNS server's IP address. Pass rules allow for certain specified traffic that matches the rule to be dropped by Snort before processing. This creates a false negative only if the DNS server's IP was used in the DoS attack.

In addition to normally occurring false positives, there are malicious attempts by black hats to overwhelm or institute a DoS attack against an IDS with a flood of false positives. Crafty hackers have devised ways to overload IDSs with false positives to cover a real attack, or to just harass the IDS analyst. One tool, appropriately titled Snot, is designed to specifically overload Snort with a hail of alerts.

Marketplace Factors

Snort is primarily an IP-centric application. Additional protocols are supported in Snort's packet decoder, and new ones are constantly added via preprocessors. Snort needs to increase the number of covered protocols to have total coverage in modern networks.

Some commercial vendors have economies of scale working against Snort. Cisco has an IDS that plugs in as a blade on a Cisco switch. This means that the Cisco IDS has direct hardware access from the switch-back plane to network traffic. Snort will have a hard time competing with this, especially as gigabit networks gradually replace 100Mb as the standard.

Summary

This chapter provided a 30,000-foot overview on how Snort functions as an intrusion detection system. Snort is distinguished as a network intrusion detection system and inherits the advantages and disadvantages associated with this genre of IDS. NIDSs have grown more popular than other types of IDSs because of their ability to provide intrusion monitoring coverage that covers large swaths of network infrastructure.

Snort is an incredibly flexible application that can be installed on every major hardware platform and operating system. It monitors for intrusions effectively even under fully saturated high-bandwidth networks. Snort is an open source application and can be modified freely and distributed free of cost. A sizable community of talented developers and users has grown around the Snort IDS and are fully committed to enhancing the application and providing expert technical support.

Snort is primarily a signature-matching IDS that uses rules to identify suspicious or malicious traffic. Rules can be created to catch out-of-spec traffic, malicious payload contents, and specific protocol elements. Custom rules can be created to match any traffic signature desired, and are used to adapt Snort to your network topology. Snort stores all captured traffic data possible, which makes the job of the IDS analyst less nebulous.

Snort has a flexible architecture that can be extended to perform new tasks. Preprocessors are plug-ins that are used to massage data before it is fed into the Snort signature-detection engine. These preprocessors are efforts to stay abreast in the ever-changing world of vulnerabilities and exposures. Preprocessors also add new protocol support for Snort, and are used to detect suspicious traffic that has no identifiable signature. Output plug-ins get intrusion data from Snort to the IDS analyst. They are configurable in many different ways to support real-time alerting and point-and-click GUIs.

Different attacks have different severity levels for each individual network at which they are launched. Snort supports customizable prioritization of alerts that allow you to decide which categories of attacks are important to you. Snort's prioritization of alerts is granular enough to allow individual attacks to be assigned a priority level.

Snort supports a distributed architecture that can be spread out over the standard three tiers. A console tier gathers and processes intrusion data, and passes it to a second server tier. The server tier organizes the data into a relational database and is responsible for real-time alerting. Additionally, the server tier houses a GUI that is used to manage alerting information. The third and final tier is a console used by the IDS analyst to interpret and act on intrusions. Hardening the hosts and utilizing encrypted sessions secures the tiers and, subsequently, Snort itself.

Although Snort is a powerful, flexible, and cost-effective IDS solution, it does have some shortcomings. Intrusion detection is reactive in nature and does not directly prevent intrusion. Intrusion detection is not an automated process; it requires a highly skilled and intelligent analyst to interpret and act on suspicious activity. IDSs are prone to false positives, which can cause the IDS analyst to lose interest in intrusion detection. A flood of false positives can be employed by hackers to overwhelm an IDS and render it useless. Snort has several options to reduce false positives without false negatives occurring, but they can make using and maintaining an IDS difficult. Snort is complex and difficult to install, even for highly skilled sysadmins. Snort is also dependent on the libpcap sniffing interface for its portability, which limits the maximum bandwidth it can process.

3

Dissecting Snort

THE CLICHÉ YOUR GRAMMAR SCHOOL TEACHERS told you, "It's what's on the inside that counts!" still applies in the real world. Snort contains many configurable internal components that can vastly influence false positives and negatives as well as general packet logging performance. Knowledge of Snort's internals is required to make Snort run and monitor for intrusions effectively. Snort is a powerful application, but it takes a little more in-depth research on your part than other, less potent, IDSs. Understanding the function of these internal components will help you customize Snort to your network and help you avoid some of the common Snort pitfalls.

Snort can be divided into five major components that are each critical to intrusion detection. The first is the packet capturing mechanism. Snort relies on an external packet capturing library (libpcap) to sniff packets. After packets have been captured in a raw form, they are passed into the packet decoder. The decoder is the first step into Snort's own architecture. The packet decoder translates specific protocol elements into an internal data structure. After the initial preparatory packet capture and decode is completed, traffic is handled by the preprocessors. Any number of pluggable preprocessors either examine or manipulate packets before handing them to the next component: the detection engine. The detection engine performs simple tests on a single aspect of each packet to detect intrusions. The last component is the output plugins, which generate alerts to present suspicious activity to you. A simplified graphical representation of the dataflow is shown in Figure 3.1.

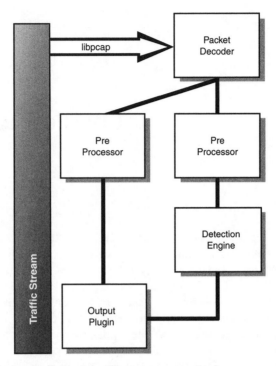

Figure 3.1   Snort component dataflow.

Feeding Snort Packets with Libpcap

To get packets into the preprocessors and then the main detection engine, some prior labor must first occur. Snort has no native packet capture facility yet; it requires an external packet sniffing library: libpcap. Libpcap was chosen for packet capture for its platform independence. It can be run on every popular combination of hardware and OS; there is even a Win32 port—winpcap. Because Snort utilizes the libpcap library to grab packets off the wire, it can leverage lipbcap's platform portability and be installed almost anywhere. Using libpcap makes Snort a truly platform-independent application.

The responsibility for grabbing packets directly from the network interface card belongs to libpcap. It makes the capture facility for raw packets provided by the underlying operating system available to other applications.

A *raw packet* is a packet that is left in its original, unmodified form as it had traveled across the network from client to server. A raw packet has all its protocol header information left intact and unaltered by the operating system. Network applications typically do not process raw packets; they depend on the OS to read protocol information and properly forward payload data to them. Snort is unusual in this sense in that it requires the opposite: it needs to have the packets in their raw state to function. Snort uses protocol header information that would have been stripped off by the operating system to detect some forms of attacks.

Using libpcap is not the most efficient way to acquire raw packets. It can process only one packet at a time, making it a bottleneck for high-bandwidth (1Gbps) monitoring situations. In the future Snort will likely implement packet capture libraries specific to an OS, or even hardware. There are several methods other than using libpcap for grabbing packets from a network interface card. Berkeley Packet Filter (BPF), Data Link Provider Interface (DLPI), and the SOCK_PACKET mechanism in the Linux kernel are other tools for grabbing raw packets.

Packet Decoder

As soon as packets have been gathered, Snort must decode the specific protocol elements for each packet. The packet decoder is actually a series of decoders that each decode specific protocol elements. It works up the Network stack, starting with lower level Data Link protocols, decoding each protocol as it moves up. A packet follows this data flow as it moves through the packet decoder (see Figure 3.2).

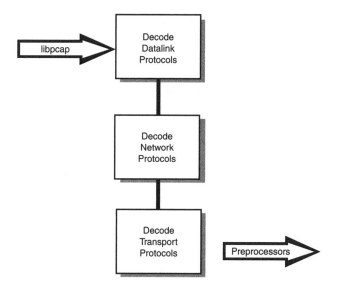

Figure 3.2 Decoder data flow.

As packets move through the various protocol decoders, a data structure is filled up with decoded packet data. As soon as packet data is stored in a data structure it is ready to be analyzed by the preprocessors and the detection engine.

Preprocessors

Snort's preprocessors fall into two categories. They can be used to either examine packets for suspicious activity or modify packets so that the detection engine can properly interpret them. A number of attacks cannot be detected by signature matching via the detection engine, so "examine" preprocessors step up to the plate and detect suspicious activity. These types of preprocessors are indispensable in discovering non-signature-based attacks. The other preprocessors are responsible for normalizing traffic so that the detection engine can accurately match signatures. These preprocessors defeat attacks that attempt to evade Snort's detection engine by manipulating traffic patterns.

Additionally, Snort cycles packets through every preprocessor to discover attacks that require more than one preprocessor to detect them. If Snort simply stopped checking for the suspicious attributes of a packet after it had set off an alert via a preprocessor, attackers could use this deficiency to hide traffic from Snort. Suppose a black hat intentionally encoded a malicious remote exploit attack in a manner that would set off a low priority alert from a preprocessor. If processing is assumed to be finished at this point and the packet is no longer cycled through the preprocessors, the remote exploit attack would register only an encoding alert. The remote exploit would go unnoticed by Snort, obscuring the true nature of the traffic.

Preprocessor parameters are configured and tuned via the snort.conf file. The same snort.conf file lets you add or remove preprocessors as you see fit.

frag2

The `frag2` preprocessor is Snort's weapon against IP fragmentation attacks. Fragmentation is a normally occurring phenomenon in IP networks. It is necessary to successfully send traffic over different types of network media. Different network-based protocols have divergent rules for the maximum allowable size or maximum transmission unit (MTU) for datagrams on their networks.

Fragmentation occurs normally when a packet's payload exceeds the MTU. On an ethernet network, any IP datagram larger than 1,500 bytes has to be fragmented. Fragmentation does not have to happen exclusively at the origination point; it can occur at an intermediate router.

After packets are fragmented, they must be reassembled at the target host. It is the reassembly process that hackers exploit to perpetrate attacks. The receiving host expects the sender to follow some rules when fragmenting. They are:

- The receiving host reassembles packets by associating a fragment with an identical fragment identification number, or fragment ID. The fragment ID is a copy of the IP identification number in the IP header.

- Each fragment must carry its position or offset in the original unfragmented packet (that is, the first fragment will have an offset of 0).

- Each fragment must display the amount of data carried in the corresponding fragment.

- If the fragment is not the last fragment to be received, it must flag the more fragments (MF) bit.

As you can see, any host that expected these rules to be followed at all times could be exploited by a malicious hacker. One simple attack devised to bypass firewalls and filtering devices uses fragmentation to overwrite TCP header data. The attack works by sending a fragmented TCP packet with header information that is allowed through the firewall. Subsequent fragments contain malicious data that would not otherwise be allowable through the firewall. If the fragmentation offset is small enough, though, the malicious packet overwrites the header information, allowing the malicious traffic through the firewall. An example is overwriting the header to change the destination port number. The attacker might change traffic from normal port 80 HTTP traffic to attack RPC on TCP port 111.

A good proportion of fragmentation attacks are DoS attacks. Host operating systems have been discovered to react unexpectedly to crafted fragmented packets. Probably the most famous type of these attacks was the Ping of Death attack. This attack used many small fragmented ICMP packets, which, when reassembled, exceeded the maximum allowable size for an IP datagram of 65,535 bytes. This caused most operating systems vulnerable to the Ping of Death to crash unexpectedly.

A hacker tool named fragroute uses fragmentation techniques to hide malicious traffic from Snort. Fragroute combines many of the previously known fragmentation evasion tactics into one tool. The various techniques can be mixed and matched together, making reconstruction of the fragmented attacks difficult. Fortunately, frag2 can now detect these types of attacks with some additional configuration options.

The frag2 preprocessor can detect attack types that are related to fragmentation, whether they are IDS evasion techniques or malicious DoS attacks. The frag2 preprocessor is important and should never be disabled. There are five options for configuring frag2. They are described in the following sections.

timeout *Seconds*

This option sets the number of seconds that a fragment is to be saved. If the fragment is not completed in the defined time allowance, it is dropped. Sixty seconds is the default, and should work well for most networks. If you are monitoring a network prone to IP fragmentation, such as a network with an abundance of NFS traffic, it is recommended that you reduce this threshold to avoid false positives. Most external monitoring sensors should not see much fragmented traffic. Some crafty black hats know that 60 seconds is the default setting for frag2, and use this information to evade frag2. It is recommended that you increase this threshold slightly to 65 seconds to combat this.

memcap *bytes*

The memory cap option limits the amount of memory the frag2 preprocessor can utilize. The default is 4,194,304 bytes, which is suitable for most fragmentation situations. Once again, if you are monitoring a network with heavy fragmentation traffic, it would be prudent to increase this amount.

detect_state_problems

This simple configuration option enables detection of overlapping fragments. Overlapping fragments have an offset that overwrites a previous fragment. They are used in firewall bypassing attacks, described previously in this section.

min_ttl *number*

The min_ttl configuration option specifies the minimum time to live (TTL) that frag2 will accept. Anything lower than *[number]* will be dropped. The default setting is 0. TTL is a death counter for packets. Every time a router forwards a packet, it decrements the TTL value and forwards it on. If the TTL reaches 0, the packet is dropped and no longer routed. TTLs were put in place to avoid situations where packets would get caught in endless loops, which could potentially create a Denial of Service situation.

Tools such as fragroute use small TTL values to set the expirations for datagrams before they reach the target host, but Snort still picks them up. This scenario is possible when a sensor lies at an intermediate point between the attacker and the target. If the target is two hops away from the sensor, the sensor and not the target interprets any packets with a TTL of 1. Packets with a TTL of 1 expire and are not forwarded on to the target. This can have the effect of inserting garbage data into an attack signature, making the signature not discernable by Snort. Snort is unable to detect the attack. Imagine that three packets make up an attack on an FTP server:

```
Packet 1 - QUOTE SITE                  - TTL = 55

Packet 2 - inserted_garbage data          - TTL = 1

Packet 3 - EXEC EXEC echo toor::0:0::/:/bin/sh >> /etc/passwd - TTL = 122
```

Snort sees the attack as the following:

```
QUOTE SITEinsert_garbage dataEXEC EXEC echo toor::0:0::/:/bin/sh >> /etc/passwd
```

Because of the *insert garbage data*, Snort cannot match a rule to this signature. However, the host still sees the real attack because the packet containing the garbage data will expire and not be forwarded:

```
QUOTE SITE EXEC EXEC echo toor::0:0::/:/bin/sh >> /etc/passwd
```

Dropping packets that have a very low TTL can avert this type of evasion. The recommended setting is 3.

ttl_limit *number*

This option specifies the maximum difference in TTL values that fragmented packets with the same fragment ID can have. The default is 5. This option was added because tools like Fragroute utilize inconsistent values for fragmented packets to evade Snort. They are vastly different than what is found in normal Internet traffic. The average change in TTL values for normal Internet traffic is somewhere in the 5–7 range. Leaving this set at the default of 5 creates some false positive noise; it is recommended to set `ttl_limit` to 8.

stream4

The `stream4` preprocessor is what Snort uses to maintain the state of TCP streams, which is used in detecting some types of information gathering attacks. Stateful inspection with `stream4` helps Snort better match attack signatures across multiple packets. This is important because attacks can be spread over many individual packets or exhibit anomalies in terms of TCP connections. The `stream4` preprocessor also lets you create rules that are state-aware via the *flow* option.

A simple example can be demonstrated with the WU-FTPDexploit. A vulnerability was discovered for all versions of WU-FTPD, which is included by default in most major Linux distributions. With this exploit, any user who can log into a vulnerable version of the WU-FTPD server can execute arbitrary code remotely with root access. The vulnerability is due to a combination of coding errors, one located within the function responsible for the remote command globbing feature, which fails to properly signal an error to its caller under certain conditions. The globbing function does not properly handle the string "~{" as an illegal parameter.

To detect the first phase of this attack, a rule must be created to trigger any time a signature matched "~{". This works fine if the entire content of the attack is in the same packet. If the attacker causes the signature to be split up, so that ~ is in one packet and the { is in the next, the signature does not trigger. With `stream4`, Snort stores the ~ portion of the signature. When the attacker sends the final piece, {, in a subsequent packet, Snort completes the signature and an alert is generated. Without stream reassembly this would not be possible.

The `stream4` preprocessor can also detect attackers doing unusual things with TCP streams in an attempt to hide information-gathering traffic. One such method of reconnaissance is a TCP stealth or half-open scan. In this method, the TCP three-way handshake is never fully completed. The attacker first sends a SYN packet as normal. When a SYN-ACK is received from the host, the service is assumed to be listening. The attacker never completes the handshake by responding with the expected ACK packet. This type of scanning could trick an IDS that is not monitoring state.

The `stream4` preprocessor is the next evolutionary step up from the `stream` preprocessor. It had to be expanded to deal with a type of stateless attack specifically created to create a Denial of Service condition with Snort. Snot attacks take a Snort's own ruleset and generate a flood of randomly chosen attack signatures. When this flood is aimed at Snort, it creates a massive amount of false positives. A Snot attack can be used to bury a legitimate attack in the noise. When a Snot attack is run, it completes only the first phase of the three-way handshake, similar to the stealth scan. You can configure `stream4` in conjunction with a command-line option to defeat Snot attacks. With the –z command-line option specified with the "est" argument, Snort ignores TCP streams that do not demonstrate normal bidirectional activity.

The `stream4` preprocessor was also rewritten to incorporate higher bandwidth conditions. With modern hardware, `stream4` can handle stateful inspection for up to 64,000 simultaneous connections. `stream4` supports 10 different configurable options, described in the following sections.

detect_scans

This option simply enables `stream4` for portscan detection. This option detects normal TCP connect scans and stealthy scans, such as the Xmas Tree, Half Open, and SYN-FIN scans. It can detect a variety of other attempts at stealthy scanning.

detect_state_problems

With this option enabled, `stream4` alerts on various state inconsistencies that black hats have in their arsenals. One of the many possible attacks this configuration option detects is a TCP reset packet evasion attempt. This works by sending forged TCP reset packets each time a TCP connection is made. If this option is not enabled, Snort might perform stream reassembly incorrectly and assume that the connection has been terminated. Snort would then think that the session had been torn down and not log future data relating to this stream. Malicious traffic could be hidden from Snort in this manner.

disable_evasion_alerts

This configuration option disables some of the alerting that Snort does for aged, less widely used IDS evasion attempts. TCP overlapping is one of these methods. It works by creating connections with overlapping but incongruous data. This may cause older intrusion detection systems to misinterpret the intent of the connection. TCP overlapping was used to create both false positives and negatives in older IDSs. Recent TCP implementations of Windows 2000 and XP send status information in this manner, which results in a noticeable number of false positives. For this reason, it may be advisable to enable this option if the number of false positives becomes too much to bear. With any of the options beginning with "disable" in Snort, it is always best to leave them enabled unless they present an unmanageable number of false positives.

min_ttl *number*

Nearly the same as the option in `frag2`. This option drops packets with a TTL less than *number*. A short TTL attack has a short enough TTL set for some packets in a stream. A router may then cause some of the packets with TTLs of zero to expire before they reach the target. If Snort is only one hop away from the target and does not check the TTLs, it will reassemble the TCP stream badly. The recommended setting for *number* is 3.

ttl_limit *number*

This option specifies the maximum difference in TTL values that fragmented packets with the same fragment ID can have. The default is 5. Fragroute utilized inconstant TTL values for fragmented packets that were way out of the range of normal Internet traffic. The average change in TTL values for normal Internet traffic is somewhere in the

5–7 range. Leaving this set at the default of 5 creates some false positive noise; it is recommended to set *number* equal to 8.

noinspect

This option disables stateful inspection of TCP streams. The `noinspect command` should be utilized only in special situations, such as testing in very high bandwidth or limited hardware.

keepstats *machine or binary*

This option logs session summary information to session.log in Snort's log directory. The `machine` switch logs in a flat file; the `binary` switch logs in unified binary output format. This log is useful for additional event correlation and forensics.

timeout *seconds*

This option sets the number of seconds for a which a session is to be saved. If the session is not completed in the defined time allowance, it is flushed. Thirty seconds is the default. If you are monitoring a network with heavy session traffic, it is recommended to increase this threshold to avoid false negatives. Some crafty black hats know that 30 seconds is the default setting for `stream4`, and use this to evade `stream4`. It is recommended that you increase this threshold slightly to 35 seconds to combat this.

memcap *bytes*

The memory cap option limits the amount of memory the `stream4` preprocessor can utilize. The default is 8,388,608 bytes, which is suitable for normal networks. Once again, if you are monitoring a network with heavy session traffic, it would be prudent to increase this amount.

log_flushed_streams

This option is used to log complete streams to disk that contain a packet that matches a signature. Without this option, Snort logs only the specific packet(s) that match the signature. This option works only when Snort is run in pcap mode.

stream4_reassemble

The `stream4_reassemble` preprocessor is closely related to `stream4`. It performs TCP stream reassembly as described earlier. Malformed packet injection is one of the many reassembly attacks. Malicious hackers attack the TCP stream reassembly process by creating packets with some valid header data such as sequence numbers, ACK numbers, source ports, and destination ports. The forged packets have a bogus payload and a checksum that fails. These crafted packets are inserted between totally valid packets. The target drops the injected crafted packets, and IDSs that do not do TCP checksum verification when reassembling packets miss the attack. Fortunately, Snort has `stream4_reassemble` to catch these attacks.

The `stream4_reassemble` preprocessor has five different configuration options, described in the next few sections.

clientonly

The default setting for `stream4_reassemble` is `clientonly`. This setting reassembles sessions only if they originate from the client side. The client network is defined elsewhere in the snort.conf file. Chapter 6 examines the definition of clients, servers, and other important hosts.

serveronly

The inverse of the `clientonly` option is `serveronly`. The `stream4_reassemble` preprocessor reassembles only sessions originating from the server side.

both

This reassembles from both client and server directions.

ports *list*

The `ports` option is used to specify which TCP destination port traffic is reassembled. The default is set for ports 21/FTP, 23/Telnet, 25/SMTP, 53/DNS, 80/HTTP, 143/IMAP, 110/POP, 111/RPC, and 513/rlogin. You can enable this port list by specifying `default` for the `[list]` parameter. You can enable reassembly for every port by specifying `all`. If you have a custom list of TCP ports on which you would like reassembly, you can list them, separated by spaces.

noalerts

This option disables alerting for reassembly attacks and evasions. If you are generating an unhealthy number of false positives related to TCP session reassembly, this should be your last resort. It is recommended that you attempt to narrow down the traffic with the `ports`, `serveronly`, and `clientonly` configuration options before disabling alerts altogether.

HTTP_decode

The `HTTP_decode` preprocessor is responsible for detecting abnormal HTTP traffic and normalizing it so that the detection engine can properly interpret it. Normalizing traffic is the process of translating an obscure character set, such as Unicode or hex, to a character set that Snort can recognize. This is necessary for Snort to be able to match signatures to malicious content. `HTTP_decode` works specifically with the URI string of an HTTP request. It generates an alert if it encounters traffic that requires decoding.

Encoding or obfuscating HTTP traffic is a method that hackers can use to disguise an attack from an IDS or even the human eye. Without `HTTP_decode`, an attack that Snort would normally catch can be obfuscated in a manner that does not match a signature, but that the target Web server still accepts as a valid URL string. Using Microsoft's IIS %u encoding, an .ida attack that would normally match a signature can be easily hidden.

Suppose you have a Snort rule designed to trigger on any URI content that matches .ida. An attacker could use %u encoding to hide the a and evade Snort with the following URL request:

```
GET /vulnerable.id%u0061 HTTP/1.0
```

After the request evaded Snort, IIS would translate this to

```
GET /vulnerable.ida HTTP/1.0
```

Encoding URLs in this manner can be used to obfuscate any type of malicious HTTP URI request. Encoded URLs are also used to coax unsophisticated Internet users into clicking on malicious hyperlinks. Cross-site scripting attacks sometime require a user to click on a link for an authentication token to be delivered to a host controlled by the attacker. These links are often encoded in hex to increase the chances of success. The HTTP_decode preprocessor can detect users clicking on hex-encoded links.

Moving beyond obfuscation, some malicious attacks utilize encoded strings. Programmers implementing application-level access controls and bug fixes often forget about encoded URI strings. The Unicode directory traversal sample attack in Chapter 1 is a good example of a coding error that resulted in a security exposure. Even though directory traversal attacks had been patched, they were still vulnerable when the / symbol was encoded in Unicode.

HTTP_decode has five different configuration options that relate to different encoding strategies attackers employ.

port list

This option is the list of source ports where HTTP_decode is to look for encoded HTTP URI requests. The default is 80. Any Web server ports should be listed here, delimited by a space.

unicode

Specifying the unicode option normalizes all Unicode strings to ASCII. Leave this option off if you do not want alerts for Unicode URI traffic.

iis_alt_unicode

Enabling this option allows HTTP_decode to detect %u encoding. Microsoft's IIS supports a little-known, proprietary method of HTTP URI encoding known as %u encoding. The legitimate purpose of this %u encoding was to represent true Unicode character strings. Because %u encoding is proprietary and not an IETF standard, most IDS systems are unaware that %u encoding existed. Attackers can use %u encoding to hide IIS attacks that would have otherwise triggered an alert. Not including this configuration option causes Snort to not generate alerts for %u encoding.

double_encode

This option detects possible double encoding attempts and normalizes double decoding attempts. In a double encoding attack, the cracker forwards an encoded HTTP URI request that has been through two rounds of encoding. The IDS detects the first round of encoding and normalizes it. The attack still evades the IDS, however, because the result of the first normalization outputs an encoded string that does not match a signature. Without this option enabled, Snort decodes a string only once and assumes there is no more nested encoding. For example, if an attacker wanted to pass in the infamous \ character with double encoding, she would encode the character in hex as %5c. To double encode, the attacker hex encodes the %5c string again. The attacker hex encodes % to %25, 5 to %35, and c to %63, resulting in %25%35%63. Thus, the cracker has double encoded the \ character as %25%35%63.

iis_flip_slash

This option detects and decodes directory separators that are obscured through the use of a Microsoft proprietary directory separator. Microsoft OSs separate directories using a \ instead of the standard /. A HTTP request requires that the direction separator be a /. This means that IIS, as well as all other Win32-based Web servers, must convert the directory separator to a /. IIS still allows the use of \ in HTTP requests, because it is considered a valid directory separator. With IIS, directory separators can be encoded as /scripts\admin.asp, which does not match a typical /scripts/admin.asp signature.

full_whitespace

This option generates alerts and normalizes strings that are obscured by the use of the /t method for formatting HTTP requests to an Apache Web server. A standard HTTP request uses spaces to separate different portions of the request. It looks like this:

```
method <whitespace> URI <whitespace> HTTP/ Version
```

The <whitespace>s are used as delimiters for extracting specific portions of the HTTP request, such as the URI string. Snort utilizes this method for extracting URI strings to match to signatures.

Apache 1.3.6 and newer permits a different nonstandard request:

```
method /t URI /t HTTP/ Version
```

This request evades any IDS that expects an HTTP request to be separated by <whitespace> rather than /t or a <tab>.

RPC_decode

This preprocessor has a similar function as HTTP_decode, but with another protocol: RPC. RPC can be used by black hats for both reconnaissance and remote exploit attacks. Attackers can use port mapping applications, such as rpcbind and portmapper, that make dynamic binding of remote services possible. The attacker can use information gathered from rpcbind to find additional targets for buffer overflows, or the attacker can attack the RPC service itself.

Malicious hackers desiring to hide RPC traffic can break up the RPC signature. The RPC signature, 0186A0, can be split up to obscure an RPC request. If the signature is spread out over many packets, Snort cannot match a valid signature. For this reason, RPC requests are normalized with the RPC_decode preprocessor. RPC_decode has one configuration option: *[ports list]* is the list of RPC ports to be normalized by RPC_decode. The default is 111 and 32771.

BO

The BO preprocessor detects Back Orifice. Back Orifice is a remote control Trojan for Windows systems. Back Orifice was a very popular Trojan when it was released, but has recently been replaced by other more advanced Trojans. Back Orifice still remains a considerable threat; it can be used by script kiddies to take total control of a remote system.

This preprocessor detects Back Orifice UDP traffic when commands are issued to the Trojan. It works by detecting the "magic cookie" that Back Orifice servers and clients require to communicate with each other. A fairly weak encryption algorithm is used to encrypt BO traffic. The entire keyspace of the Trojan's encrypted communication protocol can be brute forced with little effort. The BO preprocessor supports the brute forcing of Back Orifice's entire keyspace. It can also be configured to search for packets that use the default installation encryption key, 31337, to search for packets. Searching solely for the default key improves the performance of BO and Snort in general, but allows Back Orifice communication to slip by unnoticed if a key other than the default is used for encryption. BO supports two configuration options.

number

This option is used to set the default key used to decode Back Orifice–encrypted communication to something other than the default of 31337.

-nobrute

As explained previously, this option disables the brute forcing of the Back Orifice keyspace for a valid encryption key. This is the default setting. This setting should not be enabled unless BO is causing a significant performance impact on Snort.

Telnet_decode

This is another one of the family of decoding preprocessors. This preprocessor specifically relates to Telnet and FTP protocols. Telnet_decode decodes or removes arbitrarily inserted binary Telnet control codes in a Telnet or FTP stream. Malicious hackers insert control codes into communication in an attempt to evade Snort's watchful eye. Control code insertion is often performed with the SITE EXEC FTP command and its associated vulnerabilities. The FTP command SITE EXEC is used by attackers to execute system commands via an FTP connection. An attacker could enter an FTP command like so to retrieve a passwd file:

```
QUOTE SITE EXEC EXEC echo toor::0:0::/:/bin/sh >> /etc/passwd
```

More sophisticated hackers intersperse Telnet control codes into the command hoping to evade Snort. `Telnet_decode` prevents this by removing or decoding the malicious control codes. `Telnet_decode` has no configuration options.

ARPspoof

`ARPspoof` is a preprocessor designed to detect malicious Address Resolution Protocol (ARP) traffic. ARP is used on ethernet networks to map an IP address to a hardware MAC address. To reduce the number of ARP broadcasts on modern networks, operating systems of connected devices store a cache of ARP mappings. When a device receives an ARP reply, it updates its ARP cache with the new IP-to-MAC address mapping whether or not the device sent the ARP request.

Various attacks involve ARP; the basis of them is ARP spoofing. ARP spoofing is accomplished by crafting ARP request and reply packets. Forged ARP reply packets are stored in the ARP cache of the receiving device even if the device did not send the request.

ARP spoofing can be used to misdirect traffic, making sniffing possible on switched networks. Forged ARP replies can trick a target device into misdirecting ethernet frames intended for a legitimate device to the attackers choice of device. The legitimate device is not aware that misdirection had taken place. ARP spoofing can also be used to perform a simple yet effective DoS. The DoS happens when spoofed ARP replies that contain invalid IP-to-MAC mappings flood a device's ARP cache. This causes the target device to send traffic to non-existent devices.

The `ARPspoof` preprocessor can detect some of these types of attacks and ARP spoofing attempts. `ARPspoof` detects spoofing attempts by determining that an ethernet source address is different from the one included in the ARP message, indicating a spoofed ARP reply. Conversely, `ARPspoof` detects a destination address that differs from the one in the ARP message, indicating a spoofed ARP request.

Another type of attack `ARPspoof` detects is the ARP cache overwrite attack. The attack works by sending ARP packets received by the device for the device's own interface address but a different MAC address. This overwrites the device's own MAC address in the ARP cache with the malicious ARP request. This causes the device to be unable to send and receive any ARP packet. In turn, this causes the device and any other devices that depend on it for communication to be unable to send packets to each other.

Because ARP is a Layer 2 protocol, `ARPspoof` detects only those attacks occurring on the same physical segment as the Snort sensor. `ARPspoof` has two configuration options.

host IP address host MAC address

Each device that you wish to monitor with `ARPspoof` must be specified with its own IP-to-MAC address mapping. Each one of the devices is listed on a new line in the snort.conf file. Any time the mapping changes, you must reconfigure the file. Devices that obtain their IP address via DHCP should be converted to static IPs before `ARPspoof` is enabled.

`-unicast`

This option will enable detection of ARP `unicast` attacks. Most valid ARP requests are sent to broadcast addresses. ARP requests that are sent to a Unicast address are often the sign of an attack designed to modify ARP caches. This option is disabled by default, but should be enabled for serious ARP misuse monitoring.

ASN1_decode

`ASN1_decode` is a preprocessor designed to detect various inconsistencies in ASN.1 that may indicate malicious behavior. ASN.1 or Abstract Syntax Notation One is an international standard for coding and transmitting complex data structures. ASN.1 protocol is used by a diverse set of higher-level protocols including LDAP, SNMP, SSL, and X.509. ASN.1 is also used for communication in proprietary government and industrial applications. Portions of the U.S. power grid are controlled remotely by the ASN.1 protocol. The SS7 network that controls telephone call routing, parcel delivery, and credit card verification systems all use ASN.1. Vulnerabilities associated with ASN.1-based networks are a matter of national security and are a major concern.

A Finnish group of researchers at Oulu University discovered a wide range of ASN.1-related vulnerabilities. They were able to exploit poor coding of ASN.1 on almost every SNMP-enabled device. The exploits operate by deliberately violating the ASN.1 standard in thousands of different ways. Most of these violations take the format of extreme over-sizing or undersizing of ASN.1 messages. These cause the higher-level protocol dependent on ASN.1 to crash or create a situation where a buffer overflow occurs. This may have the effect of creating a Denial of Service condition or remotely controlling the attacked device.

The `ASN1_decode` preprocessor detects various attempts to attack ASN.1-enabled hosts by breaking the rules of the ASN.1 protocol. The OpenSSL ASN.1 DoS is an example of the type of attack `ASN1_decode` is designed to detect. OpenSSL had a vulnerability in its implementation of the ASN.1 library. This vulnerability, due to parsing errors, affects SSL, TLS, S/MIME, PKCS#7, and certificate creation routines. The certificate encodings can cause a Denial of Service to server and client implementations that depend on OpenSSL-to-secure communication over pubic networks.

`ASN1_decode` is an experimental beta preprocessor that may generate more false positives than other preprocessors. It has no configuration options at this time.

fnord

The `fnord` preprocessor is designed to detect and defeat polymorphic shell code evasion attempts. Polymorphic shell code is a new twist on an old idea. Virus creators have been designing polymorphic viruses for years. Polymorphic viruses change their signature randomly to avoid detection by static signature-based Antivirus applications. A similar method of randomizing remote exploit shell code was developed recently to evade IDSs, and released with the ADMutate tool.

ADMutate evades Snort or any other IDS by randomly polymorphing the buffer overflow signature by choosing random no-op instructions and encrypting the shellcode portion of the exploit. A buffer overflow is divided into two sections: a no-op pad or no-op sled and the shellcode payload. The no-op pad is a large section of no operation codes (that is 0×90 for Intel) specific to the target architecture. The shellcode payload is a portion of the buffer overflow where the shell gets executed and bound to a TCP port. Snort and other IDSs use the no-ops and the shellcode signature to detect buffer over-flow exploits.

ADMutate performs two actions on the buffer overflow exploit to disguise it. It randomly replaces the no-op instructions with other no-effect instructions that are functionally similar to a no-op. It then encrypts the shellcode with a fairly simple encryption algorithm (usually xor or a double xor). The purpose of encrypting is not to protect the shellcode, but rather to obscure it in a random fashion. ADMutate has to include the decryption routine with the newly formulated exploit. The decryption routine is randomly created through the use of methods similar to those employed by polymorphic viruses. This process makes the no-ops, the shellcode, and the newly added decryption engine impossible to detect for normal signature-based IDSs. Any attacker using ADMutate on previously existing exploits can happily hack away without Snort noticing.

To defeat polymorphic shellcode attacks, the `fnord` preprocessor was created. It detects a large amount of no-effect instructions grouped together for Intel, Sparc, or HP hardware architectures. It is effective at detecting polymorphed exploits, but generates some false positives.

The `fnord` preprocessor is relatively new and is potentially computationally expensive. It has no configuration options.

conversation

The `conversation` preprocessor is similar to the `stream4` and `stream4_reassemble` preprocessors. It is designed to extend session tracking beyond TCP. It tracks pseudo-sessions or conversations for any other IP protocol (such as ICMP). This is useful for detecting where communication has originated. It can also detect when new communication commences. The `conversation` preprocessor must be enabled for the `portscan2` preprocessor to function.

As of now, `conversation` is used only in conjunction with `portscan2` to detect information gathering attempts. It has three configuration options.

allowed_protocols *port list or any*

This is the list of IP protocols for which Conversation will track sessions. It can be configured with either a list of IP protocols or the any option. The number list corresponds to the IP protocol number defined in RFC 791. Some of the most common are 1/ICMP, 6/TCP, and 17/UDP. The any option tracks all protocols.

`timeout`

This option sets the number of seconds that a conversation will be saved. If the conversation is not completed in the defined time allowance, it is dropped. The default is 60 seconds. Some crafty black hats know that 60 seconds is the default setting for `conversation` and use this as an evasion technique. It is recommended to increase this threshold slightly to 65 seconds to combat this attack.

`max_conversations` *numbers*

   This is the maximum conversations that `conversation` will support simultaneously. The default is set to 65,335, which is the recommended value.

portscan2

The `portscan2` preprocessor is the successor to the original anomaly detection `portscan` preprocessor. It functions by anomaly detection as well. The original `portscan` detected reconnaissance attempts by alerting whenever packets were seen going to four different ports in less than three seconds. This set off a lot of false positives. Even though you could specify which IP addresses to ignore, a fair amount of Snort regulars would disable the preprocessor altogether. It was not a bad preprocessor by any means; it just needed some evolutionary improvements. Fortunately, `portscan2` is here to avenge the death of his father.

   The `portscan2` preprocessor works in concurrence with `conversation` to track sessions for IP protocols. It has configurable options that enable it to detect different methods of scanning that are anomalous for most IP networks. It can detect vertical portscans, or scans that sweep the entire range of ports for one host. It can also detect horizontal portscans, which scan one port across many hosts. The `portscan2` preprocessor is not as prone to false positives because it has more configuration options. It utilizes `conversation`, and is therefore aware of state. It has five different configuration options.

`scanners_max` *number*

This option sets the maximum number of possible conversations to track for reconnaissance attempts. The default setting is 3,200.

`targets_max` *number*

This is the maximum number of target hosts to be monitored. The default setting is 5,000. Even if you do not have this many possible targets, it is a good idea to keep this setting high. The attacker may be blindly scanning for IP addresses that have no host bound to them, and you would not want to miss this type of information gathering attempt.

`target_limit` *number*

This configuration option is the horizontal portscan threshold. It is the maximum number of unique hosts the conversation can attempt to access before generating an alert. The default is 5, and is the recommended setting.

`port_limit` *number*

This is the vertical portscan threshold. It is the maximum number of unique ports the conversation can attempt to access before generating an alert. The ports do not have to be on the same host to generate the alert. The default setting is 20, and is recommended.

`timeout` *seconds*

This configuration option is the length of time to hold a conversation in memory before flushing it. This is the amount of time you are giving `portscan2` to generate an alert. The default setting is 60, and is recommended.

SPADE

`SPADE` (Statistical Packet Anomaly Detection Engine) is a preprocessor that detects suspicious traffic via anomaly detection methods. `SPADE` determines whether traffic is anomalous by building a table to describe normal traffic patterns. When traffic does not match data stored in the table, `SPADE` outputs an alert.

`SPADE` functions by assigning all incoming packets an anomaly score. High anomaly scores are assigned to specific packets that are rare in occurrence. `SPADE` defines a unique packet by combining packet IP and port information. For instance, a packet with a destination IP of 192.168.1.1 and destination port of 443 is defined as one packet.

A table is constructed that reflects the occurrences of different kinds of packets over time. Recent packets are given precedent over aged packets. Over time, an alerting threshold is defined for `SPADE`. For each packet that exceeds this threshold, an alert is generated.

`SPADE` has five configuration options.

anom-report-thresh

This is the threshold at which packets are reported when the Snort process starts. If a packet has an anomaly score that exceeds this threshold, an alert is generated. If configured with -1, SPADE starts with no default alerting threshold. The default is -1.

filename

This is the filename to which alerts will be written. If SPADE is used in conjunction with an output plugin, alerts are sent as expected through the plugins.

statefile

This file is used to store the state of SPADE's anomaly table. The statefile is used to keep the anomaly table intact when the Snort process is refreshed or restarted. You can set this option to 0 if you do not wish to store a statefile.

checkpoint-freq

The option to configure how often the statefile is refreshed. *Checkpoint-freq* is the number of packets to accept before refreshing the table.

probability-mode

This is a configurable list of probability modes to use in detecting anomalous behavior. The four different modes define a SPADE "packet" differently. You configure this by choosing one of the related numbers.

- 0: A Bayes network approximation of the source IP, source port, destination IP, and destination port.
- 1: Source IP, source port, destination IP, and destination port.
- 2: Source IP, destination IP, and destination port.
- 3: Destination IP and destination port.

The default setting is 3.

The Detection Engine

The *detection engine* isthe primary Snort component. It has two major functions: rules parsing and signature detection. The detection engine builds attack signatures by parsing Snort rules. Snort rules are read line by line, and are loaded into an internal data structure. The rules are loaded only when the Snort service is started, meaning that to modify, add, or delete a rule you must refresh the Snort daemon.

The detection engine runs traffic through the now loaded rule set in the order that it loads them into memory. You can dictate which rules are run first by prioritizing and then organizing in the manner you see fit. Rules are split into two functional sections: the rule header (rule tree node) and the rule option (option tree node). The rule header contains information about the conditions for applying the signature. You can specify the protocol, source, and destination IP address ranges, the port, and the log type in the rule header. The rule header for the OpenSSH CRC32 remote exploit is:

```
alert tcp $EXTERNAL_NET any -> $HOME_NET 22
```

The rule option for the same exploit begins and ends with a parenthetical. The rule option contains the actual signature, the priority level, and some documentation about the attack.

```
(msg:"EXPLOIT ssh CRC32 overflow /bin/sh"; flow:to_server,established;
content:"/bin/sh"; reference:bugtraq,2347; reference:cve,CVE-2001-0144;
classtype:shellcode-detect; sid:1324; rev:3;)
```

The detection engine processes rule headers and rule options differently. The detection engine builds a linked list decision tree. The nodes of the tree test each incoming packet for increasingly precise signature elements. A packet is tested to see whether it is TCP; if so, it is passed to the portion of the tree that has rules for TCP. The packet is then tested to see whether it matches a source address in a rule; if so, it passes down the corresponding rule chains. This process happens until the packet either matches an attack signature or tests clean and is dropped. The important thing to remember is that Snort commences testing a packet after it has found a signature to match to the packet. Even if the packet could possibly match another signature, the detection engine moves on to the next packet. This is why it is valuable to organize rules so that the most malicious signatures are loaded first. Look for this to change in the near future; Snort's developers are hard at work implementing a last-exit strategy.

Output Plugins

Snort's output plugins are the means Snort has to get intrusion data to you. The purpose of the output plugins is to dump alerting data to another resource or file. Multiple outputting plugins can be activated to perform different functions. Loads of external applications—some even built exclusively for Snort—are designed to read Snort's output and manage intrusion data. Chapters 6 and 11 examine some of these applications.

Output plugins can be a major bottleneck for Snort. Snort can read and process packets quickly, but bogs down when trying to write to a slow database or over a network. Database output plugins are not used in high-bandwidth environments. It is recommended to configure Snort to spool to unified format and let Snort's unified log application, Barnyard, take over. Snort has 12 output plugins that push out data in different formats.

Alert_fast

`Alert_fast` is the quick and dirty outputting mechanism for Snort. It spits out alerts in a one-line file as fast as the detection engine can spawn them. With `Alert_fast` Snort does not write packet headers, making it a fast but brief method of logging. `Alert_fast` takes one configuration option.

[filename] is simply the name of the file for `Alert_fast` to log to. The log is created in the default logging directory (/var/log/snort) or the directory specified.

Alert_full

This is a somewhat antiquated logging facility for Snort, but still useful for low-bandwidth networks. `Alert_full` creates a directory for each IP that generates an alert and fills it with decoded packet dumps. It includes the packet headers in the dumps, unlike `Alert_fast`. It has one configuration option.

[filename] is simply the name of the file for `Alert_full` to log to. The log is created in the default logging directory (/var/log/snort) or the directory specified.

Alert_smb

`Alert_smb` is another antiquated output plugin. It sends windows SMB requests to Windows machines. If you take perverse pleasure in clearing message boxes hour after hour, this plugin is for you. `Alert_smb` sends alerting information in the clear, and executes an external binary with root privileges, making it a security risk in and of itself. `Alert_smb` has one configuration option.

[alertworkstationlist] is a file listing workstation to be notified. The format of the workstation file is a list of the NETBIOS names of the hosts, one per line.

Alert_unixsock

This plugin sets up a Unix domain socket and sends alerts to it. External programs/processes can listen in on this socket and receive Snort alert and packet data in real time. This plugin does not work with Windows installations, for obvious reasons. Alert_unixsock has no configuration options.

Log_tcpdump

Log_tcpdump logs packets to the famous tcpdump file format. There exists a wide assortment of applications and tools designed to read tcpdump output. This module enables you to use them in conjunction with Snort. Log_tcpdump has one configuration option.

[filename] is the name of the output file. The [filename] will have the <month><date>@<time> prepended to it. This is to keep data from separate Snort runs distinct.

CSV

The CSV plugin outputs to a comma delimited file. CSV files are easily imported into other databases and spreadsheets. The data separated by commas can be organized in any manner required. You can use CSV to write as few as one field or all 24. CSV takes two configuration options.

[filename]
This is the name of the output file.

[default | field list]
Here you can list out the fields in your desired order. The possible fields are:

timestamp	ethdst	tos
msg	ethlen	id
proto	tcpflags	dgmlen
src	tcpseq	iplen
srcport	tcpack	icmptype
dst	tcplen	icmpcode
dstport	tcpwindow	icmpid
ethsrc	ttl	icmpseq

You can modify this list to output the fields you want in the order you desire. If you specify default, CSV outputs a comma-separated file in the preceding order.

XML

The XML plugin allows you to log to Simple Network Markup Language (SNML). SNML can be used to collect data from many different sensors in a single management database. The XML plugin logs via encrypted or plain text HTTP sessions. XML has a unique sanitization feature. With the santization feature enabled, all IP addresses will be outputted with the mask, XXX.XXX.XXX.XXX. You can then anonymously submit your intrusion data for review by other entities, such as the CERT/CC (check www.cert.org for more information). CERT/CC can use this data to predict trends and monitor malicious activity on a global scale. The XML plugin has a good number of configuration options.

log or *alert*

This is used to specify whether to attach the XML output plugin to the log or alert facility. Certain rules are set to "alert" while others are set to "log"; this option outputs the chosen rule type.

parameter list

This option is a monster list of possible parameters for configuring XML to function in the way you want it to. Parameters are set in the familiar *name=value* pair. A list of names and descriptions follows:

- `file`—Filename for XML output. If this is the only parameter entered, it writes to disk, to a local file.
- `protocol`—Used to specify the protocol for logging to a remote host. Possible values are
    - `http`—Send output via HTTP posts; requires file parameter
    - `https`—Send via encrypted HTTPS posts; requires file, cert, and key parameters
    - `tcp`—Send via a TCP port; requires an external application to listen to the TCP port
- `host`—The remote host to send logs to.
- `cert`—The client certificate to be used for HTTPS communication.
- `sanitize`—An IP address range with netmask combination. The range specified will be sanitized. You can use this option several times to sanitize multiple ranges. With any alerts that are sanitized, packet payloads are not logged.
- `hex`—Include this name with no value to store binary data in hex.
- `base64`—Include this name with no value to store binary data in base64 encoding.
- `ascii`—Include this name with no value to store binary data in human-readable ASCII encoding.

- detail—Can be either full or fast. With full you log all details of the packet that Snort has available. Fast logs only timestamp, signature, source and destination IPs, source and destination ports, TCP flags, and protocol.

Alert_syslog

Alert_syslog writes to the syslog facility. A syslog server can be used to collect logging information from a variety of different devices not related to Snort, such as routers, firewalls, Web servers, and so on. Inputting Snort intrusion data into a syslog server can vastly aid in event correlation and problem identification. Writing alerting data to syslog can be used in conjunction with other tools to perform real-time alerting and notification. Alert_syslog is one of the most popular outputting plugins.

This plugin cannot be used to log to a remote syslog server if the sensor is installed on a Windows machine. You must use the command-line option for syslog (-s) to write to a remote syslog server. Alert_syslog supports the standard three syslog configuration options.

facility

This is the facility parameter that will be assigned to Alert_syslog output in the syslog server. The default is LOG_AUTH. You may want to use LOG_AUTHPRIV if others will be working with the syslog server but should not have access to intrusion data.

priority

This is the priority parameter that will be assigned to Alert_syslog output in the syslog server. The default is LOG_ALERT. This setting is a good fit for alerts; it is included with other critical events.

options

This is the option parameter that will be assigned to Alert_syslog output in the syslog server. The default is not assigned. You can use *options* to write directly to the console, or to log Snort's process ID with each alert. The *options* parameter can be used to identify multiple Snort processes on a single machine.

Database

The database output plugin logs directly to a relational database of your choice. It supports MySQL, PostgreSQL, Oracle, and UnixODBC-compliant databases such as SAPdb. Outputting to a relational database makes large amounts of intrusion data accessible. When the database plugin is placed into a database, alerts can be sorted, searched for, and prioritized in an organized manner. There are several applications that use the intrusion data in a relational database to create a management GUI. Snort data is written to the database in the table structure shown in Figure 3.3.

Snort Database ER Diagram (version 1.03): snort 1.8

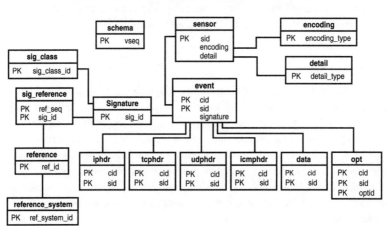

Figure 3.3   Snort database structure.

The database plugin can serve as a bottleneck in even moderately saturated networks. The plugin itself is not a bottleneck; rather, the database being written to is. When the database plugin writes to the chosen database, it must wait until the database is ready for another write. Writing to a remote database over a network can exacerbate the problem.

The database plugin has three options.

log or alert

This option lets you write alert or log data to the selected database. Remember, you can enable as many output plugins as you wish. To write both alert and log data to the same database, activate the database plugin twice, once with *alert* and once with *log*.

mysql or postgresql or unixodbc or mssql

This is the type of database you are going to write to. You can write to MySQL, PostgreSQL, Oracle, Microsoft's SQL Server, and UnixODBC-compliant databases.

parameter list

This list contains the *name=value* pairs required to successfully write to a database. The names and descriptions are as follows:

- host—This is the host where the database resides. Set to localhost if connecting to a database local to Snort.
- port—The port number to connect at the remote database host.
- dbname—The database username required to log in to the database.
- password—The password required to authenticate to the database.

- `sensor_name`—The name you want given to this sensor or Snort process in the database.
- `hex`—Include this name with no value to store binary data in hex. This is the default.
- `base64`—Include this name with no value to store binary data in base64 encoding.
- `ascii`—Include this name with no value to store binary data in human-readable ASCII encoding.
- `detail`—Can be either full or fast. With full you log all details of the packet that Snort has available. Fast logs only timestamp, signature, source and destination IPs, source and destination ports, TCP flags, and protocol.

Unified

The unified output plugin is designed specifically for speed. It is the fastest possible method of outputting Snort intrusion data. Unified writes intrusion data to its own binary format. It outputs two files: an alert file and a packet log file. The alert file contains a summary of the alert, including only the source and destination IP addresses, the protocol, the source and destination ports, and the alert message id. The log file contains the full packet information.

The purpose of the unified plugin is to allow data to be pushed out of Snort as fast as possible and to outsource plugins to a dedicated application. The application, Barnyard, reads unified output and sends data to other plugins, namely database output plugins. This gives Snort the luxury of not having to wait for a slower database to be ready to accept more input.

Unlike other plugins, the unified plugin is enabled with two different commands. The `alert_unified` command outputs alert data and the `log_unified` command outputs log data. Each produces a file that has a time signature (`monthday@hourminute-`) prepended to it. They both have one configuration option.

limit [maximum size]

The maximum size to which a file is allowed to grow. Default is 128MB.

Summary

This chapter delved deep into the inner workings of Snort. Snort acquires raw packets directly from a network interface card. The acquisition of packets is performed by the libpcap, which is external to Snort. Libpcap is portable to every popular computing platform, making Snort a truly platform-independent application.

The packet decoder is the first internal component of Snort that a sniffed packet encounters. Its purpose is to strip off the various headers. It works by decoding up the TCP/IP stack, and placing the packet in a data structure. Packets are then routed to the preprocessors.

Snort's preprocessors perform two fundamental functions. They either manipulate packets so the detection engine can properly analyze them, or they examine traffic for suspicious use that cannot be discovered by signature detection alone. Snort has a variety of preprocessors, most of which have been added to combat new methods of IDS evasion. Everything from polymorphic shellcode to fragmented packets can be detected with the aid of Snort's preprocessors. After traffic is run through the preprocessors, it is sent on to the detection engine.

The detection engine is responsible for the actual signature detection. Snort rules are loaded into the detection engine and are categorized in a tree-like data structure. This tree structure is implemented to be more efficient by minimizing the number of tests the detection engine has to perform to discover malicious activity. After malicious activity has been discovered, Snort writes intrusion data to any number of output plugins.

The output plugins are the means Snort has to get data from the detection engine to you. Snort can be configured with multiple output plugins to better facilitate intrusion data management. Output plugins can range from simple comma-delimited output to complex relational database output. An output format has been specifically designed for Snort to outsource the writing to databases, which has traditionally been a bottleneck.

4

Planning for the Snort Installation

A RECENT MAGAZINE ARTICLE REVIEWED ALL the major Intrusion Detection Systems. The test included IDSs from Cisco, Internet Security Systems, Intrusion, Lanscope, OneSecure, Network Flight Recorder, Recourse Technologies, and Snort. They connected the IDSs on nine T1 Internet connections. Within hours, every one of the tested IDSs had crashed and burned. All the IDSs had filled up their respective intrusion databases, dropped significant numbers of packets, and crashed. No private IDS DoS attack was used against them—just normal high bandwidth Internet traffic. The author of the article summarily dismissed IDSs as an immature, ineffective technology and created quite a stir in the IDS community.

This test did not prove that Intrusion Detection Systems are a failure. Rather, it proved how ineffective an IDS can be without proper planning. No matter which technology was used, be it open source or closed source, hardware-based or software-based, signature-based or anomaly-based, an IDS not properly planned for is next to worthless.

Because Intrusion Detection is a relatively new technology, persons not acquainted with the field will often assume that IDS is the proverbial silver bullet for all security problems. This attitude leads people to believe they can slap an IDS onto an existing network and walk away, having taken care of the problem. Nothing could be further from the truth. No one would assume that an email server taken out of the box and dropped in front of an Internet connection would function correctly. In the same way, you need to properly plan out IDS policy, sensor placement, incident response, and a range of other tasks.

You will have to make a number of decisions before installation that will impact Snort's scalability, security, and performance. By putting together a good plan, you will save time and reduce frustration in the future.

In reality, an IDS is a means to enforce an information security or risk management policy. You may not consider an IDS as something so abstract; you may simply see it as a tool to catch hackers. Although this statement is true, and definitely one component of the overall function of an IDS, you are in reality enforcing policy when you are using an IDS to catch hackers. If you use an IDS to catch hackers, it is being used to enforce an unauthorized access policy. Almost every organization has the need to control access to information assets, and has a policy to prevent unauthorized access. Your organization's policy may be spelled out in a policy manual, or it may be something less formal, such as the organization adhering to industry best practices. Looking at an IDS as a means to enforce policy, rather than a tool to catch hackers, will help you answer some of the difficult IDS planning questions:

- What should I be monitoring for?
- What alerts can I afford to ignore?
- Where should I place my sensors?
- What do I do now that I have discovered a security breach?

Defining an IDS Policy

In its most basic form an IDS is designed to monitor for abnormal or suspicious activity. In this monitoring for suspicious activity, the IDS must be able to determine which activity is unauthorized and which is not. This determination is done by combining knowledge of the access control policy, the culture, and the network infrastructure particular to your organization. This process of defining what is unauthorized is the core of creating the IDS policy.

This IDS policy will be implemented in the form of configuration settings and signatures on the Snort application. Applying the policy to Snort is not the final step in discovering unauthorized activity. You, the IDS analyst, must make the final decision on whether activity is unauthorized. No IDS solution can remove the necessary human component.

Activity that is considered to be unauthorized is different for every organization and for every network. Activity that is not permitted can be broken down into four areas that are relevant for a NIDS: malicious, suspicious, abnormal, and inappropriate. Each category is increasingly subjective. Activity that is malicious is likely to be unauthorized for most networks, regardless of culture, access control policy, and specific network infrastructure. There is little room for interpretation. On the other hand, definitions for abnormal and inappropriate activities are highly subjective and likely to be vastly different for each organization. Your organization's values will dictate what is inappropriate for its employees, and your unique network setup will dictate what is abnormal. Working on these issues will help you define your IDS policy and make Snort successful.

Note

The terms used to describe unauthorized activity here are not industry standard terms and may have different meanings for different people. The point of this section is to get you thinking about what is really unauthorized for your organization and what is permitted.

Malicious Activity

Malicious activity is any traffic that is cut-and-dry unauthorized. There is little room for debate on what is malicious activity; most organizations would consider malicious activity to be unauthorized at all times and in all places. Traffic that falls into this category includes remote exploits, privilege escalation attempts, and DoS attacks. Under normal circumstances, these types of traffic are unauthorized. An example of malicious activity is remote control Trojan traffic. There is no legitimate use for remote control Trojans, such as Subseven or Netbus. The IDS should monitor for these types of traffic no matter where a sensor is placed within the network infrastructure.

There are special situations where malicious activity may be permitted. Penetration tests or vulnerability assessments orchestrated by in-house or third-party security practitioners may generate this type of traffic, and would be permitted.

Suspicious Activity

Suspicious activity is anything that indicates that malicious activity is taking place, but is not malicious in of itself. Suspicious activity can take the form of network traffic that violates standard protocol implementation, such as traffic with reserved bits set or packets with both SYN and FIN flags set. Legitimate applications would never set reserved bits, as they are set aside by IANA for future use. Additionally, a packet with the SYN flag set is used to start a connection, and a FIN flag is used to terminate one. Logically, a packet should never contain both. Traffic of this nature is likely to have been crafted by an attacker and likely has no legitimate purpose.

Other types of suspicious activity include portscanning and other reconnaissance attacks. Attackers attempting to access a wide variety of ports and hosts within a short time period can indicate portscan activity. Although some normal applications and user activity can create traffic that sets off a portscan alert, it is usually worthwhile to investigate portscan attempts originating from suspicious hosts. Causing an application or host to divulge network information that should not be passed on to an external host is suspicious as well. A DNS zone transfer, where a request is sent to a DNS server to dump all hostname and IP address information to an external host, is an example of this type of reconnaissance attempt.

Almost all suspicious activity should be monitored for external connections to the organization. Traffic from business partners connected via an extranet or Internet should not exhibit suspicious activity. Suspicious activity often signifies impending malicious activity.

In most cases, you will want to monitor for suspicious activity internally as well. Out-of-spec or portscan traffic internal to your network should be cause for alarm. DNS zone transfers, for example, are routinely performed by other DNS servers or network management devices. Although internal monitoring is bound to have an abundance of false positives relating to suspicious activity, suspicious activity should always be investigated when coming from an unrecognized internal source.

Abnormal Activity

Abnormal activity is defined as activity that appears totally normal in nature but is present in suspicious or unusual circumstances. Determining which abnormal activity is unauthorized requires the greatest amount of in-depth knowledge of your organization and network infrastructure. What is abnormal for one organization may be a standard practice for another. Examples of abnormal activity include occurrences of TFTP traffic to an Internet-facing Web server that you know should not have a TFTP server installed. An inbound Windows share access from a user's desktop to a corporate partner when users are not permitted to create shares is another example.

Usually, abnormal activity is a sign that an intrusion has already occurred. It is possible that the attacker successfully attacked a host without generating an alert, or the alert was missed. It is also quite possible that an internal user made use of legitimate access to compromise the host.

Some Snort rules included with the source distribution are used to capture abnormal activity. A subset of rules stored in the ftp.rules file is used to discover abnormal FTP commands used by warez, or pirated software, traders. Warez groups search the Internet for anonymous or easily hacked FTP servers to store warez or pirated software. They then give out the FTP login information to public IRC channels or other members, turning your FTP server into a hot spot for illegal software distribution. To obscure the location of the software from sysadmins, warez groups create strange-looking directories. Sometimes the Windows file system manager is unable to delete or display the obscured directories. Because of the size of the files and the large number of users accessing them, warez traders want to find the FTP servers with the most bandwidth. They test the connection speed with a 1MB file filled with random data. These types of activities are abnormal and can be picked up by Snort.

Each network protected by an IDS has a different concept of what is considered abnormal traffic. Some software companies host an anonymous FTP server to allow customers to retrieve product updates, security patches, and trial versions. In this case, the anonymous FTP server is a critical component of ongoing business and would not be considered a security issue if properly maintained. At another organization, such as a financial institution, traffic signaling an anonymous external FTP server could be cause for great alarm and would be considered abnormal. In this case, you would want to develop custom Snort rules to monitor for anonymous FTP login traffic. Even at the software company, you may still want to develop anonymous FTP rules that would exclude the specific server that was used for customer support.

Furthermore, each sensor used in an IDS may need to have different rules implemented to determine what activity is abnormal. This sensor-level rules granularity is where you can really put your knowledge of your network and organization to best use. If your company uses Oracle Applications' One-Hour Install extensively to maintain and support your Oracle applications via built-in Web servers, you may want to disable the Snort rule that detects this traffic for internal sensors. Oracle Applications' One-Hour Install does not by default support authentication and can be used to compromise a database or application server. For sensors that are monitoring connections external to the corporate network, you would want to enable this rule to detect One-Hour Install traffic originating external to your organization.

Inappropriate Activity

Some types of activity are not intentionally malicious or harmful, but are unauthorized by the organization nonetheless. These types of inappropriate activity can be harmful to the organization, or simply a nuisance. Some types of inappropriate activity, such as use of P2P file-sharing programs, are likely to be inappropriate for most security-conscious organizations. Internet-based file-sharing programs can be used to covertly transfer confidential information through a firewall or proxy. These programs also present a threat when the user is not aware that the P2P program by default shares the entire contents of his workstation. Recently, there have been cases of malware, such as worms and viruses that are specifically created to propagate through such programs. For these reasons, P2P activity is usually considered unauthorized in the workplace.

Other types of inappropriate activity include improper Web site access by users. Examples include Web sites that distribute pornography, hacking tools, and other content that serves no legitimate work function. Remember, your organization's IP address will show up in the logs of the Web sites that your users visit, so a reputational risk exists when you allow employees to visit any Web site unmonitored. You would not want the media to find out your organization has been browsing for child pornography.

Note

Monitoring your organization's employee Internet traffic can be construed as a violation of the Wiretap Act. You can take appropriate actions to ensure the confidentiality of your company's data, but if you want to use a sniffer to watch for objectionable behavior, you need to include the fact that you are doing so in your company's policy manual or employment contract.

An IDS policy can be as simple as a few paragraphs detailing the mission and objectives of the IDS. It could also be a formal document certified by a high-ranking executive that sponsors the intrusion detection process as a whole.

Sample Policy

What follows is an informal sample policy that could be used for a small software development shop:

Alert in real time any remote buffer overflow attempts, remote control Trojan traffic occurrences, and SQL injection attempts regardless of origin. Generate alerts for any information gathering attempts external to our network, including portscans and DNS zone transfers. Alert on activity from any host establishing connectivity to our network via rlogin, Telnet, or FTP. Ignore SNMP scanning activity from 192.168.1.1, our networked device management workstation.

Deciding What to Monitor

After putting together an IDS policy centered on what activity is deemed to be unauthorized, you need to put it to practical use. The outcome of the policy should be a high-level overview of the intrusion detection capability you will strive to achieve for the organization. After this process is finished, you should apply the policy to the portions of your network infrastructure you are going to monitor. Getting more granular, you will need to decide which services will be monitored, and the specific attack signatures that will be looked for. We will get into this level of detail when you tune Snort in Chapter 10.

The ideal situation is to monitor everything. Every network device would be covered under Snort's watchful eye, and every external connection to the enterprise would be watched for attempted attacks. Although this scenario is quite possible at small organizations, it becomes a Herculean feat when there are significant numbers of connected devices present.

On the assumption that you do not have the resources to deploy an enterprise-wide Snort IDS right off the bat, we will take a look at three of the most common areas to place sensors.

External Network Connections

Network connections to external organizations or public networks are the most obvious location to monitor for intrusions. The Internet is a vast global playground for hackers and self-propagating malware that routinely attempts to achieve unauthorized access. Monitoring a connection to a third-party service provider or business partner also falls into this category. Business partners connected via extranets, VPNs, and dedicated lines are possible entry points to your network infrastructure. Although your organization may have good working security controls, you likely have less knowledge of and access to the security posture of your business partners. A black hat could compromise a service provider and leverage the extranet to your organization. For these reasons it is important to monitor external network connections.

It is also important to monitor traffic that is leaving your network. Various types of outgoing traffic can indicate a compromised host, such as remote control Trojan or abnormal traffic. Monitoring outgoing traffic could also help you find a compromised server that is being used to attack other hosts on the Internet.

Firewalls or screening routers are regularly used to protect external access points. Firewalls are often used to define what is external to an organization. When external access points are protected by firewalls, the issue arises whether to place Snort sensors on the outside or inside of the firewall. Both sensor placement scenarios have their advantages and disadvantages.

Sensors External to a Firewall

Placing the sensor external to the firewall allows it to monitor the widest range of malicious traffic intended for the organization. The sensor detects many attempted attacks that the firewall would otherwise block. The external sensor gives you the best idea of what type of attacks your network is regularly encountering, whether the attacks are successful or not.

An external sensor has a better chance of picking up on reconnaissance attacks, which are usually perpetrated by attackers with little to no knowledge of your network. Hackers seeking to gather knowledge of your network will probe for services, ports, and hosts that do not exist, which can be discovered only by an external sensor. External sensors are required to detect information gathering attempts that sweep network infrastructure protected by a firewall. Last but not least, an external sensor is privy to attacks that are intended for the firewall itself.

The downside to placing the sensor on the external side of the firewall is the number of irrelevant attacks. You will undoubtedly receive many attack alerts that are likely to be prevented by the firewall. Whether you want to be alerted for attacks that will likely be prevented is a personal decision. The external sensor is also in a risky position and has an increased chance of being attacked or compromised. Chapter 6 examines some mitigating factors that will make the sensor extremely secure. The external sensor is farther away from attacked hosts, so TTL evasion techniques can be used to obscure traffic from the external sensor.

Sensors Internal to a Firewall

A sensor placed on the internal side of a firewall monitors only traffic that has successfully passed through the firewall. Assuming the firewall was configured correctly, these types of attacks are targeted at legitimate hosts and services that could be compromised. Attacks that are detected by a sensor internal to a firewall are likely to be more severe and of higher priority. The internal sensor will not generate as many false positives as an external sensor, because the firewall is shielding it from a good proportion of attacks. It is also more secure because it is protected by the firewall and may not require security controls that are as stringent as those of the external sensor.

The disadvantage to using an internal sensor is that it cannot discover attempted attacks that are blocked by the firewall. This leaves portscanning and other reconnaissance activities to go unnoticed.

Recommended Placement Strategy

Ideally, you would want to set a sensor both in front of the firewall and behind it. By using two sensors you can catch reconnaissance and attempted attacks with the external, and be alerted to high priority attacks with the internal. The external can be configured for near real-time alerting through the use of ACID, whereas the internal can be configured to generate real-time alerts via email or pagers when an attack is detected. This method also provides a degree of redundancy: If a sensor misses an attack, you have another chance to catch it. It also enables the correlation of data between the two sensors.

If you do not have the resources available to implement two sensors, the standard practice is to place the sensor in the location where it will capture alerting data that is most pertinent to the monitoring situation. If you are using the firewall and IDS to protect an ecommerce application or Web presence, you would want to deploy the sensor external to the firewall. With the sensor external to the firewall and protected infrastructure, you will be sure to be alerted to attempted attacks and information gathering attempts. Additionally, you could develop a similar alerting facility as a dual sensor system with a single external sensor by configuring real-time alerting on all attacks that are likely to pass through the firewall.

Hmm…well, what about attacks originating inside the network that are sent out? That would be "real intrusion detection."

On the other hand, if the firewall's primary purpose is to regulate Internet access for employees, in addition to preventing unauthorized external access, the sensor would best be placed internal to the firewall. In this setup, Snort would be monitoring for inappropriate activity and attempts to attack other networks; as well as catching attacks that manage to slip by the firewall.

Internal Network Chokepoints

Core internal network chokepoints make a great location for installing IDS sensors. A heavy-duty core switch where a large proportion of the traffic flows through is an ideal location to monitor for internal attacks and inappropriate activity.

A central internal location is likely to utilize a large amount of bandwidth, which could overcome a single sensor. You would have to resort to a sensor load balancing strategy described in Chapter 5 to ensure your sensors are not overwhelmed. Another possibility is to place the sensors on a number of less powerful switches that feed into the core switch. This would achieve the goal of distributing load, but would introduce considerable duplicate intrusion data. It is likely that a few sensors could capture the same traffic as it flows through the network.

Critical Computing Resources

Areas of your organization's network that already have a significant number of security controls are another candidate for intrusion monitoring. Infrastructure that is valuable enough to be protected by DMZs, firewalls, secured routers, and hardened hosts is likely to be worthy of an IDS deployment. Databases containing confidential data or tiered external-facing Web applications are probable locations that require increased security attention. Even if you do not have a layered security infrastructure, it would be wise to deploy Snort sensors to monitor valuable or sensitive network hosts. This protects against the often-overlooked internal attack.

Designing Your Snort Architecture

Snort is an incredibly flexible and extensible application. Although this is certainly a boon for Snort users, it also creates quite a quandary for the first-time user. Choosing

the best architecture for Snort can be daunting: You want to ensure that you can successfully build a working Snort IDS without much difficulty, but you also want a system that
you can use to organically scale the IDS as a greater need for intrusion monitoring
develops.

As illustrated in Chapter 2, Snort supports an n-tier architecture. This book covers
both a single-tier setup and a three-tier installation. Snort's functionality can be spread
across multiple machines on different tiers to provide scalability, security, and performance. This three-tier setup is often referred to as *distributed Snort*.

Snort can also be collapsed onto a single tier. A three-tier deployment isn't de facto
superior to a single-tier installation. Many factors will influence whether a full-blown
three-tier architecture is required or a single-tier setup is appropriate.

Three-Tier

Each of the three tiers of a distributed Snort deployment supports a separate function.
The sensor or first tier is responsible for intrusion monitoring and data gathering. The
server or second tier houses intrusion data and provides a means to deliver data to the
IDS analyst. The Analyst Console or third tier is a dedicated workstation for the IDS
analyst to interpret intrusion data gathered across the enterprise. Snort supports an n-tier
architecture for scalability, security, and performance reasons.

Spreading Snort out over many tiers makes Snort a scaleable application. You can scale
Snort by adding resources to each tier as needed. If increased monitoring is required,
additional sensors can be installed. If an additional IDS analyst is brought on board, a
new console can be added.

In a three-tier Snort architecture, performance is enhanced as dedicated resources are
assigned to each of the major functions of a Snort installation. Each tier has its own separate set of computers that are assigned to that specific tier. This keeps functions of each
tier separate and unable to consume the system resources of another.

The three-Tier installation enables you to add some security features. When an application is separated onto different computers, it forces the attacker to compromise many
different hosts rather than one. It also allows more finely tuned access control. You can
set up one console that has only read access to the intrusion database, while another
console could be granted full access.

The enterprise Snort is typically installed in a distributed, three-tiered mode. The
flexibility and performance gained by installing Snort in a distributed fashion is easily
offset by the cost of additional hardware resources at large organizations. The three-tier
setup allows a large organization with multiple disparate physical or geographic locations
to deploy intrusion monitoring relatively painlessly. Having many separate sensors report
to single or multiple intrusion databases allows for event correlation and a true birds-eye
view of unauthorized network activity across the enterprise.

Even if you plan to have only a few sensors monitoring for traffic, it is still worthwhile to use the distributed installation. If you have more than two locations where you
would like to implement intrusion detection capability, the distributed architecture

becomes worthwhile. The time and money spent on building and monitoring for intrusions with three single-tier Snort installations is far greater than a distributed installation with three sensors.

Single Tier

A single tier or hybrid server/sensor installation is functionally similar to the three-tier deployment. If you choose to use the hybrid method and collapse all the Snort components onto a single server, you will still have a functioning Snort IDS. The single-tier installation cannot scale or perform as well as a distributed application, nor can it have the same security.

The hybrid deployment makes the most sense if you are using Snort on a relatively small network with few network-enabled devices, such as at home or at a small business. If you are planning on simply getting acquainted with Snort and the field of intrusion detection, the hybrid is a viable option. You can use it to experiment and develop intrusion analyst skills that will be useful in a corporate setting or when you decide to install a greater intrusion monitoring presence at your current position.

Monitoring Segment

Installing and deploying a separate network segment dedicated for the Snort IDS components is a simple way to segregate the IDS infrastructure from the rest of your organization. This is primarily done to secure Snort, and to provide a high level of assurance that the intrusion data is accurate. If trust is placed in an IDS to detect unauthorized activity, the system must have the highest level of integrity of any system in your network infrastructure. If an attacker can compromise network attached devices, he should not be able to compromise the system designed to detect his malicious activity. If a black hat can access the IDS components and the traffic that flows between them, he can remove alerts to cover his tracks. He can also create false alerts that lead you in the wrong direction. You need to picture the standard network infrastructure as if it had already been compromised. For these reasons it is a standard practice to create a monitoring segment.

When you develop a separate network segment, the only entry points into the Snort network are the sniffing interfaces on the sensors. These interfaces can be secured so that they function as "read only," which will make attacking the Snort segment difficult. This still leaves open the possibility of an on-site attack or physical attack. Appropriate physical security measures should be taken to protect the Snort monitoring segment.
A separate monitoring segment sounds like an expensive and complicated proposition. In reality, the segment can scale along with the Snort infrastructure. If you have a single hybrid server/sensor, the monitoring segment would consist of a single Ethernet cable. If you have a distributed deployment, with five sensors, a server, and a console, the segment would be comprised of a single connected switch. The monitoring segment becomes complicated and expensive when you need to place a sensor at a different physical or geographic location. Deploying a separate, private line for the IDS may be out of range

of even the largest IDS budgets. In this situation you may want to consider a VPN that includes firewalls at both endpoints.

Planning for Maintenance

It is easy to get caught up in the excitement of learning and implementing a new security technology and disregard the ongoing maintenance issues that will eventually arise. Sooner or later you will have to update Snort signatures and write custom rules. New versions of Snort are released frequently, meaning the actual Snort application will have to be upgraded at some point. With all good chance, your Snort deployment will be productive, and additional intrusion detection capability will need to be requested at your organization. Incorporating these tasks into a maintenance plan ensures that your Snort IDS deployment will stay relevant as time progresses.

Keeping abreast of security–related information is paramount in maintaining an up-to-date ruleset. If you aren't already subscribed to the Bugtraq mailing list, it is a good idea to sign up. Bugtraq is a mailing list that provides updates and information on security research. Individuals, corporations, security firms, white hats, and black hats all contribute to the list to bring the latest security news to you. You can subscribe at this location:

`http://online.securityfocus.com/cgi-bin/sfonline/subscribe.pl`

It is also a good idea to check the CERT coordination center at `www.cert.org` to find updated advisories. You should take a look at another site that contains an abundance of the latest exploits and hacker tools that may be used against your network:

`www.packetstormsecurity.nl`

You can easily find hundreds of other security news resources on the Internet that could be of better use to you than these recommended Web sites.

After you have brought yourself into the loop in the information security scene, it is a good idea to subscribe to the Snort mailing lists. You can do so at

`http://sourceforge.net/mail/?group_id=3357`

These mailing lists are useful for troubleshooting, obtaining help, and finding the latest unofficial Snort rules. The Snort homepage at `www.snort.org` is worth checking periodically for new tools and Snort updates. Getting in the habit of staying up to date with security news will ensure that you are always on top of the latest rule. When you are up to speed with the latest vulnerabilities and exploits, you will have a better idea of what new signatures you need to implement.

You can always write your own signatures for new rules, or you can get the latest from the Snort Web site. Setting a regular time and date to check for new signatures is a good practice for any Snort user. Implementing non-critical changes at a set time each week saves time and allows for a consistent change control process. It is easier to troubleshoot new rules when you have exact knowledge of what was changed and when. Critical changes or rule updates should always be made as soon as possible.

Some of the packages or components will likely have to be updated or patched as time progresses. The Snort application will also have to be updated. Snort is often released in beta version ahead of a stable official release. It is a good idea to set up a test system for installing major upgrades or updates. If you are testing a new version of Snort, it is recommended that you use it in a non-production environment while you work out the bugs.

As you scale your Snort installation larger, staffing needs are often overlooked. IDSs generate an abundance of alerts, but they will be of no use unless a person is present to interpret them. Alerts generated by Snort must be carefully combed over by a trained professional to determine whether a security breach has actually occurred. If you grow your Snort installation without aligning the required human resources, the IDS could loose its effectiveness. It is of great importance to make certain that staffing needs are met.

Incident Response Plan

Snort helps you discover and manage security-related events. Up until now the focus of this book has been on the gathering and alerting of intrusion related data. The relevant question remains of what to do when you detect a real intrusion. Many novice security practitioners assume that they will deal with the specifics of an incident when it actually arises. The flawed logic is that each security event is unique and that any pre-planning is useless. Security events are best handled when they are reacted to according to a previously developed plan that includes all the appropriate persons. Industry best practices and established guidelines have determined that developing an incident response plan greatly reduces the negative consequences of a security breach.

This section serves as a quick introduction to the field of incident response and forensics. Entire books have been written on both subjects, so this section will not attempt to be a complete resource.

You can increase the damage that an intrusion can cause by not having the appropriate applications and tools available prior to the security incident. When an incident occurs, the last thing you want to worry about is having the proper software and hardware available to carry out an investigation and remediation plan. Not having the tools lined up extends the time to a recovered state. Trying to assemble the correct applications and hardware required to perform an investigation may not be possible in the time frame that you would want when responding to an intrusion.

Some of the tools you will need to perform the incident response include the following:

- A reliable backup and restore application
- Software to create images and snapshots of potentially compromised systems
- A tool to compare file properties and create and compare checksums of files
- Log parsing tools or scripts
- Dedicated hardware to store all this on

You can find some of the tools at the CERT resource page online:

`http://www.cert.org/tech_tips/security_tools.html`

Without an incident response plan, important decisions that could possibly alter the extent of the damage from the intrusion are not fully thought out. When a major security breach is discovered, an organization can react in a totally unpredictable manner. Some companies get so many people involved in the incident that evidence is destroyed, or the attacker picks up on the chatter and closes up shop. Other organizations may react in an opposite fashion, where important decisionmakers are skeptical that an incident has actually occurred. Try explaining a buffer overflow attack to your CEO at 4:00 a.m. and you could likely get such a response. Even worse, in some organizations parties are unwilling to participate in a response, thinking it is not their problem. Creating an incident response plan that involves the correct people ahead of time will avert these situations.

The incident response process outline in a plan should include the following:

- The goals for the proper handling of an incident
- The priority level of information assets
- Establishing a notification chain

The Objective

The primary objective of the incident response plan is to protect assets that could be damaged or compromised. Unquestionably, the most important asset to protect is human life. If your organization is protecting systems that are relied upon for personal safety or national security (such as air traffic control, the power grid, and so on), maintaining them in a working order is of the highest priority.

The next most significant asset to be protected is confidential or sensitive data. By its very definition, confidential data must remain private and remain uncompromised. Not only must confidential data be protected from unauthorized access, it must remain intact and unaltered. If confidential data is to be protected, it must maintain the same level of integrity throughout its useful lifetime. It may be impossible to reproduce confidential data, as well, so the destruction of this type of asset must be averted. These three situations should be prioritized above all else, excluding human life, when responding to an incident.

Next, other non-confidential data must be sheltered from harm. Proprietary and other internal use data should be protected. Although it is not as important to protect non-confidential data from unauthorized access, there is still a need to keep it unaltered and intact. The preservation of data usually takes precedence over the next asset, computer systems.

Note

Data may include evidence related to the intrusion. It is worth pointing out that this data should be saved to help you discover the means the attacker used to perpetrate the intrusion.

The next priority should be the protection of damage to the systems that hold data. This includes operating systems, hardware, applications, and other resources available for data processing. Damage to systems can result in costly downtime and reputational damage.

The final and lowest priority is the protection of the availability of computing resources. During an incident it is important to protect the availability of general computing resources. A computing resource is any application, system process, or service that is used to provide access to information or process data.

Establishing a Notification Chain

The group of persons to be notified of a security breach should be planned out ahead of time to avoid scrambling for contacts and making desperate phone calls. Depending on the size of your organization, you may have to include other departments in the notification chain. Organizing a formal or informal incident response group will greatly speed up the amount of time needed to bring an incident to closure. If all the appropriate people are involved in incident planning and response, they are likely to raise fewer questions and act in a predicable manner that aids you in incident response. Groups of people who are internal to your organization and with whom you should consider making arrangements prior to an incident include:

- Managers and system professionals in your department
- Managers and system professionals who deal with systems administration or networking
- Executives
- Legal counsel

Groups of people who are external to your organization and with whom you should consider making arrangements prior to an incident include:

- Administrative and abuse contacts at your organization's ISP(s)
- Contacts at business partners or third-party service providers
- Local and federal law enforcement contacts
- Members of the press

For each group of contacts you define, you should establish two people who act as primary points of contact. You should also define what type of information would be given to the point of contact and the expected response. You would not want to share the same level of information with the press as you would with a server team manager at your organization. Additionally, you should define the type of information to release to each point of contact. You would not want to present a highly detailed technical report to most senior executives.

It is important to get the appropriate persons internal to the organization involved for both physiological and pragmatic reasons. When members of the organization are invited to an incident response team, they will be more receptive and cooperative when an incident occurs. The concept of a security breach will not be a foreign concept and will be easier to swallow if they are already indoctrinated to the idea.

It is also imperative to establish under what authority the incident handling team is operating. Issues such as who has the authority to stop business-critical processes, confiscate computer hardware, and deny access to critical systems need to be ironed out ahead of time. This type of authority has to come from the business owner or a high-ranking executive.

Involving your organization's legal counsel will help you determine the appropriate situations for legal action. Legal counsel, combined with executive guidance, will help you determine whether the company is willing to take on the public exposure of a legal course of action.

External persons to the organization can aid in incident response as well. Contacts at your company's ISP can help determine the source of incident or block traffic in the event of a DDoS attack. Business partners and third-party service providers may be the source of an attack or may be compromised along with your organization.

Establishing contact with law enforcement agencies will help you determine what sort of legal evidence will be admissible in a court of law. They can also offer advice on how to properly collect and distribute evidence in what is known as a chain of custody. If you establish the point of contact at law enforcement agencies prior to an incident you will save yourself the time in trying to determine the correct person to contact in an emergency.

Contacting members of the press should be done via a public relations professional at your organization. Realizing that a majority of organizations have no such person, there are a couple of important points to remember when working with the press. If you must release information to the press, stay clear of any technical details or information that could be of use by possible attackers. Remember, your attacker will likely be paying attention to the media. Other attackers could be enticed to commit similar attacks if technical information were released. When talking to the media, be sure to never intentionally mislead or misrepresent the facts. False information has a tendency to look worse than the real incident when it is uncovered. Customers and business partners will loose trust in the organization if such discrepancies are discovered. Another practice to avoid when working with the media is speculation. No matter how tempting, never release your thoughts about the investigation without having cold hard facts. Speculation can turn out to be wrong, and possibly viewed as an attack to discredit certain organizations or individuals.

Responding to an Incident

Knowing in advance the steps you will need to follow when responding to an incident will make you better prepared for the task when it arises. Outlining the steps in a plan or procedure that can be quickly and easily followed will lessen the chance that crucial pieces of data are overlooked.

When responding to an incident, never lose sight of the primary goal. If that goal is to restore control of the system as quickly as possible, you should not spend an inordinate amount of time gathering evidence. If the goal is to limit the extent of the damage while possibly pursuing the attacker, make sure to create images, backups, and a chain of custody to develop a solid set of evidence. A best practice is to have a redundant set of hardware available that can be used to continue business as usual while the servers affected by the intrusion are investigated. If the goal is simply to catch the intruder, sniffers could be deployed along with increased system auditing. Whatever your goal is, make sure not to get distracted with other activities that do not adhere to the stated plan.

Identifying an Incident

The first stage in responding to a security breach is to determine whether it is a true incident or a false alarm. It is quite normal for legitimate applications and user activity to appear malicious. Before taking any corrective action or initiating a notification chain, you should put forth the due diligence to ensure you have a real incident on your hands. No one wants to cry the proverbial wolf. This being said, make sure not to take the due diligence too far. If you have a gravely serious incident in progress that is likely to cause ongoing damage, it is better to raise the alarm than sit on your hands.

Before you begin the process of identifying an incident, you should start a log or journal of the events as they take place. Be sure to take down full names of people contacted and detailed event descriptions, along with time and date. The journal will serve as both a method of organizing your thoughts and a piece of evidence.

To determine whether a security event has actually occurred, you should take care to thumb through any system logs you can get your hands on. Attackers rarely exploit a system on the first try. It is often a guessing game as the black hat seeks to penetrate your network. Check for suspicious activity, such as new account creation, repeated failed logins, and data modification attempts. The absence of logs for a period of time is another good indication that a security incident has occurred. A time period where no audit trail was created by an application that regularly generates logs is a positive sign that an intrusion has occurred. You should also check the log file size; if it has shrunk an attacker could have altered the log. Unusually large logs tip you off to an intrusion as well. When an attacker attempts to brute force a password, log files can jump in size exponentially.

Penetrating a system is not an exact science. A buffer overflow may not always function in the manner the attacker wishes it to. An attacker penetrating a network could cause some noticeable performance impact that could alert you to an intrusion. Suspicious system crashes or unexplainable performance loss could be the signature of a malfunctioning compromised system.

The most apparent sign you have been intruded upon is, of course, direct evidence of an intrusion. The presence of Trojaned system files from an attacker's rootkit or a remote control Trojan are sure signs that an incident has occurred. Network interfaces set in promiscuous mode for sniffing is another positive sign. The most obvious is when the attacker intentionally leaves a calling card by defacing a Web site or leaving a message intended to taunt system owners.

Classifying the Incident

After you have determined that you have an actual incident on your hands, you need to determine the classification and scope of the incident. You should first try to discover how many hosts have been compromised and the extent to which each one has been compromised. Creating a detailed damage report will aid both in the incident response and later if legal action is taken.

If confidential or other important data is involved, the hosts should be immediately disconnected from the network to prevent further compromise or destructive behavior. Make note that any sort of continued denial of service will alert the attacker that an incident response plan is being executed. This activity may clue in savvy users of the system as well. Any host that possibly has been touched by the incident should be considered tainted and inspected. If possible, the hosts should be segregated from other untouched network components.

A significant temptation is to leave the system up and running in a compromised state in an effort to capture the attacker. Remember, with confidential or sensitive data at risk, the priority is the protection of the data, not a personal vendetta. Failing to resist the intellectual and personal challenge of tracking down the attacker when other priorities are present is the mistake incident response leaders are most likely to make. Even if you were to discover the true identity of the attacker, the legal counsel and executives in your organization might not wish to pursue legal action out of fear of negative publicity.

You should next attempt to determine the method of attack. This can be difficult, especially if the attacker has advanced skills and takes time to cover tracks. Snort should be able to provide some detailed forensic information that likely alerted you to the intrusion in the first place. Furthermore, you should make use the tools you have acquired for forensic analysis to complete this portion of the investigation.

Gathering Evidence

When gathering evidence, document every detail about the incident response. The documentation, in the form of a journal, will help you provide valuable information to others that may be later brought into the investigation. If you do not compile a detailed journal, it is likely that you will have to revisit the task and attempt to reconstruct how and when the evidence was collected. Keeping the journal current and full of details will ensure that you have an accurate log of the event, which can be used in a legal course of action or damage estimate.

In the first incidents you respond to, you are likely to make some mistakes. Keeping a journal of the events and evidence collected helps you identify what went wrong after the incident. Some of the evidence you should consider collecting includes:

- System logs from operating systems and applications (event logs, syslog entries, and so on)
- Intrusion detection alerts
- System files and potentially compromised hosts
- Actions taken by yourself in the course of the incident response
- Persons contacted, either internal or external to the organization

An important point to make is that when you collect evidence, make sure that you store it in a secure place that cannot be tampered with. Never bring evidence home with you or let it leave the workplace. Remember, your journal is a piece of evidence as well.

Restoring to a Normal State

After all the possible evidence has been gathered, it is time to remove the cause of the incident. If you are fortunate, you have discovered the cause and method of intrusion in the classifying of the incident stage. Ensure that you have gathered all the evidence that you require before cleaning up, because you are likely to destroy any and all evidence when restoring the system.

When restoring from backups, make sure that the backup you are restoring from is clean and does not reintroduce a threat to the system. You also must close the security exposure that led to the compromise. After the system is reinstalled and functioning, make sure to make a new backup before connecting the system to the network.

After the system is operational again, you should pay close attention to it to ensure it is not compromised again. It is quite possible that you unknowingly restored a bad back-up or did not discover the true vulnerability that led to the intrusion.

After completing the incident response, you should put together a formal report to be made available to the appropriate persons. The report should include the methodology and plan used to execute the incident response, as well as the scope of the damage.

Testing the Plan

After you have completed an incident response plan, the best way to ensure that you have a bulletproof plan is to run a mock incident. No test will ever be the same as a real incident, but you should make every effort to simulate a real incident. Running a test incident will make sure that the correct points of contact have been made. Run through the use of your tools and the imaging and backup procedures. It may also be advisable to coordinate the test with another team simultaneously performing a penetration test. Doing so will help to ensure that your practices and evidence capturing skills are effective.

Summary

This chapter introduced the planning tasks required to install Snort effectively. Planning is an essential stage that ensures the IDS does the work it is intended to do. Without proper planning, you are likely to encounter significant difficulties. Planning helps you answer some of the most difficult questions posed by novice Snort users, such as:

- What should I be monitoring for?
- What alerts can I afford to ignore?
- Where should I place my sensors?
- What do I do now that I have discovered a security breach?

The first step in planning is to create an IDS policy that fits into a more broad information security or risk management policy. In its most basic form, an IDS is designed to monitor for abnormal or suspicious activity. In this monitoring for suspicious activity, the IDS must be able to determine which activity is unauthorized and which is not. It does so by combining knowledge of the access control policy, the culture, and the network infrastructure peculiar to your organization. This process of defining what is unauthorized is the core of creating the IDS policy.

Activity that is not permitted can be broken down into four areas that are relevant for a NIDS. They are malicious, suspicious, abnormal, and inappropriate activity. Defining activity that falls into each category is increasingly subjective. Activity that is malicious is likely to be unauthorized for most networks, regardless of culture, access control policy, and specific network infrastructure. There is little room for interpretation. On the other hand, defining abnormal and inappropriate activity is highly subjective and likely to be vastly different for each organization.

After putting together an IDS policy centered on what activity is deemed to be unauthorized, you need to put it to practical use. The outcome of the policy should be a high-level overview of the intrusion detection capability you will strive to achieve for the organization. After this process is finished, you should apply the policy to the portions of your network infrastructure you are going to monitor.

The next step is to choose the architecture you will use for Snort. Choosing the best architecture for Snort can be daunting: You want to ensure that you can successfully build a working Snort IDS without much difficulty, but you also want a system that you can use to organically scale the IDS as a greater need for intrusion monitoring develops.

Maintenance issues related to the Snort IDS will eventually arise. Sooner or later you will have to update Snort signatures and write custom rules. New versions of Snort are released frequently, meaning the actual Snort application will have to be upgraded at some point. You may need to install additional intrusion detection capability at your organization. Including these tasks into a maintenance plan ensures that your Snort IDS deployment will stay relevant as time progresses.

Part of managing a holistic IDS solution is developing an incident response plan. Sooner or later you will have to deal with a real security breach, whether it was discovered by Snort or not. The primary objective of the incident response plan is to protect assets that could be damaged or compromised. The group of persons to be notified of a security breach should be planned out ahead of time to avoid scrambling for contacts and making desperate phone calls. Organizing a formal or informal incident response group will shorten the length of time needed to bring an incident to closure. If all the appropriate people are involved in incident planning and response, they are likely to raise fewer questions and act in a predictable manner that aids you in incident response.

Knowing in advance the steps you will need to follow when responding to an incident will make you better prepared for the task when it arises. When responding to an incident, never lose sight of the primary goal. If that goal is to restore control of the system as quickly as possible, you should not spend an inordinate amount of time gathering evidence. The first stage in responding to a security breach is to determine whether it is a true incident or a false alarm. It is quite normal for legitimate applications and user activity to appear malicious. Before taking any corrective action or initiating a notification chain, you should put forth the due diligence to ensure you have a real incident on your hands. After you have determined that you have an actual incident on your hands, you need to determine the classification and scope of the incident. You should first try to discover how many hosts have been compromised and the extent to which each one has been compromised. Creating a detailed damage report will aid in both the incident response and later if legal action is taken.

When gathering evidence, document every detail about the incident response. The documentation, in the form of a journal, will help you provide valuable information to others who may be later brought into the investigation. After all the possible evidence has been gathered, it is time to remove the cause of the incident. It is to be hoped that you have discovered the cause and method of intrusion in the classifying of the incident stage.

5

The Foundation—Hardware and Operating Systems

Snort's capability to function efficiently can be limited by the choice of the underlying hardware, operating system, and networking components. When one thinks about being able to function efficiently, raw performance is usually the first thing that comes to mind. If this is one of your first encounters with an IDS, you may assume that performance is not much of an important issue and is a topic that only expert IDS analysts should be concerned with. Nothing could be further from the truth. Remember, when Snort is not performing efficiently, it is most likely experiencing significant packet loss. If Snort is dropping packets, there is a good chance that you could miss out on suspicious activity alerts. Snort's performance is always an important issue worthy of attention.

Hardware Performance Metrics

Because each network and Snort installation is unique, it is difficult to create exact performance metrics. It is impossible to say X amount of processing power and RAM will monitor Y bandwidth for a typical Snort deployment. This can be insanely frustrating for persons new to Snort. I have seen environments where a user new to Snort had purchased expensive state-of-the-art hardware and was unable to have Snort monitor a T1 Internet connection without dropping packets. Snort's performance is derived primarily from the Snort configuration and the type of monitored traffic. With this said, there are some general, rough guidelines you can use to help you gauge what system resources Snort will require.

Ruleset and Configuration Settings

Snort's configuration settings and the rules enabled have the greatest impact on how Snort performs. Configuring Snort to output to a database rather than Barnyard can have a tremendous performance impact. Enabling a large ruleset with an abundance of rules that check traffic content (rather than protocol elements) also has a noticeable performance impact, as does monitoring two identical traffic streams with different rulesets enabled. Therefore, the amount of work that Snort has to do can be directly correlated to the choice of output plugin and enabled ruleset. More system resources are required when you run Snort in one of these situations to ensure that it can function without dropping packets.

Depending on how Snort is set up, the major internal bottlenecks can be in either the output or the packet decoder stage. If the database logging output plugin is used, instead of the more efficient Snort Unified format, the output stage is the primary bottleneck. A monitored network that has a good deal of suspicious traffic requires extensive use of the output plugins, which in this case are the least efficient components of Snort. If you have decided to use the database output plugin, make sure you have additional resources available to handle the load.

If Snort outputs with the Unified format and hands database processing off to Barnyard, the packet decoder becomes the primary bottleneck. The packet decoder is where Snort rules are implemented and signatures are matched against traffic. Deployments with extremely poorly designed custom rules can make the decoder an even greater bottleneck than the database output plugin. Any rule that requires Snort to check a packet's contents is more resource intensive than one that does not. The more rules with content checks you have enabled, the more system resources you need to make available for Snort.

Snort's internal configuration settings (described in Chapter 3), combined with the rules enabled, affect the number of hardware resources Snort will need. Settings in some of the preprocessors consume additional system resources. Beyond the obvious maximum memory cap (*memcap*) option in `frag2` and `stream4`, some configuration options consume additional system resources if enabled. The brute-forcing of Back Orifice traffic keyspace with the BO preprocessor and the monitoring of all IP protocols with the `conversation` preprocessor requires additional system resources. If you have decided to enable a good number of the preprocessor options, it is wise to make sure you have the hardware to handle it.

With this being said, some minimum requirements for the different tiered components can serve as a rough guideline for procuring equipment. The specifications are for Intel-based hardware architectures.

Sensor Hardware

It is common to make the assumption that adding processors to a multi-processor system will increase Snort's performance. Unfortunately, this assumption is not always true. Snort is not designed for multithreading or multi-processor systems and cannot take advantage of an additional processor.

This is not to say that you can't assign services ancillary to Snort to a second processor. Some advanced Snort users assign the Barnyard daemon to one processor and the Snort daemon to another. This does create some significant performance gains. It is important to remember that not all operating systems allow services to be assigned to a particular processor. Before purchasing a multi-processor system, it is prudent to check whether your OS of choice supports this type of service assignment.

For the sensor, the minimum recommended requirements are as follows. Snort can be configured to run on less powerful computer if need be.

- Processor clockspeed of at least 1GHz for an AMD Athlon or Intel Pentium 4 brand processor. Should have a bus speed of 266MHz. Duron and Celeron processors should be avoided.

- System should have a minimum of 256MB of 133MHz ECC SDRAM.

- Sensor should have at least 7,200RPM hard drives, with 10,000RPM recommended for external sensors. The hard drive does not need to be larger than 20GB in size, unless you will be logging locally.

Server Hardware

For the server, the minimum recommended requirements are as follows:

- Processor clockspeed of at least 1.5GHz for an AMD Athlon or Intel Pentium 4 brand processor. Should have a bus speed of 266MHz. Duron and Celeron processors should be avoided.

- System should have a minimum of 512MB of 133MHzECC SDRAM.

- Server should have 10,000RPM hard drives. The hard drive array should be able to accommodate 100GB.

Console Hardware

For the console, the minimum recommended requirements are as follows

- Processor clockspeed of at least 800MHz. Duron or Celeron processors are acceptable.

- System should have a minimum of 128MB of ECC SDRAM.

- Console should have a 20GB hard drive.

Network Interface Cards

The Network Interface Card (NIC) is another important hardware component that should be selected with care. NICs are often assumed to be created equal, but nothing could be further from the truth. However, it is true that most "commodity" NICs are similar in terms of performance. Any low-end NIC is a fine choice for light bandwidth monitoring situations, as long as it can handle full duplex traffic. If you are going to place sensors in an environment that stresses Snort to the maximum, it is suggested that you purchase a NIC that can unburden the system hardware from some of its duties.

There are specially created NICs for monitoring and intense traffic situations. 3Com's NICs with the 3XP processor can take away some of the duties that system hardware would often have to accomplish. This leaves more resources accessible to Snort for its activities. High-performance NICs can often be five times as costly as a low-end card, and are really necessary only when monitored bandwidth approaches 100Mbps.

Some NICs contain cryptography chipsets that offload encryption and decryption duties from the OS. These cards further increase the resources available to Snort. These are good candidates for the management NICs that connect the tier's segments. These interfaces do not present any added benefit for the sniffing NICs on sensors because they do not encrypt or decrypt data.

Picking a Platform

Factors other than raw performance should influence your platform decision. The platform choice you make will ultimately dictate how well Snort functions and the amount of effort you will have to expend to guarantee that Snort runs smoothly. The security posture, stability, and external applications available to work in concert with Snort are all influenced by platform selection.

An IDS must have one of the highest levels of assured security in a network architecture. Having a compromised IDS is much worse than having no IDS at all. After you deploy intrusion detection capability, a degree of trust grows in the idea that your network is being properly monitored for malicious activity. If the IDS is unknowingly compromised, you still have a high level of trust that your IDS and network are reasonably protected. If you had not deployed an IDS, you would surely cast a more paranoid eye on suspicious events across your network. For these reasons, it is vitally important to keep your IDS bulletproof. An essential component in keeping your IDS secure is to ensure that the underlying OS is secure.

Certain operating systems are easier to secure than others. Every operating system is bound to have security flaws, but some have a greater precedent for security flaws than others. Whenever a vulnerability is discovered for an operating system, there is usually a lag of a few days before a patch is available. Operating systems with numerous vulnerabilities therefore have more time available for attackers to exploit them. Additionally, fixing security holes is a laborious and time-consuming task. Although it may not be much work to apply security fixes for one machine, continuously updating patches can become a festering problem if your IDS grows to dozens of sensors. Patching servers takes away from better ways to spend your time.

Precedent is more accurate than predisposition.

On the whole, Unix-based operating systems have a better track record in terms of security. Making a blanket statement like this can be quite dangerous, but it is based on cold hard facts. The latest complete data from SecurityFocus.com states that in the year 2000 there were 97 vulnerabilities released for Windows Server (NT and 2000) operating systems, while there were 55 for Debian Linux, 22 for Sun Solaris, and 20 for OpenBSD. A visual representation of this data is shown in Figure 5.1.

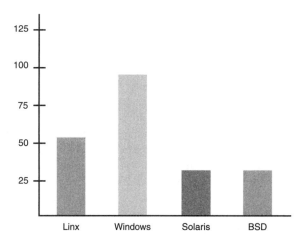

Figure 5.1   Vulnerabilities in 2000 by OS.

This could be related to Microsoft having larger market share and therefore being more thoroughly targeted by attackers. The reasons behind the disproportionate number of security holes for non-Unix operating systems is a lengthy discussion that is beyond the scope of this book. Operating system holy wars aside, if you choose Microsoft as the foundation for Snort, you will spend more time fixing security holes than if you do not. And if you happen to miss one, you leave your IDS open for compromise.

Stability is another essential factor in the OS selection process. An OS that is prone to memory leaks and crashes will not only cause headaches, it will cause you to miss vital alerts. Windows OSs are notorious for crashes. Although Windows 2000 is much better in this regard than its predecessors, it still does not match the reliability of a Unix operating system. For this reason it is again a better choice to run a Unix operating system for any mission-critical application.

Even if the OS is stable on its own, the Snort application itself may be more likely to crash on certain operating systems. This problem is exacerbated by Snort having no native facility for notifying the operator when it has crashed. You must write a script or use a tool to monitor system processes to alert yourself of a possible crash. For this reason, it is a best practice to use an OS on which Snort can run reliably. Snort was initially designed for the BSD platform, but now is just as stable on Linux or Solaris.

Snort is designed to perform only one function extremely well: monitoring network activity for intrusions. All the peripheral activities that make Snort more efficient and easier to manage are performed by other tools and applications. Open-source Unix-based operating systems have an abundance of tools available for Snort. Most of these associated applications are open source and free as well, and were designed to be run on Unix-based OSs. The most popular database for Snort is MySQL, which runs most effectively on Unix. There is a Windows port, but it crashes much more frequently than the Unix version. Although there are some exceptions, like IDS Policy Manager for

Windows, the majority of Snort-related applications are either exclusively for Unix or are most reliable when run on Unix. By choosing Linux or BSD, you are going to have more freely available tools for Snort and have a larger community to support you when something goes haywire.

Putting biases aside, from a practical standpoint, a Unix-based or, more specifically, an open-source Unix-based operating system is the best choice for the underlying Snort OS. Windows operating systems have definite advantages for other tasks, but by running Snort on Windows you are bound to create extra work and headaches for yourself. This is not to say it is totally inappropriate to run Snort on Windows. If you are totally unfamiliar with Linux or BSD, and do not have the time or patience to learn, Windows is still an option to get your feet wet with an IDS. If you are not serious about detecting intrusions, and only desire to test or play around with an IDS, Snort on Windows is a quick and easy option.

There are not as many disadvantages to using Windows for the console. Security is not as time-consuming because you should not be running much of anything on the console other than a Web browser. IDS Policy Manager for Windows is a phenomenal application for tuning and managing Snort rules and applying IDS policy in general. For these reasons, if you are more comfortable with Windows, it can be used safely as the console.

Hardening the OS

Whatever platform you choose, it is imperative that you properly prepare it before installing Snort. OSs are shipped with many services and daemons that are not necessary for Snort to function. Any unnecessary daemons running may have existing known vulnerabilities or have exposures waiting to be found. To reduce the likelihood of an exposure, it is crucial to remove all services that are not expressly required. In Snort's case, you want the OS to be as barren as possible.

The Monitoring Segment

Deploying a separate monitoring segment for an IDS is the generally accepted means of inserting an intrusion monitoring presence into network infrastructure. It is vital even for small deployments, such as Snort and all of its related applications installed on a single desktop computer. Taking the time and energy to install a separate monitoring segment enhances Snort's security and performance. A monitoring segment does not necessarily have to include expensive rewiring and additional network equipment. You can build an inexpensive and relatively secure segment with readily available equipment from your local computer shop.

The thorny part of installing a monitoring segment is the interface between it and the network to be monitored. From the IDS perspective, you want to be able to acquire every single packet that flows through the monitored segment. Tuning Snort so that it can handle all the traffic you are about to throw at it is an entirely different subject, but you must first build a foundation capable of reliably capturing traffic before concerning yourself with tuning.

The other priority is to monitor for intrusions in a secure fashion. We want to make it as difficult as possible for attackers to compromise the segment and attack Snort's infrastructure. Security can be greatly aided by properly installing the monitoring segment.

From the monitored network's perspective, and those that administer it, you want to ensure that installing intrusion detection capability will not adversely affect the network to be monitored. You want ensure that inserting sensors cannot degrade uptime or performance. We also want to take care to avoid single points of failure. A single point of failure is a component in a network topology that would cause the entire network to fail if it were removed. Single points of failure can create a denial of service situation for the monitored segment.

There are three methods of installing a monitoring segment into existing network infrastructure. They are via an inlinehub, a switch's Switched Port Analyzer (SPAN) port, and with a tap. Each method is increasingly reliable, efficient, and expensive.

Inline Hub

Monitoring with a hub is the easiest, least expensive method of inserting a monitoring segment into existing network topology. A hub utilizes shared media, meaning that all incoming packets are sent to every active port on the hub. For instance, traffic originating from the Internet sent through a hub is copied to every device attached to a port on the hub. This makes intrusion monitoring easy. You can simply plug a Snort sensor into an open port on a hub and all traffic will be copied to the sensor.

There are some rather serious disadvantages to using the hub method of monitoring. Most infrastructure that is worthy of an IDS does not typically use hubs or shared media. Hubs are generally not used in mission-critical infrastructure because they are not efficient. Hubs are prone to collisions, which degrade traffic throughput. Think of a hub like a conference call: If one person is speaking, everyone connected can understand the conversation. If another person wants to make a point, he or she must wait for the other to stop speaking. When a device tries to communicate over a hub and it is already in use, it must wait until the hub is free, causing a collision. A 100Mbps hub with 12 ports must share all its available bandwidth among the 12 connected systems. This leaves only 8.3Mbps (100Mbps divided by 12) on average for each connected system. Because hubs share their traffic, they are also prone to collisions when operating below the maximum threshold. Collisions degrade performance and significantly lower the maximum throughput.

For these reasons, almost every critical piece of network infrastructure is connected via switched media. Switched media is different than shared media in that it reserves a dedicated amount of bandwidth for each system connected to a port. A 100Mbps 12-port switch gives the full 100Mbps throughput to each port. Unfortunately, to achieve this bandwidth, packets are sent only to the port that is their intended destination. After a switch determines that a MAC address is attached to a device on a given port, it forwards all traffic for the MAC address directly to the appropriate port. This makes the installation of a sensor much more difficult.

To use a hub for monitoring in situations where switched media is used, you have to insert a hub into the monitored infrastructure. You have to split a line that serves as a choke point between two networks. For instance, you would have to attach the hub to your existing Internet connection cable and then connect a new cable to the switched media where an external firewall or servers reside. You would then connect a Snort sensor into a port on the hub, which would make monitoring external to your network possible. Figure 5.2 provides a diagram of inserting a monitoring segment via a hub.

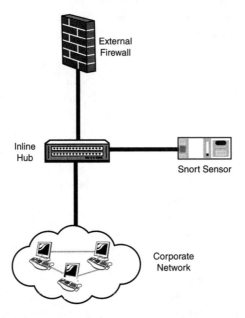

Figure 5.2 Using a hub to insert a monitoring segment.

Each time a sensor is introduced into the switched environment, a new hub is purchased and another line is severed. You may have to replicate this inline hub method several times to divide traffic into portions that the hub itself can handle. You may end up having to split intranet connections into two separate inline hubs to feed the same sensor. More importantly, the hub will degrade the traffic stream running through the hub. Since the hub cannot support full duplex, segments that require more than 100 megabits cannot have an inline hub installed. If traffic regularly approaches the 100 megabit threshold, the hub will significantly impair performance.

While the hub method is an inexpensive and easy way to introduce your monitoring segment, it introduces many single points of failure. If a hub were to unexpectedly malfunction, whether because a power cord was unplugged accidentally or a complete meltdown occurred, service would be denied to valuable infrastructure. The problem is exacerbated by the need to place the single points of failure on network choke points that are heavily used and relied upon. The probability of a hub-induced DoS multiplies with every sensor.

Using the hub method of inserting a monitoring segment opens up the possibility that an attacker could discover that an IDS is in use. As soon as an attacker knows that an IDS is being used to monitor for intrusions, he may change his behavior. The attacker would likely resort to attacks that use IDS evasion techniques. He may even attack the IDS itself, by attempting to compromise the monitoring segment or create a DoS condition on the IDS. This is a very real possibility if the hub lies external to the network and is facing the Internet. If the attacker can determine the sensor's IP address, she can launch attacks against the sensor. Even if no address is assigned, if the sensor is sniffing in stealth mode, there is still a small possibility that the IDS can be compromised by a remote exploit in libpcap, Snort, or the operating system. After an attacker has gained control of the sensor, he can establish bidirectional communication with a host he controls. He can also use the privileged position of the sensor to penetrate deeper within the network. The hub has no intrinsic security features to prevent any of this from happening.

Constructing a Unidirectional Sniffing Cable

There should never be a situation when traffic flows from the monitoring segment out to the monitored network. If traffic flows in this direction, something suspicious is occurring. To keep traffic from flowing out of the sensor, you can create what is known as a unidirectional sniffing cable. The cable is unidirectional, meaning it allows traffic to flow in only one direction. This cable prohibits traffic from flowing in the wrong direction when the cable is in use. It doesn't stop an insider from switching cables, but it greatly reduces the risk of monitoring with a hub. Creating the unidirectional sniffing cable mitigates the risk of a libpcap exploit. To create the cable you need some category 5e cable, some RJ-45 jacks, and some wire strippers and crimpers.

A standard (non-crossover) ethernet cable is laid out in a RJ-45 jack in the configuration shown in Figure 5.3, when viewed with the depressor side down.

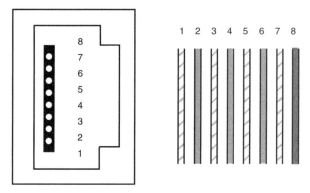

Figure 5.3   Standard ethernet pin configurations.

You should note some important details:

- Pins 1 and 2 are orange.
- Pins 3 and 6 are green.
- Pins 4 and 5 are blue.
- Pins 7 and 8 are brown.

A crossover cable is wired differently. If the cable you possess does not match this layout, you have the wrong type of cable. In the standard setup, pins 1 and 2 are transmit pins, whereas pins 3 and 6 are receive pins. To make the cable unidirectional (see Figure 5.4), you must connect pin 1 to pin 3 and pin 2 to pin 6. Make sure you do these swaps at only one end of the cable. The jack of the cable that you have modified belongs in the hub.

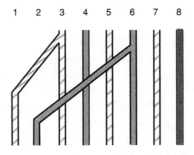

Figure 5.4   Unidirectional cable setup.

Some models of hubs determine that a cable is inserted into a port by checking whether a signal has ever been received. It is necessary, therefore, to connect the pins rather than simply clip the transmit pins on a unidirectional cable. If you were to simply disconnect the transmit pins, the hub would erroneously determine that the ethernet cable is not connected.

The sniffing cable functions only when it is used on a hub, because incoming traffic is now routed back into the hub. A switch gets confused if the port on which it sends traffic out receives the same traffic in return, and consequently shuts down the port.

Unidirectional sniffing cables are an inexpensive and necessary addition to a hub-based monitoring segment. If you upgrade to a more standard, professional setup, they can be reused as tools for pranks on your friends.

SPAN Ports

SPAN ports are another option for introducing a monitoring segment into existing network infrastructure. SPAN or mirror ports are a feature present on most midrange and high-end switches. A SPAN port can be either a dedicated port or a configurable option for all ports on a switch. The function of the SPAN port is to introduce the monitoring capability that network admins and security professionals have grown accustomed to with shared media.

A switch copies or mirrors all traffic that passes through the switch to the SPAN port. From a monitoring standpoint, the result is basically the same as plugging all segments directly into a hub. There are some notable advantages of using SPAN ports for monitoring, rather than an inline hub. The SPAN port is advantageous because on most models you can select from which non-SPAN ports you want to copy traffic. This allows you to get more granular with the type of traffic you want to monitor. If you are installing sensors internally, you may have servers that you do not want to monitor for intrusions. The SPAN port lets you do this much more easily than the chokepoint hub method.

The SPAN port does not introduce a single additional point of failure into the monitored network. This is the greatest advantage SPAN port monitoring has over hub monitoring. The SPAN port is present on the actual switch that is to be monitored, so it requires no break in a chokepoint connection. Utilizing SPAN ports to establish a monitoring segment does not degrade traffic via collisions, as using an inline hub does. The SPAN port does not introduce collisions and allows traffic to be transmitted in a normal fashion.

The SPAN port does away with the need for a unidirectional sniffing cable. The SPAN port does not accept traffic flowing toward the monitored segment. This prevents the sensor from establishing bidirectional communication with a host outside the monitoring segment.

Utilizing SPAN ports is a more scalable solution than using an inline hub. If traffic increases, you do not have to worry about adding additional hubs and single points of failure. You simply let the SPAN port take care of it. You can also add traffic streams by enabling additional segments to be mirrored. This method is useful for bringing intrusion monitoring to high-bandwidth networks. You can mirror one port, watch Snort's performance over time, and then tune as necessary. After Snort is tuned for one port, you can add others in a sensible, iterative process, rather than force Snort to drink from the proverbial fire hose.

If you have a large grouping of low-traffic SPAN port–enabled switches with no reasonable chokepoint, you can use the SPAN ports to aggregate traffic into one stream. You can aggregate them via an additional switch and then perform a second-degree SPAN port to mirror all the traffic to one port. Dedicated SPAN-Port switches are also available to aggregate traffic from the SPAN ports of many switches into a single device. Although they are somewhat pricey, they support more traffic and are more reliable than using an additional switch.

Although SPAN ports definitely hold an unmatched advantage over the use of hubs for the insertion of monitoring segments, there are some disadvantages. Enabling SPAN ports can degrade a switch's performance. Using a SPAN port can overload the switch's memory and cause its performance to drop off. Because mirroring traffic is a memory-intensive process and less critical than the primary function of transmitting traffic, the SPAN port is the first port to be affected. When the switch runs low on memory, it begins to let traffic slip by without mirroring it to the SPAN port. This is a problem that can be difficult to detect, especially if memory overloads occur randomly at peak times. Snort has no method of detecting when a switch memory overload occurs, so it is a problem that is difficult to discover unless you regularly monitor the switch for dropped packets.

Even if the switch can handle the memory requirements to SPAN multiple ports, the SPAN port has an upper limit of 100Mbps. You may think that we are getting ahead of ourselves by thinking of monitoring bandwidth over 100Mbps. Snort in its current state is unlikely to be able to handle such a deluge of traffic. This will change in the near future, as Snort's performance is significantly improved upon. Snort's commercial venture, Sourcefire, is already boasting an enterprise-class sensor that utilizes an expertly tuned version of Snort that can monitor gigabit networks. It is only a matter of time until Snort can do the same.

Another problem with SPAN ports is that some brands do not mirror layer 1 and 2 traffic. Attacks at low layers are somewhat rare, but can often be very serious if undetected. Just about any sniffer designed to function on switched networks, such as dsniff, goes unnoticed. ARP attacks are orchestrated at layer 2, and renders the use of the `ARPspoof` preprocessor worthless. Some vendors are beginning to mirror layer 1 and 2 traffic to SPAN ports, and in the future we can expect this to become the norm for switches.

Taps

Installing a tap is the third and final method of inserting a monitoring segment. Using taps is the most expensive way to place monitoring segments. A tap has all the advantages of an inline hub and a SPAN port combined. A tap is a device that sits inline on a chokepoint cable, much like a hub.

Because of its internal design, a tap does not introduce an additional single point of failure. Taps have this advantage because they can maintain what is known as *passive link integrity*. If the tap were to loose power or somehow malfunction, traffic would flow through the device uninterrupted. This is a major advantage over both the hub and SPAN port methods. Passive link integrity makes the tap the most reliable and least intrusive monitoring tool.

A tap can be purchased that allows either unidirectional or bidirectional traffic flow. You should purchase unidirectional taps for intrusion monitoring to mitigate the risk of bidirectional sensor traffic flow. There are a few situations where you may want bidirectional flow, such as for inline packet scrubbing and intrusion prevention, so it can be advantageous to purchase a tap that can accommodate both settings.

A tap has an advantage over both inline hubs and SPAN ports in that it cannot impact or degrade the traffic that flows through it. A tap does not degrade traffic by introducing packet collisions like a hub. The tap is a separate device from a switch, so it does not impact devices that are designed to move and monitor traffic. The tap also mirrors layer 1 and 2 traffic, unlike a SPAN port. This enables you to detect ARP attacks and other low-level network-based attacks. A tap is the only device that can guarantee that the sensor receives every packet that flows through the line, while not introducing performance penalties to the monitored network.

The primary disadvantage of a tap is its cost. A tap can easily cost more than 10 times as much as an inline hub and is about twice as expensive as a switch with a SPAN port. For these reasons, they are suitable for only medium to large organizations with a considerable security budget. The other methods are appropriate for small businesses and home networks.

Distributing Traffic to Multiple Sensors

If you are deploying an IDS at a large organization, there is a good chance that you will be faced with a situation where you will need to monitor network traffic at a single location, and that traffic will exceed the theoretical capacity of a lone Snort sensor. In high-bandwidth situations, it is tempting to tune Snort by trimming a large quantity of rules from the ruleset so that a single sensor can accommodate the rush of traffic. It is equally tempting to turn off preprocessors that generate non-critical alerts, such as portscan2. Although these actions are better than dropping packets or not monitoring at all, there are solutions that allow the sensor to remain in its most potent form.

Large organizations today often have a central backbone that supports gigabit networking. A backbone that is responsible for carrying all the organization's communication makes a great target for intrusion monitoring. The problematic issue remains, though, that a single Snort sensor cannot handle gigabit traffic. There are methods to split prohibitively high-bandwidth traffic to a number of sensors via hardware.

One possible method of dividing up traffic is to assign different traffic segments to each sensor. If you were to configure two sensors, one to interpret traffic from 0.0.0.0/4 and another to process traffic from 128.0.0.0/4, you could effectively divide traffic between sensors. Because of Snort's internal structure, the preprocessors in both sensors interpret traffic. This method partially distributes the load between two sensors. There are other more effective and expensive means of distributing traffic.

IDS load-balancing hardware is available that evenly distributes traffic to a grouping of sensors. This ensures that no single sensor will be overwhelmed with traffic. The load balancer can support up to eight sensors monitoring the same network.

The load balancer is deployed in combination with a tap, either gigabit or full duplex. The tap is inserted in the usual manner described previously. The load balancer receives all the traffic from the tap and marshals it out to sensor groupings. The load balancer functions by assigning each sensor a monitor link; the sensors can be grouped together and their traffic flow regulated.

For a load balancer to be used in an IDS setting it must support stateful mirroring. Stateful mirroring ensures that a sensor that is tracking a session continues to receive the same session data as the load balancer divides up traffic. If the load balancer were to randomly distribute packets, streams would be broken up and intrusion detection would be severely hampered. Attackers could easily send session-based attacks, knowing that they would have a good chance of passing undetected. For this reason it is imperative to have stateful mirroring technology present in any load balancer considered.

Load balancers also provide redundancy. By creating extra intrusion monitoring capacity via additional sensors, you can ensure that a hardware failure or system crash does not disrupt the IDS as a whole. It also enables you to test new sensor configurations and beta versions of Snort in a controlled environment, relieving you from having to be concerned with losing monitoring capability with an untested upgrade. Load balancing across multiple sensors helps thwart the inevitable traffic spikes and malicious resource depletion DoS attacks. Having extra IDS capacity at an important network chokepoint can never be a disadvantage.

Like taps, load balancing's major disadvantage is its cost. A load balancer with a gigabit tap can easily be more expensive than the Snort sensor group utilizing it. Load balancing is something that should be considered only when traffic approaches full duplex or gigabit levels.

Summary

This chapter focused on the hardware and software required to build a Snort architecture. The proper system resources have to be made available for Snort to avoid situations where packet loss and subsequently false negatives occur. It is difficult to gauge the system resources that Snort will require. Widely varying factors, such as Snort's internal configuration and the content of the monitored traffic, will greatly influence the system resources that Snort will require.

The Snort sensor and the server require the most hardware resources because they are resource-intensive platforms. The console does not have such stringent hardware requirements. An often-overlooked hardware purchasing decision is the NICA NIC, which can be used to offload some of the processing that the system would otherwise have to do.

Snort can run on many different platforms, but the best choice for Snort is Unix. Unix platforms are more secure and stable and have more freely available ancillary Snort applications. Open-source Unix platforms such as Linux and BSD are the preferred platforms for Snort.

Installing a monitoring segment is a necessary task in a Snort deployment. There are three methods of inserting the monitoring segment into existing network infrastructure. The methods—hubs, SPAN ports, and taps—are increasingly secure, reliable, and expensive. The lowest-cost method, using an inline hub on a network choke point, utilizes the inherent properties of the hub to monitor for intrusions. Hub monitoring requires the construction of a unidirectional sniffing cable to properly secure the sensor. Hub monitoring creates single points of failure in the network to be monitored and can degrade traffic.

SPAN ports are a feature of modern switches, which allow selected traffic to be mirrored to a special port. The SPAN port passes all traffic through the switch mirrored to it. SPAN ports are advantageous because they require a unidirectional sniffing cable and do not degrade traffic. SPAN ports can overwhelm the switching device's memory. When the switch approaches its memory limit, it ceases to mirror all traffic to the SPAN port. SPAN ports do not mirror layer 1 and 2 traffic and cannot output traffic in excess of full duplex.

Taps are the most expensive but most secure and reliable method of inserting a monitoring segment. Taps maintain passive link integrity, so if the tap were to lose power or malfunction in some way, traffic would flow through them uninterrupted. Taps do not degrade traffic and mirror layer 1 and 2 traffic to the sensor. Taps are the preferred method of monitoring.

Another hardware device used in intrusion detection is an IDS load balancer. The load balancer evenly distributes traffic to multiple sensors. This enables many sensors to monitor a single high-bandwidth traffic stream. Gigabit networks can be monitored in this fashion. IDS load balancers can also be used for greater redundancy, and to test new sensor configurations.

6

Building the Server

THIS CHAPTER IS A COMPLETE GUIDE to deploying a Snort server. The primary function of the Snort server is to serve as a collection and distribution point for intrusion data. The server receives alerts generated by any number of sensors and stores them in the intrusion database. The alerts can then be logically organized and distributed to you via the management GUI.

By the end of this chapter, you will have a fully functional Snort server. One thing to note, however, is that you need to have some basic knowledge of Unix commands to follow this guide. If you are unsure about a command you can turn to a number of reference books or online resources.

Installation Guide Notes

The Snort server installation guide outlined in the following pages is built on the Linux platform. Linux is chosen because of its stability, security, large supportive community, and the vast quantity of available applications. Although there are other choices that are of equal stability and security, Linux is the most widely accepted open source platform today.

More specifically, the Red Hat distribution version 7.3 has been chosen for its popularity and the fee-based technical support. In using a distribution other than Red Hat, you will find that the installation process varies slightly but should still function. Although you most likely will never need the pay-for technical support Red Hat provides, it is comforting to know it is there if you need it.

Red Hat Linux 7.3

Red Hat Linux is available freely for download. You can also purchase the distribution at most computer stores. Installing Red Hat is a straightforward process if you have installed Linux before. If you do not have experience installing Linux, rest assured; the installation process is graphical and fairly intuitive. If you get stuck somewhere in the initial install (for example, if the video card is not supported by X Windows), remember that numerous resources on the Internet are available to help you out. During the installation process choose the default options unless the instructions in this chapter specify differently.

Partitioning Strategy

The Snort server must have the maximum amount of hard drive space available for the intrusion database. This chapter adheres to a partitioning strategy that supports this. When you arrive at the Partitioning Strategy screen, choose to Manually Partition. You need to create the following four partitions, using the New button to create each one:

- **Boot Partition**. 40MB in size and a mount point of /boot.
- **Swap Partition**. Select filesytem type Swap for this partition and 1024MB in size.
- **Var Partition**. This partition should be a third of the total drive size, or 5GB at minimum. Set mount point to /var.
- **Main Partition**. Use the Fill to Maximum Allowable Size checkbox to partition the rest of the hard drive.

Network Configuration

Under the IP address setup information for eth0, you should deselect the Configure Using DHCP option. DHCP is used to automatically obtain and assign an IP address to a host. The DHCP server could potentially assign a different address to the server if it were to be rebooted. With a new IP address, the server would lose contact with the sensors. You would then have to change settings on the sensors that make use of a hard-coded IP address. It is a better strategy to define a static IP address.

The IP information defined for the server should be a private RFC1918 address. The valid RFC1918 ranges are:

- 10.0.0.0–10.255.255.255
- 172.16.0.0–172.31.255.255
- 192.168.0.0–192.168.255.255

These groupings of addresses are not routable on the Internet under most normal circumstances. This makes accessing devices on the IDS segment more difficult for external attackers. Although this is not a foolproof security control, it is an additional layer in a defense in-depth security strategy.

Firewall Configuration

Under firewall configuration, you should select No Firewall. The server should not be acting as a firewall, and should not have any services that need to be blocked.

Furthermore, the server should be residing on the IDS segment that is separate from all other network infrastructure. If you wish to place the server behind a firewall to be accessed by analyst consoles, the firewall should be configured as a separate device.

Time Zone Selection

Keeping time in sync between the Snort sensors and servers makes event correlation possible. Without accurate synchronization, it is difficult to piece security events together.

> **Investigating Incidents and Correct Time**
>
> Accurate time is especially important when investigating a security incident that involves external parties. Large organizations, particularly ISPs, can have a tremendous number of users or customers making use of the same pool of IP addresses. These addresses can be reassigned to different persons several times in the space of a minute. If your IDS has not accurately synced time with a reliable external time server, the external party cannot positively determine who was using the offending IP address at the requested time.
>
> Inaccurate time can make it impossible to link an exact person to the attacking IP address. Although you may be able to determine that it was very likely that your attacker was in possession of the attacking IP address, you introduce inconsistencies in your evidence if you do not have perfectly accurate time. This could be problematic if you were to bring legal action against the suspected attacker.

Network Time Protocol (NTP) is the tool for accurate time synchronization. You need to select the UTC offset tab and single out your correct offset. Additionally, you should check the System Clock Uses UTC check box.

Account Configuration

When creating accounts for the server, or for any critical security device, you should choose strong passwords for the user accounts. Strong passwords are over 10 characters long and have a mixture of alphanumeric (that is, ABC123) and special characters (such as *!@#&). The stronger the password, the more computationally expensive is it to work through every password combination with a password cracker.

Package Group Selection

The following package groups should be selected:
- Classic X Windows
- X Windows
- KDE or GNOME
- Network Support
- Messaging Web Tools
- Authoring and Publishing
- Emacs

- Utilities
- Software Development

The purpose of installing X Windows is to make use of a graphical server hardening tool in a later step. If you feel comfortable using this tool in a non-graphical mode that does not contain the same internal documentation, by all means remove X Windows. X serves only to degrade performance if you do not need it.

Post-Installation Tasks

There are a few simple but important post-installation tasks that are essential for priming the server. The first and most important task is to bring the server up to a current patch level. Not only do the patches close some serious security holes, but they fix some bugs that could reduce the server's performance and functionality. If you are installing on a distribution other than Red Hat, the process of updating Linux varies slightly. Most Linux distributions (Mandrake, Debian, and so on) have an update tool that can be used to patch the server automatically. All distributions have a manual method of downloading patches to update software.

You can either use the Red Hat network to automatically update the server for you, or select the patches you need from the following URL:

```
http://rhn.redhat.com/errata/rh73-errata.html
```

Security patches are denoted with an open padlock icon, whereas bug fixes are associated with the spider-looking bug icon. Simply scroll through the list and install the patches that are necessary.

After you have updated Red Hat to a bug-free and secure level, it is time to harden the server. Both manual and semi-automated processes are effective means for hardening any Linux distribution. An important fact to remember is that a completely hardened server is not a functional one. The process of hardening gradually eliminates access and increases the target's security controls. A fully hardened machine denies access to everyone. What we are shooting for is a server that is hardened enough to prevent most types of misuse, but can still perform the functions it is required to do. Finding that thin line between overly hardened and open access is a tough one, but with some practice you can determine where that line exists.

If you are an experienced user, or desire to sharpen your Linux security skills, you can work through one of the many online guides for Linux hardening. Following the steps outlined at sans.org will result in a well hardened Snort server. You can check out the guide at the following URL:

```
http://www.sans.org/linux.htm
```

Bastille Linux

Bastille Linux is a set of scripts that automatically harden a Red Hat or Mandrake Linux machine. It can be used to harden the HP-UX OS as well. Bastille Linux is a viable option if you prefer to use a more automated method of hardening, or want to ensure that you have not accidentally missed something when hardening manually.

A fair warning: Bastille Linux is not foolproof. It applies the best security practices that have been developed by the Linux community for hardening. It cannot detect every possible configuration that should be locked down. Additionally, Bastille can change settings that are needed for normal Snort Server use. An automated hardening tool can never replace general system security knowledge, but can serve as a great starting point or working guide for the uninitiated.

The best feature of Bastille is that the entire installation process can be rolled back. If you run the script and a necessary application is no longer functioning, you can download the "undo" script. It rolls back every change Bastille makes so you can re-harden the host.

The graphical version of Bastille has exceptional internal documentation. When you use the graphical interface, Bastille explains what the function you are enabling does. This makes it a great tool for learning Linux security. If you are experienced with hardening Linux and do not require the documentation, use the text-only version of Bastille.

You can download Bastille Linux at

```
http://www.bastille-linux.org/
```

You need to acquire three files from the Web site:

- The Bastille Linux RPM
- The Bastille Perl-Tk graphical module
- The Perl-Tk RPM

After you have downloaded the three files you need to install them. For this situation you will use the Red Hat Package Manager (RPM) to automatically install Bastille. This is one of the few packages or applications that you will install in this automated manner. Run the RPM install command with the –nodeps option from the download directory.

```
rpm -ivh —nodeps perl-Tk-800.022-4mdk.i586.rpm
```

The –nodeps prevents the installation from failing if the required package dependencies are not satisfied. Package dependencies are put in place to prevent a package from being installed that requires another package if it is to function. In this case, you should ignore such requirements. After the Perl-Tk package has installed, install Bastille Linux and the graphical interface. Execute this command from the download directory:

```
rpm -ivh Bastille-1.3.0-1.0.i386.rpm Bastille-Tk-module-1.3.0-1.0.i386.rpm
```

You now have Bastille installed. To start the hardening process enter the `InteractiveBastille` command as root from a command prompt. This loads the graphical interface for Bastille, see Figure 6.1.

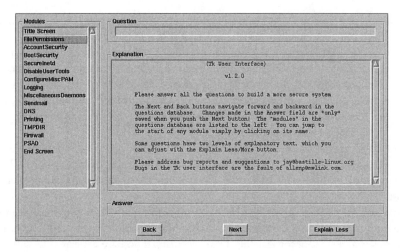

Figure 6.1   Bastille Linux GUI.

Bastille loads the hardening options in a questionnaire format. It explains the option and asks you whether you want to enable it. You are going to want to enable them all by selecting the Yes check box, except for a few. The exceptions stated in the following sections provide more hassle than security.

File Permissions

Select all except:

- Reservation of ping for root-level accounts
- Reservation of traceroute for root-level accounts.

Ping and traceroute are not much of risk. If someone has compromised your server, you have other things to worry about than ping.

Account Security

Select all except `restricting remote root login`.

By disabling remote logon as root you are in effect forcing any user with root privileges to log on remotely as an ordinary user. The user would have to switch to a root account after logging in. This prevents attackers possessing only the root password from logging in. Disabling remote root login is a somewhat weak security control and can make maintenance a hassle. If you feel that you should have to log in twice to get remote root access, you should select the remote root login restriction option.

Boot Security

Select all except `Disabling CTRL-ALT-DELETE Reboot`. Disabling CTRL-ALT-DELETE simply makes it more difficult to reboot the server. If someone has physical access to reboot your server via a keyboard, he or she can most likely cut the power source. This has the same effect as CTRL-ALT-DELETE.

Secure Inetd

Select all except `Defaulting to Deny` for TCP Wrappers and Xinetd.

Disable User Tools

Select all except `Disabling the GCC Compiler`. Disabling GCC is a good thing to do after you have compiled and installed the necessary Snort server packages. You may want to revisit this option after the entire installation process is complete.

Configure Miscellaneous Parameters

Select all except `Limit Resource Usage`. Limiting resource usage, such as a maximum file size of 100MB and other controls this option performs, makes the server function poorly. The performance of the database used to store intrusion data is severely hamstrung if you limit resource usage.

Miscellaneous Daemons

Select all except `Disable GPM`. Using the mouse in text applications via GPM is a useful feature that does not pose a significant security risk.

Sendmail

Select all except `Prevent Sendmail from Running in Daemon Mode`. Even though sendmail has a terrible security track record, the Snort server needs it. Sendmail needs to run in daemon mode to send alerts real time.

Firewall

Disable all. You do not want a firewall running on the server.

PortScan Attack Detector (PSAD)

Disable all. Snort sensors are to be the primary method of detecting portscans across network infrastructure.

Completing the Bastille Linux Hardening

After you have selected the options you want, Bastille runs the script. If you later realize that you hardened the server too tightly and some process does not function you can roll back the changes. Simply download the "undo" script at

`http://www.bastille-linux.org/UndoBastille`

You can then re-run Bastille and deselect the option you mistakenly enabled.

Installing the Snort Server Components

This rather large section walks you through the steps in building the Snort Server from scratch. You should now have a lean, hardened Linux machine primed for action. If you have decided to use a distribution other than Red Hat, the following instructions may vary slightly. The locations of files, directories and other components may be different on other distributions.

It is important to follow the steps in this guide in consecutive order. Some of the packages must have another package installed for them to compile and install. It is important to have these dependencies satisfied; if not there is a good chance the installation will fail.

When gathering packages for the Snort Server, you may find a version of a package that is more current than the one used in this book. When encountering this situation, it is a good idea to use the most current version rather than the version specified in this book. Most open source programs are improved upon with each subsequent version. Newer versions are likely to be more stable and secure as bug fixes and security patches are rolled into existing code. If you encounter difficulties with the newer version, you can always find the version specified in the book to ensure you will have a working Snort server.

For the majority of applications in this book, it is recommended to compile source code and install rather than use RPMs (Red Hat Package Modules). If you are unfamiliar with Red Hat, RPMs can be used to automatically install software. The entire installation process is hidden from you, and requires only that you have the correct dependencies available.

RPMs are truly a great idea. They can make using Linux much easier, but they have some significant disadvantages. First of all, RPMs are not available for all packages. There will come a point in your Linux administering career where you will have to install software that does not have an RPM. It is best to learn how to do it. RPMs are usually not as current as source distributions. RPMs are not challenging to create; most open source developers would rather concentrate on developing new code for the application. So there can be a lag between when an updated version of software is released and the RPM is updated. Often, RPMs do not contain important bug fixes for compatibility issues and security updates. Additionally, RPMs install a default set of software. They may install software or code that you do not want on your system. There is no way to conveniently edit the RPM or select installation options, so you are stuck with whatever the RPM builder has decided should be in the RPM.

For these reasons, the instructions in this chapter compile and install from source code for the Snort setup. Working with source code is not as difficult as it sounds, and does not take up an inordinate amount of time. It involves only a few extra commands for each package.

Installing OpenSSL

OpenSSL Project is an open source toolkit for implementing Secure Sockets Layer (SSL) and Transport Layer Security (TLS). Furthermore, OpenSSL contains a general-purpose encryption library with support for strong encryption algorithms. The SSL protocol is widely known for the encryption of HTTP sessions, but it can be used in other settings. OpenSSL is widely accepted because it is secure and can be used without much difficulty. SSL can be used to encrypt most any type of TCP session with the help of an additional package, stunnel.

For the Snort server, OpenSSL provides the encryption for the sensor-to-server session. Alerts generated by Snort and Barnyard on a sensor are posted via a TCP session to the intrusion database residing on the server. Encrypting this session is important for a few reasons. The authentication information that is used to identify the sensor to the database is passed in cleartext. An attacker could sniff the logins and passwords and access the intrusion event database with the same privileges as a sensor. The attacker could insert false positives or otherwise cause damage to the IDS. In addition to authentication information, the intrusion data itself is sent in the clear. The attacker could read the data to see whether attacks were being picked up on, or use the data to map the network for vulnerable hosts. For these reasons, we recommend using OpenSSL to encrypt the sensor-to-server sessions.

OpenSSL is also used to encrypt the server-to-console sessions. Because the console uses a Web browser to access intrusion data, OpenSSL is used in the more traditional role of encrypting HTTP sessions. Server-to-console sessions are encrypted for the same reasons the sensor-to-server sessions are.

You can begin the OpenSSL installation by downloading the source code at

`http://www.openssl.org/source/`

Notice there are two versions of the source code: OpenSSL and OpenSSL-engine. The OpenSSL code is the correct source for this setting. The OpenSSL-engine is similar to the OpenSSL codebase, but has additional code for use with hardware encryptors. Download the compressed file to a directory for storing source code (such as `/usr/local/tarballs`). The compressed file is often referred to as a tarball. After you have downloaded the file, you must uncompress it. Do so by issuing this command:

`tar -xzvf openssl-0.9.6g.tar.gz`

This `tar` command uncompresses the OpenSSL tarball and places the contents in a directory named openssl-0.9.6g. The –x option specifies that the files will be extracted. The –z option filters the compressed file through `gzip` before extracting with `tar`. This is needed to uncompress the .gz portion of the archive. Change to the newly created directory, and prep the source code for compiling by using the following command:

`./configure -DSSL_FORBID_ENULL`

The –DSSL_FORBID-ENULL option prevents OpenSSL from permitting null ciphers in the SSL cipher suite. Null ciphers permit unencrypted, cleartext data to be outputted. Null ciphers negate the purpose of using OpenSSL, so it is best not to allow their use. After the source has been prepared, compile the source with

`make`

And then install the source using

`make install`

If everything runs smoothly, you should now have OpenSSL installed on the Snort server.

By default, OpenSSL is installed in the `/usr/local/ssl` directory. OpenSSL is comprised of a few important files that include the following:

- `libcrypto.a`. General encryption routines for encryption ciphers (libdes, RC4/2, Blowfish, IDEA), Message Digests (MD5, SHA), public keys (RSA, DSA, Diffie-Hellman), X.509 certificates (encrypting/decrypting via private key), and various other routines.
- `openssl`. A tool used to access OpenSSL routines, available in `libcrypto.a`.
- `libssl.a`. The code for SSL versions 1 and 2 and code for TLS.

You need to complete one last setup to let other packages know that the OpenSSL package is available. Most Linux applications require libraries to execute. Programs are by default compiled to use one or many dynamically linked libraries (DLLs). This is done so that you can update a library and all the packages that use the library will use the updated version.

Red Hat searches a file, `/etc/ld.so.conf`, when a program starts up. You want OpenSSL to be included in this list of libraries, so you need to edit the ld.so.conf to include OpenSSL. Open it for editing by typing the following:

emacs /etc/ld.so.conf &

Emacs is a powerful text editor available for most Unix systems. The ampersand places the emacs job in the background so you can still use the command prompt. If you wish to recover the emacs session, simply type `fg` *job number*. After you have emacs running, you need to add the line `/usr/local/lib` to `ld.so.conf`. Save and exit. Run the ldconfig command to update the new shared libraries. You have now successfully installed OpenSSL.

Installing Stunnel

Stunnel is used to establish and maintain encrypted sessions. The Stunnel program is an SSL encryption wrapper. It encrypts sessions between remote clients and local or remote servers. Stunnel is used to make non-SSL-aware services that are running communicate with clients over a secure SSL channel.

Stunnel can be used to add SSL capability to commonly used `inetd` daemons, such as POP-2 and IMAP servers, without having to modify the program's source. Stunnel can be used to protect any protocol that uses TCP and does not require two channels to communicate (such as FTP). Stunnel itself does not provide any cryptographic routines. It requires a supplementary library to perform the encryption and decryption of data. OpenSSL is a leading choice for the cryptographic library, which you have already compiled and installed in the previous step. Stunnel has no limitations on the type of cryptographic algorithm to be used.

Stunnel supports session caching. Whenever an SSL connection is established, a fair amount of negotiation must take place. The server and client must decide on which cryptographic ciphers to use, the SSL version they can mutually support, and other tasks related to setting up the secure session. This information is stored in what is known as a session ID. Both the server and the client store the session ID in a cache. The session ID is stored so the computationally expensive process of SSL negotiation can be avoided after the SSL session has been established.

If the client offers the session ID to the server, and the server recognizes it, the session is maintained. If the client does not have a valid session ID or if the server does not recognize the session ID forwarded, the SSL session has to be torn down. The negotiation process must now be repeated. Stunnel utilizes session caching on both the server and client side to remain efficient.

Stunnel has three basic functions that relate to the encryption of transmitted data:

- It can receive unencrypted data and deliver it to a SSL server.
- Stunnel can accept encrypted data and launch an appropriate program to make use of the encrypted channel.
- Finally, it can receive encrypted data and send decrypted data to the remote host.

With the Snort server, you will be using the first two Stunnel functions. You can download Stunnel at `http://www.stunnel.org/download/source.html`.

After downloading the Stunnel tarball to your download directory, you must untar it in a similar manner that OpenSSL was unpacked.

```
tar -xzvf stunnel-3.22.tar.gz
```

After it uncompresses, change to the new Stunnel source directory, `Stunnel-3.22.tar.gz`. From here, you want to type:

```
./configure
```

If you get an error message (something to the effect of `Cannot find SSL library installation dir`), there is no need to worry. This error message most likely means you have installed OpenSSL to a non-standard directory. If you have installed OpenSSL in a different directory, you need to specify the `-with-ssl` option like so:

```
./configure -with-ssl=path/to/ssl/libraries
```

Next, you simply want to compile:

```
make
```

And finally install:

```
make install
```

Now you have a working version of Stunnel installed on your machine. You now must perform some post-installation configuration.

Each Stunnel server must have a private key to function. The key is contained in a PEM file that Stunnel uses to define its identity. PEM stands for Privacy Enhanced Mail, which has evolved into an accepted key format for uses other than email.

This private key is placed in the directory:

`/usr/local/ssl/certs/stunnel.pem`

The problem is that this default key is the same for every installation of Stunnel. The default key is publicly available on the Stunnel.org Web site, meaning that anyone can use it to intercept and decrypt your session data. You cannot use this private key if you expect your sensor-to-server sessions to be secure. Fortunately, creating a new private key is a simple process, as illustrated in Figure 6.2. Type the following command from the Stunnel source directory:

make cert

Figure 6.2   Creating a new Stunnel certificate.

This overwrites the stunnel.pem file with a new private key that will be valid for one year. It uses the SSL library by default to generate the key. You are then asked a series of questions to generate the key. Enter the physical location information as you see fit. The important question is the last one; it asks for your common name or Fully Qualified Domain Name (FQDN). You should ensure that the FQDN is the Snort server's actual host name. You can type the `hostname` command to find this name if you do not already know it. If you do not have the correct hostname specified, Stunnel clients receive errors when connecting to the server.

You also need to change the permissions for the stunnel.pem file. As a security precaution, Stunnel does not run if the file is accessible by anyone other than root. There is no password protection on the file, so anyone who can read the file can intercept communication and compromise Snort's security. For this reason, Stunnel requires you to correctly set the permissions for stunnel.pem. You can correct the permissions with the following command:

`chmod 600 /usr/local/ssl/certs/stunnel.pem`

The final step in configuring Stunnel is to list the new secured version of MySQL in the /etc/services file. The services file is used to contain known services available. Edit the file via emacs or your favorite text editor and insert this line:

```
mysqls 3307/tcp
```

This completes the Stunnel installation for the Snort server.
You can start Stunnel by using the following command:

```
/usr/local/stunnel/sbin/stunnel -d mysqls -r 127.0.0.1:3306
-p /usr/local/ssl/certs/stunnel.pem &
```

The -d option runs Stunnel in daemon mode. The -r is used to specify the remote service (mysql, 3306/tcp, in this case), to which connections to the service specified with the -d option (mysqls) will be forwarded. The -p is the location of the newly created Stunnel certificate.

Installing OpenSSH

There are likely to be situations where you will need to log into the Snort server remotely. You may place the server in a production environment or a rack that is not in a convenient physical location. The situation may arise where you will have to move large files, such as log files or intrusion data, to and from the server. There are also circumstances where you would like to perform maintenance or troubleshooting activity, and desire to do so from the Analyst's console. Traditionally, such activities require the use of unencrypted, insecure protocols. With OpenSSH, we can perform remote maintenance without risking the Snort server.

OpenSSH is an open source implementation of the Secure Shell (SSH) protocol. SSH is a transparent method of securely establishing communication and transferring data between a client and server. OpenSSH provides the same functionality as other less secure protocols, such as

- Telnet
- FTP
- rlogin
- rcp
- rsh

OpenSSH maintains security by encrypting both authentication and session data. Antiqued protocols (Telnet, FTP, and so on) send their username and password combos in the clear. Additionally, data transferred with these protocols is sent in clear text. The possibility of an attacker gathering authentication credentials or intrusion data becomes a very real possibility with unencrypted protocols. This makes the antiquated protocols an unacceptable means of remotely updating or managing the Snort server. For these reasons you should use the secure OpenSSH for all remote management tasks.

OpenSSH is actually a suite of programs. It contains six programs and three setup and maintenance utilities.

ssh

The ssh program is the client-side application used to log into and execute commands on a remote machine. It is a replacement for insecure rlogin and rsh methods of remote command execution. The ssh program provides secure, encrypted communication between two hosts over an unknown or insecure network.

It also supports X11 connections and arbitrary TCP/IP port forwarding through the encrypted tunnel. The ssh application connects and logs into the remote host using one of various different authentication methods. You should use those available to version 2 of the SSH protocol. SSHv.2 supports strong encryption that uses DSA public keys. It also supports verifiable integrity of the connection.

scp

The scp program securely copies files between hosts on a network. It is an extension of the ssh program that is used for data transfer. It relies on ssh for authentication and encryption, therefore providing the same security as ssh. The scp program is a replacement for the antiquated rcp. Unlike rcp, scp prompts for authentication information if required.

sshd

The sshd (SSH daemon) is the daemon or server program for ssh. The daemon is the program responsible for listening for connections from ssh clients. Each time an incoming connection is found, it spawns a new daemon dedicated to the new connection. When the session has completed or timed out, the daemon is torn down. Each spawned daemon handles all the ssh duties for each individual session. The sshd program is installed on the Snort server to be used for remote maintenance and troubleshooting.

The sshd daemon is started at boot time from the /etc/rc file. You can edit this file if you choose to change this option.

sftp

The sftp program is a secure file transfer program, similar to FTP. It performs all normal FTP functions over an encrypted ssh transport. It can also use many features unique to ssh, such as public key authentication and on-the-fly data compression. On-the-fly data compression compresses data using gzip before transmitting, and then decompresses it when it reaches the client. With compression enabled, significant bandwidth savings can be achieved at the expense of processing power.

sftp-server

The sftp-server program provides the sftp protocol information for sshd. You do not need to interact with sftp-server directly; its functionality is accessed through sshd. It is called through a subsystem operation within sshd.

ssh-agent

The ssh-agent tool is used to hold private keys used for RSA public key authentication. Ssh-agent is started in the beginning of every login session, and all other programs are started as clients to the ssh-agent tool. Through use of environment variables the agent is located and automatically used for authentication when logging in to other ssh daemons using ssh.

ssh-add

The ssh-add tool simply adds DSA key identities to the authentication agent, ssh-agent.

ssh-keygen

The ssh-keygen tool generates authentication keys for ssh. It can also be used to manage and convert keys between ssh protocol versions. It can be used to create RSA or DSA keys.

Implementing OpenSSH

Now that you are familiar with the basics of OpenSSH, it is time to download and install it. Get OpenSSH for Red Hat at

```
http://www.openssh.org/portable.html
```

The Importance of Verifying Your Packages

All open source packages are distributed with some sort of integrity verification scheme. Some use a hash, such as MD5, and others use a gnupg signature. The purpose of integrity verification is to ensure that the package to be downloaded has not been tampered with. If someone were to insert malicious code and turn the package into a Trojan, the integrity signature would no longer match. Open source projects often store the signatures on a physically separate server. This is done to add another layer of security: If the server that holds the package is compromised, the signature cannot be changed as well. If the attacker compromises both servers, then the system fails. People who download packages rarely check for integrity. OpenSSH was Trojaned in a method similar to what's already been described. A black hat compromised a OpenBSD FTP server that housed the OpenSSH source download, most likely using the Apache chunked encoding exploit. The attacker placed a remotely controlled Trojan into OpenSSH. It took almost three days for the Trojan to be discovered. Thousands of downloads took place during this time period, and many systems were Trojaned. The malicious code was discovered only when users were having trouble running the Trojaned version. It was then noticed that the code did not match the gnupg signature. So to stay secure, it is worth your time to check the integrity of every package you download.

After you download the correct version of OpenSSH, you need to uncompress the tarball.

```
tar -xzf openssh-3.4p1.tar.gz
```

Change to the new source directory:

```
cd openssh-3.4p1
```

Follow the same configuration, compilation, and installation steps:

```
./configure
make
make install
```

Now you should have OpenSSH properly installed. If you are using a different version of Red Hat or have an entirely different distribution, you may have received an error relating to the zlib compression library. If so, you need to download zlib from

```
http://www.gzip.org/zlib/
```

Install it using the normal ./configure, make, and make install process. After you are finished, OpenSSH installs properly.

You must now generate your DSA keys. Use

```
ssh-keygen
```

You can now run sshd by executing the commands:

```
/usr/local/sbin/sshd
/usr/local/bin/egd.pl
```

The OpenSSH daemon is now ready to accept incoming OpenSSH connections.

Downloading Apache

Apache has been the world's most popular Web server since April of 1996. Apache maintains around 60% of the market share. You can check accurate Web server market share statistics at:

```
http://www.netcraft.com/survey/.
```

It was named Apache because it grew out of a large collection of patched code, making it a-patchy or an "apache" Web server. Like Snort, Apache is open source and extendable. There are many side projects for the core Apache HTTP server, such as an XML server, an SSL server, and numerous application servers.

There are a number of other components for the Snort server that utilize the Apache source code. For these programs to compile correctly, you need to have the source code readily available. Download the latest version of Apache from

```
http://www.apache.org/dyn/closer.cgi/httpd/
```

Uncompress the tarball:

```
tar -xzf apache_1.3.26.tar.gz
```

Make sure to make note of the path to the source directory; you will need it in the next few steps.

Installing MySQL

MySQL is the most popular open source SQL database. MySQL is a relational database management system. It is relatively fast, reliable, and easy to use. MySQL was originally developed to handle databases larger than most contemporary requirements, so it can handle large volumes of data. It has been used to power demanding production environments for several years, including top Web sites such as Yahoo! Finance. Though under constant development, MySQL Server today offers a rich and useful set of functions.

MySQL is a multi-threaded SQL server that supports a vast array of auxiliary applications and tools. It is compatible with thousands of applications and is used in countless coding examples.

Download MySQL at

```
http://www.mysql.com/downloads/mirrors.html
```

After the download is complete, decompress the tarball:

```
tar -xzf mysql-3.23.52.tar.gz
```

Now go to the source directory:

```
cd mysql-3.23.52
```

Installing MySQL is slightly different; it must know where the Apache source code is:

```
./configure
```

If your Apache source directory is something other than /usr/local/apache_ 1.3.26/, be sure to change the --with-apache to reflect the changes. If you wish, you can add a --prefix=/storage/dir/ option to place MySQL outside the normal /usr/local/ installation directory.

Now, follow the usual compilation and installation instructions:

```
make
make install
```

After you have installed MySQL you need to perform some additional installation steps. The first task is to create a group and user account to run MySQL. You do this with the following two commands:

```
groupadd mysql
useradd -g mysql mysql
```

The first command creates the mysql group, whereas the second creates the mysql user as a member of the mysql group. Next, we need to properly set up the MySQL files we created.

```
chown -R root /usr/local/mysql
```

You also need to give the mysql user access to the actual location of the mysql databases.

```
chown -R mysql /usr/local/mysql/var
```

Finally, you should grant access to the `mysql` group.

```
chgrp -R mysql /usr/local/mysql
```

MySQL does not run if it does not have the correct access to the directories specified. If you have used the `--prefix=` command when compiling, make sure you have made the corresponding changes to the previous commands.

You now have a working MySQL server installed on the Snort server. You need to do some quick hardening of the server before you set up the intrusion database. First, you must start the MySQL daemon.

```
/usr/local/mysql/bin/safe_mysqld &
```

The daemon starts; hit Return a few times to get back to a command prompt. Your first duty is to change the MySQL root password to something secure. Make sure to pick a strong password, and one that is different than the Linux root password. Do so with this command:

```
/usr/local/mysql/bin/mysqladmin -u root secure_password
```

After you have changed the root password, you need to log in as root, as shown in Figure 6.3.

```
/usr/local/mysql/bin/mysql -u root -p secure_password
```

You are now logged in to the MySQL shell.

```
mysql >
```

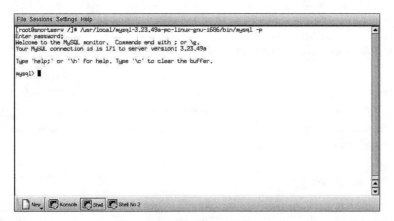

Figure 6.3   Logging into MySQL.

You need to remove default users who are a security risk. Change to the `mysql` database.

```
\u mysql
```

You now need to remove all users with blank usernames.

```
DELETE FROM user WHERE user='';
```

Remember to always add the semicolon to any SQL command in MySQL. Now you remove all users with blank passwords.

```
DELETE FROM user WHERE password='';
exit;
```

This is a simple way to do a light hardening for MySQL. It is advisable to find a more thorough hardening guide online. Next, you need to create the Snort database schema. Fortunately, Snort has a prewritten script designed for MySQL that you can use to import the database schema. First, download and uncompress Snort. Go to

```
http://www.snort.org/dl/
```

Untar it and change to the Snort contrib directory with

```
tar -xzf snort-1.9.0.tar.gz
cd snort-1.9.0/contrib
```

Now you need to log back in to MySQL.

```
/usr/local/mysql/bin/mysql -p secure_password
```

At the MySQL shell, you now must create the database to hold all the intrusion data.

```
create database snortdb;
```

Now you must switch to the new snortdb.

```
connect snortdb;
```

Next you will create the Snort database schema.

```
source create_mysql;
```

If you did not log into MySQL from the Snort contrib directory, the preceding command will fail. Use `source/path/to/snort/contrib/dir/create_mysql;` instead.

After you have created the primary intrusion database, you need to create a database used for storing intrusion information for the long term. This is done to solve both data management and forensic issues. To keep the intrusion database efficient, alert data needs to be pruned from the intrusion database. Trimming the intrusion database also makes identifying events easier and causes searches to run faster. You can simply delete alerts, but by doing so you can destroy valuable forensic evidence if a security incident is discovered in the future. For these reasons you should create a separate archiving database. At the MySQL prompt enter the following command:

```
create database snortarchivedb;
```

Now you must switch to the new archive database.

```
connect snortarchivedb;
```

Finally you create the Snort database schema.

```
source create_mysql;
```

Next, you need to create a user that the sensors will use to log in to the database. Most analysts name this user "snort" or something similar. Please do not choose "snort" for the login, because this is commonly used and easily guessed.

You should also create a separate user for ACID that has a different set of privileges. The ACID user must have the capability to delete alerts, whereas the Snort user should not. If a hacker can compromise and control the sensor, he can easily read the Snort username and password because it is stored in the clear on the sensor. If the Snort user does not have the DELETE privilege, the attacker cannot destroy the entire intrusion database as easily.

```
mysql> GRANT INSERT, SELECT ON *.* TO unique_snort_username@localhost

IDENTIFIED BY 'strong_password' WITH GRANT OPTION;


mysql> GRANT INSERT, SELECT ON *.* TO unique_snort_username@"%"

IDENTIFIED BY 'strong_password' WITH GRANT OPTION;

mysql> GRANT ALL PRIVILEGES ON *.* TO unique_ACID_username@localhost

IDENTIFIED BY 'strong_password' WITH GRANT OPTION;


mysql> GRANT ALL PRIVILEGES ON *.* TO unique_ACID_username@"%"

IDENTIFIED BY 'strong_password' WITH GRANT OPTION;
```

You have now completed the installation and configuration of MySQL. MySQL comes with a benchmarking tool to test the performance of your specific MySQL installation. If you would like to test the performance of MySQL, enter these commands:

```
cd /usr/local/mysql/sql-bench
./run-all-tests
```

Configuring mod_ssl

Mod_ssl is Apache's interface to OpenSSL. Apache can be extended via various modules or mods. There are several hundred mods for Apache, mod_ssl being one of them. Mod_ssl is not a standalone program. It is simply a module for Apache that allows the use of the OpenSSL libraries. This section shows you how to acquire the mod_ssl source and prepare it to be compiled with Apache. For this reason, it is important to have mod_ssl available and configured before compiling Apache. Download mod_ssl from

```
http://www.modssl.org/source/
```

Untar and change to the new directory.

```
tar -xzf mod_ssl-2.8.10-1.3.26.tar.gz
cd mod_ssl-2.8.10-1.3.26
```

Next, you need to configure mod_ssl. It is crucial to include the `--with-apache=` option. Make sure that the directory contains the Apache source or the configuration will fail.

```
./configure –with-apache=/usr/local/apache_1.3.26
```

If you receive an error relating to OpenSSL, you may have to supply the directory of the OpenSSL source. The following command sets the OpenSSL source directory to its default location. If you have the source in a different directory, make the appropriate changes.

```
./configure –with-apache=/usr/local/apache_1.3.26
–with-ssl=/usr/local/ssl
```

You now have mod_ssl ready to be compiled along with Apache.

Installing gd

gd is a graphics library used by many popular programming languages to create images on the fly. It enables a programming language, such as PHP, to quickly draw complicated graphics with relative ease. gd is not intended to be a print-quality graphics package or a painting program. It is used to create simple graphics, such as charts, graphs, and line art. The gd library can be used to create JPG, PNG, or WBMP images. It does not support the popular GIF format due to copyright restrictions. gd is used primarily in Web applications to create simple graphical representations.

When used with a Web application, gd can be used to create graphics on the fly. It can take a large, difficult-to-visualize dataset and create an image that graphically represents the data. Because it is controlled by application logic, the graphics can be automatically updated on the fly when new data becomes available.

The Web-based management GUI you will be deploying, ACID, can utilize the gd library to create graphical representations of intrusion data. ACID can create graphs and charts that help you grasp threat trends over time. This is an effective way of presenting intrusion data to less technical persons at your organization. It is also useful in forecasting attack trends in the future. To use the charting features of ACID, you must install gd. The other ACID components can function without the gd library.

gd is dependent on three libraries to function. The first, zlib, is a compression library. You may have already installed it in a previous step. If not, you can download it at

```
http://www.gzip.org/zlib/
```

Uncompress, configure, compile and install as usual:

```
tar -xzf zlib-1.1.4.tar.gz
cd zlib-1.1.4
./configure
make
make install
```

The second library required is LibPNG. LibPNG is the library for creating PNG files. You can download it at

```
http://www.libpng.org/pub/png/libpng.html
```

After you have downloaded it, uncompress and change directory and install with the familiar commands:

```
tar -xzf libpng-1.2.4.tar.gz
cd libpng-1.2.4
```

You will now need to find a file named makefile.linux in the \scripts directory. Copy the makefile.linux to the LibPNG source root directory.

```
cp makefile.linux ../makefile
```

After you have done so, compile and install:

```
./configure
make
make install
```

The third and final component, the JPEG compression library, can be found at

```
http://www.ijg.org/files/
```

Uncompress, configure, compile, and install:

```
tar -xzf jpegsrc.v6b.tar.gz
cd jpegsrc.v6b
./configure
make
make install
```

You are now ready to install gd. Gd is available for download at

```
http://www.boutell.com/gd/
```

Extract the tarball and install. There is no configure script for gd.

```
tar -xzf gd-1.8.4.tar.gz
cd gd-1.8.4
make
make install
```

You have successfully installed gd.

PHP

PHP is an application server used to process code written in the PHP programming language. PHP is one of the many popular embedded HTML scripting languages. PHP has become a popular alternative to mod_perl and Active Server Pages (ASP) for its simplicity and C-like syntax. This does not mean that PHP is not a powerful and robust language. It can be used to put together dynamic Web applications in a relatively short amount of time. PHP can stand for Personal Home Page or PHP Hypertext Preprocessor, depending on who you talk to.

ACID, the Snort Server management GUI, is built with the PHP language. ACID uses PHP to dynamically create Web pages from intrusion data collected by the sensors. PHP is also used to create the search interface. To use ACID, you must have a PHP application server available.

PHP requires many of the packages that you have already installed to be in place. If you have followed all the earlier steps, there should be no compilation errors. Download PHP from

```
http://www.php.net/downloads.php
```

Uncompress and move to the source directory:

```
tar -xzf php-4.2.2.tar.gz
cd php-4.2.2
```

To configure PHP, you must specify the source directories of some vital components:

```
./configure --with-mysql=/usr/local/mysql
--with-apache==/usr/local/apache_1.3.26 --with-gd=/usr/local/gd-1.8.4
 --with-openssl --disable-debug
```

The `--with-mysql=`, `--with-apache` and `--with-gd=` options are the respective locations of MySQL. The *–disable-debug* takes PHP out of debug mode, which is needed only if you are going to be doing development on the PHP application server itself.

Now you must compile and install:

```
make
make install
```

After you have PHP installed, you need to edit the php.ini file. The php.ini file is where all the configuration settings for PHP are located. Go to your PHP source directory, most likely `/usr/local/php-4.2.2/`, and copy and rename the php.ini-dist to the following location using this command:

```
cp php.ini-dist /usr/local/lib/php.ini
```

Note, there is a `php.ini-recommened`. This is a locked-down and hardened version of php.ini and is usually used when configuring PHP. Unfortunately, ACID does not work with php.ini-recommended, so you will have to lock down the php.ini-dist yourself. Open the php.ini for editing with emacs or your chosen text editor. Make sure you are editing the php.ini located at */usr/local/lib/php.ini*; otherwise PHP cannot interpret your changes.

The first two options you need to change are located in the Paths and Directories section. Under the option `include_path`, include this statement:

```
include_path =
.:./php:/usr/local/include:/usr/include:/usr/local/apache/htdocs/acid
```

Even though you have not installed ACID at this point, you are going to have to insert its include path here. If you do install ACID in a different directory, make sure to come back and edit the preceding statement.

The next option, `extension_dir`, must be set to the following:

```
extension_dir =./php
```

You want to log errors that occur in PHP scripts, so you need to turn the logging of errors on. This is done by setting the following:

```
log_errors = On
```

Now that you have errors turned on, you do not want to display them to end users. You can suppress errors with this configuration line:

```
display_errors = off
```

You log all errors to a php error log file.

```
error_log = /var/adm/php_errors
```

You can choose which level of error reporting you want to receive by setting `error_reporting`. To log all errors, be they critical or not, set to `E_ALL`. If you would rather receive only critical errors, set to `E_ALL & ~E_NOTICE`.

```
error_reporting = E_ALL
```

You can also hide the existence of the PHP server from HTTP headers with this configuration option:

```
expose_php = Off
```

PHP is set by default to allow a script access anywhere within the file system. If a PHP script is somehow compromised, the attacker can use the script to change file system settings or export information he should not have. You can restrict script access to only the directory root that PHP scripts will be placed in.

```
open_basedir = /user/local/apache/htdocs
```

ACID supports no user input checking. If a malicious user were to gain access to ACID, he would be able to perform SQL injection attacks easily. You can use a feature of PHP to escape most malicious user input. Turning magic quotes off has the desired effect:

```
magic_quotes_gpc = Off
```

> ### SQL Injection
>
> SQL injection is an attack perpetrated against unsecured Web applications. It occurs when the attacker is
> able to insert into a data input field arbitrary SQL statements that will change the intended function of the
> query and the Web application as a whole. Take the following SQL statement that is used to authenticate
> users and return their credit card numbers:
>
> ```
> select cc_num from users where username ='user_input'
>  and password = 'user_input'
> ```
>
> If the *userinput* fields in the Web application are not properly secured, the attacker can insert SQL logic into
> the above SQL statement. If the attacker entered `'or  1=1—` in the username field, the SQL statement
> would now be:
>
> ```
> select cc_num from users where username =''or 1=1—' and password = 'user_input'
> ```
>
> The — characters are used by MS SQL server to comment out code, or to stop interpreting code for the con-
> tiguous line. The actual code executed by the SQL server would be
>
> ```
> select cc_num from users where username =''or 1=1—'
> ```
>
> Now that the statement has been changed, the SQL server returns cc_num if 1=1, which it always does.
> The SQL server returns the first cc_num field it has stored in the users table.
>
> When SQL Injection is possible, it can be used to place almost any imaginable SQL statement into a query.
> The attacker can use the xp_cmdshell to execute remote commands at the operating system level. She
> could also inject SQL commands to shut down the SQL server, export sensitive data, and enumerate the
> entire database table structure. For these reasons, it is critically important for Web applications to filter
> characters used to execute SQL injection.

There were numerous exploits for earlier versions of PHP related to uploads via an
HTTP POST. Even though PHP is now secure, it is a good idea to disable the capability
to upload files, because you will not need to do so via PHP.

```
file_uploads = off
```

At some point in the future, ACID will be able to run in PHP's safe mode. As of right
now, enabling safe mode for PHP causes ACID to malfunction. You can enable safe
mode at some point in the future with

```
safe_mode = On
```

For now, verify that that safe mode is set to off:

```
safe_mode = Off
```

Php.ini configuration is now complete. Save the php.ini file.

Installing Apache

You have already downloaded and uncompressed Apache in a previous step. For this step,
you compile and install Apache using all the packages you have gathered previously. The

configuration command is slightly different than that for the other packages you have installed. You need to precede the `./configure` with the location of the OpenSSL library. Run the following command all as one line, as shown:

```
SSL_BASE=/usr/local/ssl ./configure --prefix=/usr/local/apache
--enable-module=ssl --disable-module=status
```

The `--prexfix=` sets the location of the Apache installation files. The `--disable-module=status` prevents the server activity and performance from being published to an easily accessible Web page. Next you need to compile Apache with the usual command:

```
make
```

Now that Apache is properly compiled, you need to make an SSL certificate. This is an easy step; simply enter the following command:

```
make certificate
```

Enter your personal information as you deem fit. After this step is complete, you can install Apache and set the appropriate permissions for the Apache daemon:

```
make install
chmod 0511 /usr/local/apache/bin/httpd
```

Apache installs with a set of unnecessary test pages. You should delete all the test files located in the /usr/local/apache/htdocs/ directory:

Now that you have Apache installed with all the important components—mod_ssl, PHP, MySQL, and so on—you need to make some configuration changes. The first step is to add a plotting and graphing library, PHPlot, to Apache. You need to create a home for PHPlot in the Apache root Web directory.

```
cd /usr/local/apache/htdocs
```

Next you need to create two new directories to hold PHPlot.

```
mkdir PHP
cd PHP
mkdir PHPLOT
```

Now you need to download the current version of PHPlot at

```
http://sourceforge.net/project/showfiles.php?group_id=14653
```

Uncompress the source to the `/usr/local/apache/htdocs/PHP/PHPLOT` directory.

After you have PHPlot installed, you need to make some changes to httpd.conf. Much like php.ini for PHP, httpd.conf is the master configuration file for Apache. You can find it at `/usr/local/apache/conf/httpd.conf`. Open it for editing because you need to make some changes.

ACID has no native password protection. You need to install your own password protection using Apaches built-in authorization scheme. You will configure the actual password settings later, but first you must force all HTTP sessions to authenticate. This is done via the `AllowOverride` option. Find the `AllowOverride` option and change it to

```
AllowOverride AuthConfig
```

In addition to the `expose_php` option in the php.ini file, you need to suppress Apache banner advertising to prevent information gathering attacks. To do so, you should change the following option:

```
ServerSignature Off
```

If Apache has not yet been configured to recognize PHP extensions, you can do so with the next two configuration changes:

```
AddType application/x-httpd-php .php. php3
AddType application/x-httpd-php-source .phps
```

.htaccess

An `.htaccess` file is a simple means of forcing authentication to Web pages served by an Apache server. The `.htaccess` file is used to restrict or allow access to directories and or directory contents. You will be using `.htaccess` to password-protect ACID. The configuration change you made to `AllowOverride` in httpd.conf makes `.htaccess` authentication possible. The same functionality can be supported using `httpd.conf` settings, but `.htaccess` is the preferable method.

The first step in setting up `.htaccess` authentication is to create a `.htpasswd` file. The `.htpasswd` file is a flat file that contains the username and password combos for each user you will be granting access to ACID. Change the directory to your Apache root, the default being `/usr/local/apache/`. Make absolutely sure never to place the .htpasswd file in a directory accessible via a browser (such as `/usr/local/apache/htdocs`). If you place it in Apache's document root, anyone could download the .htpasswd file and use it to access ACID. Run the following command:

```
/usr/local/apache/bin/htpasswd -c filename user
```

The *filename* is the name you use for the `.htpasswd` file; it is commonly called .htpasswd. The `user` is the username that you will be using to log in to ACID. The `-c` option creates a new file, if you do not include the `-c` the username and password will be appended to the file. Use the `-c` for only the first user; otherwise you will overwrite the existing file. You are then prompted to enter a password for the ACID user and then asked to verify the password a second time. Repeat the command for each user that is to be granted access to ACID.

Now that you have defined who should have access to ACID, you must designate what they can have access to. To do so, you need to create an `.htaccess` file. Navigate to the directory you plan to install ACID (such as `/usr/local/apache/htdocs/acid`). If you have not created this directory yet, do so now. Open a text editor and enter the following lines:

```
AUTHUSERFILE /usr/local/apache/.htpasswd
AUTHNAME "ACID"
AuthType Basic

<Limit GET>
require user username
</Limit>

SSLRequireSSL
```

Save the file as .htaccess. The AUTHUSERFILE option points Apache to the location of the .htpasswd file. This is the file you created before this step. The AUTHNAME option is the name of the "realm" that will be displayed in the grey dialog box. The AUTHTYPE is the type of authentication to be used. This example uses basic. Basic authentication uses Base64 encoding to encode the password. It does not encrypt or hash the password, meaning it could be captured and decoded. A more secure method is to use a one-way hash, such as MD5, to encrypt the password.

The Limit tags restrict the access that the required user gets to that directory. For example, the username acid can only use the HTTP GET command in the ACID directory.

The require user line specifies the users in the .htpasswd who are permitted to access files in the directory where the file you are editing resides.

The <Limit> tags define the access that the *username* is permitted to have for the directory. In this .htaccess file, the user *username* only can use the HTTP GET command in the /usr/local/apache/htdocs/acid directory. The SSLRequireSSL line requires that any connection made to the ACID directory must utilize SSL.

You have now completed the Apache installation and configuration. At this point it is a good idea to check to see whether everything has been installed correctly. You can start up Apache with the following command:

```
usr/local/apache/bin/apachectl start
```

Shut down Apache cleanly with the next command:

```
usr/local/apache/bin/apachectl stop
```

Start Apache in SSL mode with this command:

```
usr/local/apache/bin/apachectl startssl
```

If everything starts without errors, check your .htaccess authentication by navigating to the new Apache server:

```
http://hostname or IP address/acid
```

You should be prompted with a gray dialog box for authentication information (see Figure 6.4).

Figure 6.4   .htaccess authentication.

If you are not prompted for a password, go back and check your work. You can check to make sure gd and PHPlot are functioning by bringing up a test page at the following URL:

```
http://hostname or IP address/phplot/examples/test_setup.php
```

You should get a test graphic. There may be an error message resembling GIF NOT ENABLED. This error is expected, because gd no longer supports the GIF format. You do not need GIF support for PHPlot anyway, so ignore the error.

Installing ADODB

The database access functions for PHP are not standardized. Each database type (MySQL, PostgreSQL, Oracle, and so on) has a different method of accessing the individual database with PHP. To develop PHP code that can access many different types of databases, you must use a library to provide a generic interface for all databases. This allows users of PHP applications to select a database that best suits the application.

The library that offers generic database access is the ADODB library. It supports every database under the sun: MySQL, Oracle, SQL Server, Sybase, Sybase SQL Anywhere, Informix, PostgreSQL, FrontBase, Interbase (Firebird and Borland variants), Foxpro, Access, ADO, and ODBC.

Even though this example uses MySQL, ACID can be used with many different types of databases. The ADODB library makes this possible.

ADODB must be installed in Apache's document root. Create a directory of your choice to store the ADODB code:

```
mkdir /usr/local/apache/htdocs/php/adodb
```

Next you must download the latest version of ADODB at

```
http://php.weblogs.com/ADODB
```

Extract the contents of the tarball to the directory listed in the preceding URL. Next you need to edit the ADODB configuration file, adodb.inc.php. You must let ADODB know where it is located within the filesystem. Open this file with a text editor and find the line that contains the following:

```
$ADODB_DIR = dirname(__FILE__);
```

Change this line to reflect the directory where you have placed ADODB:

```
$ADODB_DIR = '/usr/local/apache/htdocs/php/adodb';
```

Save the file and exit. ADODB installation is complete.

Installing ACID

The Analysis Console for Intrusion Databases (ACID) is the primary means you have to interact with Snort data. You will do most of your intrusion detection work through ACID.

As previously stated, ACID is a PHP-based analysis engine. It is designed to process a database of security events generated by security devices, such as IDSs and firewalls. ACID can be used to export security incidents in a timely manner via email. ACID can be run on most operating systems, including Linux, BSD, Solaris, and Windows. ACID is an open-source application released under the GPL. Roman Danyliw at the CERT Coordination Center created ACID, and remains its principal developer.

You have all the supporting applications required to install a secure version of ACID. Download the latest version of ACID from

```
http://www.andrew.cmu.edu/~rdanyliw/snort/snortacid.html
```

If you have not already created the directory to house ACID, you should do so now. The commonly used directory is

```
/usr/local/apache/htdocs/acid/
```

But it can be any directory protected by .htaccess and within the Apache document root. Obfuscating the ACID directory's name will never hurt you. After you have created the directory, uncompress and copy the ACID files into it. After you have the ACID files in place, you need to set the permissions on the files and the ACID directory. Do so with the next two commands.

```
chmod 755 /usr/local/apache/htdocs/acid
chmod 644 /usr/local/apache/htdocs/acid/*
```

Now that ACID has been properly installed, you need to configure ACID. A large list of configuration options is stored in the acid_conf.php file. Open this file for editing. The remainder of this section is a list of the configuration options in the acid_conf.php and how to configure them. Make sure to encapsulate all values with a double quote(") and terminate them with a semicolon (;).

DBlib_path

This path is the location of the ADODB library. If you installed ADODB according to the previous instructions, you should set the Dblib_path value to

```
/usr/local/apache/htdocs/php/adodb
```

If you decided to install it elsewhere, make changes accordingly.

DBtype

The type of database ACID will be interfacing. Leave this set to the default of mysql unless you have chosen a different underlying database.

alert_dbname

This is the name of the database that will contain the alert data. If you have followed the conventions in this book, it should be set to "snortdb".

alert_host

The location of the intrusion database. If ACID resides on the same physical server as the database, set this to `localhost`.

alert_port

The remote port for ACID to connect to if the database is not stored locally. Leave this blank.

alert_user

The username required to log in to the database. You created this in the MySQL installation section.

alert_password

The password required to log in to the database. You created this in the MySQL installation section.

archive_dbname

The type of database ACID will be interfacing. Leave this set to the default of *mysql* unless you have chosen a different underlying database.

archive_host

The location of the intrusion database. If ACID resides on the same physical server as the database, set this to `localhost`.

archive_port

The remote port for ACID to connect to if the database is not stored locally. If you have set MySQL to listen on a port other than 3306, make the appropriate change here. Otherwise, leave archive_port blank.

archive_user

The username required to log in to the database. You created this in the MySQL installation section.

archive_password

The password required to log in to the database. You created this in the MySQL installation section.

db_connect_method

This is the method in which ACID's PHP code utilizes connections to the database. If you set db_connect_method to 1, ACID will use a persistent connection. A persistent connection is a link to a SQL server that does not close when the execution of the PHP script ends. When a persistent connection is requested, the PHP application server checks whether an identical persistent connection exists from a previous script execution. If a connection is available, it utilizes it to make the connection. If the connection is not available, it creates a new one. This offloads much of the connection processing from the database to PHP. For the Snort server, you want to lighten the load on MySQL as much as you can. You should set db_connect_method to 1.

If you would like to transfer processing back to the PHP application server, choose option 2 for non-persistent connections.

chartlib_path

The path to the PHPlot files. This should be

```
/usr/local/apache/htdocs/php/phplot
```

chart_file_format

The file format to create ACID's charts. You can choose either png or jpeg. The default is png.

chart_bg_color_default, chart_lgrid_color_default, chart_bar_color_default

These settings are arrays that determine the default color settings for any chart built with PHPlot and ACID. You specify color with an RGB array (red, green, blue). Chart_bg_color_default sets the color of the default gridline, whereas chart_lgrid_color_default does the same for gridline colors. The chart_bar_color_default sets colors for bar and line colors.

MAX_ROWS

The maximum number of elements you can use to build a search in ACID. With ACID, you can build complex searches using 37 different criteria. If the number of criteria you choose to search with exceeds MAX_ROWS, the search does not execute. The default setting is 10; a recommendation is 15.

show_rows

The maximum number of resultset rows to display per screen after a search is performed. You can still view alert data, via standard next and previous buttons. Any number between 50 and 100 is a reasonable setting.

last_num_alerts

ACID has a quick link on the main index page to the most recent alerts stored in the database. The last_num_alerts dictates how many alerts are to be presented in the most recent alerts page. The default is 15; this should be set to 50.

last_num_ualerts, last_num_uports, last_num_uaddr

These options set the number of alerts presented, much like the last_num_alerts. Last_num_ualerts sets the number of unique alerts displayed; last_num_uports defines the number of unique alerts for each port; and last_num_uaddr displays the number of unique alerts for an IP address. The default is 15; they should be set to 50.

freq_num_alerts, freq_num_uaddr, freq_num_uports

These settings closely resemble the previous settings. They are for the most frequent alert links from the main index page. Again, the default is 15; they should be set to 50.

debug_mode

This option sets the level of internal debugging information posted to the ACID Web interface. Unless you are going to be making changes to the ACID source, leave this option set to 0. If you decide you want debugging, set it to 1. If you want verbose debugging data, set debug_mode to 2.

html_no_cache

This setting uses ACID to send a no-cache directive to the browser. If you are using Internet Explorer, and allow IE to cache ACID pages, you may not see the most current alerting information. If you are planning on using IE with ACID, set this to 1; for other browsers leave it at 0.

sql_trace_mode

This option logs all SQL commands to a file specified in sql_trace_file. Useful for debugging.

sql_trace_file

The file to which to log SQL commands.

refresh_stat_page

This setting enables the automatic refreshing or reloading of the browser. When the browser is refreshed, any new alerts become accessible to ACID. Set this to 1.

stat_page_refresh_time

If you have set refresh_stat_page to 1, you must define a time between browser refreshes. This is done with the stat_page_refresh_time option. Specify the time in seconds.

max_script_runtime

Sets the maximum amount of time that an ACID page can take to load. Deleting or archiving large sets of rules can take a very long time. If you set max_script_runtime too low, the script times out and the delete or archive request is incomplete. Set the value to 300.

ip_address_input

This option lets you divide the IP address input for the query builder into octets. This allows you increased granularity when searching for IP addresses. If you want to search by octets, set this option to 1. If searching by the entire IP address suits you, set ip_address_input to 2.

use_sig_list

With use_sig_list, you can have all possible signatures loaded into a drop-down combo box instead of having to specify the signature yourself. This is a great option to enable if you have not had experience with the Snort signature names or want to save some time. You can enable all signatures with a 2 value. If you want to see only signatures created by the detection engine and no pre-processor signatures, set it to a 1. If you do not want signatures prepopulated, set use_sig_list to a 0. The recommended setting is 2.

resolve_IP

This option resolves IP addresses to their fully qualified domain names if possible. Resolution of IP addresses is a useful feature of ACID. It is recommended to turn this option on by setting it to 1. Turn resolve_IP off by specifying 0.

show_summary_stats

This setting displays meta data pertaining to the summary stats on each query results page. This feature is by default disabled. Set to 1 to enable it.

dns_cache_lifetime, whois_cache_lifetime

These options set the amount of time in minutes before the resolved DNS and whois cache expire. The cache is implemented for performance reasons. The default settings for these options are acceptable.

portscan_file

This is the location of the log file for the portscan preprocessor. As of this writing, ACID supports only portscan and not the newer portscan2. If you have enabled this option, it can be used to correlate portscanning events across your network infrastructure.

event_cache_autoupdate

This setting automatically updates the cache of events loaded into ACID every page load. This notifies you of new alerts as you are working within ACID. Even though there is a performance penalty for enabling this option, it is advisable to enable it. Leave this at the default setting of 1.

maintain_history

This option lets you maintain the history of ACID pages you have viewed in a PHP session variable. If you disable this option, you cannot use the Back button on your browser to retrieve information. You get the session expired error page. Enable this option with a 1.

main_page_detail

This is the level of detail to be displayed on the index page. If you want merely a count of the alerts and links to the search builder and other basic functions, set this to 0. If you want full summary statistics and links, set main_page_detail to 1.

external_whois_link, external_dns_link, external_all_link, external_port_link

These are the external links that are used to refer to public data sources on the Internet. These links are attached to an alert event. They can rapidly help in gauging the origin and malicious nature of an alert. The external_whois_link links out to an external whois database, which provides information on domain and IP address ownership. The external_dns_link looks up DNS information on an external site. The external_all_link is specifically created for samspade.org, which is used to link to samspade.org's show me everything listing. The external_port_link is a ports database lookup link for identifying to what service the specific port is usually bound. The default setting is samspade.org for the Whois, DNS, and all links. The ports link references the portsdb.org site.

action_email_from

The action_email_from is the email address to be used in the From field for emailed alerts.

Acid and Emailing Alerts

ACID supports the emailing of alerts. Do not confuse this with real-time notification of security events. The emailing process with ACID is neither automatic nor actually in real time. You can email alerts from ACID after they have been generated by Snort. Email functionality is primarily used to export intrusion data from ACID. This is not meant to be a means of bulk data export, but rather to be used in an emergency situation as part of an incident response.

Exporting alerts via email is the most convenient method of displaying multiple alerts on one page with complete packet headers and payloads. This helps you get an overall picture of the attack. You can more readily search for new attack patterns and correlate separate alerts. Without this functionality you would have to flip through several alerts on different Web pages, which is quite inconvenient.

action_email_subject

This is the subject to be used in the email message.

action_email_msg

This is additional text to be used in the email message.

action_email_mode

The method for determining which alerts will be delivered in the email. You can set to 1 for the alerts to be included in the body of the email, or 2 for the alerts to be sent as an attachment.

Completing the Installation

After you have configured ACID, you need to run a final setup script. This script is run from within ACID, so you must have Apache started in SSL mode. Navigate to the ACID main page and log in:

```
https://localhost/acid/
```

The main index page gives an error along the lines of the underlying database table structure appearing to be invalid. Don't panic; this is expected. The page forwards you to the ACID DB setup script. The ACID DB setup script creates four tables that ACID requires to manage alerts. It also adds indexes to the MySQL Snort tables, which increase query speed. Execute the script by clicking the Create ACID AG button.

If the script has executed successfully, a status page is displayed with DONE indicated for the various table creation tasks. If the script fails, check to make sure you have enabled the proper permissions for the MySQL account that ACID has been configured to use in acid_conf.php. The account needs to have INSERT, SELECT, and DELETE permissions.

The installation of ACID and the Snort server is now complete. Congratulations!

Summary

This chapter presented a thorough, step-by-step guide to building a Snort server. A Snort server should be built off a hardened version of the chosen operating system. This chapter walked through the use of Red Hat Linux 7.3 for the Snort server. The first steps are to update and patch Red Hat and to harden the installation. Bastille Linux is an open source tool available to the hardening process. After the OS is installed and brought up to speed, the Snort packages are ready to be installed. Packages should be compiled and installed from source rather than installed from an RPM.

OpenSSL Project is an open source toolkit for implementing Secure Sockets Layer (SSL) and Transport Layer Security (TLS). Furthermore, OpenSSL contains a general purpose encryption library with support for strong encryption algorithms. OpenSSL source is used by Stunnel and mod_ssl to encrypt traffic. Stunnel is used to establish and maintain encrypted sessions. The Stunnel program is an SSL encryption wrapper. It encrypts sessions between remote clients and local or remote servers. Stunnel is used to encrypt communication between the Snort server and sensors. OpenSSH is an open source implementation of the Secure Shell (SSH) protocol. SSH is a transparent method of securely establishing communication and transferring data between a client and server. OpenSSH provides the same functionality as other less secure protocols and is used to maintain the Snort server remotely.

Apache's source code is needed by mod_ssl, so it must be downloaded and uncompressed before the installation of these two packages. Apache has been the world's most popular Web server since April of 1996. MySQL is a relational database management system that is used to house the intrusion database. Mod_ssl is Apache's interface to

OpenSSL. Mod_ssl is not a standalone program. It is simply a module for Apache that allows the use of the OpenSSL libraries.

The next packages configured, compiled, and installed are required components of the ACID management GUI. The first is a graphics creation library, gd. Gd is a graphics library used by many popular programming languages to create images on the fly. It enables a programming language, such as PHP, to quickly draw complicated graphics with relative ease. PHP is an application server used to process code written in the PHP programming language. The PHP language is one of many popular HTML embedded scripting languages.

The next step is to install Apache by using all the packages that have been gathered previously. The first step in installing Apache is to add a plotting and graphing library, PHPlot. Then you must create and install a .htaccess file. An .htaccess file is a simple means of forcing authentication to Web pages served by an Apache server. After Apache is installed, the generic database access library, ADODB, is implemented.

The Snort server is now ready to have ACID installed. ACID is a PHP-based analysis engine. It is designed to process a database of security events generated by security devices, such as IDSs and firewalls. The setup, configuration, and customization of ACID is performed with the acid_conf.php file. The Snort Server is now complete.

7

Building the Sensor

THIS CHAPTER IS A COMPLETE GUIDE to deploying a Snort sensor. The Snort application itself is installed on the sensor. The sensor collects data from the monitored segment by sniffing packets. The packets are then fed directly into the Snort application. Snort interprets the nature of sniffed packets and generates alerts when suspicious activity is detected. The alerts are then posted to the Snort server. In the following installation, you will be logging to the Snort Unified format. You will then configure Barnyard to continuously process the alerts created by Snort. Barnyard will post alerts into the MySQL database residing on the Snort server. Sensors must be connected to the same network segments to be monitored for intrusions. Naturally security is a priority. The sensor will be hardened and will only have Snort and its supporting applications installed. Like the Snort server, you will be using Red Hat Linux 7.3 for the underlying operating system for the sensor.

You need to ensure you have two network cards installed in the sensor. One will be used for the sniffing interface and one for the management interface. You will configure the sniffing interface to attach to the monitored segment, whereas the management interface will connect to the monitoring segment. The sniffing NIC will be configured to run in stealth mode, meaning it has no IP address assigned to it. On the other hand, the management interface has an IP address assigned to it so that it can communicate with both the sensor and the console. Alerting data is passed out of this interface up to the server. The console utilizes the management interface to remotely administer the sensor. It is easier to have both NICs installed on the sensor prior to installing Linux. Linux discovers and installs the NICs automatically, saving you some work.

Installation Guide Notes

The Snort sensor installation guide outlined in the following pages is built on the Linux platform. Linux is chosen because of its stability, security, large community, and the vast quantity of available applications.

More specifically, the Red Hat distribution version 7.3 has been chosen for its popularity and the fee-based technical support.

Red Hat Linux 7.3

Begin the installation of Red Hat Linux with the media you acquired for the server and console builds. During the installation process choose the default options unless you are directed differently in the following sections.

Network Configuration

For the sake of this setup, you will assign eth0 as the management NIC and eth1 as the sniffing NIC. This means you should not assign an IP address to eth1. Leave the IP addresses fields blank. Under the IP address setup information for eth0, you also should deselect the Configure Using DHCP option. When choosing an IP address for the management NIC, choose a private RFC1918 address, as you did for the server. The valid RFC1918 ranges are

- 10.0.0.0–10.255.255.255
- 172.16.0.0–172.31.255.255
- 192.168.0.0–192.168.255.255

Firewall Configuration

Under firewall configuration, you should select No Firewall.

Time Zone Selection

Keeping time in sync between the Snort sensors and servers makes event correlation possible. Without accurate synchronization, it is difficult to piece security events together. The NTP section in this chapter looks further into time syncing. For the time being, you need to select the UTC Offset tab and single out your correct offset. Additionally, you should check the System Clock Uses UTC check box.

Account Configuration

When creating accounts for the server, or for any critical security device, you should choose strong passwords for the user accounts. Strong passwords are over 14 characters long and have a mixture of alphanumeric (that is, ABC123) and special characters (that is, *!@#&). The stronger the password, the more computationally expensive it is to work through every password combination with a password cracker.

Package Group Selection

The following package groups should be selected:
- Network Support
- Messaging Web Tools

- Emacs
- Software Development

Post-Installation Tasks

As with the server, there are a few important post-installation tasks for the sensor. The first and most important task is to bring the server up to a current patch level.

You can either use the Red Hat network to automatically update the server for you, or you can select the patches you need from the following URL:

```
http://rhn.redhat.com/errata/rh73-errata.html
```

After you have updated Red Hat to a bug-free and secure level, it is time to remove some unnecessary packages that may have been installed. libcap and tcpdump may have been installed with the operating system, and need to be removed. You will be building and installing a more current version of libcap than the version shipped with Red Hat. You can remove the libcap and tcpdump packages with these two commands:

```
rpm -e libpcap
rpm -e tcpdump
```

The tcpdump and libpcap packages are now removed.

The next step is to harden the server. Both manual and semi-automated processes are effective means for hardening Red Hat Linux. If you used Bastille Linux for the server, you may want to try a manual hardening procedure. Following the steps outlined at sans.org will result in a well-hardened Snort server. You can check out the guide at

```
http://www.sans.org/linux.htm
```

Bastille Linux

Bastille Linux can be used to bring the sensor up to a hardened state. Because the sensor is in a position of high risk, it should be hardened tighter than the other machines you have built. You will work through a more restrictive configuration for the sensor. Remember, you can always roll back the hardening process by using the undo script.

You can download Bastille Linux at

```
http://www.bastille-linux.org/
```

You need to acquire three files from the Web site:

- The Bastille Linux RPM
- The Bastille Perl-Tk graphical module
- The Perl-Tk RPM

After you have downloadeded the three files you need to install them. For this situation you will use the Red Hat Package Manager (RPM) to automatically install Bastille. This is one of the few packages or applications that you will install in this automated manner.

Run the RPM install command with the –nodeps option from the download directory, as follows:

```
rpm -ivh --nodeps perl-Tk-800.022-4mdk.i586.rpm
```

The –nodeps prevents the installation from failing if the required package dependencies are not satisfied. After the Perl-Tk package has installed, install Bastille Linux and the graphical interface. Execute this command from the download directory:

```
rpm -ivh Bastille-1.3.0-1.0.i386.rpm Bastille-Tk-module-1.3.0-1.0.i386.rpm
```

You now have Bastille installed. To start the hardening process enter the InteractiveBastille command as root from a command prompt. You are going to want to enable them all, except for a few, by selecting the Yes check box. The exceptions stated in the following sections provide more hassle than security.

File Permissions
Enable all.

Account Security
Enable all except Restricting Remote Root Login.

By disabling remote logon as root you are in effect forcing any user with root privileges to log on remotely as an ordinary user. The user would have to switch to a root account after logging in. This prevents attackers who posses only the root password from logging in. Disabling remote root login is a somewhat weak security control and can make maintenance a hassle. If you feel that you should have to login in twice to get remote root access, you should select the remote root login restriction option.

Boot Security
Enable all except Disabling CTRL-ALT-DELETE Reboot.

Disabling CTRL-ALT-DELETE simply makes it more difficult to reboot the server. Anyone who has physical access to reboot your server via a keyboard can probably cut the power source. This would have the same effect as CTRL-ALT-DELETE.

Secure Inetd
Enable all except Defaulting to Deny for TCP Wrappers and Xinetd.

Disable User Tools
Enable all except Disabling the GCC Compiler.

Disabling GCC is a good idea to do after you have compiled and installed the necessary Snort server packages. You may want to revisit this option after the entire installation process is complete.

Configure Miscellaneous Parameters
Enable all except Limit Resource Usage.

Limiting resource usage, such as by establishing a maximum file size of 100MB and other controls that this option performs, will make the sensor function poorly. The performance of the Snort application is severely hamstrung if you limit resource usage.

Miscellaneous Daemons

Enable all except Disable GPM.

Using the mouse in text applications via GPM is a useful feature that does not pose a significant security risk.

Sendmail

Enable all.

Firewall

Disable all. You do not want a firewall running on the sensor.

PortScan Attack Detector (PSAD)

Disable all. Snort sensors will be your primary tool for detecting portscans across network infrastructure.

Completing the Bastille Linux Hardening

After you have selected the options you want, you commit and Bastille runs the script. If you later realize that you hardened the server too tightly and some process does not function you can roll back the changes. Simply download the "undo" script at

`http://www.bastille-linux.org/UndoBastille`

You can then re-run Bastille and deselect the option you mistakenly enabled.

Installing the Snort Sensor Components

This section walks you through the steps in building the Snort Sensor from scratch. You will configure, compile, and install most packages as you did with the server and console.

Again, it is important to follow the steps in this guide in consecutive order. Some of the packages must have another package installed for them to compile and install. It is important to have these dependencies satisfied; if they are not the installation may not function as expected.

Installing libpcap

Snort has no native packet capture facility; it requires an external packet sniffing library, libpcap. libpcap is responsible for grabbing packets directly from the network interface card. It makes the raw packet capture facility provided by the underlying operating system available to other applications.

For Snort to function, you must have libpcap properly installed. You can download it at

```
http://www.tcpdump.org/release/
```

Get the most current stable version and uncompress the tarball.

```
tar -xzf libpcap-0.7.1.tar.gz
```

Change to the new directory and configure, compile, and install.

```
./configure
make
make install
```

You have now finished the installation of libpcap.

Installing tcpdump

Installation of the tcpdump package is optional. tcpdump is a powerful tool that utilizes libpcap to sniff network packets. Tcpdump operates by placing the network card in promiscuous mode. Although tcpdump is not required for the Snort sensor deployment you are building, it is a handy tool that can be used for a variety of intrusion detection–related functions.

tcpdump can be run as a standalone packet sniffer independent of Snort. Snort records only traffic that matches an alert. You could conceivably configure Snort to alert on every packet, but this method of sniffing can be cumbersome. You are likely to be confronted with a situation where you would like to capture packets outside of Snort. A standalone sniffer can be used to gather detailed network information without requiring you to modify or reconfigure Snort.

tcpdump is useful for troubleshooting your sensor setup. If Snort is not capturing packets, you can use tcpdump to ensure that you have installed the hardware and software properly.

You can also use tcpdump to read output files generated by Snort. At some point you may wish to log to tcpdump format for troubleshooting reasons. If you suspect that Barnyard or an output plugin is not functioning correctly you can attempt to log to tcpdump format to verify that Snort is indeed functioning.

You can download it at

```
http://www.tcpdump.org/release/
```

Get the most current stable version and uncompress the tarball.

```
tar -xzf tcpdump-3.5.2.tar.gz
```

Change to the new directory and configure, compile, and install.

```
./configure
make
make install
```

tcpdump is now installed.

tcpdump is a fairly simple yet powerful tool. You can use tcpdump in its most simple form by running the `tcpdump` command and specifying the interface to use:

```
tcpdump -i eth0
```

If this proves to be too much traffic, you can add a filter to monitor for only a specific source IP:

```
tcpdump -i eth0 'src host HOST_IP_ADDRESS'
```

The previous commands send data to the standard output. If you would rather write to a file and investigate the traffic later, you can use a command like this:

```
tcpdump -i eth0 -w filename.dump
```

You can use tcpdump again to read the file at a later point in time:

```
tcpdump -r filename.dump
```

This is by no means a comprehensive tutorial on tcpdump; you should be able to find numerous resources online to aid in using tcpdump for intrusion detection.

Installing OpenSSL

OpenSSL is used in conjunction with Stunnel to encrypt the sensor-to-server communication. You need to install OpenSSL in a similar manner as you did the server. You can begin the OpenSSL installation by downloading the source code at

```
http://www.openssl.org/source/
```

Remember to obtain the OpenSSL source rather than the OpenSSL-engine source. After you have the tarball, uncompress it by issuing this command:

```
tar -xzf openssl-0.9.6g.tar.gz
```

Change to the new directory, and prepare the source code for compiling by using the following command:

```
./configure
```

After the source has been prepared, compile the source with

```
make
```

And then install the source using

```
make install
```

If everything runs smoothly, you should now have OpenSSL installed on the Snort server. You need to edit the ld.so.conf to include OpenSSL. Open it for editing by typing

```
emacs /etc/ld.so.conf &
```

Add the line /usr/local/lib to ld.so.conf. Save and exit. Run the command

```
ldconfig
```

to update for the new shared libraries. You have now successfully installed OpenSSL.

Installing Stunnel

Stunnel is used to establish and maintain encrypted sessions. You will be using the client portion of Stunnel for the sensor. You are going to be encrypting the MySQL session. You can download Stunnel at

```
http://www.stunnel.org/download/source.html
```

After downloading the Stunnel tarball to your download directory, you must untar it in a similar manner as you did OpenSSL.

```
tar -xzf stunnel-3.22.tar.gz
```

After it uncompresses, change to the new Stunnel source directory, /Stunnel-3.22.tar.gz. From here, you want to configure:

```
./configure
```

If you get an error message—something to the effect of `Cannot find SSL library installation dir`—there is no need to worry. This error message most likely means you have installed OpenSSL to a non-standard directory. If you have installed OpenSSL in a different directory, you need to specify the `-with-ssl` option like so:

```
./configure -with-ssl=path/to/ssl/libraries
```

Next, you simply want to compile:

```
make
```

And finally install:

```
make install
```

Now you have a working version of Stunnel installed on the sensor. You need to create a user and group for the Stunnel client to run as. You can do so by issuing these commands:

```
groupadd stunnel_group
useradd -g stunnel_group stunnel
```

The first command creates the group stunnel_group, and the second creates a user stunnel, who is a member of the stunnel_group. After you have the groups created you can start up the Stunnel client.

To start Stunnel on the sensor use the following command:

```
/usr/local/stunnel/sbin/stunnel -c -d 127.0.0.1:3306 -r
```

```
 Snort_Server_IP:3307 -s stunnel_user -g stunnel_group &
```

This command starts up a Stunnel in client mode. The –c switch specifies client mode, whereas –d runs Stunnel in daemon mode. The options for the –d switch are the local loopback interface and the mysql port. For the –r switch you must insert the IP address of the Snort server and the remote mysqls port. The –s and –g are the respective username and groupname of the accounts to run Stunnel.

This completes the Stunnel installation for the Snort server.

Installing OpenSSH

An OpenSSH daemon must run on every Snort console for remote management to be possible. You can connect to the sensor from the console in the same manner as you do for the server. Get OpenSSH for Red Hat at

```
http://www.openssh.org/portable.html
```

After you have downloaded OpenSSH, you need to uncompress the tarball.

```
tar -xzf openssh-3.4p1.tar.gz
```

Change to the new source directory:

```
cd openssh-3.4p1
```

Follow the same configuration, compilation, and installation steps:

```
./configure
make
make install
```

Now you should have OpenSSH properly installed. If you are using a different version of Red Hat or have an entirely different distribution, you may have received an error relating to the zlib compression library. If so, you need to download zlib from

```
http://www.gzip.org/zlib/
```

Install it using the normal ./configure, make, and make install process. When you are finished, OpenSSH will properly install.

You must now generate your DSA keys. Use

```
ssh-keygen
```

You can now run sshd by executing the following commands:

```
/usr/local/sbin/sshd
/usr/local/bin/egd.pl
```

The OpenSSH daemon is now ready to accept incoming OpenSSH connections.

Installing the MySQL Client

The MySQL client is required for an application to remotely connect to a MySQL server. Barnyard needs to post alerting data to MySQL, so you must install the MySQL client libraries and programs. To install the client, you have to download the entire MySQL server and client source. You can then use a configuration option to prevent the installation of the server.

Download MySQL at

```
http://www.mysql.com/downloads/mirrors.html
```

After the download is complete, decompress the tarball:

```
tar -xzf mysql-3.23.52.tar.gz
```

Now go to the source directory:

```
cd mysql-3.23.52
```

You need to configure MySQL to compile only the client application.

```
./configure --without-server --prefix=/usr/local/mysql
```

Now compile and install.

```
make
make install
```

The MySQL client is now installed.

Installing NTP

NTP or *Network Time Protocol* is used to keep time in sync between multiple physically separated devices. Synchronous time is essential for event correlation. Event correlation is the act of associating sub-events gathered by different devices to piece together an event. Many security events pieced together become an incident. This process is extremely difficult if each device is set to a different time. One device may record a piece of an attack at 14:20:01:01, whereas another device may record the other portion at 14:21:04:32. This may not have much impact on small environments where only a few events are generated every minute. But if you are at a medium-sized or larger environment, where hundreds or thousands of extraneous events are recorded in a similar time frame, time synchronization becomes a priority. Distinguishing the few sub-events that make up an event becomes an impossibility if time syncing does not happen.

NTP is used to keep time in sync between multiple devices. You will use it to sync the time of all the sensors. If you will be importing data from other devices (such as firewalls) into the intrusion database, be sure to install NTP or a similar service on them. NTP is one of the few packages you can install using a RPM. Get the latest NTP RPM from either rpmfind.net or the Red Hat Web site. After you have acquired the correct RPM, install it using this command:

```
rpm -ivh ntp-4.1.1-1.i386.rpm
```

After it is installed, you need to specify with which time server you will be syncing. An important point to note: If you decided to sync all the sensors to the Snort server, you must sync the server with a reliable outside time provider. Otherwise, event correlation with different organizations, such as ISPs, CERTs, and business partners, is impossible. Reliable event correlation is required for an effective incident response plan. You can get a list of publicly available time servers at

```
http://www.eecis.udel.edu/~mills/ntp/servers.htm
```

Or you can create, use, or install your own internal time server. Next you need to edit the ntp.conf file located at /etc/ntp.conf. Change the following line to let NTP know which time server you will be using:

```
server chosen_time_server.com
```

The `chosen_time_server` should be internal to your organization. Optionally, you can use the Red Hat utility dateconfig. It is a graphical utility that allows you to set your system clock to an NTP server. It also has a listing of NTP servers to choose from.

After you have configured NTP, you can start it with the following command:

```
/etc/rc.d/init.d/ntpd start
```

NTP installation is now complete.

Installing Snort

Now for the moment you have been waiting for: the installation of the Snort application itself. You should have a good understanding of what Snort is, what it can do, and how it functions at this point.

> **Note**
> An important fact to point out at this juncture: If you follow the installation guide in this section you will have a completely detuned installation of Snort. This results in a large number of false positives. The installation intentionally maximizes the ratio of false positives to false negatives. It is advisable to start each sensor with this configuration and slowly work to a more finely tuned state.

This default setting is the recommended configuration state for a new sensor. False negatives are much worse than false positives. Although false positives can be irritating and downright frustrating at times, there are proactive steps you can take to reduce them. You can slowly modify rules and tune preprocessors to trim out alerts that you have verified to be benign. However, by their very definition, it is much more difficult to detect false negatives. There is also no measurable, organized method of reducing them. Often it will take realization that the host has been compromised to detect false negatives. For these reasons, you should cast the widest net and ensnare the greatest number of alerts when you first implement a new sensor. Chapter 10 works through the tuning of Snort.

The first step is to download the latest and greatest version of Snort from the Snort community Web site:

```
http://www.snort.org/dl/
```

Untar and change to the new directory.

```
tar -xzf snort-1.9.0.tar.gz
cd snort-1.9.0
```

The next step is to configure Snort to be used with MySQL. If you plan using Barnyard, you should omit the --with-mysql switch.

```
./configure --with-mysql
```

Now follow the normal compilation and installation steps.

```
make
make install
```

The Snort application is now installed. Next you need to create the group and the user that will run the Snort process.

```
groupadd snort_group
useradd -g snort_group snort_user
```

It is a good idea to create a depository for the rules and configuration files that make up Snort. This makes it much easier to manage them with a tool such as IDS Policy Manager or via SSH. Create the rules directory with the following command:

```
mkdir /etc/snort/conf
```

You are going to have to store usernames and passwords in the clear in this directory, so you want to implement a restrictive permissions.

```
chmod 700 /etc/snort/conf
```

After you have created a directory for the rules and configuration files, you move the appropriate files into the corresponding directory. From the directory that contains the Snort source, issue these commands:

```
cp snort.conf /etc/snort/conf/
cp classification.config /etc/snort/conf/
cp reference.config /etc/snort/conf/
cp sid-msg.map /etc/snort/conf
cp gen-msg.map /etc/snort/conf
```

The signatures included in the Snort source distribution are current for the day the version was released. Hence, they are most likely out of date and not the most current signatures available. You can download a fresh ruleset from

```
http://www.snort.org/dl/snapshots
```

Extract the rule files.

```
tar -xzf snortrules.tar.gz
```

Switch to the rules directory and move the rules to the /etc/snort/conf directory.

```
cd snortrules
mv * /etc/snort/conf
```

You have completed the installation of Snort.

Configuring snort.conf

Snort.conf is the chief entry point for configuring Snort's settings. It is the main configuration file for Snort. You use it to specify ranges of IP addresses to monitor, preprocessors to enable, output plugins to utilize, and rules to use.

What follows is a walk-through of the snort.conf file and the recommended settings.

Setting Network Variables

The network variables are a group of options that give Snort some basic information about the network to be monitored. They set the ranges of IP addresses to be monitored and the common ports for heavily used services. These settings will give Snort a rough overview of how your network is setup. They are also used as variables in rules, so you want to be as accurate as possible. Take this rule for example:

```
alert tcp $EXTERNAL_NET any -> $HTTP_SERVERS $HTTP_PORTS

(msg:"WEB-PHP php.exe access"; flow:to_server,established;

uricontent:"/php.exe ";)
```

This rule detects attacks that make use of a vulnerability in the php.exe executable. It allows the attacker to remotely view or download any file on the target host. This is done by simply appending a filepath after php.exe in the URL, like so:

```
http://www.victimhost.com/php/php.exe?c:\confidential_information.txt
```

Notice that this rule makes use of both the $HTTP_SERVERS and $HTTP_PORTS variables. These variables are set in the snort.conf file. At first glance you may think you only need to set $HTTP_PORTS to 80 and 443. There are a bevy of HTTP-based device management tools, some of which may utilize a scripting language such as PHP. If you had a PHP management device that ran on Windows on a usual port, such as 3276/TCP, Snort would miss attacks aimed at this device. The point to remember is if you casually assign snort.conf variables to only the most common ports, without doing a fair amount of research on the network to be monitored, you could be inadvertently setting up Snort for false negatives.

HOME_NET

This variable denotes the range of internal IP addresses for Snort to monitor for intrusions. Snort does not watch anything outside of the range specified by the HOME_NET variable. You can specify one of four different types of IP address ranges. The first is a simple address range:

192.168.1.1/24

Address ranges must be specified in CIDR format. The second is a list of CIDR address ranges:

[192.168.1.1/24,10.0.0.1/24]

HOME_NET is very picky about how you list CIDR address ranges. Notice that you must include the brackets [], with ranges delimited by a comma with no spaces. Be careful to follow this exact syntax. The third method of specifying internal address ranges uses a local interface.

$interface_ADDRESS

You can use this option to have Snort always use the IP address and netmask of the specified interface. Remember, most likely you have eth1 set as the sniffing interface, so if you choose to use this option, set HOME_NET to $eth1_ADDRESS. If you have the sniffing interface in stealth mode (that is, no IP address assigned), this method will not work. The fourth and final option is guaranteed to watch the most amount of traffic.

Setting HOME_NET to any will monitor every internal IP address. This is the setting that we want to use. As you tune Snort you may want to revisit this option and have the sensor monitor a smaller address range. You can also use the CIDR options to split the internal address range between a number of sensors. Your HOME_NET variable declaration should look like this:

var HOME_NET any

EXTERNAL_NET

This variable is an analogy for the HOME_NET variable for external addresses. This range of addresses external to your network will be monitored for intrusions. It supports the same four options as HOME_NET. Because you are configuring snort.conf for the first time, you want to set this to any. Your EXTERNAL_NET variable declaration should look like this:

var EXTERNAL_NET any

You could optionally configure EXTERNAL_NET to !$HOME_NET. This has the effect of monitoring every packet that is not included in what you defined as HOME_NET. If you do decide to set EXTERNAL_NET to !$HOME_NET, you should make absolutely positive you do not have HOME_NET set to any. The inverse of any is nothing, meaning you will monitor for nothing if you configure these variables in that fashion.

`HTTP_PORTS`

The variable used to name ports on which your organization runs HTTP services. Snort examines these ports for HTTP-based rules. As of this writing, Snort supports only four types of port assignments for variables. You can list a single port, such as

`80`

Additionally, you can monitor a sequential range of ports. This example would monitor for ports 1 through 1024:

`1:1024`

You can also use a less-than-or-equal-to range of ports. This example monitors for every port equal to or below 1024:

`:1024`

The final method combines any of the previous three with a negation operator to signify everything except the port or range of ports specified.

`!80`

In the near future, Snort will support a non-sequential port list. If this feature has been added, you will be able to create a list of ports to monitor for HTTP attacks. The obvious choices for the `$HTTP_PORTS` variable are `80`, `8080`, and `443`. Some easily overlooked common HTTP ports you may want to include as well include the following:

- **591**. Filemaker Pro uses port 591 to publish a Web version of a Filemaker database.
- **593**. The Windows RPC endpoint mapper enables RPC clients to determine the port number currently assigned to a particular RPC service.
- **900**. Client authentication to a Check Point brand of firewall over HTTP.
- **1580**. Web admin interface for IBM Tivoli Storage Manager (TSM).
- **2301**. Web admin interface for Compaq Insight Manager.
- **2381**. SSL-enabled Web admin interface for Compaq's Insight Manager.
- **2693**. Belarc Web license manager HTTP server.
- **8880**. Apache-based Web admin interface for HP OpenView.

Your `HTTP_PORTS` variable declaration should look like this:

`var HTTP_PORTS 80`

`SMTP`

This variable is used to identify SMTP servers within your network that you would like Snort to monitor. Snort monitors traffic that is sent to these IP addresses for SMTP attacks. It applies rules that specify the `$SMTP` variable. Here you have an example of an SMTP rule:

```
alert tcp $EXTERNAL_NET any -> $SMTP 25

(msg:"SMTP expn cybercop attempt"; flow:to_server,established;

content:"expn cybercop";)
```

This rule is a signature for an attacker who is using the CyberCop vulnerability assessment tool. This particular test probes the SMTP server for the EXPN vulnerability. EXPN is a command that can be used to gain information about usernames or mail routing from the SMTP server.

If you accidentally leave out an SMTP server address when defining the SMTP variable, you could open yourself up to false negatives. Attackers often attempt blind reconnaissance attacks against services that do not exist. Additionally, script kiddies often attempt to exploit services that do not exist on your network. If you define the exact addresses of the SMTP servers, you miss these attempted attacks. For this reason, you should define the SMTP variable as `$HOME_NET`. This checks for SMTP attacks against any IP address you have set equal to `$HOME_NET`. When you are ready to tune Snort, you can revisit this variable. Your SMTP variable declaration should match the following:

```
var SMTP $HOME_NET
```

HTTP_SERVERS

This variable has the same function as the `SMTP` variable. It is set to the IP addresses of HTTP servers within your organization. It is recommended to first set this variable equal to `$HOME_NET`. Your `HTTP_SERVERS` variable declaration should match the following:

```
var HTTP_SERVERS $HOME_NET
```

SQL_SERVERS

Set `SQL_SERVERS` to the IP addresses of various SQL servers within your organization. It is recommended to first set this variable equal to `$HOME_NET`. Your `SQL_SERVERS` variable declaration should match the following:

```
var SQL_SERVERS $HOME_NET
```

DNS_SERVERS

Set `DNS_SERVERS` to the IP addresses of various DNS servers within your organization. DNS servers are a major source of false positives for most networks, regardless of the network layout. For the DNS servers, you should break pace and actually identify the DNS server IP address within your organization. Your `DNS_SERVERS` variable declaration should match the following:

```
var DNS_SERVERS list_of_DNS_IP_addresses
```

RULE_PATH

This variable lets Snort know the location of the rule files on the sensor. Make sure to set this to the directory you created for Snort configuration and rule files. If you have followed the example in this book the RULE_PATH would be:

```
var RULE_PATH /etc/snort/conf
```

SHELLCODE_PORTS

These are ports that Snort will monitor for shellcode, or more specifically no-op (No Operation) sleds. Shellcode or no-op sleds are often present in the signature of buffer overflow attacks. Exploits pad the stack with no-ops so that the return address need not be exact. A class of Snort rules relies on the shellcode signature to identify these types of attacks. Unfortunately, NFS, binary email attachments, and other binary communication often match a shellcode signature. Because of the high degree of false positives related to shellcode signatures, you should detail which ports not to look for shellcode attacks.

For the SHELLCODE_PORTS variable, the same port assignment rules must be used as the HTTP_PORTS variable. Unfortunately, you can specify only a single port or range of ports with the current version of Snort. For now, set SHELLCODE_PORTS to everything but port 80 with this setting:

```
!80
```

When Snort can accept a list of ports, you may want to include these ports:

- !119. The NNTP port. Binary files are often transmitted via NNTP.
- !515. The printer spooler TCP port.

Your SHELLCODE_PORTS variable declaration should look like this:

```
var SHELLCODE_PORTS !80
```

ORACLE_PORTS

This variable is used by Snort to identify the ports that Oracle is run on at your organization. Snort uses this variable to detect suspicious or malicious Oracle activity. If you run Oracle on something other than the default port of 1521 at your company, be sure to set it here. Your ORACLE_PORTS variable declaration should look like this:

```
var ORACLE_PORTS 1521
```

Configuring Preprocessors

Adhering to the strategy of minimizing false negatives at the expense of maximizing false positives, we will configure the preprocessors to be particularly sensitive. If you need to refresh your memory on the function of a certain preprocessor, refer to Chapter 3.

`frag2`

`frag2` is Snort's IP defragmentation preprocessor. It is used to normalize fragmented packets. Set the `frag2` options equal to the following settings:

- Set timeout equal to 35.
- Leave memcap at its default setting of 4194304.
- Set `min_ttl` to 3.
- Set `ttl_limit` to 8.

The `frag2` line is the following:

```
preprocessor frag2: timeout 35, memcap 4194304, min_ttl 3, ttl_limit 8
```

`stream4`

`stream4` is what Snort uses to maintain the state of TCP streams. Configure these `stream4` options:

- Set timeout equal to 35.
- Enable `detect_scans`.
- Enable `detect_state_problems`.
- Leave memcap at its default setting of 8388608.
- Set `min_ttl` to 3.
- Set `ttl_limit` to 8.

The remaining options can be disregarded for the time being. The `stream4` preprocessor configuration line should be set to the following:

```
preprocessor stream4: detect_scans, timeout 35, memcap 8388608, min_ttl 3,
ttl_limit 8
```

`stream4_reassemble`

`stream4_reassemble` is closely related to the `stream4` preprocessor. It performs TCP stream reassembly. You should configure these options:

- Enable both.
- Set ports to all.

If you are running the sensor on close to the minimum hardware setup or are monitoring a high bandwidth network, you may have to set ports equal to all to reduce the amount of reassembly processing. The remaining options can be disregarded. The `stream4` preprocessor configuration line should be set to the following:

```
preprocessor stream4_reassemble: both, ports all
```

`http_decode`

The `http_decode` preprocessor is responsible for detecting abnormal HTTP traffic and normalizing it. You should configure these options:

- Enable `unicode`.
- Enable `iis_alt_unicode`.
- Enable `double_encode`.
- Enable `iis_flip_slash`.
- Enable `full_whitespace`.

You also need to set which ports on which `http_decode` will be normalizing traffic. The most common list is 80, 443, and 8080. If you use any ports for HTTP servers outside this list (for example, 2301 for Compaq Insight Manager), be sure to include them. Use the following line for `http_decode`:

```
preprocessor http_decode: 80 443 8080 unicode iis_alt_unicode

double_encode iis_flip_slash full_whitespace
```

`rpc_decode`

The `rpc_decode` preprocessor is used to decode RPC traffic that has been suspiciously manipulated. To configure the preprocessor, simply list the ports your organization uses for RPCs. Use the following if you have no other RPC daemons running on non-standard ports.

```
preprocessor rpc_decode: 111 32771
```

`bo`

The bo preprocessor detects the Back Orifice remote control Trojan for Windows systems. We will configure bo to use the default settings. If you are using a sensor in less than ideal conditions, (for example, with limited resources or for monitoring medium to high bandwidth) it is advisable to enable the `-nobrute` option. Doing so causes bo to use significantly less system resources. The following simple line suffices for the bo preprocessor:

```
preprocessor bo
```

`telnet_decode`

`telnet_decode` decodes or removes arbitrarily inserted binary Telnet control codes in a Telnet or FTP stream. This preprocessor has no configuration options. Use this line to enable `telnet_decode`:

```
preprocessor telnet_decode
```

arpspoof

arpspoof is a preprocessor designed to detect malicious ARP traffic. You should enable
the –unicast option to detect ARP unicast request monitoring. Enable arpspoof
with this line:

```
preprocessor arpspoof -unicast
```

To enable the preprocessor, you must list the IP addresses and their associated MAC
addresses in separate lines, like so:

```
preprocessor arpspoof_detect_host: 192.168.1.1 00:06:5B:18:EF:10
preprocessor arpspoof_detect_host: 192.168.1.2 01:AF:05:11:BC:10
```

To find MAC addresses on Windows systems use the ipconfig /all command
from a command prompt. On Linux run the ifconfig –a command at the shell
prompt.

asn1_decode

asn1_decode is a preprocessor designed to detect various inconsistencies in ASN.1 that
may indicate malicious behavior. It requires no options to enable:

```
preprocessor asn1_decode
```

fnord

fnord is a preprocessor designed to detect and defeat polymorphic shell code evasion
attempts. It requires no options to enable it. Do so with the following snort.conf line:

```
preprocessor fnord
```

conversation

This preprocessor tracks conversations for any IP traffic. It is a prerequisite for running
portscan2. You should configure these options:

- Set allowed_ip_protocols to all.
- Configure timeout to equal 65.
- Set max_conversations to 65335.

If you would rather track conversations for the three most common IP protocols, set
allowed_ip_protocols to 1, 6, 17. This enables conversation tracking for TCP, UDP,
and ICMP. You should then include the alert_odd_protocols option. This alerts you
whenever a IP protocol other than 1, 6, or 17 is detected. Use the following line to
enable conversation:

```
preprocessor conversation: allowed_ip_protocols all,

timeout 65, max_conversations 65335
```

`portscan2`

`portscan2` works in concurrence with the conversation preprocessor to track sessions for IP protocols. It has configurable options that enable it to detect different methods of scanning that are anomalous for most IP networks. Implement the following configurations for `portscan2`:

- Set `scanners_max` to 3200.
- Set `targets_max` to 5000.
- Configure `target_limit` to be 5.
- Set `port_limit` equal to 20.
- Configure timeout equal to be 60.

You should also add a second `portscan2` directive that specifies the IP addresses to ignore portscanning activity from. You should initially set this to any DNS servers you have, and add to it as needed.

Use the following lines to implement the `portscan2` preprocessor:

```
preprocessor portscan2: scanners_max 3200, targets_max 5000,
target_limit 5, port_limit 20, timeout 60
preprocessor portscan2-ignorehosts DNS_server_IP_address_range
```

Setting up Output Plugins

Although there are a plethora of options for setting up output plugins, you are going to make use of only one plugin for the sensor. You have two options for populating the Snort server with data. The first is to use the database output plugin provided by Snort to log alerts to the MySQL database. Keep in mind that this setup will create a major bottleneck at the output state. MySQL is exceptionally fast and efficient at querying for data. SQL statements that use SELECT with MySQL are incredibly fast. However, inserting and updating data in MySQL is a completely different story. MySQL is awfully slow when it comes to UPDATE and INSERT statements. When Snort is writing data to the database, it uses INSERT statements, which causes the database server to bog down. Snort must then wait until MySQL is ready to accept new data, and the Snort process itself is slowed. Outputting directly from Snort is not the most efficient or preferable method. For these reasons, it is best to outsource the outputting of alerts to Barnyard. This second logging option is possible when Snort outputs to the Snort Unified format. Snort is then free to process traffic and create alerts as fast as it can. Barnyard takes the time to insert the data into MySQL as a separate process that will not impact Snort's performance.

Either option will get you up and running. If you are monitoring a high-bandwidth connection or one that you suspect will generate a lot of alerts, output to Snort Unified and use Barnyard. Even if you are now monitoring a low-traffic network, using Barnyard ensures that your sensor can cope with a sudden increase in traffic. If you are setting Snort up on a home network or simply want to verify that everything is working, go ahead and use the database plugin.

Using the Database Plugin

The `database` output plugin logs directly to the MySQL database. You need to specify the local loopback address for the database communication to be encrypted with Stunnel. Configure the following options for the `database` plugin:

- Set the `output facility` to `alert`.
- Make the `database type` equal to `mysql`.
- Set the `host` to `127.0.0.1`.
- Set the `dbname` to `snortdb` or the name you have chosen for the intrusion database.
- Set `user` equal to `snortdb_username` or the MySQL username you created in Chapter 6 for the Snort sensor.
- Set `password` equal to `snortdb_password` or the MySQL password for `snortdb_username` you created for the Snort sensor.
- Configure `sensor_name` to be the name that you are going to choose for this Snort sensor.
- Set `encoding` equal to `ascii` to log in ASCII rather than binary format.

Your database plugin line should look like the following:

```
output database: alert, mysql, host=127.0.0.1 dbname=snortdb

user=snortdb_username password= snortdb_password

sensor_name=creative_sensor_name, encoding=ascii
```

The database output plugin is now configured.

Using the Unified Plugin

The goal of the `unified` plugin is to enable Snort to process traffic as fast as possible. The `unified` format is a variant of the `tcpdump` binary format.

There are two options for the unified format: `log_unified` and `alert_unified`. The `alert_unified` setting was created to allow super-fast outputting of intrusion alerts. Data outputted with `alert_unified` does not contain complete packet detail, allowing Snort to write alerts with blazing speed. It is intended for real-time notification purposes only. You should not use this option if you intend to do any sort of forensic work with the data.

`Log_unified` outputs full packet information. This is the setting that you need to use for this configuration of the `unified` plugin. You must specify two additional options for the `log_unified` to function:

- Set `filename` equal to `snort.unified.log` or the filename you want to use to spool alerts to.
- Set `limit` to a value equal to or greater than `128`.

Your Unified output plugin line should look like this:

```
output log_unified: filename snort.unified.log, limit 256
```

Enabling Document Linking and Alert Prioritization

Two supplemental files are used to prioritize alerts and link external documentation to Snort rules. The `classification.config` file is used to both classify and prioritize alerts. It is from this file that you can group alerts by what they have in common. Additionally, you use `classification.config` to assign alerting priorities to the alert groups. The priorities are used to distinguish which rules will trigger a real time notification.

The other file, reference.config, is used to define the base URL links for external documentation. This file contains keys that are used in rules to represent various public documentation resources on the Internet.

To enable document linking and alert prioritization, include the following two lines:

```
include classification.config
include reference.config
```

Configuring the Ruleset

The final step in setting up the snort.conf file is to configure the rules that you will use. Use the include `$RULE_PATH/rulefile.rules` format to enable rule files. To stay with the philosophy of minimizing false negatives, you should enable the entire rule set. You can do this by enabling every rule that has been commented out. Remove the pound (#) character that has been placed in front of the following lines:

```
include $RULE_PATH/web-attacks.rules
include $RULE_PATH/backdoor.rules
include $RULE_PATH/shellcode.rules
include $RULE_PATH/policy.rules
include $RULE_PATH/porn.rules
include $RULE_PATH/info.rules
include $RULE_PATH/icmp-info.rules
include $RULE_PATH/virus.rules
include $RULE_PATH/chat.rules
include $RULE_PATH/multimedia.rules
include $RULE_PATH/p2p.rules
```

Be prepared for a flood of false positives and possible dropped packets by enabling the above rules. You will trim the rules down to manageable levels in Chapter 9 by using both automated tools and manual editing.

Running Snort

You should now have a fully operational Snort application. If you have chosen the Barnyard option, you will have to do some additional work to get Snort up and running in production mode. It is still worth your time to follow some of the steps to ensure everything is working correctly. If you have chosen to log straight from the database plugin, you will be able to start up Snort in full production mode in this step.

Snort is controlled via some command line options. You need to give Snort the following information from the command line:

- The location of the snort.conf file.
- The logging directory.
- The sniffing interface name.
- The UID and GID of the Snort user and group.

Your command line to run Snort should look like this:

```
usr/local/snort/bin/snort -c /usr/local/snort/conf/snort.conf -l

-i eth1 -u snort_user -g snort_group -D
```

Snort should start running. Notice Snort is not run in the background with the ampersand (&) appended to the command right now. When you are sure you have Snort up and running correctly you can move it to the background by appending the ampersand.

Run a tool to generate some alerts, such as NMAP or SuperScan, and check ACID to ensure that the process is working. If you are using Barnyard, you will have to complete the next few steps before you can view any alerts. If you would like to do a quick test to ensure that Snort is functioning, try

```
snort -vde
```

which will run Snort in sniffer mode. You should see traffic scroll by the console.

Implementing Barnyard

Installing and configuring Barnyard is a relatively straightforward and simple task. Barnyard was designed to have limited but powerful functionality. It is intended to perform only one function, and do it very well: the generation of alerts from Snort intrusion data. Barnyard has no other planned features, with the exception of processing alerts stored in the Snort Unified format.

Barnyard has three basic modes of operation:

- One-shot
- Continual
- Continual with checkpointing

One-shot mode is used to process a Snort unified file in a single run. Barnyard processes the file, generates alerts, and then exits. When Barnyard is set in continual mode, it starts with a file and continuously processes data as it is created by Snort. The final option, continual mode with checkpointing, runs similarly to continual mode. Barnyard process-es data as it is generated by Snort. Additionally, continual mode with checkpointing uses a checkpoint file to keep track of where it has last processed data within the unified file. If the Barnyard daemon were to end while the checkpoint file is in use, it would resume processing at the last entry as listed in the checkpoint file.

To install Barnyard you must first download the source from the Snort Web site.

```
http://www.snort.org/dl/barnyard/
```

Untar with the usual options.

```
tar -xvf barnyard-0.1.0-rc2.tar.gz
```

After you are in the source directory, you must configure Barnyard with MySQL sup-port for it to work with the Snort server. Use the following configure command:

```
./configure --enable-mysql
```

Now compile and install.

```
make
make install
```

Barnyard is now installed.

Configuring barnyard.conf

Like Snort, Barnyard's settings are controlled via a .conf file. You need to edit some of the configuration options through this file. Open the `barnyard.conf` file for editing.

When you are ready to edit `barnyard.conf`, change the settings discussed in the following sections.

daemon

This option enables Barnyard in daemon mode.

hostname

Set the `config hostname` equal to the `localhost`. Use this command line:

```
config hostname: snorthost
```

interface

Make sure to set `interface` equal to the sniffing interface. If you have followed this guide, it should be eth1.

```
config interface: eth1
```

filter

Comment out any filter directive by using the pound (#) symbol.

The default setting is to filter port 22, used by SSH. If you were to use SSH to access the sensor through the same interface Snort is sniffing with, you could cause an alert to be generated. If this alert were to be presented during the same SSH session, it would be picked up by Snort and generate another alert. This new alert would generate another alert, and so on and so forth. This would create an infinite loop that would create a DoS on the sensor until the session was terminated. It would also make connecting to the sensor via SSH an impossibility. Because you have a separate management interface, this self-inflicted DoS will not happen.

dp_alert

The `dp_alert` data processor is designed to read the alert format generated by Snort's unified output plug-in. Enable it with this line:

```
processor dp_alert
```

dp_log

This data processor is similar in function to `dp_alert`. It is designed to read the log format generated by Snort's unified output plug-in. Enable it with this line:

```
processor dp_log
```

dp_stream_stat

Same as the two preceding data processors, except that `dp_stream_stat` reads the `stream4` data. Enable it with this line:

```
processor dp_stream_stat
```

Output Plugins

Make sure to comment out all output plugins except for the `acid_db`. If you leave the others enabled, you will waste processing power.

acid_db

`acid_db` is the plugin used to output into an intrusion database. It is similar in function to Snort's database plugin. You need to enable the following parameters in order for `acid_db` to work:

- `$db_flavor`. Used to define the type of database to be outputted to, most likely MySQL.
- `$sensor_id`. An integer used to represent the sensor within ACID. Ensure that you use an integer, not a character or string. If you fail to use an integer, Barnyard crashes.
- `$database`. The name of the Snort database within MySQL.
- `$server`. The servername that the database resides on that you wish to log to.
- `$user`. The username required to log into the database.

- $password. The password required to log into the database.

- $detail. The level of completeness of information to be outputted in alerts post-
  ed to ACID.

You should put together a directive that looks like the following line:

```
output log_acid_db: mysql, sensor_id 1, database snortdb,

server 127.0.0.1, user snortdb_user, password snortdb_password, detail full
```

Running Barnyard

As stated previously in this section, Barnyard has three major modes of operation. Like
Snort, these modes and others are controlled via the command line string. You can control how Barnyard functions with the following command line options.

`-c /path/to/barnyard.conf`

This option tells Barnyard the location of the `barnyard.conf` file. This is a required
option.

`-d /path/to/snort/unified/data`

This option lets Barnyard know the location of the Snort `unified` format files. All
`unified` files must be located within this directory root. This option is required.

`-f unified.snort.file`

This option notifies Barnyard of the base name of the Unified file when run in continual mode. Snort appends a Unix timestamp to the end of each Snort Unified file; the base
name is this filename without the appended timestamp.

In one-shot mode, Barnyard processes only the file specified with `-f`. This option is
required.

`-g /path/to/gen-msg.map`

With this option you tell Barnyard where to find the `gen-msg.map` file. This file is used
to correlate the error messages generated by Snort's preprocessors to human-readable
alert messages. This file is included with Snort, not Barnyard.

`-h`

Displays Barnyard usage–related data.

`-L /location/to/store/filename.log`

Lets Barnyard know where to place logfiles generated with output options other than
`acid_db`.

`-o`

This option runs Barnyard in one-shot mode as described earlier. It processes the file specified with `-f`.

`-R`

Run Barnyard in debug mode.

`-s /path/to/sid-msg.map`

This option is used to notify Barnyard of the location of the `sid-msg.map` file. This file is similar in function to `gen-msg.map`: It correlates alerts generated by Snort with a human-readable alert message.

`-t timestamp`

This option sets earliest timestamp value (see `-f`) that Barnyard will use for alert processing. Any file created earlier than the specified timestamp is processed. Any file older than the timestamp is not interpreted. Barnyard processes any `unified` file that exactly matches the timestamp value.

`-w /path/to/filename`

The option turns on the checkpointing feature. It is also used to tell Barnyard the name of the checkpoint file to be used. This is also called a "waldo" file, hence the `-w`. The waldo file is used to make record of the last alert processed in a file. If you do not use a waldo file, Barnyard has to run through a log file in its entirety, which is likely to post to the intrusion database many alerts that were already there.

Starting the Barnyard Process

You should now be able to start the Barnyard process by using the following command:

```
barnyard -c /usr/local/snort/barnyard/barnyard.conf -d /var/log/snort/
```

```
-s /usr/local/snort/sid-msg.map -g /usr/local/snort/gen-msg.map
```

```
-f snort.unified.log
```

You can now use ACID to verify that the entire Snort sensor and server functions. When you have Barnyard up and running, you must remember to periodically issue a HUP (hang up on) command to the Snort process. The HUP restarts Snort with the same parameters that you started it with. Restarting Snort in this manner forces Snort to create a new logfile. If you do not hang up on Snort, the log file will reach its maximum size and Snort will no longer be able to process data.

Automating with barnyard.server

`barnyard.server` is a script written to aid users in the maintenance of the Barnyard daemon. It is quite a handy tool. It can automate the starting and stopping of the

Barnyard process. `barnyard.server` can also be configured to email you whenever the process ends unexpectedly. It is fairly simple to use; it has the same configuration options as the Barnyard command line. `barnyard.server` is not a required component, so you can skip this step if you like.

Get `barnyard.server` at:

`http://www.snort.org/dl/barnyard/contrib/`

Uncompress the `barnyard.server` script and move it to the barnyard directory. You need to edit `barnyard.server` with a mix of command line options.

Open `baryard.server` for editing. First, change to bash instead of ksh. The remaining fields simply map to the various command line options with which you are now familiar. Use the same options that you used to start Barnyard in the previous step. The only new line to fill out is the email address that will be notified when Barnyard crashes.

Using `barnyard.server` is fairly straightforward. It supports the following commands:

- `start`. Turns the Barnyard process on.
- `stop`. Halts the Barnyard process.
- `restart`. Stops and then starts Barnyard.
- `status`. Checks to see whether Barnyard is running.
- `failcheck`. Checks to see whether Barnyard is running and reports any failures.

You issue these commands by running the script with the command appended like so:

`barnyard.server restart`

Summary

This chapter is a complete guide to deploying a Snort sensor. Linux is chosen as the underlying OS for the sensor. The sensor is hardened and will have only Snort and its supporting applications installed.

A host of supporting packages are required to support Snort. Snort has no native packet capture facility; it requires an external packet sniffing library, libpcap. Libpcap is responsible for grabbing packets directly from the network interface card. OpenSSL is used in conjunction with stunnel to encrypt the sensor to encrypt sensor-to-server communication. An OpenSSH daemon must run on every Snort console for remote management to be possible. The MySQL client is required for an application to remotely connect to a MySQL server. Barnyard needs to post alerting data to MySQL, so you must install the MySQL client libraries and programs. NTP is used to keep time in sync between multiple physically separated sensors. Synchronous time is essential for event correlation.

After the required packages are installed, it is time to implement Snort. The described installation of Snort intentionally maximizes the ratio of false positives to false negatives. Next, Snort must be configured. Snort.conf is the chief entry point for configuring Snort's settings. Snort.conf is used to specify ranges of IP addresses to monitor, pre-processors to enable, output plugins to utilize, and rules to use. A complete walk-through of Snort.conf is included in the chapter.

Two separate outputting options are described in the chapter. Using both the `database` plugin and the Snort unified plugin are detailed. The `database` output plugin logs directly to the MySQL database. The `unified` plugin is used to log to Barnyard, and is the preferable method of logging.

After Snort is deployed, Barnyard is installed to process the Snort logs. Barnyard has three basic modes of operation. They are one-shot, continual, and continual with check-pointing. Barnyard is installed and configured via a similar `barnyard.conf` script. Instructions for the use of the `barnyard.server` script are detailed. `barnyard.server` was written to aid users in the maintenance of the Barnyard daemon.

8

Building the Analyst's Console

NOW THAT YOU HAVE SUCCESSFULLY COMPLETED the building of the Snort server and sensor, it is now time to put the analyst's console together. The primary purpose of the console is to provide an isolated environment for you to perform intrusion detection duties and maintain the Snort components. From the console you will be accessing ACID, maintaining the Snort server(s), and modifying configuration settings and rulesets on the sensors. Because the console plays no role in the actual detection or management of intrusion data, it is acceptable to use a less powerful machine or a Windows operating system.

If you or your organization can afford it, it is best to have the analyst's console separate and free of all other applications. It should also be connected solely to the monitoring segment. Keeping the monitoring segment totally isolated protects the monitoring segment from any internally orchestrated attacks. An isolated segment lessens the possibility of an attacker bypassing the numerous layers of firewalls and security by compromising the IDS. With sensors located outside external access points, this is a real possibility.

The console has a short list of required software. The two necessary components are a Web browser and an SSH client. Both of these are available for every operating system. This means that you have free rein to choose the operating system you feel most comfortable with. The best option is to set the console up to dual boot both Linux and Windows.

The primary reason to have a Windows partition on the analyst's console is to make use of the IDS Policy Manager. Unfortunately, IDS Policy Manager is not portable to any Unix operating system, and is very difficult if not impossible to run with WINE. WINE, which ironically stands for WINE Is Not an Emulator, is a pseudo-emulator used to run Windows programs on Linux.

IDS Policy Manager is an amazing tool for updating and upgrading Snort sensor configurations. It has an easy-to-use graphical interface that makes maintaining sensors simple. If you choose not to install Windows there is an alternative graphical sensor update tool for Linux: Webmin. Webmin is used to administer a variety of daemons via a Web interface. Webmin requires you to install an HTTP server on the sensor, which can be considered a security risk. It is also not as full-featured and current as IDS Policy Manager. Webmin has some advantages in that it can be used to update configuration settings outside the Snort application. Both Webmin and IDS Policy Manager support encrypted console-to-sensor sessions. Chapter 13, "Upgrading and Maintaining Snort," examines IDS Policy Manager and Webmin in greater detail.

When not updating the sensors, you can boot back into Linux. With Linux you can take advantage of powerful Unix command-line utilities for manipulating data. You can also use it to upgrade or maintain the sensors and servers via SSH. By keeping the everyday OS Linux, you are keeping the console in a more secure controlled environment.

Windows

If you choose to install a Windows partition, or have the console support only Windows, you should follow a few basic guidelines. You should pick a Windows 2000 codebase OS for the analyst's console, such as Windows 2000 Professional or Windows XP. IDS Policy Manager runs on only these versions of Windows. Windows 2000 also has increased stability over other versions. After you have installed Windows, you need to harden it. The Center for Internet Security has thorough guidelines for hardening Windows systems. You can find a detailed guide and a tool to discover the gaps between the state of your system and secured configuration at

`http://www.cisecurity.org/bench_win2000.html`

Installing SSH

You need to install a version of SSH for Windows. If the console is a dedicated Windows machine, you will need SSH to manage the server and sensors. If you are planning on using only a Windows partition to make use of IDS Policy Manager, you still must install SSH. IDS Policy Manager uses secure copy (SCP), explained earlier in Chapter 6, "Building the Server," to encrypt session information. There are many good choices for a Windows SSH client. You can use either an open source or free version, such as OpenSSH or PuTTY. Or you can buy a closed source proprietary version, such as SSH or F-Secure. Download the Windows port of OpenSSH at

`http://www.networksimplicity.com/openssh/`

Simply run the executable and follow the onscreen instructions. Make sure to install the client portion by itself; the server portion is not needed. After you have installed OpenSSH, you must use the command prompt to use any of the SSH suite of programs. If you would rather use a SSH client with a GUI interface, PuTTY is the choice for you. You can get PuTTY at

`http://www.chiark.greenend.org.uk/~sgtatham/putty/download.html`

Using PuTTY is as simple as clicking on the executable. You will be presented with an easy-to-use GUI that can be used to make both Telnet and SSH connections.

Web Browser

The only other piece of software needed for the console is a Web browser. Microsoft's Internet Explorer works well with ACID now that a no-caching directive can be outputted from ACID. Remember to set `html_no_cache` in `acid_conf.php` to 1 if you are going to make use of IE. You can just as easily use Mozilla or Netscape.

Linux

If you plan on using Linux for the analyst's console there are steps that mirror the Windows installation. Assuming you are using Red Hat 7.3, install the following package groups:

- Printing Support
- Classic X Windows
- X Windows
- KDE or GNOME
- Network Support
- Messaging Web Tools
- Authoring and Publishing
- Emacs
- Utilities
- Software Development

These package groups should give you everything you need to run the console. After you have Red Hat installed, download and install Bastille Linux as described in Chapter 6, "Building the Server." After hardening with Bastille, you are ready to install OpenSSH.

Installing OpenSSH

For the console, follow the directions for building and installing OpenSSH detailed in the "Implementing OpenSSH" section in Chapter 6. You should omit the following two commands that enable sshd:

```
/usr/local/sbin/sshd
/usr/local/bin/egd.pl
```

There is no reason to have the SSH daemon running on the console. All connections should originate at the console and terminate at the server or sensor.

Web Browser

The last package needed for the Linux console is a Web browser. Mozilla works well with ACID regardless of how the `html_no_cache` in `acid_conf.php` is set.

Testing the Console

For this step you are going to perform a real upgrade to the server to test your newly installed SSH client. It is possible to add an additional layer of security to the Snort environment via `.htaccess` IP address restrictions. Restricting by IP address will make it more difficult for unskilled persons to access ACID. You can add lines to the `.htaccess` file on the server that will only allow the IP address of the console.

For a change of pace, we will use the Windows version of PuTTY to connect to the SSH server on the Snort server. Running the PuTTY executable will bring up the configuration and login screen (see Figure 8.1).

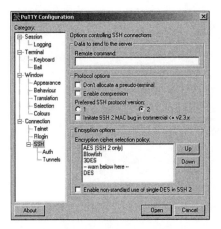

Figure 8.1   PuTTY configuration.

On the Session screen, enter the IP address of the Snort server and switch the Protocol radio button to be set to SSH. Navigate to the SSH screen, where you need to change the Perferred SSH Protocol Version to 2. On the Auth submenu, check the Attempt Keyboard Interactive Authentication check box. After you have made the changes, click on the Open button to connect.

The first time you connect to the Snort server you will receive a warning window that reads as follows:

The server's host key is not cached in the registry. You have no guarantee that the server is the computer you think it is. The server's key fingerprint is

```
ssh-rsa 1024 4a:e1:1c:a2:c4:b2:11:52:7b:c2:11:cf:1c:17:6a:7b
```

You should then verify this key with the Snort server. If it matches, you can select the Yes option, which will store the key on the console. If at some point in the future you receive the key warning again, it could be a sign that your Snort server has been compromised. After verifying the key, you now log in with your username and password.

After you have established an SSH connection to the server, download the
`.htaccess` file from

```
/usr/local/apache/htdocs/acid/.htaccess
```

Edit the `.htaccess` to include the following lines within the Limit tags:

```
<Limit GET>
require user username
order deny, allow
deny from all
allow from xxx.xxx.xxx.xxx
</Limit>
```

Where *xxx.xxx.xxx.xxx* is the IP address assigned to the console. The order line
specifies the order in which subsequent IP allow and deny lines will be interpreted. For
this example, I want to default deny every IP and then only allow those that I specify.
The allow line specifies the IP addresses permitted to authenticate. These simple IP
address restrictions are not foolproof security; there are many different methods of cir-
cumventing this layer of security.

The building of the analyst's console is now complete.

Working with ACID

ACID is the primary tool you will be using to work with intrusion data gathered by
Snort. ACID has a number of useful features that will aid in intrusion detection and
forensic work.

ACID presents alerts and intrusion data in a manner that makes the raw data outputted from Snort easier to understand (see Figure 8.2). Data is arranged in a logical
fashion that facilitates quick decision making. Packets are displayed in an easy-to-
understand manner that clearly documents the information in the packet.

ACID provides detailed documentation that will give you insight into a new or
unrecognized alert. Most Snort signatures contain documentation "keys" that ACID can
interpret. ACID uses these "keys" to match the signature to various public signature databases on the Internet. Each time an alert is displayed, links corresponding to the attack
signature are displayed. This method of using external Internet resources is much more
effective than using internal documentation. Lengthy signature documentation cannot be
stored in the actual signature for performance reasons. If signature documentation were
stored in the ACID application itself, you would be required to update ACID quite often
to keep up with the flood of new signature information. Most importantly, external
Internet intrusion databases are the most current and extensive resources available. There
is no need to reinvent the wheel, so to speak, when numerous free resources already
exist. The most popular linked databases are

```
http://www.whitehats.com
http://www.securityfocus.com
http://cve.mitre.org
```

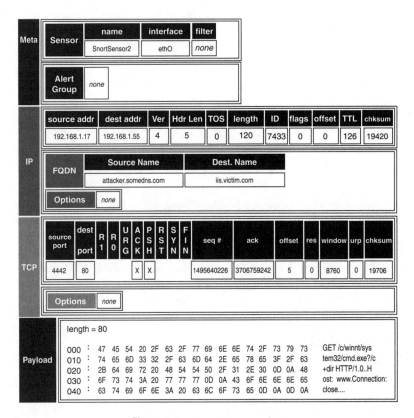

		name	interface	filter
Meta	**Sensor**	SnortSensor2	ethO	*none*
	Alert Group	*none*		

		source addr	dest addr	Ver	Hdr Len	TOS	length	ID	flags	offset	TTL	chksum
IP		192.168.1.17	192.168.1.55	4	5	0	120	7433	0	0	126	19420

	FQDN	Source Name	Dest. Name
		attacker.somedns.com	iis.victim.com
	Options	*none*	

	source port	dest port	R 1	R 0	U R G	A C K	P S H	R S T	S Y N	F I N	seq #	ack	offset	res	window	urp	chksum
TCP	4442	80				X	X				1495640226	3706759242	5	0	8760	0	19706

Options	*none*

length = 80

Payload	000 :	47 45 54 20 2F 63 2F 77 69 6E 6E 74 2F 73 79 73	GET /c/winnt/sys
	010 :	74 65 6D 33 32 2F 63 6D 64 2E 65 78 65 3F 2F 63	tem32/cmd.exe?/c
	020 :	2B 64 69 72 20 48 54 54 50 2F 31 2E 30 0D 0A 48	+dir HTTP/1.0..H
	030 :	6F 73 74 3A 20 77 77 77 0D 0A 43 6F 6E 6E 65 65	ost: www.Connection:
	040 :	63 74 69 6F 6E 3A 20 63 6C 6F 73 65 0D 0A 0D 0A	close....

Figure 8.2 A suspicious packet.

ACID also supports linking to a specific URL that provides deeper insight into the alert. Some alerts have links to vendor statements and patches for the specific attack, whereas others point to security research that can provide detailed information about the attack.

Additionally, ACID contains links to resources for identifying TCP or UDP ports and IP address ownership. It is impossible to remember every service that runs on every possible port. For this reason, every port listed in an alert is linked out to a comprehensive port database on the Internet. This feature lets you quickly access up-to-date information on ports you are unfamiliar with. IP address ownership can help you identify whether the IP address was spoofed or not. If the IP address is reserved or from a source unlikely to be attacking you (such as the IP address of `whitehouse.gov`), you can assume it was spoofed. If the address is possibly the real source of the attack, you can use this information to track down your attacker and pursue corrective action.

Searching

If you have taken a peek at the search interface for ACID, you may have already noticed that it is nothing like a typical search engine. The ACID search interface is fairly complex and extremely powerful. ACID assumes that the user is a technical person with the ability to build and execute complex logical queries. The search interface is designed to give the intrusion analyst the maximum number of features and the highest criteria selection granularity. When you use ACID to search, you first build a query and then execute it. You construct the query by selecting the criteria to be searched on and the data to be searched for.

You can specify a multitude of logical operations on most alert event criteria. Some criteria are static and defined by ACID, whereas others allow or require your input. You can search on four basic categories of criteria. You create queries from these four categories in a top-down logical fashion. The four categories are metadata, IP header data, network layer protocol, and payload data.

Metadata

In addition to gathering intrusion or alerting data, Snort generates some useful information about the intrusion data collected. Metadata is definitional data that provides information about intrusion data gathered by Snort. Metadata is needed because not all the information required to monitor for intrusions is available in captured packets. Information, such as the time the traffic was recorded, is necessary for event correlation and intrusion detection as a whole. The meta criteria searchable by ACID are the same data collected by Snort. You can build queries with the following criteria:

- Sensor. Query for alerts generated by the chosen sensor. Sensors can be placed at different locations within the network infrastructure. Alerts that may be critical for an external sensor, such as Windows share access attempts, may be benign for an internal sensor.

- Alert Group. Search for alerts that are contained in the specified alert group. Alert groups are assembled collections of alerts that form an "incident." We will take a detailed look at alert groups later in this chapter.

- Signature. Query for alerts that match a specific Snort signature. Narrowing alerts down by signature will help you quickly point out possibly compromised servers. If you know a set range of IP addresses are vulnerable to a specific attack, you can use this option to discover which hosts may have been compromised.

- Classification. Return alerts that are of only a certain alert type (such as DoS). This option has a similar use as searching by signature. Classification criteria can be useful in rediscovering the earlier steps of an attack. If you were to receive a number of DoS attacks that were targeted at specific services and sent only to vulnerable servers, you could conclude that some reconnaissance had been previously performed. Even if the DoS attacks used spoofed source IP addresses, the reconnaissance must have used a real source address. You could use the classification criteria to narrow down on reconnaissance attacks within a set time frame.

- Alert Time. A specific time or range of time within which to query for alerts. You are bound to have a large number of alerts over time, and there will always be situations where you would like to search for alerts over a given time period.

IP Header Data

IP header data is data containing the header portion of an IP datagram. You can query for specific IP header data to zero in further on the alerts that you are seeking. Sorting out false positives by IP datagram headers is a must. You can use any of the subsequent IP header criteria to build your searches.

- Address. You can identify alerts that match a specific address or a range of addresses. IP addresses can be searched for in just the source, the destination, or both source and destination fields. You must list ranges of IP addresses in CIDR format. If you are unfamiliar with CIDR notation, there are numerous guides online that will bring you up to speed in a matter of minutes.

- Field Data. Return only alerts that match one of the six specific IP header fields. The six fields are Type of Service, Time to Live, Fragment ID, Fragmentation Offset, Checksum, and Header Length. You must specify the data within the fields for which you want to search. Abnormal field data is often an indicator of an attack or IDS evasion attempt. Short TTLs are indicative of IDS evasion, fragmentation is often a sign of DoS attacks, and failed checksum data is a characteristic of forged packets.

Network Layer Protocol

You can choose from one of three layer four protocols to build your query. ICMP, TCP, and UDP are searchable. For TCP you can build a query that contains any number of the following three criteria:

- TCP Port. You can search for a specific source or destination port or range of ports. This is useful for zeroing in on possibly compromised services.

- TCP Flags. Returns alerts that match one or more of the eight TCP flags. For instance, if you wanted to search for an NMAP Xmas tree scan, you would select the FIN, URG, and PUSH flags.

- TCP Field Data. Build a query that matches specific TCP header field data. The TCP headers you can search for are Sequence Number, Acknowledgement Number, Data Offset, Reserved Bits, Window, Checksum, and Urgent Pointer. You can search for as many of the TCP field data elements you wish.

If you switch to UDP you can use either of the following criteria in a query:

- UDP Port. Similar to TCP port criteria, you can search for a specific source or destination port or range of ports.

- UDP Field Data. Used to create a search that contains either UDP length or checksum. Strange UDP lengths and failed checksums can be indicative of a specific tool or attack. For example, a UDP packet of length zero can be used to create a DoS situation on unpatched versions of the Raptor Firewall.

If you choose to include ICMP data in building your query, there is a single criteria element you can use repeatedly to build your search.

- ICMP Field Data. The field data stored in an ICMP header. You can search for Type, Code, Sequence number, ID, and Checksum. If, for example, you wanted to single out only ICMP echo requests to search for possible ICMP covert channels, you could set the Type field equal to eight.

Payload Data

You can search all alerts for strings of data stored in the packet payload. The payload contains data that the application layer program will make use of. Payloads can include everything from buffer overflows to Trojan traffic signatures. You will often want to identify specific strings or elements within a packet's payload. With ACID, you can enter in any type of string in either ASCII format or Hex. ACID will convert between the two formats, if requested, before executing the query.

Constructing Queries with Logical Operators

ACID uses an extended set of logical operators to build queries. The logical operators define the relationship between the criteria elements you have chosen to build the query. The logical operators help you further refine and pinpoint the exact alerts you want to view. The operators closely resemble the syntax of the SQL language. Not surprisingly, these operators are parsed into a SQL statement. The statement is executed by ACID to retrieve the alerts you want.

You will obviously be familiar with some operators, but some others are unique to ACID and most likely will be foreign to you. A listing of the operators and a description follows.

- = The familiar equality operator.
- != The inverse of the equality operator: the inequality operator.
- > Greater than.
- >= Greater than or equal to.
- < Less than.
- <= Less than or equal to.
- has A sub-string search relationship between the criteria and the user inputted string. If the user input matches any portion of data stored in a string, the alert is returned in query results. The has operator is not case-sensitive. In conversion to SQL syntax, the has will be converted to a LIKE for query execution. This operator is available only in the payload criteria section. For example, if you wanted to find any payload that attempted to access the Windows command executable, you would create a payload has statement that included the cmd.exe. Any alert that had cmd.exe in its payload would be returned. Additionally, alerts that contain

cMd.eXe would be returned, as would alerts that contain GET /scripts/
..%5c../winnt/system32/cmd.exe?/c+dir c+dir HTTP/1.0 in the payload. Using has for payload search strings is a good method of finding exact
strings within a group of similar alerts.

- has NOT   The inverse of the has operator. It has an inverse sub-string search
  relationship between the criteria and the user inputted string. If you included the
  has NOT operator in a payload search string, ACID would return every alert
  except alerts that matched the string. The cmd.exe would return everything but
  alerts that contained attempted Windows command executables are used in the
  packet payload.

- is   The selected criteria elements must match the user input exactly. This operator is used in the TCP flag criteria relationship. If you were to check one of the
  TCP flag check boxes, alerts would be returned that contained the selected flag
  and no others. For example, if you were to check both the SYN and FIN check
  boxes, alerts would be returned that contained exclusively SIN and FIN flags and
  no others. Alerts that contained SYN, FIN, and ACK flags would not be retuned.
  Similarly, packets that contained only a SIN flag would not be returned. It is easy
  to confuse the is logical operator with something that it is not. Make sure to
  remember that you will be returning only exactly what you have specified when
  using is.

- contains   This logical operator is used in the same criteria element as the is
  operator: TCP flags. The contains operator is not as strict as is. Any alert that is
  composed of the selected TCP flags and any other flags will be returned. For
  example, if you were to check both the SYN and FIN check boxes, alerts would be
  returned that contained SIN, FIN, and any other flags. Alerts that contained SYN,
  FIN, and ACK flags would be retuned. Packets that contained only a SIN flag
  would not be returned.

- exactly   This operator matches the contents of the user input exactly to the
  criteria to be queried. The exactly logical operator is used with the signature
  metadata criteria. It is not case-sensitive. For example, if you wanted to find only
  Code Red 2 root.exe access attempts with exactly you would enter WEB-IIS
  CodeRed v2 root.exe access to return Code Red version 2 root.exe access
  attempts. If you entered IIS the results would be an empty set.

- roughly   A sub-string search relationship between the criteria and the user
  inputted string. The roughly logical operator is similar to exactly in that it is
  used with signature metadata criteria. If the user input matches any portion of the
  data stored in a string, the alert will be returned in query results. The roughly
  operator is not case-sensitive. Like the has operator, in conversion to SQL syntax,
  the roughly logical operator will be converted to a LIKE for query execution.
  For instance, if you wanted to find every alert that was for Internet Information
  Server, you would use the roughly operator with iis as the input. This would

return every alert that had `iis` or `IIS` in the signature string. It would not match `Internet Information Server`.

An important fact to point out is that not all logical operators can be used in each criteria relationship. Sometimes an operator will not construct a valid SQL query or is not needed. Logical operators are hard-coded into ACID, so you do not have to concern yourself with possibly choosing an illegal operator. An example is the IP address criteria. You can search for IP addresses that are either equal to or not equal to an IP address or range of addresses you specify. The less than or greater than operators are not needed because you can use the CIDR notation to identify IP address ranges.

Any time more than one of the same criteria elements are used, another logical operator must be inserted for the query to execute. These are the AND and OR operators. They are used in specifying ranges of criteria. If you wanted to search a range of UDP ports, you would create one criteria indicating the lower bound, and the greater than operator and one criteria would indicate the upper bound with a less than operator (see Figure 8.3). To complete the query, you would use the AND operator to return only the range.

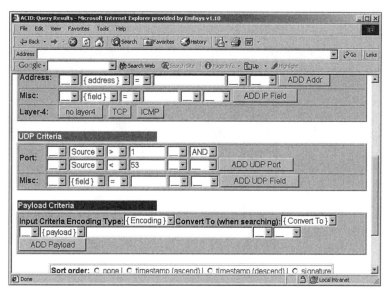

Figure 8.3 UDP port range query.

The OR operator is used to return alerts that match more than one criteria. If you wanted to match payloads that contained either `.ida` extension attempts or SAM file access attempts, you would construct the two payload criteria elements and use the OR operator to return alerts that contained both payloads. The query would look like Figure 8.4.

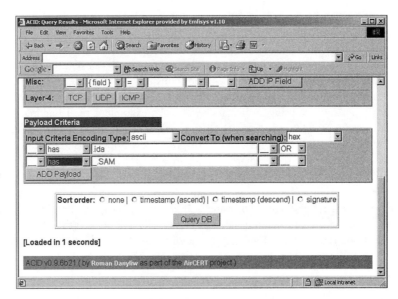

Figure 8.4   Returning two payload criteria.

You may have noticed the parentheses and underscores that precede and follow most of the criteria. These are used to establish precedence and are required when you use more than two instances of the same criteria.

Using the parentheses to indicate which portion of the query is executed first is simple after you understand how they work. Imagine you wanted to search for UDP destination ports that were between 1 and 1024. You also wanted to include port 5520 in the query. To make this query, you must use precedence and hence parentheses. First, let's take a look at the wrong way to create the query you want (see Figure 8.5).

This example leaves out the parentheses, so the SQL server cannot properly build the query. If you leave out the parentheses, or place them in the wrong order, the query is likely to fail to execute. You will get a list of descriptive SQL errors pertaining to the failed query. An example follows.

```
You have an error in your SQL syntax near '(AND(( (acid_event.ip_src>=2703692288
AND acid_event.ip_src<=2703692543))
(AND(( ' at line 1
```

You must establish which portions of the query will be executed first. You do so by changing the underscores to the appropriate parentheses (see Figure 8.6).

This will output the expected results of alerts containing UDP ports from 1–1024 and port 5520.

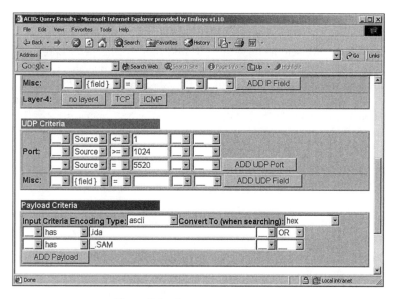

Figure 8.5   Incorrect query syntax.

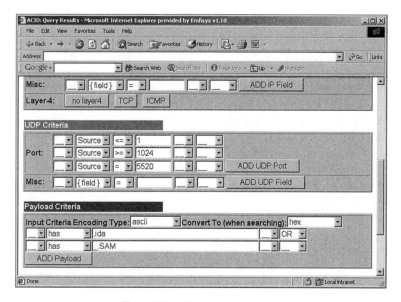

Figure 8.6   Correct query syntax.

Constructing ranges of time or single-time events is straightforward now that you are warmed up to ACID's logical operators. If you want to return alerts that occurred during a single instance of time (that is, a specific hour, day, month, or year), you would simply set the equality operator (=) and the time period you wanted. If you wanted to query all alerts that occurred before a certain date or time, you use the less than or equal to operator (<=). Conversely, if you wanted to find alert that happened after a certain point in time you would you use the greater than or equal to operator (>=). Constructing ranges of time is done in the same fashion as querying for ranges of ports. You utilize a greater than or equal to operator and a less than or equal to operator to mark the upper and lower bounds. Make sure to use the AND operator between the two time criteria. You can use the equality operator and the OR to search two or more specific points in time.

You can sort your query results in one of four different manners.

- None. Simply dump the alerts in the order in which they are stored in the intrusion database.

- Timestamp (ascend). Return alerts in ascending order according to the time they were generated.

- Timestamp (decend). Return alerts in descending order according to the time they were generated.

- Signature. Output alerts grouped alphabetically by signature.

Alert Groups

An *alert group (AG)* is a functionality of ACID that allows alerts to be clustered into a grouping you define. AGs can be used to gather multiple alerts that compose a security incident. Putting the puzzle pieces together from a successful or attempted intrusion requires the use of alert groups. If you were to find a compromised server you would then have to search back in ACID to find the alert for the attack. The alert would be added to a new AG. Then you could search for various other unsuccessful or successful attacks perpetrated by the same hacker. You then would add these alerts to the AG. You could even reach farther back into the intrusion database and find the reconnaissance and information gathering attacks and add these to the alert group. You would then have composed a working log of the security incident that you could readily access in the future. If you had not created the AG, it would be a painstaking process to return to the intrusion database and re-create the event each time you needed information pertaining to it.

You can also use AGs to insert your own comments or notes about the incident. The comments will be stored with the AG for future reference. You may save your AGs for a length of time and then have trouble piecing the incident back together. Comments are also useful to add as you build the incident and perform research.

An alert group can be as small as one alert or as large as the entire intrusion database. If you simply want to add additional documentation to a single alert, you can do this with alert groups. Alerts can also be a part of as many AGs as necessary. The actual alert is never modified when it is added to an AG.

An alert group has three metadata fields that describe and organize the AG:

- `ID Number`. A sequential numerical identifier assigned by ACID for the AG.
- `Name`. The name assigned to the alert group by the intrusion analyst.
- `Description`. An open text field to insert whatever comments and notes the analyst deems appropriate.

Creating and populating an AG is a simple task. From the Alert Group Maintenance menu, click on the Create link. This will bring you to the Create Group page. Here you can enter the short descriptive name of the AG and a description. Do not concern yourself with putting in accurate information at this point; you can always return and edit the Name and Description fields at a later point. You have now created the AG.

The next logical task is to fill the AG with alerts. For the sake of this example, we will simply dump the most recent alerts into the AG. Normally you would want to put together a more meaningful and logical group of alerts. Return back to the ACID home page and select the Most Recent Alerts link. You can also launch a query to fill your test AG if you want. From here switch to the Add to AG (by Name) on the dropdown combo box at the bottom of the page. Enter the name of the AG you created in the previous step, and click on the All on Screen button. All the alerts are placed into the new AG. If you have already put some of the alerts into the AG, it returns an error. The duplicate alerts are not inserted into the AG. This is a useful feature if you want to add new alerts in a query in a fast and easy manner without having to take the time to trim out duplicate alerts.

After you have added the alerts, switch back to the Alert Group Maintenance page. Select the new AG you have created and the alerts appear in the order they were added. At the bottom of the screen you can find the familiar action menu. You have four possible actions to perform on the AG:

- Delete Alerts. This action deletes alerts permanently from the intrusion database. Be careful—this does not simply remove the alerts from the AG; it removes them permanently from the Snort server.
- Email Alerts (full). This action emails the alerts to the email address configured in `acid_conf.php`. It emails a full description of the alerts, either in the email body or as an attachment. This is a quick and easy way to export data from ACID.
- Email Alerts (summary). Functionally the same as Email Alerts (full), but only a summary of alert information rather than the entire detailed packet capture.
- Clear from AG. This action removes the alerts from the current AG but does not delete them from the intrusion database.

If you return to the Alert Group Maintenance page, you can maintain the actual AGs themselves by clicking on the List All link. From here you can edit descriptions and AG names. You can also clear all the alerts from an AG, as well as remove the AG permanently.

Summary

The primary purpose of the console is to provide an isolated environment for you to perform intrusion detection duties and maintain the Snort components. If you or your organization can afford it, it is best to keep the analyst's console separate from all other applications and connected to just the monitoring segment. The two necessary components for the console are a Web browser and an SSH client. The console can use either a Linux or Microsoft OS. The ideal setup is a dual boot machine that has both OSs on separate partitions. The primary reason to have a Windows partition on the analyst's console is to make use of IDS Policy Manager.

After the console is installed, a real upgrading example is used to test the console. A layer of security is added to the Snort environment via `.htaccess` IP address restrictions. The `.htacess` file stored on the server is edited via an SSH connection from the console.

Next is a tutorial on the ACID management GUI. ACID provides detailed documentation that offers insight into a new or unrecognized alert. Each time an alert is displayed, links corresponding to the attack signature are displayed. The ACID search interface is fairly complex and extremely powerful. ACID assumes that the user is a technical person with the ability to build and execute complex logical queries. You construct queries by selecting the criteria to be searched on and the data to be searched for. ACID uses an extended set of logical operators to build queries. The logical operators define the relationship between the criteria elements you have chosen to build the query. Queries fail to execute if the logical operators chosen are incorrect.

ACID supports some internal documentation features and incident management components with alert groups. An alert group (AG) is a functionality of ACID that enables alerts to be clustered into a grouping you define. AGs can be used to gather multiple alerts that compose a security incident.

9

Additional Installation Methods

$\mathbf{S}$NORT IS A VERSATILE APPLICATION THAT CAN be implemented in a wide assortment of diverse platforms. You have walked through a Snort installation on a distributed Linux-based system in the previous three chapters. Although this Snort architecture is widely implemented and popular, it may not be the best option for you or your organization. In this chapter you will see some other ways to install Snort. This chapter is by no means comprehensive; it is meant to be a launching pad to get you going in the right direction.

All the Snort components can be installed on one machine. You may not have the hardware resources to spread the Snort deployment over three or more separate computers. It can be quite costly to deploy three or more machines at a small company or at home. If your organization has yet to see the proven benefit of an Intrusion Detection System, you may need to run a trial pilot with limited resources before a larger Snort installation is possible. In these cases you may wish to collapse the entire three-tiered structure down onto a single box. A hybrid server/sensor Snort installation is not much more difficult to put together than the distributed architecture. However, there are some security, performance, and scalability issues with the hybrid architecture.

Linux is one of many platform options you have for Snort. It is possible that you are more comfortable with a commercial Unix operating system, such as Solaris, or a different open source Unix OS, such as FreeBSD. There are numerous Snort installations on Solaris and HP-UX. Running Snort on a BSD variant has many of the same benefits of running on Linux. Or Unix administration may not be one of your strong skills, so you could also choose to use Windows for the underlying OS. Snort has also been ported to Windows, along with some of the programs required to run ACID.

The Hybrid Server/Sensor

Installing the hybrid server/sensor collapses all the Snort components for both the server and sensor onto a single computer. There is nothing inherently wrong with the hybrid setup; the end result is nearly the same as the distributed installation. Some benefits of a distributed Snort deployment must be given up, though, to create a hybrid server/sensor.

The hybrid makes your Snort installation much more difficult to scale. Placing intrusion monitoring throughout different locations in your network infrastructure becomes a hassle. Rather than simply install a sensor image on a new machine and insert a monitoring segment, you must find a way to bring the monitored network to the hybrid Snort machine. This may be as simple as plugging into an open port on a hub, or as complicated as installing an entirely new network infrastructure. If your organization is spread out over many physical or geographic locations, scaling Snort with the hybrid becomes extremely expensive and difficult. The most logical option would be to deploy another hybrid server/sensor, in which case you would have been better off starting with the three-tier architecture.

With the hybrid, the performance of your Snort application can be impacted by the other components. If you are archiving a MySQL database, which would consume most of the system resources, Snort may not have the processing power it needs to detect intrusions. This could cause Snort to drop packets and miss possible attacks. Having the components separated onto different functional tiers solves this problem.

The hybrid is less secure than a distributed Snort installation. Because the entire intrusion database is placed on the same machine as Snort, an attacker who compromises one component could have access to the entire Snort installation. The database will be placed in an environment with greater risk when connected directly to the monitored segment.

If these are all issues that you can live with, the hybrid is a logical choice for you. Additionally, the hybrid server/sensor makes a good test system to familiarize yourself with Snort.

You install the hybrid by implementing both the server and sensor setup on a single machine. For the sake of brevity, use the installation instructions in Chapters 6 and 7. Only what should be done differently is described in this section.

First of all, you should update Red Hat for security patches and bugs. Next, harden the hybrid with Bastille Linux, using the requirements for the server. You will not need the components used to establish secure communication between sensor and server. With this said, there is no need to install Stunnel or an additional MySQL client. You can skip these steps.

If you are not going to access the hybrid from a remote location via a console, you can eliminate the `OpenSSL`, `OpenSSH`, and `mod_ssl` components. With these components gone, compile Apache by using a different `configure` command:

```
./configure --prefix=/usr/local/apache --disable-module=status
```

You can skip the `make certificate` step as well.

When creating the `.htaccess` file, you should allow only users physically at a computer to be able to log into ACID. Do this by adding the local loopback address as the only valid address for authentication:

```
allow from 127.0.0.1
```

All the other steps should be followed according to the directions in Chapters 6 and 7.

Snort on OpenBSD

OpenBSD is one of many choices for a Unix-based operating system for Snort. OpenBSD has a reputation for adhering to the highest standards of security for an operating system. The goal of the OpenBSD team is to provide the most secure OS out of the box. The OpenBSD team performs comprehensive line-by-line analysis of every piece of software included with the OS. OpenBSD does not come with as many programs as other operating systems, but you can be sure that you are starting out with a secure system if you use OpenBSD. Because OpenBSD is not as popular as other variants of BSD, it can be difficult to find packages.

Before installing OpenBSD you should check to make sure the hardware you have is supported by OpenBSD. Unfortunately, OpenBSD does not support as many hardware devices as Linux or Windows. Check the supported hardware list for Intel architectures at

```
http://www.openbsd.org/i386.html
```

After you have verified that your hardware will function, go ahead and install OpenBSD. You can either order media directly from the development team or download a bootable floppy image. The OpenBSD team survives only by donations and CD media purchases, so it's not a bad idea to spend the $40 for the CD package. If you would rather download the OS, you can get it on any one of many FTP mirrors:

```
http://www.openbsd.org/ftp.html
```

After you have installed OpenBSD, run the `adduser` command to add the Snort user. This Snort user will run the Snort application instead of root. The user should have access to only the appropriate directories (such as logging and the like).

Create directories to hold the Snort application, logs, and configuration files:

```
/etc/snort/conf
```

```
/var/log/snort
```

```
/etc/snort/html
```

You can install software on OpenBSD via ports. The `ports` collection offers an easy automated method of installing applications, similar to that of RPMs in Linux. Although they are convenient, ports share some of the same disadvantages of RPMs. They lag behind current releases and do not always include the most desirable configuration options. Installing from source is a much better option. If you want to use the Snort port for OpenBSD, you can at

```
http://www.snort.org/dl/binaries/
```

You can install the ports by using the following command:

```
pkg_add snort-1.9.0-openbsd-3.1.tgz
```

After Snort is installed, download the .rules and .config files from

```
http://www.snort.org/dl/signatures/
```

Untar and move the files to the /etc/snort/conf dir. Open the main configuration file, snort.conf, for editing. Check out Chapter 7 for a full tutorial on setting the snort.conf file up. For a quick setup, change the following lines:

```
var HOME_NET any
```

```
var RULE_PATH /etc/snort/conf
```

Finally, uncomment all of the .rules files that have been commented out.

Snort is now installed. To start Snort in daemon mode execute the following command:

```
/usr/local/bin/snort -D -c /etc/snort/snort.conf
```

```
-i interface_name -u snort_user
```

SnortSnarf

To process the Snort logs we are going to make use of a Perl script, SnortSnarf. You could just as easily use the MySQL/ACID with OpenBSD. SnortSnarf can be used on a Linux system as well. In the effort to demonstrate that there are options other than MySQL and ACID, I use SnortSnarf to process intrusion data in this chapter.

SnortSnarf, created by Silicon Defense, parses Snort logfiles into HTML. You can serve the HTML up with a Web server to view logs remotely, or simply view them locally with a Web browser. Make sure you set up the appropriate security controls if you are going to make SnortSnarf files accessible via a Web server. SnortSnarf references the rules you have loaded in the snort.conf file. Download SnortSnarf from

```
http://www.silicondefense.com/software/snortsnarf/
```

```
Uncompress the tarball and change to the SnortSnarf directory. From here you will
have to install a time package, Time::JulianDay, that SnortSnarf requires. Switch
to the Time-modules directory and issues the following commands to install
Time::JulianDay.perl Makefile.PL
```

```
make
```

```
make install
```

After the time module is installed, you can run SnortSnarf to process the Snort alerts. Run SnortSnarf with the following command:

```
./snortsnarf.pl -rulesfile /etc/snort/snort.conf -dns
```

```
-d /etc/snort/html /var/log/snort/alert
```

This command will process the alert files located at /var/log/snort/alert and drop the HTML into /etc/snort/html. The -dns option resolves IP addresses to their corresponding domain names. Make sure you have a robust DNS server to point to, because the running of this script will place a large load on the server. It is common practice to automate the creation of the SnortSnarf HTML via a cron job. This reduces processing overhead and keeps the SnortSnarf files up to date.

Snort on Windows

For a long time, the only way to install Snort was on a Unix OS. Fortunately for Windows users, one of the two companies that built a business out of providing Snort-related support, Silicon Defense, put together a Windows port of Snort. This was done to bring Snort to a wider community of computer users. They also developed a binary distribution of Snort for Windows that will automate a good portion of the Snort installation process. I make use of the binary in this chapter to save time.

The Snort Windows port works only on Windows 2000, NT, and XP operating systems. The best choice for the Windows OS is Windows 2000 Professional. It is one of the most stable Windows OSs out of the box, and does not include superfluous software like the 2000 Server series. Windows 2000 Server, NT, and XP are not recommended.

The rest of this section provides a step-by-step guide to installing Snort on a Windows computer. All Snort components will be installed on the same machine in this example.

Setting Up the Windows Installation

To install Snort on Windows you must first start out with a clean installation of Windows 2000 Professional. Make sure to use a strong password when setting up the administrator account. After you have installed Windows, you need to update Windows via the Windows Update tool. Simply click the Start button and select Windows Update. You are taken to the Windows Update Web page, which has instructions for making Windows current.

Install the changes Windows Update recommends and let Windows reboot.

You should harden Windows before installing the Snort application. You can harden Windows via either a manual or semi-automated process. The SANS organization has a detailed hardening guide that you can use to manually harden Windows. Get the guide at

```
http://www.sans.org/SCORE/checklists/AuditingWindows2000.doc
```

You can also use a tool that will help identify the gaps between the current system and a secure state. The Center for Internet Security's Scoring Tool produces reports that detail the security settings you should implement. The tool is helpful for identifying patches required and secure policy discrepancies on the host system. Even with the tool, you still have to perform the lockdown steps manually. Download the Scoring Tool from

`http://www.cisecurity.org/bench_win2000.html`

A group of files and templates is available on this page. You should download the executable, `CIS-Win.exe`, which includes the entire package. It contains the Scoring Tool, policy templates, and detailed documentation.

The Scoring Tool includes the `HFNetChk` XML patch status tool developed by Shavlik Technologies in conjunction with Microsoft. `HFNetChk` checks the host's patch status and compares it with the master list of hotfixes and patches continuously updated by Microsoft. `HFNetChk` checks the patch list stored at Microsoft.com, so make sure to have the machine connected to the Internet behind a firewall. This is a great way to ensure that Snort will start out securely patched.

Run CIS-Win.exe to install the Scoring Tool.

After you have the Scoring Tool and the associated documentation installed, launch the program. It should present a window with the scoring program (see Figure 9.1).

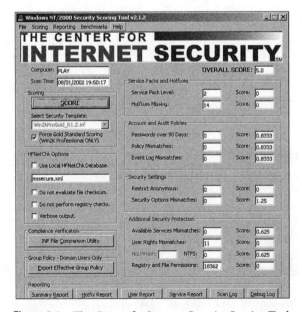

Figure 9.1   The Center for Internet Security Scoring Tool.

The intended purpose of the Scoring Tool is to generate a simple score that gives the user a quantitative number to use to judge the host's security posture. Although this is a useful feature, the most appropriate use is for identifying security gaps. Click on the INF File Comparison Utility button to compare the state of your Windows installation to the recommended security postures for a Windows host. For this example, I use the INFs compiled by the National Security Agency (NSA). Scroll down to the NSA-w2k_ server.inf file and click the Compare button. The Scoring Tool compares the settings on the host to the NSA recommended security controls. A report with the results opens in a browser. Use this guide to make the appropriate changes to the Registry and user permissions.

Next, click the Score button to start the scoring program. A certificate authorization dialog box should open up for the MSSecure XML File. This is used by the HFNetChk tool to update the list of security hotfixes and patches available from Microsoft. You need to accept the certificate for the Scoring Tool to run.

After the tool has completed its checks, it creates a number of reports you can use to bring Windows 2000 to a secure state. The two reports this example is concerned with are the Hotfix report and the Service report.

- Hotfix report. This report details which hotfixes and patches are not up-to-date for the Windows operating system and any other core Microsoft programs installed (such as Internet Explorer). The report should tell you whether the most recent Service Pack has been installed. It also offers links directly to the hotfixes that need to be installed. You should install every hotfix and patch available in the report.

- Service report. This report identifies any unusual services that are running on the host and may need to be disabled or removed. If any services are not needed, remove them (such as SNMP Agent).

Installing the Underlying Programs

You should now have a hardened Windows 2000 Professional machine primed for action. Several components are required for Snort to function. And other programs make using Snort a more pleasant experience.

Installing OpenSSH

OpenSSH is a open source implementation of the SSH protocol. SSH is used in place of insecure, antiquated protocols such as FTP and Telnet. For a more in-depth discussion of SSH and OpenSSH, refer to Chapter 6. You can use SSH to manage the Snort installation remotely.

Download the Windows port of OpenSSH at

```
http://www.networksimplicity.com/openssh/
```

Run the setup.exe file to install OpenSSH. Make sure both client and server check boxes are checked during the installation process. When completed, it installs the OpenSSH files for you and generates the DSA encryption key used for secure communication.

Before configuring and starting the OpenSSH service, you must reboot the computer. After the machine has booted, add a username and password for the account that you would like to use for accessing OpenSSH. You can add users in Windows 2000 Professional with the Users and Passwords tool located in the Control Panel. When the user is added, open a command prompt and navigate to the following directory:

```
cd \Program Files\networksimplicity\ssh
```

You must add the user you created with the Users and Passwords tool to the group of users allowed to access the Snort OpenSSH server. This is done with the `mkpasswd` tool, which adds users local to a Windows computer or domain to the OpenSSH server's list of permitted users. Add the Snort SSH user with this command:

```
mkpasswd -l -u snort_user >> ..\etc\passwd
```

The `-l` switch adds a local user to the Windows computer to the OpenSSH server. If this computer is part of a Windows Domain, could use the `-d` switch to add a domain user. You can now start OpenSSH as a service by using the following command from the command prompt:

```
net start opensshd
```

You should receive a message: `The OpenSSH Server service was started successfully`. You can now log in to the OpenSSH server remotely by using the user account you created.

Installing `WinPcap`

`WinPcap` is the Windows port of the `libpcap` packet capture library. It performs the same function as `libpcap`, capturing packets in their raw form. Snort needs `WinPcap` to sniff raw packets because it has no native raw packet capture utility.

Get WinPcap at

```
http://winpcap.polito.it/install/default.htm
```

Download the WinPcap autoinstaller (not the developer's pack), and run the executable. When WinPcap has been installed, reboot the computer.

Installing MySQL

MySQL is the most popular open source SQL database. MySQL is a relational database management system. MySQL is chosen because it is relatively fast, reliable, and easy to use. This example uses MySQL to store intrusion data that will be managed via the ACID application.

Download the MySQL Win32 binary at

```
http://www.mysql.com/downloads/mysql-3.23.html
```

Uncompress the zip file and run the `setup.exe` program to start the process. During the installation process, be sure to choose Typical for the MySQL type.

Navigate to `c:\mysql\bin` and run the `winmysqladmin.exe` program. `WinMySQLadmin` is a graphical interface for managing MySQL that is easy to use. It can be used to control most of the settings for MySQL, including the creation of databases. You can also use it to create reports on data stored in any of the databases.

When you first start `WinMySQLadmin`, you have to create a username and password to log in. Create a user named `snort` and a password. The Snort application uses this username and password combo to log in to the database.

After creating the user, click on the `my.ini` Setup tab. In the lower left corner is a Create ShortCut on Start Menu button. Click this button to have MySQL and WinMySQLadmin start when Windows boots up.

Next it's time to create the actual intrusion database. Click on the Databases tab (see Figure 9.2).

Figure 9.2 `WinMySQLadmin` creating a database.

This example uses snortdb for the name of the database. You can choose a different name if it suits you, make sure to remember the name you chose; you will need it later.

You need to log in to MySQL and set the permissions for the Snort user you created previously. You must access MySQL via the command line to change permissions. Open a command prompt and go to the `C:\MySQL\bin` directory. Run the following command to access MySQL:

```
mysql
```

After you have entered the `mysql>` prompt, change to the database that holds the user account information:

```
use mysql
```

Now, grant privileges the Snort user requires.

```
grant insert, select, create, on snortdb.* to snort_user@localhost;
```

You need to create the Snort database structure on the snortdb database. A script that will automatically create the database for you is included in the Snort source code distribution. Download the Snort source code from

```
http://www.snort.org/dl/
```

Uncompress the `.tar.gz` file. If you are having trouble opening the file, download WinRAR from

```
http://www.rarlab.com/download.htm
```

WinRAR can open almost every type of compression. You can use it free for 30 days. In the Snort source distribution you will find a Contrib folder. There is a scripted called `create_mysql`, which creates all the necessary tables and database structures for Snort. Copy `create_mysql` to the `c:\mysql\bin\` directory. Open a command prompt again and run the script with the following command:

```
mysql -u snort snortdb < c:\mysql\bin\create_mysql
```

You can check to make sure the script ran correctly by viewing the snortdb database with the `WinMySQLadmin` tool.

MySQL is now installed and configured.

Installing Apache

Apache is a Web server, originally designed for Unix OSs. This chapter uses the Windows version of Apache. Apache is open source and free of cost, so you do not have to purchase Windows 2000 Server to run a Web server. Additionally, it is more secure and stable than Microsoft IIS. This does not mean that IIS cannot be secured; it is just more work. If you are an expert with IIS, you can secure it, install the PHP module, and make use of ACID.

In this chapter, Apache is used to serve the Web-based ACID program up via a browser. Get the latest Apache `.msi` binary from

```
http://www.apache.org/dist/httpd/binaries/win32/
```

The `.msi` binary makes use of the Windows installer to complete the installation process.

The installer asks you traditional licensing questions and then takes you to the server information step. Here you should enter the server information as you see fit. It is important to check the Run as a Service for All Users radio button. This automatically starts Apache when Windows boots and runs Apache as a service independent of the logged on user. Finish the installation process by leaving the default settings intact.

After you have Apache installed, you need to create a few directories for PHP and ACID to reside in. Create the following directories:

```
c:\php
```

```
c:\php\acid
```

```
c:\phpapp
```

```
c:\adodb
```

After you have created these directories, open the Apache configuration file, `httpd.conf`, with WordPad. It is located in this directory:

```
c:\Program Files\Apache Group\Apache\Conf
```

You can also access `httpd.conf` by selecting Start, Programs, Apache HTTP Server, Configure Apache Server, Edit The `httpd.conf` Configuration File.

Enable the Word Wrap option for easier viewing. The fastest and least frustrating way to edit the `httpd.conf` file is by searching for particular strings. `Httpd.conf` is quite large and it takes a long time to find individual configuration lines. The first string to search for is `ServerName`. Find the following line:

```
#ServerName new.host.name
```

And change it to the following:

```
ServerName localhost
```

Next, search for `DocumentRoot` and add the following line:

```
DocumentRoot c:/php
```

Search down the `httpd.conf` file for the string, LoadModule. Here you will find a list of LoadModule directives. You need to add PHP scripting support to Apache, so add the following line to the end of the list:

```
LoadModule php4_module "modules/php4apache.dll"
```

Below the `LoadModules`, you will find a section composed of `AddModules`. Insert the following line to add PHP support:

```
AddModule mod_php4.c
```

Next search for `AddType` and add the following lines to the `AddType` list:

```
ScriptAlias /php4/ "C:/phpapp/"
AddType application/x-httpd-php .php
AddType application/x-httpd-php .php3
AddType application/x-httpd-php .php4
Action application/x-httpd-php "/php4/php.exe "
```

Apache is now installed.

Installing PHP

PHP started as a small project to improve a personal home page (which is where PHP comes from) and grew into one of the most powerful and popular Web scripting languages. PHP is an alterative to ASP and JSP that uses familiar C language syntax. ACID is written in PHP, so you must install it for ACID to function.

Get PHP Win32 binaries from

```
http://www.php.net/downloads.php
```

Make sure to download the current PHP zip package, not the Windows installer. Extract the files to the directory you created, called `c:\phpapp`. In this directory you will find a file named `php.ini-dist`. Rename this file to `php.ini`. Open this file for editing with WordPad. Search for the `doc_root` line. Change this line to read as follows:

```
doc_root = c:\php
```

Search again for `extension_dir`. Change it to the following:

```
extension_dir = c:\phpapp
```

Save the file and exit. Now you need to move some of the PHP files to their final resting place. Move the `php.ini` file to

```
C:\winnt\
```

To avoid confusion, it is best to actually move the `php.ini` rather than simply copy it. If you were to copy to the new location, you might get confused as to which `php.ini` was being interpreted by PHP. Now move `php4ts.dll` to

```
C:\winnt\system32\
```

Finally, move `php4apache.dll` to

```
C:\Program Files\Apache Group\Apache\Modules
```

PHP is now installed.

Installing ADODB

The database access functions for PHP are not standardized. Each database type (MySQL, PostgreSQL, Oracle, and so on) has a different method of accessing the individual database with PHP. To develop PHP code that can access many different types of databases, a library must be used to provide a generic interface for all databases. The library that offers generic database access is the ADODB library. Get ADODB from

```
http://php.weblogs.com/ADODB
```

Place ADODB into a directory (such as `c:\adodb`).

Next you need to edit the ADODB configuration file, `adodb.inc.php`. You must let ADODB know where it is located within the file system. Open this file with a text editor and find the line that contains the following:

```
$ADODB_DIR = dirname(__FILE__);
```

Change this line to reflect the directory where you have placed ADODB.

```
$ADODB_DIR = 'c:\adodb\';
```

Save the file and exit. ADODB installation is complete.

Installing ACID

The Analysis Console for Intrusion Databases (ACID) is the primary means you have to interact with Snort data. You will do most of your intrusion detection work through ACID. As previously stated, ACID is a PHP-based analysis engine. It is designed to process a database of security events generated by security devices, such as IDSs and firewalls.

ACID installation is fairly simple. Go to the ACID homepage:

```
http://www.andrew.cmu.edu/~rdanyliw/snort/snortacid.html
```

Uncompress the file and place the files in the directory you created for ACID, c:\php\acid. Open the `acid_conf.php` file for editing.

```
$DBlib_path = "c:\adodb";

$Dbtype = "mysql";

$alert_dbname = "snortdb";

$alert_host = "localhost";

$alert_port = "";

$alert_user "snort_user";

$alert_password "snort_password";
```

Where snort_user and snort_password are the username and passwords used to authenticate to the database. Save the file and exit. ACID is now configured and installed.

Installing the Snort Application

Installing Snort on Windows is made easy with the precompiled binary. Get the latest Snort Windows binary from

```
http://www.silicondefense.com/techsupport/downloads.htm
```

Make sure to download the binary with MySQL support, not the bare bones release. Uncompress the zip file and move the components into the following directories:

- Move snort.exe and snort.conf into c:\snort
- All .rules and .config files into c:\snort\rules
- Create a logging directory: c:\snort\logs

Next you need to configure Snort via the `snort.conf` file. Open `snort.conf` in WordPad. You need to specify the range of IP addresses that you want to monitor for intrusions. Do this via the $HOME_NET variable. You can specify a range of IP addresses in CIDR format or monitor all traffic using any. Start with the following line; you can always change it later:

```
var HOME_NET any
```

Next you need to let Snort know the location of the `.rules` files. This is done with the RULE_PATH line. Change the RULE_PATH line to read:

```
var RULE_PATH c:/snort/rules
```

Notice the required use of the Unix forward slash. Next you must set Snort to log to the MySQL database. Simply add this output plugin to do so:

```
output database: log, mysql, user=snort_user password=snort_password

dbname=snortdb host=localhost
```

For the last step you need to show Snort the correct location of `classification.conf` and `reference.config`. Prepend the `RULE_PATH` variable to both lines:

```
include $RULE_PATH/classification.config
include $RULE_PATH/reference.config
```

You now have the required settings for the `snort.conf` file. If you wish to delve deeper into the configuration options for `snort.conf`, check out the detailed description in Chapter 6.

You should now have fully functional Snort installation. Start Snort from the command line:

```
snort -c c:\snort\snort.conf -l C:\snort\logs -i1
```

The `-c` specifies the location of the `snort.conf` file to use; the `-l` identifies the location of the logging directory. Pay close attention to the `-i`: It is the NIC to use for sniffing. You can find the NIC number of the sniffing interface by executing an `ipconfig /all`. To stop the Snort process, you must kill it via the Task Manager.

Installing IDScenter

IDScenter is a management tool specifically designed for Snort Windows installations. IDScenter has a graphical interface to Snort's configuration files and provides some additional functionality not included with the Snort binary. Before IDScenter, a lot of these ancillary features required manual scripting.

IDScenter has some built-in alert notification features. You can set it up to notify you of important alerts via an audible alarm, email, or any external program you wish to run. IDScenter can be set to compress and rotate log files automatically. This can help you conserve space and save time when managing Snort.

IDScenter has a configuration wizard you can use to set variables, enable and configure preprocessors, and set output plugins in the `snort.conf` file. You should have the basic settings in place, but you can use this wizard to tune Snort at a later time. It also supports an easy point-and-click interface for the Snort ruleset. You can easily add, delete, or modify rules. IDScenter can be configured to restart the Snort process if it were to crash.

Additionally, IDScenter supports some more risky and dangerous settings. You can configure it automatically to block addresses via BlackIce or run a script to reconfigure routers or firewalls. The danger with enabling these functions is that an attacker could set off alerts from spoofed IP addresses that are needed for legitimate activity. The attacker could send attacks that would block external DNS servers, corporate partners, and so on. False positives could have the same effect.

Get IDScenter at

`http://www.packx.net/packx/html/en/idscenter/index-idscenter.htm`

Uncompress and install IDScenter. When it is installed you will see a icon in the system tray that represents IDScenter. Double-click it to bring up the program (see Figure 9.3).

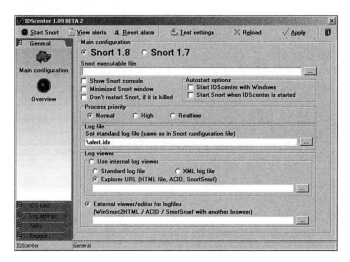

Figure 9.3   The IDScenter application.

From the General tab you have two options: Main Configuration and Overview.

Click on Main Configuration. Set the location of the Snort executable file, `c:\snort\snort.exe`. Next, check these three check boxes:

- Show Snort Console
- Start IDScenter with Windows
- Start Snort when IDScenter Is Started

Autostarting is a good idea; if the Snort machine ever reboots, Snort will continue to function. Next, set the Snort process to High. This will give it resource priority over other applications. Set the logfile location to `c:\snort\logs\alert.ids`.

Move to the Overview button. From here you can see any of the errors that the Snort process generates. The only setting you have to configure is the Snort command line option. Set it to

```
snort.exe -c c:\snort\snort.conf -l c:\snort\logs -i1
```

Next, click on the IDS Rules tab. Set the Configuration file line equal to

```
c:\snort\conf\snort.conf
```

On this tab you can set network variables, preprocessors, output plugins, and rules files. The network variables section automatically brings up IP addresses assigned to the Snort computer. It also helps you build CIDR address ranges. You can also set up pre-processors to your liking in this section. It is recommended that you turn every pre-processor on. Later, as you tune Snort, you can remove or configure those that are generating too many false positives.

The output plugins should already have been created when you edited `snort.conf` manually. Select the Rules/Signatures button and use the check boxes to enable every `.rules` file. Again, we will trim the ruleset considerably in Chapter 10.

The log settings can be used to append command line options to the Snort command. You can also use the logging parameters to log to the Windows Event Log. This is useful if you regularly monitor the Event Log. If you click on the Log Rotation button you can access the Snort log rotation and compression facility. By enabling log rotation, you can save disk space and automatically archive Snort logs for future reference. IDScenter will rotate through 10 different logs. After it reaches the 10th log, it overwrites the first log. You can set the log rotation time interval to one that suits your needs.

Move to the Alerts tab to configure the IDScenter real-time notification facility. Check the Database Alert Detection check box and fill in the corresponding fields. With IDScenter, you have four choices for real-time notification. You can enable as many of these as you see fit.

Audible Alert

You can choose to be notified via a sound when IDScenter picks up on an alert. This feature is useful only if you are constantly in the same physical location as the hybrid Snort device. It is more of a novelty than a useful feature. You can choose to either sound a default beep or set the audible alert to the `.wav` file of your choice.

Program Execution

IDScenter can be configured to run a particular script or executable. You can create a list of commands and store them in a batch file to be executed. You could possibly reconfig-ure network devices, activate a paging program, or take any other action you would like.

Block Traffic with BlackIce

BlackIce is a simple home-use IDS and firewall combination program. It is relatively inexpensive (less than $50 U.S.), and can be used to block traffic from a particular address. This function works only if traffic is routed directly through the hybrid server/sensor, or if you have installed Snort to monitor for intrusions on a single machine. This could be used to turn Snort into a psuedo-HIDS for Windows machines.

Configuring BlackIce to block IP addresses that generate alerts is generally a bad practice. If an attacker discovered that you were blocking addresses that generated alerts, she could send forged malicious packets that had the source IP address of a vital network component. Doing this would create a DoS situation. Even if the packets were created by legitimate traffic, false positives could create the same DoS situation. We will examine using Snort as an "intrusion prevention" application in the Advanced Topics section in Chapter 14.

Alerts via Email

IDScenter supports the real-time delivery of alerts via email. You can specify as many email addresses to receive alerts as need be. You have two options for email alert delivery. You can attach the entire alert file to the email. This option is acceptable for low-alerting environments where the alert file is not large. Another option is to simply append a pre-set number of lines in the file to the body of the email. Setting this option to 20 ensures that you get a good look at the traffic that is generating an alert.

Summary

This chapter presented some of the alternative methods of installing Snort. Three popular methods of installing Snort that are different from the distributed Linux setup were detailed. There are unique tools available for the different setups.

Snort can be installed as a hybrid server/sensor. In this situation, all the Snort components are collapsed onto a single machine. Some benefits of a distributed Snort deployment must be given up to create a hybrid server/sensor. Scalability, performance, and security are compromised when using the hybrid installation.

OpenBSD is one of many choices for a Unix-based operating system for Snort. OpenBSD has a reputation for adhering to the highest standards of security for any OS. This makes OpenBSD a prime choice for a Snort installation. Installing Snort on OpenBSD is detailed, as well the SnortSnarf. SnortSnarf is Perl script that parses Snort logs and outputs HTML. It is also used to resolve IP addresses to their corresponding domain names.

The third and final installation method illustrated in this chapter is Snort deployed on Windows. Installing Snort on Windows is done via a compiled binary supplied by Silicon Defense. Snort is installed with MySQL, Apache, and ACID. This gives nearly the same functionality as a Unix-based installation.

IDScenter is an application developed specifically for Snort on Windows. It enables you to easily add ancillary functionality, such as real-time alerting. IDScenter provides a GUI for setting up most of the Snort functions. IDScenter can provide real-time alerting via an audible alert, external script, BlackIce integration, or email.

10

Tuning and Reducing
False Positives

TUNING AND REDUCING FALSE POSITIVES IS A TASK that you will have to undertake for almost every situation in which Snort is used to monitor for intrusions. Tuning Snort has become increasingly important in recent years as the number of possible attacks increases, along with the amount of bandwidth Snort is expected to monitor. As time progresses, more network-based attacks and IDS evasion techniques will be discovered, requiring additional rules and preprocessors to detect them. These additional features will cause an even greater resource strain for the Snort application. The use of computer networks to perform business tasks is increasing as well. Even with the collapse of the late 90s "New Economy," bandwidth usage at most organizations is growing at a meteoric rate. Snort will have to monitor an increased amount of bandwidth as time progresses. Both of these factors contribute to the increased importance of tuning Snort.

If Snort has been built and configured in the manner described in the previous chapters, you will have a totally de-tuned Snort installation on your hands. In this setup, Snort is configured to have the absolute minimum amount of false negatives at the expense of considerable number of false positives. This setup is an ideal starting point, from which you can build to create a completely tuned Snort installation.

It's important to keep in mind that you should resort to trimming Snort's functionality (rules, traffic delivered to Snort, and so on) only if Snort is dropping packets. This chapter assumes that you have enabled the default settings described in previous chapters, and Snort has been overwhelmed.

The tuning process has two goals. The first is to reduce the number of packets dropped to negligible amount or zero. The second is to reduce the number of false positives to one you can manage, without compromising Snort's ability to detect malicious traffic. Reducing dropped packets to zero is the priority. Snort is of little use if it is unable to intercept potentially hostile traffic. For this reason you must first get Snort working in a manner where it is not dropping packets and then move on to reducing false positives.

Identifying the number of false positives that is considered manageable is really left up to you. If you can handle paging through hundreds of pages of false alarms in ACID, you need to ensure only that Snort is not dropping packets. Most Snort users are busy people and would like to reduce the amount of erroneous information that Snort generates. False positives are a burden, in addition to the time they waste. If you configure Snort for real-time monitoring, you could potentially react to a false alarm and damage your own credibility, as well as that of the IDS. False positives also distract you from real security events and eventually lead to frustration and possibly disinterest in intrusion detection.

The act of tuning Snort is actually a matter of configuring Snort to ignore certain types of traffic. Right now, Snort should be configured to detect every attack it possibly can. The goal of the tuning process is to pinpoint segments of the total detectable alerts that are highly prone to false positives and unlikely to generate a real alert. You then remove these segments of traffic from the range of possible attacks, allowing Snort to concentrate on segments that are more likely to contain real attacks.

This process of refining the Snort configuration options to yield a highly tuned Snort deployment is an iterative one. Because there is no reliable method to test a Snort installation in isolation, you must place the sensor on a live production network to receive relevant alerting data. You then should tune a component of Snort, place it back on the production network, and observe the changes. Cycling through the tuning steps in this method is the only way to accurately tune Snort.

Because of the infinite range of possible network configurations, every Snort tuning process is different. A type of traffic that generates an enormous number of false positives for one network may remain completely quiet on another. This chapter focuses on general best practices for tuning Snort and offers concrete examples when useful. And remember, you should always prioritize your better judgment over something written in a book that is intended for a general audience.

Pre-Tuning Activities

After you have Snort installed and running, it is advisable to check whether Snort is dropping packets. There is no way to determine whether Snort is in a packet loss situation automatically. Additionally there is no feature to alert you if this precarious situation is occurring. As of now, no IDS currently supports this functionality, but it is likely to be implemented by many different vendors in the near future. You can force the Snort process to display status information on Linux systems with the following command:

```
killall -USR1 snort
```

This sends status information to the standard output or syslog for any process named snort. You could optionally specify the exact Snort daemon by specifying the process ID (PID), found by issuing this command:

```
ps ax | grep snort
```

You can then display status with this command, which works on most Unix-based systems:

```
kill -SIGUSR1 snort_PID
```

Snort then dumps its internal statistics to the screen or syslog. If you are working with Red Hat, you can read the syslog messages at /var/log/messages.

If you move the Snort process to the foreground or never placed it in the background (by appending the & symbol), you should get a screen that looks like Figure 10.1.

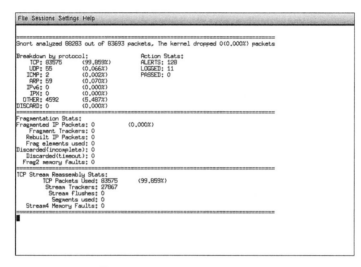

Figure 10.1   Snort internal statistics.

Don't concern yourself with the bulk of the information displayed; you should be concerned with only the first two lines at the moment. They should tell you the number of packets Snort has processed since the daemon was started and the percentage that have been dropped. You hope the percentage you are looking at is 0. If not, you have some work cut out for you. If you have a small percentage, such as .01 (1 in 10,000), of dropped packets, you may be able to get away with a small number of dropped packets. Another way to think of the dropped packets percentage is that it's saying you are potentially missing the reported percentage of attacks.

The most fundamental change you can make to improve Snort's performance and to reduce packet loss is to make use of Barnyard to process alerts. If you are not making use of the Snort Unified format for outputting and outsourcing the posting of alerts via Barnyard, and Snort is dropping packets, you should do so now. Check in Chapter 7 for the Barnyard installation process.

> **Note**
> First resorting to Barnyard for performance gains assumes that Snort is running on a computer specifically
> dedicated to Snort (a sensor). If there are other applications running on the same machine, you should
> inspect them for memory and processor use, and consider outsourcing resource-intensive applications to a
> different computer.

After you have Barnyard installed, you should run Snort for a period of time to collect a reasonable number of alerts. After Snort has run, force the process to display internal statistics again to view the packet loss percentage. If Snort has ceased to drop packets, you can concentrate on reducing false positives at this point. Otherwise you will have to perform additional tuning by configuring preprocessors, rulesets, and other activities described throughout this chapter.

Tuning the Network for Snort

One of the most basic approaches to tuning Snort is to change the amount and type of data that is delivered to a Snort sensor. Certain types of traffic consume a disproportionate amount of bandwidth for the amount of malicious traffic contained within them. If you are looking to remove segments of traffic from reaching Snort, these are potential candidates.

Multicast traffic is such a category of traffic. Streaming media applications, such as Real or Windows Media, often make use of multicasting to reduce the bandwidth required to present such data. Multicast traffic is more efficient for streaming media applications because a streaming media server will not have to service each client connection individually. The details of multicast traffic are out of the scope of this book; the issue relevant to Snort tuning is that multicast traffic is bandwidth intensive and is less likely to harbor malicious traffic.

Some switch vendors, such as Cisco and Nortel, have a line of switches that can be configured not to forward multicast traffic. You can simply create an access control list that filters the offending traffic. Some specific products can even stipulate on which port not to send multicast traffic. The SPAN port the sensor is attached to could be configured to not forward multicast. Doing so should reduce the amount of traffic Snort has to process.

Removing multicast traffic at the network level, before it is sniffed by Snort, can dramatically reduce the amount of traffic Snort has to process. This is largely dependent on how much multicast traffic your network has. Traditional multicast applications such as the aforementioned streaming media applications can be blocked, as well as other products that make use of multicast traffic. An example of an additional application that makes use of multicast is Symantec's Ghost Enterprise Edition. Ghost uses multicast to simultaneously deploy a single image to many different computers efficiently.

You could implement the filtering of multicast traffic at the kernel or Snort level, but you would still cause a resource drain on the Snort machine. Outsourcing the filtering of traffic to another device frees up the resources of the sensor, and should be used whenever possible.

Other types of traffic can be filtered with network components to reduce the amount of traffic delivered to Snort. If there is a range of IP addresses that you do not need to monitor, you should by all means filter this traffic before it hits the Snort sensor. If a specific group of hosts generates a disproportionate number of false positives, and you can afford to not monitor traffic originating from them for malicious traffic, you should configure the switch to drop packets from the hosts before it reaches the sensor port.

If Snort is still dropping packets, you should consider filtering out encrypted network traffic. Snort cannot process encrypted traffic content, which makes it a prime candidate for filtering. Any attack that utilizes content, such as remote buffer overflow attacks and some DoS attacks, will be encrypted and not detected by Snort. Such encrypted attacks are best discovered by a HIDS.

Attacks that make use of protocol inconsistencies, such as sending traffic with both the same source and destination address, can still be detected by Snort when traffic is encrypted. Attacks that happen before authentication is completed or before encryption is enabled can be detected as well. Again, filtering out encrypted traffic is a decision you have to make after taking into account the range of monitoring you want in place at your organization. If you are likely to receive an attack from a host that utilizes encrypted traffic, you should not implement this type of filtering.

If you do not have the capability of filtering traffic at the network level, methods of doing so with Snort are covered in the next section.

Filtering Traffic with Snort

There are two methods of limiting the source of traffic that Snort processes. You can create BPF (Berkeley Packet Filter) statements, which Snort uses to restrict the source of traffic it will process. Alternatively, you can configure the network variables in the Snort configuration file to limit traffic Snort processes.

Restricting the amount of traffic Snort must process naturally reduces the amount of work Snort has to do. If there are hosts that do not need intrusion detection coverage, you can filter them out with BPFs or network variables. These filtering methods can be used to ignore a host or range of hosts that are creating too much false positive noise.

Network Variables

Configuring Snort's network variables is a fairly straightforward and simple method of tuning Snort. Although it is not as effective as trimming and reorganizing the ruleset, tuning the network variables makes a noticeable difference in packet loss and excessive false positive situations. You can access the network variables in the `snort.conf` file.

If you were not able to filter unwanted IP addresses or IP address ranges with a network device, you can make use of the HOME_NET variable to define the ranges to be monitored. You can use HOME_NET to filter out hosts that create excessive false positives or encrypted traffic, as well as hosts you do not want or need to monitor for intrusions. Remember, HOME_NET is used to specify internal addresses to be checked for intrusions.

Filtering with HOME_NET still requires the packets to be loaded into Snort and then dropped, so there is a performance difference between using HOME_NET and a network device to filter traffic.

If there are external hosts to your network that you like to exclude from monitoring, you can make use of the EXTERNAL_NET variable. Set EXTERNAL_NET to hosts from which you would like to monitor traffic.

To reduce false positives and conserve resources you should attempt to find the addresses of as many HTTP, SMTP, SQL, and DNS services as possible. Beyond the obvious Web servers used for traditional means, you should take care to identify Web servers that are used for remote management and other duties. Some printers, firewalls, routers, and other network devices make heavy use of Web servers for remote management. SMTP servers are sometimes located on proxy servers and other mail filtering servers and devices, so they should be included in the list as well. It is important to identify both obvious and less obvious locations for DNS servers, such as Windows 2000 active directory servers. Even though they are not actual DNS servers, other network management stations that create a huge number of portscan false positives should be added to the DNS list. When you have a comprehensive list complied, insert these values into the corresponding network variables in the snort.conf file.

After you have made these changes you should let Snort process traffic for a period of time. After a representative example of the traffic you are going to monitor has been processed by Snort, check to see whether packets are still being dropped. You should also check to see whether false positives have been reduced to a level that you can manage.

BPFs

Berkeley Packet Filters (BPFs) function by filtering out traffic at the libpcap level, meaning they are removed long before Snort processes them. The standard BPF syntax can be used with Snort.

Snort can accept BPF statements by either appending them to the Snort command line or via a file. If you have only one BPF statement to add, it is easier to simply append it to the Snort command line. If you wanted to ignore traffic from 192.168.1.1 and 10.0.0.1, you execute the Snort command like so:

```
snort <other options> not (host 192.168.1.1 or host 10.0.0.1)
```

If you have a long list of BPF statements, then a file is a better option. Let Snort know you want to use a BPF file with the -F filename option at the command line. The new Snort command line could look like the following:

```
snort <other options> -F filters.bpf
```

Note

The −F option is capitalized.

You then create a carriage return–delimited list of filters and name it `filters.bpf`. BPFs are useful in that you can identify a particular protocol to ignore. You can get even more granular by choosing to ignore a particular protocol from a host or range of hosts. To ignore ICMP echo requests from 192.168.1.1, you could add the following line to a BPF file:

```
not (icmp[0] = 8 and host 192.168.1.1)
```

Tuning the Preprocessors

If you are still dropping packets at this point you will have to make some configuration changes to the preprocessors. The first and most important task to perform when tuning the preprocessors is to ensure that you have sufficient memory allocated for the preprocessors. Without the correct memory reserved, certain preprocessors can be placed in a situation where they are not processing every packet that Snort sniffs. This is functionally equivalent to the preprocessor being disabled for a percentage of the time. Attacks that need a preprocessor to be discovered could easily slip by. This is worsened by attacks that span many packets: If a preprocessor does not have enough memory to normalize one packet out of a range of packets, Snort could miss out on the entire attack. It is possible that an attack could be spread out over hundreds of packets, and if the preprocessor were unable to normalize one of the hundreds because of insufficient memory allocation, the attack would pass by Snort unnoticed. Other tasks, such as determining the proper resources made available for particular preprocessors and tuning them to avoid false positives are covered in this section as well.

bo

A good place to start when tuning preprocessors is with `bo`. `bo` is a resource-intensive preprocessor that rarely detects malicious activity in the wild. A simple option that can result in significant performance gains is to turn off the brute forcing of Back Orifice–encrypted traffic keyspace. The `nobrute` option is fairly easy to implement: Simply append the `-nobrute` option to the `bo` preprocessor directive.

Another possibility is to completely comment out the `bo` preprocessor to eliminate any overhead caused by `bo`. If your organization has a well-maintained antivirus solution that is proven to be applied to every computer, this may be an option because Back Orifice is detected by almost every major antivirus software package.

`arpspoof`, `asn1_decode`, and `fnord`

The `arpspoof`, `asn1_decode`, and `fnord` preprocessors are not as robust as other preprocessors. These preprocessors consume a disproportionate number processor cycles for the malicious activity coverage they provide. They are more likely to create false positives and negatives than the other, more stable, preprocessors. Like `bo`, these are good candidates for removal if not needed.

It is likely that `arpspoof`, `asn1_decode`, and `fnord` will be solidified in the near future or depreciated and no longer included in the Snort source. If one of these preprocessors creates a flood of false positives, it would be prudent to disable it until they are further refined.

There are some situations that are likely to lead to false positives for these preprocessors. The `asn1_decode` preprocessor generates false positives for a wide variety of traffic, including harmless SNMP and SSL traffic. Many vendors have poor implementations of these protocols that violate the Abstract Syntax Notation One protocol. Violating the protocol in certain methods causes `asn1_decode` to report an attack.

`Fnord` detects polymorphic shellcode by searching for a long string of no operation commands or commands that have the same function as a no operation. Large binary files, such as email attachments, are likely to set off an alert from `fnord`.

frag2

Some of the preprocessors, such as `frag2`, receive a limited amount of use unless the network protected by Snort is under attack from a specific type of attack. To realistically gauge how Snort will handle such an attack you have to create a similar type of attack against your network. As an example, we will perform a fragmentation attack by using fragroute, a tool designed to create a wide variety of different fragmentation attacks. Before we do any kind of serious stress testing, though, you should examine `frag2` to see whether it can handle fragmentation on your network without the fragroute attack. Although it is unlikely you will ever need to monitor a network that regularly exceeds the amount of memory set aside for `frag2`, it is worth taking a few minutes to make sure.

Run the usual `killall -USR1 snort` command to view Snort's internal statistics. You should see a section entitled `Fragmentation Stats:`. This section reports `frag2`'s efficiency. The section you are concerned with is the memory faults counter. If the `frag2` memory faults counter reports a value greater than zero, you do not have enough memory allocated for `frag2`. Memory faults occur when there is not enough memory reserved for `frag2`. To remedy this, track down the `frag2` configuration line in the `snort.conf` file and increase the `memcap` value. Increase it by one million bytes and then retest until you are no longer reporting memory faults.

We are now going to test to see how your Snort application functions under a fragmentation attack. To run the fragmentation tool, fragroute, you need to download and install three dependencies: `libdnet`, `libpcap`, and `libevent`. Fragroute and the dependencies are available only in source code form. You should be well versed in installing Linux packages from source after building the Snort tiers, therefore detailed information will not be provided. (Learning how to install from source instead of RPMs does have advantages.) You can get `libdnet` at

http://libdnet.sourceforge.net/

Simply configure, make, and make install. Get the familiar libpcap at

http://www.tcpdump.org/release/

Again configure, make, and make install. Get the last dependency, `libevent`, at:

```
http://monkey.org/~provos/libevent/
```

Configure, make, and make install `libevent`. Next you should download the fragroute application from Dug Song's Web site:

```
http://monkey.org/~dugsong/fragroute/
```

Do the same configure, make, and make install process.

Fragroute functions by intercepting outgoing network traffic. It then applies a configurable number of fragmentation rules to it. The traffic is then fragmented or manipulated as it is sent to the target host. To test fragroute, issue the following command:

```
Fragroute -f fragroute.conf 192.168.1.2
```

Where 192.168.1.2 is an IP address that Snort is monitoring. If you receive an error that tells you it is tunable to establish a route, you may need to do so by pinging the target or establishing a valid route in another method. After fragroute is running, you need to create some traffic for it to intercept and modify. If you simply ping or point your Web browser to the target, you should see a list of intercepted traffic that has been modified by fragroute, as in Figure 10.2.

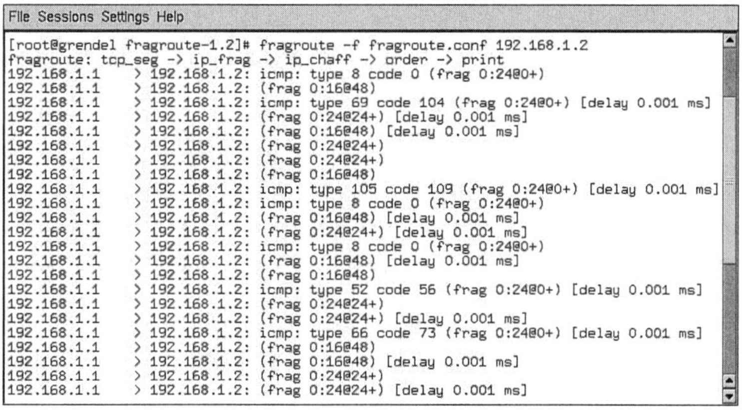

Figure 10.2   Fragoute in action.

Fragroute also comes with some predefined rules that were once able to totally evade Snort. Go to the scripts directory and open a file named `README.snort`. In this file you will find various fragmentation and manipulation attacks that we will use to test Snort. Load some of these different options into a separate `.conf` file and run the fragroute test again. When you are comfortable using fragroute, you should attempt to stress test Snort with a hail of fragmentation attacks. Enable fragroute and then run an nmap or Nessus scan against an address range protected by Snort. This should simulate an attacker attempting to use fragroute to map out a network without alerting Snort.

After running the fragrouter tool and nmap, check the Snort fragmentation stats. If your settings for `frag2` have held up to the fragmentation attack, meaning you have zero memory faults, you can begin the process of tuning `frag2` for false positives. Otherwise you may want to increase the amount of memory `frag2` has reserved for it.

If you have a false positive problem related to fragmentation, you have two options. One is to configure the Snort network variables to ignore the host that is generating the false alerts. If this is not an option, or if you would rather attempt to remove false positives and still monitor the host, you will need to tune `frag2`.

Start out by increasing the `timeout` value by five and `memcap` by one million bytes. Increasing the `timeout` value will increase the length of time that a fragmented packet is stored while waiting for the remainder of the fragmented chain of packets to be intercepted. Increasing `memcap` will ensure that you have enough memory to support the increased number of resources required to store packets for this length of time. When you set `memcap` to a value, this amount of memory will be reserved for `frag2` regardless of whether it ever is used. Let Snort run for a period of time and cycle through by incrementing by five seconds and one million bytes until you have an acceptable level of false fragmentation positives. Try not to go overboard with this method; you do not want to inadvertently allow `frag2` to consume too much memory that could be better used by other preprocessors or the detection engine.

Note
The IP stacks on potential target hosts have fragmentation timeouts of their own. Configuring Snort to exceed this timeout value has limited value.

The other two options to adjust to reduce false positives are `min_ttl` and `ttl_limit`. When either of the values set to these options is exceeded, an alert is generated. The setting chosen for `min_ttl` was 3, and this should be an acceptable setting for most networks. You should never drop below 3, as you are likely to introduce false negatives as well as allow fragroute-type attacks to go unnoticed. If you are receiving an unusual amount of `min_ttl`-related false positives, and you have fully investigated that they are actually false positives, you could raise the value up to between 5 and 10. The `ttl_limit` is much more likely to create genuine false positives because of router flap.

Router Flap
When routes on the Internet suddenly appear or disappear, frequently packets may be forwarded through drastically different routes on the Internet. When packets are forwarded through different routes on the Internet, they can possibly have widely varying TTL values. Some packets may find a direct route and have a large TTL, whereas others may have to traverse many different hops to reach the same destination. This phenomenon is known as *router flap*. Router flap occurs when large numbers of routers on the Internet are temporarily overwhelmed or otherwise momentarily unavailable. Router flap can cause routers to cease to function if they must spend all their resources calculating new routes. This was a major problem when the Internet was in its infancy, but still poses problems for IDS analysts.

If `ttl_limit` is generating an unbearable number of false positives, you can set its value to something higher than the recommended default of 8. If you set it higher than 12, it becomes somewhat useless in detecting fragroute type TTL evasion attempts.

stream4

`stream4` is another preprocessor that is tuned in a manner similar to `frag2`. It has the familiar `memcap`, `timeout`, `min_ttl`, and `ttl_limit` options you tuned with `frag2`. They are used to control the amount of memory set aside for `stream4` and the time to hold a packet in memory before flushing it. If Snort is dropping packets you may want to reduce the amount of memory reserved for `stream4` with the `memcap` option. Check the number of memory faults, and make every effort to keep this value at zero.

If you followed the setup instructions, `stream4`'s current configuration is likely to generate a decent amount of false positives. If `stream4` is not pumping out false positives, you should leave it configured as is, with every option enabled. If you are receiving a significant number of false positives that are due to overlapping TCP sequences, you may want to include the `disable_evasion_alerts` option in the `stream4` configuration line. This option forces Snort to ignore traffic of this type. The primary culprits when TCP overlaps false positives are Windows 2000 and XP hosts. These operating systems often send status information after an RST packet, which violates the recommended RFC implementation of the TCP protocol. For this reason, `disable_evasion_alerts` is best left off the `stream4` directive on sensors facing external networks, where such alerts are more likely to be real attacks. An internal sensor may see a large number of non-malicious Windows 2000 TCP overlaps, in which case you should append the `disable_evasion_alerts` directive to the `stream4` line.

Another option that can be removed from the `stream4` configuration line to reduce false positives is `detect_state_problems`. This option is used to detect various state inconsistencies that can be used to evade Snort's attack detection. Unfortunately, there are a lot of unusual types of legitimate TCP/IP traffic that also set off this alarm. For this reason, `detect_state_problems` is a candidate for removal.

You can use the same tuning method for configuring the `min_ttl` and `ttl_limit` options as you did for `frag2`. To perform the same type of stress test for `stream4`, you could make use of the Hammerhead tool. Hammerhead is primarily used to stress test Web servers, but it can work nicely as a generic TCP session stressing tool. Get Hammerhead at

`http://hammerhead.sourceforge.net/`

After you have run the stress test, check to see whether `stream4` has any memory faults. If you have memory faults, you should increase the memory available with the `memcap` option.

In addition to the configuration options in `snort.conf`, there is a command line option that can be used to control how `stream4` handles TCP traffic. To eliminate false positives and defeat Snot attacks, you can use the `-z` switch to alert only on TCP streams that have established a complete three-way handshake. This option does not affect other

IP protocols; they are still processed normally. Normal traffic usually completes the three-way handshake. By forcing Snort to ignore traffic that does not complete the handshake, you can eliminate false positive flood attacks that function by sending only the initial SYN packet and never completing the handshake. Set the switch to the following to detect attacks only on established TCP sessions:

`-z est`

stream4_reassemble

`stream4_reassemble` is closely related to `stream4`. It does not have as many options and is fairly straightforward to configure. One point to note: If you do not want to generate alerts on stream reassembly you should enable the `noalert` option rather than remove the entire `stream4_reassemble` directive from `snort.conf`. `stream4` may not function correctly with `stream4_reassemble` missing.

If you want to limit the resources consumed by `stream4_reassemble`, you should consider reducing the number of ports from every port to the default range of ports. If this also proves to be too much, you could enter a list of ports that have potentially vulnerable services running on them. You could also set the `clientonly` or `serveronly` option to limit the direction of traffic to reassemble. If the bulk of TCP sessions to be concerned about are initiated externally to the sensor, you may want to enable `clientonly`. Conversely, if sessions are initiated internally, you should enable `serveronly`.

http_decode, rpc_decode, and telnet_decode

The `http_decode`, `rpc_decode`, and `telnet_decode` preprocessors are all tuned in a similar manner. If you are not running a HTTP server, RPC service, or Telnet server at your organization, every alert caught by these preprocessors could technically be considered a false positive. Whether you still want to receive alerts for attacks on services that do not exist on your network is a decision that is different for every IDS analyst. If you feel that the probability of an attempted attack is not high enough to merit an alert, then by all means disable the appropriate preprocessor.

If you feel that being alerted to an attacker that is possibly attempting to discover vulnerable services or hosts is important, you should enable these preprocessors. Even if you do not have these services installed, unrecognized Telnet or HTTP traffic is cause for alarm. An attacker could enable one of these services to use in an attack. They could be used to remotely control or move data from the compromised host. However, most likely you would want this classification of alerts to be a low priority if an RPC, HTTP, or Telnet service is not present on your network.

You can get granular with both `http_decode` and `rpc_decode` to filter specific attack types. With `rpc_decode` you can specify the ports to monitor for attacks. The `http_decode` preprocessor lets you pick and choose which type of HTTP normalization to enable. For example, if you do not run an IIS HTTP server, you could disable the `iis_alt_unicode` and `iis_flip_slash` options to not alert on IIS-specific attacks.

`portscan2` **and** `conversation`

You can tune these two preprocessors by simply adjusting the parameters that are used to start them up. A mistake commonly made by novice Snort users is to detune the `portscan2` preprocessor to accommodate one or a small number of hosts that routinely generate `portscan2` false positives. By doing so, the analyst creates a false negative situation. Real portscan attacks will almost always fall below the threshold of a machine generating a heavy load of false positives. A better option is to filter out these hosts using a network device or Snort itself. You can also use the `ignorehosts` option to ignore portscanning activity from a range of IP addresses.

To tune `portscan2` you should evaluate whether the false positives are generated from horizontal or vertical scans. A *horizontal scan* searches for the same port on many different hosts. A *vertical scan* searches the same host for many different ports. Network management devices that access multiple machines in a short period often set off a horizontal portscan false positive. Servers with a large number of services enabled on the same host generate a vertical portscan false positive. To eliminate horizontal false positives, increase the `target_limit` value until you have successfully tuned `portscan2` to stop reporting false positives. If you would like to eliminate vertical false positives, you should increase the `port_limit` value until the same desired effect is reached. Remember, you should always have a healthy number of false positives from the `portscan2` preprocessor.

If `portscan2` or conversation is causing Snort to drop packets or otherwise function inefficiently, you can decrease the number of IP protocols for which to track conversations. Change the setting from `any` to `1 6 17` to monitor the most heavily used protocols. You could also reduce the `max_conversations` and `scanners_max` to a lower number to reduce the amount of memory these preprocessors can use.

Refining the Ruleset

Tuning and trimming the Snort ruleset has the greatest impact on Snort's performance and the number of false positives. If you can apply your knowledge of your network infrastructure and IDS policy to the ruleset, you will undoubtedly have a high-performance IDS on your hands, capable of dealing with all but the heaviest of loads. To understand how to correctly organize and trim the ruleset, you should have a basic understanding of how Snort processes rules.

As alluded to briefly in Chapter 3, Snort rules are made up of two components: the Rule Header and Rule Option, as shown in Figure 10.3.

The *Rule Header* defines the type of alert and which protocols, IP addresses, and IP protocol ports are to be monitored for the signature. Think of the Rule Header as metadata that lets Snort know where to apply the signature. The Rule Header is essentially everything that comes before the first parentheses. The *Rule Option* is the actual signature and assigned priority of the attack. The Rule Option also contains links to external documentation resources on the Internet.

alert tcp $EXTERNAL_NET any-> $HOME_NET 22

Rule Header

Rule Option

(msg:"EXPLOIT ssh CRC32 overflow /bin/sh";
flow:to_server, established; content:"/bin/sh";)

Figure 10.3   Snort Rule Header and Rule Option.

The Rule Headers and Rule Options are mapped into an internal data structure when the ruleset is loaded into memory. The Rule Header is mapped to an internal data structure within Snort known as a Rule Tree Node (RTN). The RTNs are linked together into one dimension on a three-dimensional linked list. Each protocol (TCP, UDP, and so on) has its own linked list made up of the corresponding RTNs. The second dimension is mapped from the Rule Option in the form of an Option Tree Node (OTN). The third and final dimension is a group of function pointers that determine which options should be applied to a packet to be inspected. This linked list of RTNs, OTNs, and function pointers is essentially the data structure that the detection engine uses.

Examining the life of a packet as it travels through the detection engine will help you understand how Snort processes rules. Understanding how Snort processes rules is important in tuning the ruleset.

When the detection engine processes a packet, it first checks to determine what protocol the packet uses. After the protocol is determined, the packet is sent to the corresponding linked list. The packet is then checked against each RTN until a match is found. After a match is found, the packet is passed by the OTNs. OTNs that utilize Boolean or mathematical operators are executed in a short time with little overhead. OTNs that are composed of only these types of tests are not computationally expensive and execute quickly. The IP reserved bit rule is an example:

```
alert ip $EXTERNAL_NET any -> $HOME_NET any (fragbits:R;)
```

This rule checks to see only whether a packet has the Reserved Bit set, which would indicate suspicious traffic.

OTNs that utilize any of the content checking options (uricontent, content-list, content) are much more computationally expensive and require more resources than OTNs that do not. Content options are expensive because they force Snort to make use of the pattern matching engine, which is resource intensive. When a packet matches an OTN, an alert is generated and passed to the output stage. If the packet does not match an OTN, it is flushed from memory.

This process has implications for tuning. If you want to reduce the overhead Snort requires, you should closely examine rules that utilize content checks and remove those that are unnecessary. Unfortunately, somewhere around 70% of the Snort rules make use of one of the three content options.

If Snort is dropping packets, you should prioritize rules into categories to identify content rules that are not as critical for your environment. You should begin by removing rules that alert to non-malicious behavior, such as inappropriate Internet activity. Check Appendix B for a more detailed description of the various rules files. It is best to comment out rules by using the '#' character rather than by deleting them. This makes the process of re-enabling the rule much easier in the future. In addition to removing rules that are not necessary for your organization, you may want to inspect these .rules files for content rules that alert you to less serious activity. You should disable these rules only if you absolutely have to (such as to prevent packet loss) .

chat.rules

This rules file contains rules that pertain to potentially inappropriate Internet activity. Rules that detect various instant messenger applications, such as AOL Instant Messenger, MSN, ICQ, and IRC, are found in this file. If your IDS policy does not include monitoring for this type of activity, you should remove these rules. If Snort is dropping packets, these rules are a good candidate to remove because they do not detect outrightly malicious unauthorized activity. You should leave the IRC, AIM, and MSN buffer overflow rules intact if at all possible because these detect more serious activity.

ddos.rules

This category of rules alerts you to traffic related to DDoS tools. Some of the rules alert you to communication between DDoS agents and servers. Others alert you to an actual DDoS attack perpetrated by one of these tools. These rules can detect whether one of your hosts is compromised and is being used as a DDoS agent, or whether someone on your network is using a DDoS server to perpetrate attacks. A few of these rules alert you to a DDoS attack against your network. You may want to disable some of the rules that check for agent-to-server communication if you have an effective antivirus policy at your organization.

ftp.rules

Although the bulk of the rules in this file are necessary to detect FTP-related attacks, a number of content rules in this file relate to inappropriate or information-gathering activity. If you need to reduce the rules in this file, the warez rules and FTP scan rules are a logical point to start.

icmp-info.rules

Some content rules in this file alert you only to different tools being used to ping hosts on your network. Be careful to comment out rules that utilize content options because these are the potential resource hogs.

icmp-info.rules

Consider pruning the ICMP PING rules. These rules alert you when the indicated device has issued a ping. This could be the result of some suspicious activity, but is not necessarily malicious.

info.rules

These rules detect potentially suspicious activity, such as a failed login attempt to an FTP server. These rules generate a lot of false positives and can consume an abundance of resources. They make another good candidate for trimming. You can always re-enable and edit a specific rule to watch over a particular host if the need presents itself.

misc.rules

In this file you will find a hodgepodge of rules that did not fit into any of the other files. It is likely that some of these will be irrelevant for your network.

multimedia.rules

Here you will find another grouping of Snort rules that deal exclusively with possibly inappropriate Internet activity. You may want to disable these rules if streaming media is allowable at your organization. They also make a potential target for trimming content rules to conserve resources.

other-ids.rules

The rules in this file alert you to the presence of another IDS on your network. This could be cause for alarm if the IDS is unauthorized. This is a highly unlikely situation; these rules are primarily used by penetration testers to discover what type of IDS is being used by the target network. You can safely disable these rules if you are not concerned with rogue IDS installations at your organization.

p2p.rules

This file contains rules that detect peer-to-peer file sharing programs. If your IDS policy permits such activity, you can remove these rules. You may also want to prune out rules that relate to P2P applications that are no longer available or in wide use. These rules can be removed to limit resource expenditure.

policy.rules

Similar to the `info.rules` file, this file contains rules that alert you to suspicious activity that may relate to Appropriate Use Policy (AUP) violations. You should consider whether such rules are needed; they are likely to generate false positives and consume resources because they all utilize content options.

porn.rules

This is a grouping of rules that will detect inappropriate Web usage. These rules detect Web content related to pornography. There are a lot of content rules in this file, so you may want to trim out some of the lesser-used terms. A heavy pornography user will eventually hit on one or more of the frequently used terms. This file should be a lower priority than those that deal with other malicious traffic and could possibly be removed in its entirety.

shellcode.rules

The rules in this file check all traffic for shellcode. If you have this file enabled in `snort.conf` you have already witnessed the flood of false positives. The rules in this file should not be enabled for every host. You should decide which hosts and services you would like to monitor for shellcode, and make the appropriate changes to the rules. These rules are also resource intensive, so limit their use to where they are expressly required.

Hosts on which you may consider enabling shellcode rules are external-facing Web servers, database servers that hold confidential data, or other critically important services and hosts on your network. You should avoid enabling shellcode rules on mail servers, as binary attachments are likely to set off a flood of false positives.

virus.rules

This file contains a collection of rules designed to detect viruses and worms. If you have adequate antivirus coverage at your organization with centralized reporting, you may not need the extra coverage Snort provides. In such a situation, you could disable the entire virus rules file. If you would like to use Snort to monitor for viruses and worms, you should take a close look at the signatures enabled. Some of the rules detect worms that are no longer in heavy circulation in the wild, and could be removed.

Organize Your Rules

After you have trimmed your ruleset, you need to organize the rules in a logical, efficient manner. The goal of organizing the rules is to have rules that utilize content options execute last. You want Snort to check packets against rules that are not resource intensive first, with the hope that the packets will trigger on an OTN before reaching the computationally expensive content options. It is quite a task to merge all the rules into a single file, with the Boolean and mathematical rules first. You may want to wait until you have the ruleset solidified after a few weeks of use before attempting such a task.

Another strategy is to create rules that use non-content-based rules to alert on protocols that should not be present on your network. The hope is that malicious traffic will trigger on one of these rules first, and not have to run through an expensive content-checking rule. For this strategy to be effective, you would have to reorganize the ruleset so that these protocol-checking rules come first.

When Snort is tuned properly for your network and is no longer dropping packets, you should move on to the activity of reducing false positives. You can reduce some false positives by configuring network variables and preprocessors. A popular way to remove false positives is to create what is known as a pass rule.

A *pass rule* is one of the possible rule categories, such as alert and log. It is the inverse of an alert rule; a pass rule tells Snort to ignore any packets that match the pass rule. You can use a pass rule to ignore certain types of traffic from specific hosts. If you wanted to ignore SSH traffic sent from a single server, you could do so with a pass rule.

If you are getting a number of false positives from a single host, you could write a pass rule to ignore all traffic from that host. Doing so is simple; add the following pass rule to ignore all TCP traffic from a host located at 192.168.1.1.

```
pass tcp 192.168.1.1 any -> any any;
```

You can get more granular if you want. If you wanted to ignore traffic from the same host destined for Telnet servers you could do so:

```
pass tcp 192.168.1.1 any -> any 23;
```

You can also append content options to pass rules. If the traffic matches the rule header and the content option, it will be ignored. If the same host were to constantly issue false positives relating to unauthorized Telnet login attempts, you could add this content rule:

```
pass tcp any 23 -> 192.168.1.1 any (content: "Login failed"; nocase;
flow:from_server,established;)
```

Notice the rule is for traffic that originates at a Telnet server and is sent to the host. We want to ignore traffic in this direction because the content that sets off the suspicious activity alert is sent from the server to the host. The `nocase` option makes the content string not case-sensitive, and the `flow` option makes the pass rule valid only for established traffic flow from the server to the host.

Pass rules can be used in many different situations to eliminate repetitive false positive offenders. If you decide to use pass rules, you need to change the order in which Snort processes rules. By default, Snort processes alert rules, then pass rules, and then finally log rules. If you create a pass rule that matches an alert rule, packets that match both the alert and pass rule will still be logged as an alert to the output plugin you have chosen. This processing order is in place to avoid false negatives. This protects you from accidentally creating a bad pass rule that would inadvertently cause Snort to ignore traffic that it should not. In the first pass rule example, if you had forgotten to specify the IP address of the host you wanted to ignore, you could accidentally ignore all TCP traffic. This rule would do exactly that:

```
pass tcp any any -> any any;
```

You must always be extremely careful with pass rules, and you should always test them to make sure you have not accidentally introduced false negatives.

After you have some practice writing pass rules, you should change the order in which Snort processes alerts. You can change the alert order to process pass rules first, so that the alert order would be pass, alert, log. You can do so by running Snort with the –o command line option.

Designing a Targeted Ruleset

There may come a point where you would want to develop a targeted ruleset that will alert only on services and hosts that actually exist. The targeted ruleset has rules enabled only for services that are present on your network. If a rule does not match a service existing on a host, it is disabled. This activity can trim the ruleset's size considerably. With a targeted ruleset, you are less likely to discover attempted attacks. The hacker would have to attempt to attack a legitimate service on a legitimate host to be noticed by Snort.

There are a number of different conditions where a targeted ruleset is appropriate. If you have placed a sensor on the internal side of a firewall, you may want to develop a targeted ruleset to watch traffic that is not blocked by the firewall. It would make little sense to expend all the resources necessary to check each packet against rules that will never be triggered. Along the lines of performance, you may not have the resources available on the sensor to monitor for every rule. Choosing only those that match an existing service and host will alert you to the most serious of attacks. You would be alerted to attacks that have the potential to compromise a host, and nothing else.

The targeted ruleset is also useful in cutting down on false positives. If you are monitoring a network that bombards you with false positives, a targeted ruleset will greatly trim the amount you receive. Finally, some IDS analysts consider attempted attacks unimportant, and for some reason or another do not want to be notified of them. Some are sure that their network is secure enough to withstand attacks by hackers not skilled enough to find a legitimate target to attack. The analyst may be concerned only with attackers that are skilled enough to discover a service that is exploitable. A targeted rule-set will ensure you are not alerted to attempted attacks against nonexistent targets.

If you are protecting a small network, you may want to create the targeted ruleset manually. If you have a limited number of hosts, creating the ruleset should not take more than a few hours to implement and test. The best way to determine what ports are open on different hosts is to use a portscanning tool to discover them. The most popular portscanning tool is NMAP. Get NMAP at

```
http://www.insecure.org/nmap/nmap_download.html
```

You can either download the RPM or install it from the source. NMAP comes with a graphical front end, but the command line mode is relatively easy to use. It also has some features that are used to attempt to evade an IDS. These features are out of the scope of this book, but are worth investigating, because you are sure to see them at some point in your intrusion detection work. Issue this command to scan a Class C range of hosts:

```
nmap -sT -sU -O -p 1-65530 -v -v 192.168.1.1/24 -oN target_list.nmap
```

This NMAP command scans both TCP and UDP ports with the -sT and -sU switches, respectively. It scans every port for both TCP and UDP, 1 through 65530. The command uses verbose mode, -v -v, which scrolls the scan results past the standard out as they come in. It scans a range of IP addresses, 192.168.1.1 through 192.168.1.255, and logs the results to a file named target_list.nmap. You can then use the results of this scan to build your targeted ruleset.

If you have a much larger network for which you would like to build a targeted ruleset, you can make use of a tool, snortrules, written by Roman Danyliw of ACID fame. Snortrules takes the output from an NMAP scan and edits a Snort rules file. It takes action on rules that do not match a particular service. Snortrules can either remove rules or flag them as not applicable. If you choose the not applicable option, the rule will still be triggered on, but the description will be changed to read not applicable to the current network.

Snortrules has a short list of available options:

- The -a option lets snortrules know what you want to do with a rule that does not match an existing service. You can either remove the rule or keep the rule and change the alerting message. The -a switch can be set to either 'x' or 'f', giving -ax or -af. The -ax removes rules, whereas the -af keeps the rules but flags the alerting message.

- -net is the name of the variable that represents the internal network. Unless you have specified something else in snort.conf, this should be set to HOME_NET. It is case-sensitive, so be sure to capitalize when needed.

- -in is the name of the .rules file to use as input. The rules in this file will be acted upon.

- The -out switch is set to the output file that will contain the new targeted ruleset.

You also need to have NMAP installed to run snortrules. Download snortrules from

```
http://www.andrew.cmu.edu/~rdanyliw/snort/snortrules.html
```

After you have compiled the source, get ready to fire up NMAP. Issue the following command from the directory in which snortrules resides.

```
nmap -sT -sU -O -p 1-65530 192.168.1.1/24 | snortrules -ax
-net HOME_NET -in exploit.rules -out exploit_targeted.rules
```

This command runs NMAP as already described and pipes the output to snortrules. It examines the `exploit.rules` file and removes any non-applicable rules with the `-ax` switch. It sets the internal network address range to `HOME_NET` and saves the results in `exploit_targeted.rules`. If you would like to combine all the rules files and then run snortrules once, you can concatenate the files into one large file and then run snortrules against it:

```
cat *.rules > master_file.rules
nmap -sT -sU -O -p 1-65530 192.168.1.1/24 | snortrules -ax
-net HOME_NET -in master_file.rules -out master_file_targeted.rules
```

Remember to edit `snort.conf` to include your new targeted master rules file.

Limitations in the Targeted Ruleset

A few limitations exist with the targeted ruleset implementation that are worth mentioning. Network configurations are rarely static for any lengthy period. If you compile the list of available services one day, the network could change on the next day, making your targeted list out of date. If you decide to use the targeted ruleset method for your sensor, you should adopt a regular schedule to update the list as appropriate. You could automate this task via a cron job that would automatically rescan the network and create the new rules file.

The other, more dangerous, possibility is that an attacker would manage to utilize a port or host you are not monitoring in some phase of an attack. This is possible if the port was not open at the time of scanning, but was subsequently opened by the attacker. If the attacker were able to install a Trojan, either by tempting an unsuspecting person to open an email attachment, or by sitting at the console and installing it, you would not be able to detect the intrusion. The attacker would be able to carry out any sort of remote control tasks on the compromised host without your knowledge. For this reason you may want to re-enable any Trojan traffic rules after snortrules has finished parsing the rules file. This still does not cover an attacker using a legitimate service, such as Telnet or TFTP, to orchestrate the attack. Regularly rescanning the network is the only way to avert such a precarious scenario.

Tuning MySQL

MySQL is the most common database platform used to hold a Snort intrusion database. Although the exact tuning commands will differ for individual databases, the performance tuning concepts are similar for most databases. The default installation and configuration of MySQL is not the most efficient possible. There are some methods of influencing the behavior of MySQL that can result in substantial performance gains if Barnyard is not being used.

One method of increasing performance is to add indexes to some of the tables that Snort uses. Indexes are used to increase the speed at which MySQL returns data. When an index is created, MySQL can skip over lots of data to find exactly the data that is required. Without an index, it must scan through the entire dataset to find the correct piece of data.

You should create three indexes to improve performance. They are:

- `tcphdr.tcp_sport`
- `tcphdr.tcp_dport`
- `acid_ag_alert.ag_sid + acid_ag_alert.ag_cid`

To create these indexes, you need to log into the MySQL command prompt. From this prompt, you can create the `tcphdr.tcp_sport` index with the following command:

```
mysql> create index index_tcp_sport on tcphdr(tcp_sport);
```

Create the `tcphdr.tcp_dport` with this command:

```
mysql> create index index_tcp_dport on tcphdr(tcp_dport);
```

The final index is a compound index, which you can create with this command:

```
mysql> create index index_cpd_sid_cid on acid_ag_alert(ag_sid,ag_cid);
```

You can now verify that the indexes have been created. Use the `show index` command to view the indexes.

```
mysql> show index tcphdr
mysql> show index acid_ag_alert
```

After you have the indexes created, it is wise to alter how MySQL handles memory. You can check how MySQL is performing in terms of memory management by entering this command from the command prompt:

```
mysqladmin variables
```

> **Note**
> The MySQL daemon needs to be running for this command to execute.

The two variables you should know are `key_buffer_size` and `table_cache`. You need to increase these to tune MySQL for the Snort environment. Because MySQL in a Snort setup uses a relatively small number of connections that primarily utilize INSERT statements, you should increase the amount of memory for both `key_buffer_size` and `table_cache`. You can increase the amount of memory for these two variables and others by appending new values to the `safe_mysqld` startup command. If you have a system with at least 256MB of RAM, you could use the following command line to start MySQL:

```
safe_mysqld -O key_buffer=96M -O table_cache=64 -O sort_buffer=8M -O
read_buffer_size=1M record_buffer=2M record_rnd_buffer=2M &
```

If you have more RAM, you could increase these values if you do not achieve the desired performance boost.

Another tidbit for tuning the MySQL server applies only to hybrid server/sensor installations. If you are running MySQL on the same machine as the Snort application, make use of sockets rather than TCP/IP when connecting to MySQL. You can do this by specifying `localhost` in `snort.conf` or `barnyard.conf` as the host to log to, instead of an IP address. This will automatically log via sockets instead of TCP/IP.

The regular use of the intrusion database will cause its performance to degrade over time. This happens much in the same way a disk drive becomes fragmented. After time, tables that contain variable-length rows accumulate significant amounts of unused space. You can compact the database and remove unused space with the `OPTIMIZE` command.

When a table is being optimized it is locked and cannot be accessed. Data can be forever lost. As long as you know about this situation you can take steps to avert a momentary outage. You can temporarily log to the archive database or create a new database for the transition. You can write a simple shell script to run through all the tables and optimize them. The following script optimizes all the tables in the database named snortdb.

```
for table in 'echo show tables|mysql snortdb|tail +2'
do
  echo optimize table $table|mysql snortdb
done
```

Tuning ACID

Under a large working load, ACID's capability to load pages in a timely manner can deteriorate. When the intrusion database becomes significantly large, ACID has to query through a vast amount of data with relatively complex queries. You can use two strategies to reduce the amount of processing ACID has to do, and in turn decrease page load time. The most basic method is to reduce the amount of data ACID has to search through. You can move intrusion data to the archive database or delete it altogether. The other possibility is to reduce the caching of certain types of data, which will reduce the amount of overhead each page uses to load.

Archiving Alerts

Ideally you want to archive alerts first and then later delete unwanted alerts from the archive. It is difficult to predict what crucial piece of evidence will be required at some point in the future. Crafty hackers sometimes perpetrate a reconnaissance attack and then wait a day or a week to execute the actual attack. You should try to store intrusion data for at least a month before deleting it.

An exception to this storage practice is false positives. There is little to no reason to archive false positives. Deleting false positives as soon as they are discovered goes a long way to keeping the intrusion database functional.

You should have the archive database created in MySQL and ready for action. If you have not created the archive database, refer back to Chapter 6. Archiving is a fairly simple task. You first need to create a query that matches the data you want to archive. After the query has executed, you must choose the Archive option in the Action drop-down combo box.

You have the option of copying the intrusion data into the archive database and leaving it intact in the primary alerting database. You could also move the selected data into the archive database, effectively clearing the data from the alerting database. To improve the performance of ACID you should select the Move option.

You next need to specify which alerts in the query will be archived. You can select individual alerts via the check box on the left side, archive all alerts present on the screen, or archive the entire query.

Deleting Alerts

The deletion of alerts is done much in the same manner as archiving them. You simply need to create a query that matches the data you want to delete. After you have executed the query, you need to set the Action drop-down combo box to Delete. You next need to specify which alerts in the query will be deleted. The same three options are present: You can select individual alerts via the check box on the left side, archive all alerts present on the screen, or archive the entire query.

Tuning the Caching Features

In addition to the size of the intrusion database, the caching features of ACID are most likely to be responsible for slow page loading. For example, ACID caches previously visited pages to allow the use of the Back button on the browser. Without the caching of previous pages, the Back button would return pages that have expired and have no data. Caching the history of pages causes the PHP session used by ACID to grow to 18KB for each page load. This can slow page loading considerably when all this information has to be stored and retrieved each time a page is loaded. You can disable the page history caching feature by editing `acid_conf.php` and setting the `$maintain_history` variable to `0`.

Another caching feature that significantly slows down page loading time is the Event Cache Auto Update feature. The Event Cache checks for new alerts each time a page is loaded. This provides near real-time alerting of events when ACID is being used. Searching the database for new alerts each time a page is loaded can have an impact on how fast the page loads. You can disable the Event Cache with the `$event_cache_auto_update` variable in `acid_conf.php`. Remember, if you disable the Auto Update feature, ACID loses some of its real-time alerting features.

You can update the cache manually by navigating to the following URL in a browser:

```
http://192.168.1.1/acid/acid_maintenance.php?submit=Update+Alert+Cache
```

You could also use the command-line Web browser, lynx, to load the page:

```
lynx -source http://192.168.1.1/acid_maintenance.php?
submit=Update+Alert+Cache > /dev/nul
```

You can automate this page load via a cron job if you wish. Another caching function that ACID performs that can slow down page load time is the DNS and whois cache. Each time a new IP address is loaded that has not yet been mapped to a DNS entry, ACID must look up the appropriate DNS entry. If the DNS server is down, unreachable, or slow, the time to resolve a large number of IP addresses can be lengthy. The whois cache usually takes an even greater amount of time to resolve, which can also impact performance. You can disable the DNS and whois cache by setting the `$resolve_ip` variable equal to 0. You can load the DNS and whois cache manually by navigating to the following two URLs:

```
http://192.168.1.1/acid/acid_maintenance.php?submit=Update+IP+Cache
http://192.168.1.1/acid/acid_maintenance.php?submit=Update+Whois+Cache
```

You can add these to the same Event Cache cron job with lynx if you wish.

Many other features of ACID can be switched off to improve performance. If you need even faster loading of pages, refer to the `acid_conf.php` documentation in Chapter 6 and turn off the features you do not need.

Summary

This chapter is a guide to tuning Snort and the components that influence Snort's behavior. There are two goals of the tuning process. The first is to reduce the number of packets dropped to a negligible amount or to zero. The second is to reduce the number of false positives to one you can manage, without compromising Snort's capability to detect malicious traffic.

You can check whether Snort is dropping packets by issuing a command that forces Snort to output its internal statistics. You can use this information to tune and track your progress in the tuning of Snort. The most basic and fundamental change you can make to improve Snort's performance and to reduce packet loss is to make use of Barnyard to process alerts. Another simple approach to tuning Snort is to change the amount and type of data that is delivered to a Snort sensor. Certain types of traffic are resource intensive and are unlikely to yield a true attack. By tuning out unwanted data, you can improve the performance of Snort and reduce the amount of packet loss.

If you cannot filter out traffic by using a network device, you can change the Snort network variables to have the same effect. Tuning and trimming the Snort ruleset has the greatest impact on Snort's performance and on the number of false positives. If you can apply your knowledge of your network infrastructure and IDS policy to the ruleset, you will undoubtedly have a high-performance IDS on your hands, capable of dealing with all but the heaviest of loads. If you want to reduce the overhead Snort requires you should closely examine rules that utilize content checks and remove those that are unnecessary. A number of rules identified in the chapter pinpoint areas where you can remove content rules.

When Snort is tuned properly for your network and is no longer dropping packets, you should move on to the activity of reducing false positives. You can reduce some false positives by configuring network variables and preprocessors. A popular way to remove false positives is to create what is known as a pass rule. The inverse of an alert rule, a pass rule tells Snort to ignore any packets that match the pass rule.

There may come a time when you want to develop a targeted ruleset that alerts only on services and hosts that actually exist. The targeted ruleset has rules enabled only for services that are present on your network. If a rule does not match a service existing on a host, it is disabled. You can use NMPA to discover services. You can manually edit the rules file or you can make use of an automated tool, snortrules. Snortrules takes the output from an NMAP scan and edits a Snort `.rules` file.

If you are still dropping packets at this point, you will have to make some configuration changes to the preprocessors. The first and most important task to perform when tuning the preprocessors is to ensure that you have sufficient memory allocated for the preprocessors. You can get statistics on some of the preprocessors by using a method that is similar to the one you use to discover dropped packets.

The default installation and configuration of MySQL is not the most efficient possible. Some methods of influencing the behavior of MySQL can result in substantial performance gains. One method of increasing performance is to add indexes to some of the tables that Snort uses. Another is to alter how MySQL manages memory. Both topics are covered in the chapter.

Under a large working load, ACID's capability to load pages in a timely manner can deteriorate. When the intrusion database becomes significantly large, ACID has to query through a vast amount of data with relatively complex queries. You can choose between two strategies to reduce the amount of processing ACID has to do, and in turn decrease page load time. The most basic method is to reduce the amount of data ACID has to search through. You can move intrusion data to the archive database or delete it altogether. The other possibility is to reduce the caching of certain types of data, which reduces the amount of overhead each page uses to load.

11

Real-Time Alerting

SNORT IS BUILT TO PERFORM ONE TASK and perform it very well. It does a magnificent job of detecting intrusions. Anything beyond intrusion detection is left up to the IDS analyst to handle. It is expected that you will add the features that make the IDS a truly pragmatic application. You have traveled down this road already, with the creation of an intrusion database to store alerting information and the installation of ACID to manage the collected data. Another powerful feature that should be added to Snort is real-time alerting.

Real-time alerting is a feature of an IDS or any other monitoring application that notifies a person of an event in an acceptably short amount of time. The amount of time that is acceptable is different for every person. Factors from the importance of the monitored system to the job duties of the responsible person can influence what is considered "real-time." For some IDS analysts, checking ACID a few times each day will suffice. Other IDS analysts require real-time alerting that notifies them of a critical security event within seconds. It is this type of real-time alerting that is covered in this chapter.

Even if you do not plan to make use of real-time alerting at this point, you may want to deploy the capability for real-time alerting. If a critical situation presents itself, it is beneficial to be able to notify the right person. Although you may not want to be notified for each critical alert, there will likely be a point where a unique circumstance presents itself. When a vulnerability is released and an exploit is in use in the wild before a vendor has released a patch, you would probably want to be notified of suspicious activity on hosts that are known to be affected. Real-time alerting can be useful in incident response because you would want to be notified of possible new security breaches during the course of an incident. Installing the capability for real-time alerting assures you that you can deploy real-time alerting quickly in an emergency situation.

An Overview of Real-Time Alerting with Snort

Real-time alerting with Snort is highly customizable. You can pick and choose which alerts to be notified of in real time. Assigning a priority to each rule or classification of rule enables you to do this. Each rule can have an individual priority attached to it, and every rule can be included in a classification of rules that has a priority attached to it.

Rules can be prioritized so that one priority of rule can be sent to one person while a different priority is sent to another. You can set up a third-party Snort application to notify yourself of malicious remote buffer overflow activity, while alerting an entirely different person to inappropriate Internet activity. With the customizable prioritization of alerts, you can notify yourself of different rules in different manners. One priority of rules can be sent to an email address that notifies you via pager while another can simply send you an email.

The most popular method of deploying real-time alerting capability on a Snort IDS is with *swatch* (Simple Watcher) or *syslog-ng* (syslog-next generation). Swatch and syslog-ng monitor Snort syslog output for a predetermined string. When they find the string, they execute a command. The command can be any available command on the system. Typically, a command is executed that sends an email. Other popular options include pager applications and audible alerts. Using swatch and syslog for real-time alerting is an ideal solution for a hybrid server/sensor installation. The syslog daemon is probably installed by default on the hybrid, meaning you merely have to set up swatch, configure Snort or Barnyard to log to syslog, and install an application for mailing alerts.

Syslog-ng is the better choice for the distributed three-tier Snort setup. If you have Snort installed in a distributed three-tier setup, you will want to collect syslog alerts in a central location. Logically, the Snort server is the ideal location for collecting alerts from the sensors. The server then monitors for critical alerts and emails them to the appropriate person. Installing a mailing application and swatch on each sensor creates a lot of unnecessary work, so syslog-ng is used to collect alerts. The syslog-ng client accepts alerting data from Snort and passes it to a centralized syslog-ng logging server. Stunnel is used to encrypt the client-to-server syslog-ng sessions. From the logging server, syslog-ng calls a simple shell script that passes alerts on to the mailing application.

Prioritization of Alerts

Before getting into the details of deploying real-time alerting capability for Snort, you must decide which alerts are critical enough for you to be notified of. Snort is versatile in the prioritization of alerts; you can select individual rule categories for which you want to be notified. You can also select individual rules to be notified of as well. A priority specified in a rule overrides any specified in the rule's category.

The alerting application, be it syslog-ng or swatch, monitors the log for a specific string. When this string is found, it executes the mailing application and sends an email with data from the actual alert. The string for which you should set these applications to search is the priority level of the alert. You can configure what action to take based on the priority of alert. For example, alerts with a priority of 1 could execute a paging program. Alerts with a priority of 2 could be sent to an email account that is checked frequently. A subsequent priority level of 3 could be sent to a network abuse admin.

The exact rule classifications and rules to be alerted of in real time are different for each Snort installation. You, the IDS Analyst, should make the decision concerning what is important enough to be notified of in real time. That being said, there are some general guidelines that you can use to determine what type of alerts you should be notified of in real time.

Incidents

Alerts deserving of a high priority and real-time alerting are usually those that are likely to indicate a security incident. If a rule triggers on remote control Trojan traffic, it is likely that a host has been compromised and requires immediate attention. Attack response traffic, such as pages or commands that are commonly called when a black hat successfully tests for an exposure, is a prime candidate for real-time alert. Any type of rule that is likely to result in a compromised host, such as an attack that is perpetrated against a known unpatched host, should generate immediate notification.

Targeted Attacks

Other possible categories of alerts to be notified of in real time are those that signify an attack is underway that could compromise a host. If a hacker is attempting specific attacks against certain versions of software residing on hosts that exist at your organization, you may want to include these rules in a real-time alerting strategy. This follows the logic that an attacker may have developed some prior knowledge of your network to determine the correct hosts to attack. Although the hacker could simply be guessing, it is likely that the hacker is determined to penetrate your network and is worthy of action. These attacks have a greater chance of success. In these cases you should identify rules that match existing hosts, services, and software versions and assign them a high priority.

Custom Rules

Other custom rules you have developed for your local environment, such as suspicious TFTP sessions from an external host, should be configured for real-time alerting. Custom rules are often created to bring greater monitoring coverage to a particular host, which implies that alerts generated are of a high priority. Custom rules created for these situations are ideal for real-time alerting.

After you have decided on what rules to alert, you need to make a decision on who to alert and which types of alerts the appropriate persons should receive. If you are going to notify a single person or group of persons to security events, set all the rules and rule categories that require real-time alerting to the same priority level. If you have more than one group or person to notify, you should assign a priority level to each person or group.

Alerting a Group

When a group of people is on the distribution list for Snort alerts, you must be careful to spell out responsibilities ahead of time. A clear alerting strategy can prevent numerous problems when alerting to a group. All too often a group of people receives an alert, and then one person acts on it without notifying others. The first analyst to act on the alert could take corrective action that would confuse and frustrate the other analysts. I have been witness to an analyst on the third shift who deleted alerts before others could react, totally confusing the rest of the IDS team. The IDS team suspected for a time that a Snort server had been compromised.

Another, far worse, scenario is that members of a group receiving real-time alerts will assume that another member has already taken action and will ignore a critical alert. It is important to establish these job responsibilities ahead of time to avoid this type of confusion.

If you are planning on installing more than one real-time alerting method, such as via email and pager, you need to further divvy up the rules between the different alerting methods. After you have this squared away, you can move on to implementing your alerting strategy in Snort.

Prioritizing with `classification.config`

You can edit the priority levels for rule categories in the `classification.config` file. Open the file, located at `/etc/snort/conf/`, and examine the different categories of rules. In the following examples, real-time notification is set for any rule with a priority level of 1. Change any of the classifications that you want to be notified of in this file to a priority of 1. For example, if you want to be notified of all successful DoS attacks, change the following line:

```
config classification: successful-dos,Denial of Service,2
```

To

```
config classification: successful-dos,Denial of Service,1
```

If the classifications are not granular enough, you can create your own. Simply create the rule classification in `classification.config` and assign it a priority like so:

```
config classification: attack-response,Successful Attack Response,1
```

Note

Notice the classification keyword contains no spaces, and there are no spaces between the delimiting commas.

Next you need to insert the new classification keyword into the rules that correspond to your new category. In this example the `classtype` option is changed in the following two rules:

```
alert tcp $HTTP_SERVERS $HTTP_PORTS -> $EXTERNAL_NET any
(msg:"ATTACK RESPONSES http dir listing"; content: "Volume Serial Number";
```

```
flow:from_server,established; classtype: attack-response;)
alert tcp $HTTP_SERVERS $HTTP_PORTS -> $EXTERNAL_NET any
(msg:"ATTACK RESPONSES command completed"; content:"Command completed";
nocase; flow:from_server,established; classtype: attack-response;)
```

You would now be alerted to these types of successful attack responses in real time.

The `priority` Option

You can also change the classification for individual rules. Assigning a priority option to the rule changes the priority for the specified rule. If you assign a priority to a rule and the rule has a classtype option with a different priority assigned to it, the priority option takes precedence. If you wanted to assign a different priority for the previous HTTP directory listing rule, you could make the following change:

```
alert tcp $HTTP_SERVERS $HTTP_PORTS -> $EXTERNAL_NET any
(msg:"ATTACK RESPONSES command completed"; content:"Command completed";
nocase; flow:from_server,established; classtype: attack-response; priority:2)
```

This would set the priority level to 2. Using the priority option method is useful in identifying rules that are critically important to your environment.

Alerting with the Hybrid

Deploying real-time alerting with the hybrid server/sensor is relatively easy. You need to install a mailing application, such as sendmail, to use real-time alerting via email. If you want to install another application, such as a pager or SMS gateway, you should do so. There are numerous resources online and in print for installing and configuring sendmail. The documentation included with the source distribution is fairly detailed and should get you up and running. You can get the sendmail application and associated documentation at

```
http://www.sendmail.org/
```

After you have deployed sendmail, you should take care to secure it. Sendmail has a relatively miserable history of security exposures and should be properly hardened.

After sendmail is secure, you need to configure Snort to send alerts to syslog. Sending alerts to syslog is accomplished via the output plugin, alert_syslog. Open up `snort.conf` or `barnyard.conf` and enable the alert_syslog output plugin by uncommenting the configuration line. If you have Barnyard installed, you should make the changes to Barnyard rather than Snort. Your configuration line should read as follows:

```
output alert_syslog: LOG_AUTH LOG_ALERT
```

Now you should generate some suspicious traffic either manually or with NMAP. Check to make sure Snort is logging to syslog by opening the following file:

```
/var/log/snort/alert
```

You should see a list of alerts with a priority assigned to each one. You should see alerts similar to the following:

```
[**] [1:1704:1] WEB-CGI cal_make.pl directory traversal attempt [**]
[Classification: Web Application Attack] [Priority: 1]
09/16-10:04:15.816116 192.168.1.1:3140 -> 192.168.1.2:80
TCP TTL:128 TOS:0x0 ID:12817 IpLen:20 DgmLen:131 DF
***AP*** Seq: 0xDEFC8E6D  Ack: 0x1A519F30  Win: 0x4470  TcpLen: 20
[Xref => http://cve.mitre.org/cgi-bin/cvename.cgi?name=CVE-2001-0463]
[Xref => http://www.securityfocus.com/bid/2663]

[**] [1:1122:2] WEB-MISC /etc/passwd [**]
[Classification: Attempted Information Leak] [Priority: 2]
09/16-10:04:15.826116 192.168.1.1:3143 -> 192.168.1.2:80
TCP TTL:128 TOS:0x0 ID:12832 IpLen:20 DgmLen:149 DF
***AP*** Seq: 0xDEFF5454  Ack: 0x1A51AF74  Win: 0x4470  TcpLen: 20

[**] [1:1730:1] WEB-CGI ustorekeeper.pl directory traversal [**]
[Classification: Web Application Attack] [Priority: 1]
09/16-10:04:15.836116 192.168.1.1:3144 -> 192.168.1.2:80
TCP TTL:128 TOS:0x0 ID:12837 IpLen:20 DgmLen:141 DF
***AP*** Seq: 0xDEFFEE00  Ack: 0x1AB7B107  Win: 0x4470  TcpLen: 20

[**] [1:1721:1] WEB-CGI adcycle access [**]
[Classification:  sid] [Priority: 2]
09/16-10:04:15.846116 192.168.1.1:3148 -> 192.168.1.2:80
TCP TTL:128 TOS:0x0 ID:12857 IpLen:20 DgmLen:76 DF
***AP*** Seq: 0xDF035110  Ack: 0x1A9AEFA4  Win: 0x4470  TcpLen: 20
```

Installing Swatch

Now that you are logging alerts, you need to install swatch to monitor syslog. Swatch requires four Perl modules in order to function. They are:

- Date::Calc
- Date::Parse
- File::Tail
- Time::HiRes

Most Linux distributions include these modules. In case your flavor does not, you can get these modules from

```
http://search.cpan.org
```

To install them, run through the following list of commands to compile and install the modules:

```
perl Makefile.PL
make
```

```
make test
make install
make realclean
```

After you have the modules installed, you can download swatch. It is located at

`http://www.oit.ucsb.edu/~eta/swatch/`

You can install swatch by using the same commands you used to install the Perl modules.

Configuring Swatch

Swatch is controlled from command-line arguments and configuration files, much like Snort and Barnyard. The configuration file for swatch is named `.swatchrc`. In the `.swatchrc` file you specify a string for swatch to monitor the log for and the action to take.

Some of the commands you could use to build real-time alerting include the following:

- `watchfor`   This is the required command that tells swatch what string to monitor for in the log. You can specify any string. For the purposes of this book we will search only for strings that match a certain priority number. The following example is a `watchfor` command to monitor for alerts with a priority of 1.

  `watchfor  /Priority\: 1/`

  You can find a tutorial on building regular expressions that are used in pattern matching at `http://japhy.perlmonk.org/book/`.

- `echo`   The echo command echoes the matched line. This can be used to append alerting information into the body of the email, or to a text field in a pager.

- `exec`   This command is used to execute an external program. If you have a paging program or any other script you want to execute, use the exec followed by the full path to the program. You can add a `$N` or `$0` to the exec command, which appends N lines or the entire alert to the executed command.

- `mail`   The `mail` option sends an email either to the local system or to a specified email address. You can store a group of email addresses in the alias file located at `/etc/aliases`, and use the alias to represent the group of email addresses.

- `throttle`   This command limits the number of alerts to be acted on. When the throttle is set, alerts that match the string are not acted on in the specified time. You can use this to avoid stressing your mail server and overloading your account.

You can use other commands for more advanced features of swatch, but the preceding are all you will need to send alerts via email or pager.

With these commands you can install real-time alerting in many different manners. Open up the `.swatchrc` file for editing and add the following commands:

```
watchfor    /Priority\: 1/
echo=normal
mail=user\@domain.com,subject=Snort Security Alert!
```

> **Note**
> You must escape the @ symbol with a backslash.

This configuration watches for any alert with a priority of 1 and emails user@domain.com with the alert. If you wanted to call a paging program you could replace the mail command with an exec command. QuickPage is a paging gateway that can be integrated with sendmail. You can get QuickPage at

http://www.qpage.org

To send emails via QuickPage to a text pager, you could add these commands:

```
watchfor    /Priority\: 1/
echo=normal
exec /usr/local/bin/qpage -f snort@domain.com -p IDS_admin '$0'
throttle 00:00:10
```

This command calls the QuickPage program and sends a page to IDS_admin, from the email address snort@domain.com. It makes use of the $0 to send the entire alert to the qpage command. With the throttle command, swatch ignores any alert of priority level 1 for 10 seconds after the page has been sent. You could also use swatch to ring the local PC bell with this command:

```
watchfor    /Priority\: 2/
bell 5
```

This command rings the PC bell five times for each alert with a priority of 2.

> **Note**
> This is sure to ruin any rapport you have developed with your co-workers.

You are not limited to one command set; you could implement all three if you wanted to.

After you have the .swatchrc file configured to alert you in a manner you see fit, you can move on to running swatch. Swatch has a few command-line options you should be made aware of.

-c

This option specifies the location of the .swatchrc file.

---input-record-separator

With this command-line option you can specify the delimiting boundary for each alert. By default it is the newline character, \n.

`-p`

The –p is used to read information outputted directly from a command. You can use this to monitor the output of a command for specific events.

`-t`

This option specifies the file to be monitored for security events.

`---daemon`

Append this switch to enable daemon mode.

A sample swatch startup command follows:

```
./swatch -c /usr/local/.swatchrc /var/log/snort/alert —daemon
```

This command runs swatch in daemon mode using the configuration file located at /usr/local/.swatchrc. It will monitor the syslog file at /var/log/. If you run this command, you will notice that swatch sends only the first line of the alert, as follows:

```
[**] [1:1704:1] WEB-CGI cal_make.pl directory traversal attempt [**]
```

It does so because the default input record separator is used, \n. If you would like to see additional meta information, such as IP addresses, time, TCP flags, and so on, you need to append additional lines of the alert.

To send the entire alert, make use of the tail command and swatch's piping feature:

```
./swatch -c /usr/local/.swatchrc —input-record-separator="\n\n"
-p="tail -f /var/log/snort/alert" —daemon
```

The –p switch watches the alert file with the `tail` command for new data. It uses a double carriage return, \n\n, for record separation. You should now receive the entire alert:

```
[**] [1:1704:1] WEB-CGI cal_make.pl directory traversal attempt [**]
[Classification: Web Application Attack] [Priority: 1]
09/16-10:04:15.816116 192.168.1.1:3140 -> 192.168.1.2:80
TCP TTL:128 TOS:0x0 ID:12817 IpLen:20 DgmLen:131 DF
***AP*** Seq: 0xDEFC8E6D  Ack: 0x1A519F30  Win: 0x4470  TcpLen: 20
[Xref => http://cve.mitre.org/cgi-bin/cvename.cgi?name=CVE-2001-0463]
[Xref => http://www.securityfocus.com/bid/2663]
```

This completes the swatch installation and real-time monitoring for hybrid server/sensors.

Alerting with Distributed Snort

To deploy real-time monitoring capability in a three-tier Snort setup you use a different method than with the hybrid. It would be a waste of time and resources to install a mailing application (such as sendmail) and swatch on each sensor. But making a single change to swatch and sendmail configurations across multiple sensors is bound to create confusion and possibly mistakes. To solve this problem, you can make use of syslog-ng and Stunnel to forward alerts securely from the sensors to the Snort server. You could optionally install another server to handle the alert collection and mailing functionality, in which case you would forward alerts to this new server.

Syslog-ng is a replacement for the syslog logging facility used by many different applications on Unix systems. Error messages and security alerts from applications or the operating system are posted to syslog. The original syslog has only 20 possible event types, which are known as facilities. Each facility has a priority assigned to it. The facilities are generic and are used by many different applications, so you will have many different applications reporting events to syslog with the same facility. With many applications reported as the same facility, it becomes difficult to search for events generated by a specific application. Filtering is difficult when you have a large amount of data stored in a syslog file. Syslog-ng solves this problem by making the filtering process much more granular. With syslog-ng, you can filter events based on the content of the event as well as the facility and priority. You can make use of regular expressions to filter events, which is not possible with the original syslog.

Syslog-ng supports some additional features that make it ideal for the Snort environment. The source of alerts from the original syslog can be obscured if the alerts are forwarded over more than one host or forwarded with Stunnel. If you collect alerts from many different machines on one host, syslog reports the correct logging host. But if you forward these syslog alerts again to a master host, the alerts appear to come from the second host. In a large Snort environment, where multiple logging servers are used, this can make determining the source of the alert difficult. Syslog-ng solves this problem by storing the complete hostname, along with time the alert was generated on the local host.

The original syslog sends alerts via UDP. This is problematic, because Stunnel does not currently support the encryption of UDP traffic. You could install a UDP tunneling package specifically for syslog sessions, such as Zebedee, to fix this problem. It is easier to upgrade to syslog-ng, which uses TCP, and make use of the Stunnel package you have already installed.

Syslog-ng also has native support for emailing alerts. You can add lines in the configuration file to automatically mail alerts that match a particular string. This eliminates the need to install swatch.

Configuring Snort and Installing Sendmail

You need to install a mailing application, such as sendmail, to use real-time alerting via email. If you want to install another application, such as a pager or SMS gateway, you should do so. There are numerous resources online and in print for installing and configuring sendmail. The documentation included with the source distribution is fairly detailed and should get you up and running. You can get the sendmail application and associated documentation at

```
http://www.sendmail.org/
```

After you have deployed sendmail, you should take care to secure it. Sendmail has a relatively miserable history of security exposures and should be properly hardened.

After sendmail is secure, you need to configure Snort to send alerts to syslog. Sending alerts to syslog is accomplished via the output plugin, alert_syslog. Open up snort.conf and enable the alert_syslog output plugin by uncommenting the configuration line. Your configuration line should read:

```
output alert_syslog: LOG_AUTH LOG_ALERT
```

The stage is now set for the installation of syslog-ng.

Installing syslog-ng on a Sensor

The first step to deploying syslog-ng is to install and configure the package on the sensors. Syslog-ng is dependent on the libol package. You must install it before attempting to install syslog-ng. Download the latest version of libol at:

```
http://www.balabit.hu/downloads/syslog-ng/libol/
```

Run the familiar `configure`, `make`, and `make install` commands to install the libol package. After you have this completed, download syslog-ng from

```
http://www.balabit.hu/en/downloads/syslog-ng/
```

You can run through the usual `configure`, `make`, and `make install` commands to install the package.

Configuring syslog-ng for the Sensor

syslog-ng is controlled via a configuration file, `syslog-ng.conf`. You will be writing this file from scratch. The examples in this book use the ports typically used by rservices (512, 513, 514) for syslog-ng. You should not be using any of the rservices on the Snort tiers because they are insecure. If you want to use ports other than those specified in the examples, you are free to do so.

To begin to configure syslog-ng for the sensor you must create a configuration file. Create a syslog-ng configuration file located at

```
/etc/syslog-ng/syslog-ng.conf
```

> **Note**
>
> You want to create a new file, not use one of the default or sample `syslog-ng.conf` files included with the package.

The purpose of the `syslog-ng.conf` file is to let syslog-ng know where to look for syslog information and what to do with it after it is discovered. You do so by adding sources and destinations and then associating a source with a destination. The sources are potential locations from which syslog-ng can receive alerts, and destinations are areas to which they should be output.

Associating a source with a destination tells syslog-ng exactly where to look for alerts and where to send them. The two actions are not mutually exclusive; after you define a source you can associate it with as many destinations as your heart desires. The same holds true for sources.

The first line you need to build is a source line. It is used to identify the source of the syslog-ng alerts to the syslog-ng application. You need to name the source with an identifier as well. A good guideline for naming is to use the name of the sensor, then an underscore, and finally the integer the sensor uses in ACID.

> **Note**
>
> This is only to help you remember what you have done at a later date; it is not required that you follow this guideline.

The following format provides an example:

```
source identifier {source-driver(parameter);};
```

The `source-driver` is where you want syslog-ng to look for alerts. The `source-driver` can be the local machine, a TCP port, or even a file. You can specify as many source-drivers as you wish. For the sensor installation of syslog-ng, you should accept alerts from the local system. Use the following configuration line to accept alerts from the local system:

```
source sensor_7 { unix-stream("/dev/log"); internal(); };
```

The name of the sensor is `sensor`, which corresponds with the integer of 7 in ACID, so the identifier is `sensor_7`. The `unix-stream("/dev/log")` source-driver tells syslog-ng that this is a Linux system and to listen for alerts in `SOCK_STREAM` mode. If you are using a BSD variant you would change this to `unix-dgram("/dev/log")`. The internal command tells syslog-ng to also listen for messages generated internally in syslog-ng.

The next line to create is the destination to which the alerts are to be sent. On the sensor, all alerts should be forwarded directly to the Snort server. This is specified with a destination line, which has the following format:

```
destination identifier {destination-driver(parameter);};
```

The identifier is the name of the Snort server. The destination is the IP address and port that corresponds to the syslog-ng service that will be installed on the server. You should insert a line similar to the following:

```
destination snort_server { tcp("Snort_Server_IP" port (514)); };
```

This line sends alerts to a syslog-ng daemon listening on port 514/TCP located at *Snort_Server_IP*. The final configuration line you need to add, `log`, lets syslog-ng know which sources you want to correspond to which destinations. In this case there is only have one source and one destination, so only a single configuration line is needed. The log configuration line has the following format:

```
log { source(source_name); filter(filter_name); destination(destination_name) };
```

Because we are not using any filters at this point, we can ignore the filter options. We will need to filter syslog alerts later on to support real-time alerting. To construct the log line you simply utilize the source and destination lines you created previously:

```
log { source(sensor_7); destination(snort_server); };
```

This completes the configuration of syslog-ng on the sensor. We will have to revisit this file later to enable Stunnel. To start syslog-ng, run the following command:

```
/usr/local/sbin/syslog-ng
```

Installing Syslog-ng on the Server

You can follow the same process for installing syslog-ng on the server as you did for the sensors. Download and install libol, then install syslog-ng.

Configuring Syslog-ng for the Server

Configuring syslog-ng for the Snort server is relatively painless now that you understand how to configure a `syslog-ng.conf` file. Create a syslog-ng configuration file located at

```
/etc/syslog-ng/syslog-ng.conf
```

Open this file for editing. The first step is to create a source line that listens to both a TCP port and the local syslog-ng application. We want to see alerts that are incoming from the sensors, as well as any related to the syslog-ng application itself. Use the following source line:

```
source sensors { unix-stream("/dev/log"); internal();
tcp(ip(Snort_Server_IP) port(514) max-connections(7) };
```

This command listens for alerts generated locally by syslog-ng. It also listens for alerts via TCP to port 514 to the interface with the IP address of *Snort_Server_IP* assigned to it. You should change this IP address to match the IP of the management NIC you use to control the sensors. The `max-connections()` option sets the maximum number of sensors that can connect to the syslog-ng server.

The next line to create is the destination configuration line. You should send alerts to a logfile local to the server. Do so with this line:

```
destination localhost { file("/var/log/snort.log")); };
```

This writes all the logs from the sensors to the log file located where specified. To complete the posting of alerts to a local file, add a log statement to associate the source and destination:

```
log { source(sensors); destination(localhost); };
```

You should now test Snort by sending traffic to generate alerts and by checking the
/var/log/snort.log file. If everything is working correctly, you can move on to
configuring real-time alerting with syslog-ng.

Configuring Syslog-ng for Real-Time Alerting

Configuring the syslog-ng to send alerts via email or pager involves creating a simple
shell script that is executed by syslog-ng when a string is matched. The shell script in
turn executes the mailing or paging application. Some additional configuration lines are
required as well.

The first thing is to add the configuration lines, and then create the shell script. Open
the syslog-ng.conf file for editing. You will use the source line that is used to log to
the local snort.log file, so you need not create a new source line. The destination for
the alerts is the shell script you have yet to create. Use this destination line to execute
the script:

```
destination email_alert_script { program("/usr/local/bin/alert_mail.sh"); };
```

The program option specifies the command to be executed that will receive the
alerts. Be sure to include the full path.

Next, you need to create a filter that matches only your high-priority Snort alerts. If
you want to match all Snort alerts with a priority of 1, you create this filter line:

```
filter high_priority { match("\\[Priority: 1\\]"); };
```

Notice that you must escape the bracket symbols with a double backslash, \\. Create
filters for each of the priorities on which you want to alert.

Now you must add the final log statement to tie the source, destination, and filter
lines together.

```
log { source(sensors); filter(high_priority);
destination(email_alert_script); };
```

This completes the setup of the syslog-ng.conf file. Exit and restart syslog-ng.

The final piece of the puzzle is to write the simple shell script that syslog-ng is to
execute. Open /usr/local/bin/alert_mail.sh for editing. Enter the following
script:

```
#!/bin/sh
while read line; do
        echo $line | mail -s "High Priority Snort Alert" IDS_admin@domain.com
done
```

This script emails the alert to IDS_admin@domain.com with the subject of "High
Priority Snort Alert." You can change this script to your liking if you are using a paging
package or mailing application other than sendmail. You can easily alert on other priorities by creating new filters and new log statements. You should test to ensure that the
real-time alerting is functioning and then move on to encrypting the syslog-ng communication via Stunnel.

Encrypting Syslog-ng Sessions with Stunnel

You should already have Stunnel installed and configured on the Snort sensors and server. If you have yet to install Stunnel, you should revisit Chapters 6 and 7 for the installation instructions. To make use of Stunnel you have to make changes to the `syslog-ng.conf` files on both the sensors and the server.

Open the `syslog-ng.conf` file on the sensor for editing. The first step is to include a global option that preserves the correct name of the local syslog-ng machine. If you do not set this option, all the alerts will have the hostname set as `localhost`, making it difficult to determine which sensor has generated the alert.

```
options { keep_hostname(yes); };
```

Next you will need to create a new destination line. You want to route traffic from syslog-ng so that Stunnel can read it, encrypt it, and forward the traffic on to the server. Add a new destination line that reads as follows:

```
destination stunnel { tcp("127.0.0.1" port (513)); };
```

This destination sends alerts to the localhost (127.0.0.1) on port 513. Next, you need to change the existing log line to use the new destination. Change it to

```
log { source(sensor_7); destination(stunnel); };
```

Save and exit the `syslog-ng.conf` file. Restart the syslog-ng process so that syslog-ng recognizes the new configuration file.

Now you must start a Stunnel daemon to handle the encrypted syslog-ng traffic. Run the following command:

```
/usr/local/stunnel/sbin/stunnel -c -d 127.0.0.1:513 -r \
Snort_Server_IP:512 -s stunnel_user -g stunnel_group &
```

This command sets Stunnel in client mode with the −c switch. It forwards syslog-ng traffic sent to port 513 on the localhost to the Snort server located at *Snort_Server_IP*. It also runs the daemon as *stunnel_user*, which is a member of *stunnel_group*. Stunnel is now configured for the sensor.

Moving to the Snort server, you need to make similar changes to the syslog-ng configuration file. Open the `syslog-ng.conf` file for editing. On the server, Stunnel accepts the traffic and forwards it to the local syslog-ng TCP port. The first step is to create a new source line that reflects the change. Add the following source line:

```
source stunnel { unix-stream("/dev/log"); internal();
tcp(ip(127.0.0.1) port(514) max-connections(7) };
```

Now you need to alter the log line to reflect the new source. Change your existing log line to the following:

```
log { source(stunnel); destination(localhost); };
```

Save and exit, and restart the syslog-ng daemon. You are now ready to log from Stunnel to the local syslog-ng service. The final step is to start the Stunnel daemon on the server by using the following command line:

```
/usr/local/stunnel/sbin/stunnel -d 512 -r 127.0.0.1:514
-p /usr/local/ssl/certs/stunnel.pem &
```

This command starts Stunnel listening on port 512 for incoming syslog-ng traffic. It then forwards traffic to the local syslog-ng server running on port 514. This completes the configuration of Stunnel. Alerts will now traverse the network encrypted.

Closing the Loop

The distributed Snort setup you have is relatively resistant to session-based attacks. The MySQL connection is encrypted, the syslog-ng session is encrypted, and the ACID browser session is encrypted. Although the setup you have installed is by no means bulletproof, it should make the interception and modification of alerts relatively difficult for most intruders. The only major hole you could possibly have in the system is the real-time alerting emails.

If you have bothered to encrypt all these connections, you should close the loop and encrypt the real-time email alerts. Check the documentation for your mailing application for instructions on installing an encrypted email system.

Summary

This chapter contains both an overview of real-time alerting strategies with Snort and how to configure them. Real-time alerting with Snort is highly customizable. You can pick and choose which alerts to be notified of in real time. Rules can be prioritized so that one priority of rule can be sent to one person while a different priority is sent to another.

Priority levels are managed through rule categories in the `classification. config` file. If the classifications are not granular enough, you can create your own. You can also change the classification for individual rules. Assigning a priority option to the rule changes the priority for the specified rule.

Deploying real-time alerting with the hybrid server/sensor is accomplished with syslog, swatch, and a mailing application such as sendmail. The installation and configuration of swatch is covered in this chapter. The configuration file for swatch is named `.swatchrc`. In the `.swatchrc` file you specify a string for swatch to monitor the log for and the action to take. Swatch can be configured to alert via pager, email, or audible alert.

To deploy real-time monitoring capability in a three-tier Snort setup you use a different method than you do with the hybrid. It would be a waste of time and resources to install sendmail and swatch on each sensor. Syslog-ng and Stunnel are used to forward alerts securely from the sensors to the Snort server. Syslog-ng is a replacement for the syslog logging facility used by many different applications on Unix systems. Syslog-ng supports some additional features that make it ideal for the Snort environment.

The first step to deploying syslog-ng is to install and configure the package on the sensors. The chapter walks through an example that details creating the appropriate source, destination, and log lines that are used to configure syslog-ng on the sensor. After the sensors are installed and configured, the Snort servers are configured. The installation and configuration for the server is similar to the sensor.

Configuring the syslog-ng to send alerts via email or pager involves creating a simple shell script that is executed by syslog-ng when a string is matched. The shell script in turn executes the mailing or paging application. Configuration lines, including a `source`, `destination`, and `log` line, are used. A new configuration line, `filter`, is used to monitor for a specific string.

Stunnel should have been installed and configured on the Snort sensors and server in Chapters 6 and 7. To make use of Stunnel you have to make changes to the `syslog-ng.conf` files on both the sensors and the server. The first step is to include a global option that preserves the correct name of the local syslog-ng machine. New source, destination, and log lines are required to enable Stunnel. The final step is to start Stunnel daemons that encrypt and decrypt the syslog-ng sessions.

12

Basic Rule Writing

THE EASE WITH WHICH SNORT RULES can be written has arguably been the most influential factor in Snort's tremendous adoption in the information security community over the last few years. The decision of Snort's creator, Marty Roesch, to create a simple and extensible rules creation syntax has allowed Snort users worldwide to create one of the most comprehensive signature sets available for any IDS. Each rule can be modified individually, making the modified rule increasingly relevant to the network infrastructure Snort is protecting. Additionally, rules can be created from scratch and used within Snort. Enabling users to create custom rules make Snort a truly pragmatic security application.

The ruleset has made Snort the envy of many commercial IDS companies. The closed-source IDS market leader, ISS, has implemented a feature on their IDSs, Trons (Snort spelled backwards), which parses and loads Snort rules. It can accept almost any type of Snort rule, either from the official ruleset or a custom rule. The Trons module does not perform packet normalization that is required for the rules to work properly (such as stateful inspection, defragmentation, and so on), so it can be considered only an interesting feature rather than a serious intrusion detection application. The Trons module shows how important the Snort rules writing language is to an IDS.

Every IDS analyst that runs Snort should have some handle on how to write Snort rules. You need not become an expert rule developer, but a basic understanding of how to write rules is essential. With a limited understanding you can modify existing rules to better monitor your network. You could easily get by with using the official ruleset and modifying individual rules when required. You can also create simple rules that can be very effective in detecting malicious activity that is unique to your organization.

Fundamental Rule Writing Concepts

When writing a Snort rule, keep in mind that you are in reality building a traffic signature. The purpose of this signature is to discover a specific type of traffic by matching all traffic against it. With this in mind, there is often a gap between what you intend the rule to trigger on and what type of traffic actually triggers the rule.

The goal in creating effective signatures is to write rules that match exclusively the network traffic you want to discover. Unfortunately, this goal is almost impossible to attain; each rule is likely to trigger on traffic other than what you would intend it to. When writing a rule, you should make a best effort to narrow down the rule to trigger on only the isolated traffic patterns of which you want to be alerted. You should also take care not to add too many traffic proprieties, which would cause legitimate attacks to not match the rule.

To write rules that will trigger only on the traffic you intend them to, you must research and discover properties of the traffic that are unique. The individual properties of the traffic need not be unique themselves, but the combination of them should be. Take, for example, cross-site scripting attack traffic.

Cross-site scripting (XSS) occurs when a Web site allows malicious script to be inserted into a dynamically created Web page. If user input is not properly checked, the attacker can embed script that will force the Web application to act in an unintended manner. XSS attacks can be used to steal cookies used for authentication, access portions of the Web site that are restricted, and otherwise attack Web applications. The majority of XSS attacks require scripting tags inserted into a particular page request. You can use this feature of XSS attacks to write a rule. Tags such as <SCRIPT>, <OBJECT>, <APPLET>, and <EMBED> are required to insert an XSS script into a Web application. For this example, you can create a rule that should trigger when the <SCRIPT> tag is discovered. First you create a rule to trigger on traffic with "<SCRIPT>" content:

```
alert tcp any any -> any any
(content:"<SCRIPT>"; msg:"WEB-MISC XSS attempt";)
```

This rule triggers on XSS attacks, but unfortunately also triggers on many other types of benign traffic. If someone were to send an email with embedded JavaScript, the alert would be triggered, causing a false positive. To prevent this from happening, you need to change the rule to trigger only on Web traffic:

```
alert tcp $EXTERNAL_NET any -> $HTTP_SERVERS $HTTP_PORTS
(content:"<SCRIPT>"; msg:"WEB-MISC XSS attempt";)
```

Now this rule triggers only when the <SCRIPT> content is detected in relation to an HTTP session from a Web server. It triggers when the traffic originates at an external IP address ($EXTERNAL_NET), and is sent to your Web servers ($HTTP_SERVERS) on the ports on which an HTTP service runs ($HTTP_PORTS). If you have correctly identified all the Web servers at your organization and the ports on which they run, the XSS rule triggers only when sent to Web servers. After loading this rule, though, you would notice that a large number of false positives are generated whenever a page is requested that contains JavaScript. You need to further refine the rule and discover properties of XSS traffic that are unique.

XSS occurs when the client embeds the <SCRIPT> tag in a request. If the server sends the <SCRIPT> tag in response to a request, it is probably benign traffic (JavaScript) and not an XSS attack. You can use this property of an XSS attack to further refine the rule:

```
alert tcp $EXTERNAL_NET any -> $HTTP_SERVERS $HTTP_PORTS
(msg:"WEB-MISC XSS attempt"; flow:to_server,established; content:"<SCRIPT>";)
```

This revised rule makes use of the `flow` option, which uses Snort's TCP reassembly features to identify the direction of traffic flow. The flow options specified, `to_server` and `established`, apply the rule only to sessions that originate at the client and are sent to the server. This is where an XSS attack will occur: Traffic flowing in the opposite direction is likely to be a normal HTTP session containing JavaScript tags.

Now that the rule has identified the properties that describe XSS attack traffic, you need to make sure an attacker cannot evade the rule by taking advantage of case sensitivity. The content option is case-sensitive, whereas HTML is not, so an attacker could evade this rule by changing the script tag to be `<ScRiPt>` or `<script>`. To remedy this, make the content option not case-sensitive:

```
alert tcp $EXTERNAL_NET any -> $HTTP_SERVERS $HTTP_PORTS
(msg:"WEB-MISC XSS attempt"; flow:to_server,established;
content:"<SCRIPT>"; nocase;)
```

To finish up the rule, assign it a high priority.

```
alert tcp $EXTERNAL_NET any -> $HTTP_SERVERS $HTTP_PORTS
(msg:"WEB-MISC XSS attempt"; flow:to_server,established;
content:"<SCRIPT>"; nocase; priority:1;)
```

This completes the writing of an XSS rule.

Rule Syntax

Snort rules have a basic syntax that must be adhered to for the rule to properly match a traffic signature. Violating the Snort rules syntax can cause a rule to not load into the detection engine. If a rule does manage to load, incorrect rule syntax may result in unpredictable and unintended consequences. The rule could trigger on a large amount of benign traffic, causing a hail of false positives. This could potentially overload the intrusion database. The rule could trigger on randomly occurring traffic patterns, which have the potential to cause unnecessary panic when an alert is generated.

Even worse, some rules load, but never trigger on the traffic they are designed to detect. The IDS analyst may assume the rule is functioning correctly and miss out on the alert. The same scenario can occur in the case of a pass rule, where a poorly written rule can cause a significant amount of potentially malicious traffic to be ignored. It is therefore important to make sure your rules are written in the correct syntax. It is a good practice to check rules over and test them before implementing the rules in a production situation.

Snort Rules

The most basic syntactical requirement of a Snort rule is that it be in a single line, even though they have been separated into multiple lines in this book for formatting purposes. If you attempt to make a rule more legible by inserting a carriage return, you will effectively split the rule in two and cause it to not load. If you must separate the rule into more than one line, you must append a backslash to the end of the line to let Snort know to continue on the next line.

The Rule Header

As you may remember from Chapter 10, "Tuning and Reducing False Positives," a Snort rule is divided into two sections, the rule header and the rule option. The rule header defines the type of alert and which protocols, IP addresses, and IP protocol ports are to be monitored for the signature. The rule header is the portion of the rule up to the first parentheses. Think of the rule header as metadata that lets Snort know under what situations to apply the rule. The rule header on the final example XSS rule is

```
alert tcp $EXTERNAL_NET any -> $HTTP_SERVERS $HTTP_PORTS
```

The rule header is essentially everything that comes before the first parentheses. The syntax of the rule header is

```
rule_action protocol source_address_range source_port_range
direction_operator destination_address_range destination_port_range
```

The rule action, protocol, and direction operator are normally chosen from a static list of possible values. Snort dictates these statically because the rule can trigger only a limited number of possible actions, and Snort can monitor for only a limited number of protocols. The remaining parameters can be assigned to a variable (such as $HOME_NET), an IP address or port, or a range of IP addresses and ports. The following sections describe these rule header parameters.

Rule Action

The first parameter, rule action, lets Snort know what to do when a packet matches the rule. There are three built-in options for the rule action. They are

- **Alert** Alert is used to generate an alert and then log the packet. Most critical rules are set to `alert`. Packets with the `alert` parameter set will be sent to the alerting output mechanism.
- **Log** Log simply logs the packet without alerting on it.
- **Pass** Pass is used to inform Snort that you want to disregard any packet that matches the signature. Pass rules are primarily used to eliminate false positives. Pass rules can be dangerous; a single poorly written `pass` rule can hide malicious traffic from Snort. Pass rules should always be tested without the –o Snort command-line option, to ensure that they are not filtering out relevant alerts. After the rule has been properly tested, the –o command line can be reimplemented.

The Snort Inline patch, covered in Chapter 14, "Advanced Topics," adds another rule option, `drop`. Drop is used to block the matching packets and not allow them to pass by the Snort Gateway IDS.

You can also create your own rule actions. The purpose of creating your own rule action is to force the rule to output to a different output plugin than the default. It is common practice to use a different output plugin to test a new rule. You can call the ruletype option to create your own rule action. If you wanted to use a rule action to log new rules in tcpdump format, you would write the following statement:

```
ruletype test

{
  type log output
  log_tcpdump: rule_test.log
}
```

Protocol

This rule header parameter is used to identify to which protocol or suite of protocols the rule will be applied. Currently Snort can monitor three protocols for traffic: TCP, UDP, and ICMP, which are the primary protocols used in Internet traffic. IP should be used as the protocol option if you are attempting to detect IP protocol attacks.

Direction Operator

The direction operator is used to tell Snort in which direction to apply the rule. You can apply the rule in one direction with the `->` operator, or both directions with the `<>` operator. If you want to reverse the direction, switch the source and destination addresses and ports. Changing the `->` to `<-` is no longer supported; all rules must use the `->` to signify unidirectional traffic flow.

Source and Destination IP Addresses

These two rule headers are the IP addresses or range of IP addresses to which Snort will apply the rule. You can specify a single address by simply placing it in either the source or destination IP address as needed. To list a range of IP addresses, you must specify the address and the CIDR netmask, like so:

```
192.168.1.1/24
```

You can make a list of both ranges of IP addresses and single addresses as well:

```
192.168.1.1/24,10.0.0.1
```

You can also set the IP addresses equal to a variable, possibly one that you have already defined:

```
$EXTERNAL_NET
```

If you want Snort to inspect every IP address, you can use the any value:

```
any
```

Last, if you would like Snort to monitor all addresses except a particular address or range of addresses, you can use the inverse operator (!):

```
!EXTERNAL_NET
```

or:

```
!192.168.1.1./24
```

> **Note**
>
> Double-check what your variables are set to before using the inverse operator. If you have a variable set to any, and you take the inverse (!any), you will force Snort to monitor for no addresses.

Source and Destination Ports

Identifying the source and destination ports to which Snort is to apply the rule is similar to making the IP address declarations. You can list a single port:

```
21
```

A range of ports, separated by a colon:

```
1:1024
```

This would apply the rule to any port from 1 to 1024. You can signify an open ended range of ports as well:

```
:512
```

This would apply the rule for any port below or equal to 512 (1 to 512). You can do the same in the opposite direction:

```
1024:
```

This applies the rule to ports 1024 and above (1024 to 65530). You can use the same inverse operator used for IP addresses (!), to specify all ports except the ones specified:

```
!1:1024
```

This would apply the rule to everything but ports 1 through 1024 (1025 to 65530).

The Rule Option

The rule option is the actual signature and the assigned priority. The signature portion of the rule option is represented with one or more option keywords. These option keywords are used to build the traffic signature for which you would like the detection engine to monitor. When more than one option keyword that relates to a signature is used, they can be considered to form a logical AND statement. Take the XSS example:

```
(msg:"WEB-MISC XSS attempt"; flow:to_server,established; content:"<SCRIPT>";
nocase; priority:1;)
```

The option keywords that relate to a signature in the XSS example are `flow`, `content`, and `nocase`. Together they state that the detection engine should match established sessions sent to a server *and* containing <SCRIPT> in the packet payload *and* to ignore case when searching for the <SCRIPT> content. The remaining keyword options, `msg` and `priority`, are used to write a message to the alert output and prioritize the rule.

The option keywords make up the bulk of the rule. They are used to create the actual traffic signature, and provide information to Snort about the rule. If you can master the use of the different option keywords, you can write almost any Snort rule.

Option keywords can be grouped into eight functional categories, discussed in the following section.

Content-Related Option Keywords

The most important keyword options are associated with content-checking options. Content keyword options are used to monitor for a specific pattern in the packet's payload. These options are used in around 75% of the rules in the official Snort ruleset.

Content keyword options are also the most resource intensive, so you should avoid their use whenever possible. When you do have to include a content option in a rule, you should make an effort to limit the amount of data in the payload the content option must search. You can use the `offset`, `depth`, and `flow` keywords to search a particular section of the payload. This will dramatically improve the performance of a content-based rule.

content

The `content` keyword is the primary content-matching keyword option. When the content specified by this option is discovered in a packet, an alert is generated. The `content` option is case-sensitive by default, although this can be changed with the `nocase` keyword.

The string for which to search with the content option can be either binary or ASCII. Content options that use ASCII are simply stated in the keyword like so:

```
content:"CF_SETDATASOURCEPASSWORD()";
```

This content is related to a Cold Fusion exploit that would allow an attacker to gain unauthorized access to a host via an undocumented administration feature. When specifying the content in binary format, you must preprend and append the string with a pipe (|). An example of using hex content follows:

```
content:"|0A 00 00 01 85 04 00 00 80 72 6F 6F 74 00|";
```

This is the bytecode representation of a MySQL root login attempt. You can also use more than one string in a content keyword, and the pattern can be represented in a mix of binary and ASCII strings. The next example uses both hex and ASCII content to reduce false positives:

```
content:"|0f 00 00 00 03|show databases";
```

This pattern triggers on any attempt to list the databases in a MySQL environment.

You can also use the inverse operator (!), to tell Snort to alert on packets that do not match the specified pattern. If, for some reason, you wanted to be alerted when packets were discovered that did not attempt to list MySQL databases, you could use the inverse operator:

```
content:  !"|0f 00 00 00 03|show databases";
```

The inverse operator is primarily used when the content option keyword is used with many other keywords.

uricontent

The `uricontent` option is another popular content-related keyword option. It is used to trigger alerts specifically on the URI portion of a request. A URI is a superset of the more common HTTP URL.

You should use the `uricontent` option rather than the `content` keyword option when you want to alert only on URI requests. `uricontent` does not alert on server responses. If you were to use the same pattern in the content option, you would generate false positives from legitimate traffic. Because the `uricontent` keyword option has to check only the URI portion of a request, it is not as computationally expensive as the `content` keyword option. Patterns are expressed in the same manner as in the previous `content` keyword option.

content-list

The `content-list` option is a pointer to a file that contains a list of carriage return–delimited content patterns. The `content-list` patterns should be enclosed with a double quote ("). This option is primarily used with the `react` keyword option.

You can build a list of content strings to check for (gambling, pornography, and so on) and then use the `react` keyword to break down the TCP connection and issue a warning to the offending IP address. You are not required to use the `react` keyword with `content-list`. You can use the inverse operator as well to cause Snort to alert whenever a pattern is not found in the list. You can specify the `content-list` keyword option like so:

```
content-list:  "inappropriate_content.txt";
```

The `inappropriate_content.txt` file could be created in the following format:

```
#This is the inappropriate content list file for Snort
"porn"
"warez"
"hotmail"
"www.inappropriatesite.com"
#EOF
```

`nocase`

The nocase keyword option is used to match patterns regardless of case. nocase helps Snort detect attacks that attempt to evade a signature by mixing up the case of an attack in an unusual method.

> **Note**
>
> ocase modifies the preceding content or uricontent option. You need to specify nocase for each content or uricontent option:
>
> content: "preserve_case"; content: "IgNoRe CaSe"; nocase;

`offset`

The offset keyword option works in conjunction with the content keyword. You must specify a content keyword option to use offset. offset is used to limit the amount of data in the packet payload to which the content pattern will be applied. The offset keyword sets the starting point within the payload—not the start of the packet—to begin matching patterns.

This keyword is used to make a content keyword less resource intensive. You can use it in situations where you are positive that the content pattern will never occur in the predefined number of bytes at the beginning of the payload. For example, to skip over the first 10 bytes in the payload, you would include the following offset in the rule:

offset: 10;

> **Note**
>
> Just as with nocase, offset modifies the preceding content or uricontent option.

`depth`

Depth is similar to the offset keyword option. It restricts the amount of the payload to which the content pattern is applied, making the content keyword less resource intensive. depth specifies the number of bytes, starting from the beginning of the payload, against which to match. A good proportion of attacks take place in the first few bytes of the packet payload; the depth keyword can be used to make these rules more accurate and efficient. The following depth keyword would tell Snort to search for content matches only in the first 20 bytes:

depth: 9;

You can use a combination of the depth and offset keywords to limit content pattern matching to a range of bytes within the payload. If you wanted to apply the content pattern matching from the 20th byte to the 60th byte, you would use these option keywords:

```
offset: 20;
depth: 40;
```

> **Note**
> When used with the offset keyword, the depth keyword counts from the offset.

regex

The regex keyword lets Snort know that you will be using a regular expression character in the content string. regex does not permit true regular expressions, but rather the familiar * and ? characters to be used in a content string. The * represents any number of characters, whereas the ? represents a single character.

If you want to match content for requests to a specific directory but any number of files that share the same extension, you would use the following content keyword:

```
content:"/jsp/snp/*.snp";
```

And enable regex characters with

```
regex;
```

This would match any request for an .snp file located in the /jsp/snp/ directory. regex is a computationally expensive keyword, so you should use it only when absolutely required. In the preceding example, you could use a single content keyword to notify all .snp file–related requests:

```
content:".snp";
```

If this creates too many false positives (that is, there are many legitimate .snp requests), you would then move to the more restrictive regex configuration.

> **Note**
> Regex modifies only the content option that it follows.

Session-Related Option Keywords

Rules can apply themselves to certain portions of a TCP session. Naturally, these options apply only to TCP rules. Session-related keyword options help eliminate false positives. In some cases, session keywords make rules possible that used to generate an unacceptable amount of noise. To use these keywords you must have the stream4 and stream4_reassembly preprocessors enabled.

flow

A good number of session-related keywords have been consolidated under the newer flow option. Flow works in conjunction with the TCP reassembly features of Snort to apply a rule to a specific direction of traffic flow. This lets you apply a rule only to a request portion of a TCP session. Singling out a direction of traffic flow is highly useful in detecting Web application attacks, such as the XSS example used previously.

Flow has many different options that can be used to apply a rule to the direction of traffic, the state of the TCP three-way handshake, and status of the TCP stream reassembly process. You can enable flow with as many of these configuration options as required. There are four directional possibilities:

- to_client
- to_server
- from_client
- from_server

These parameters are self-explanatory: They apply the rule to the corresponding direction of traffic. You can use more than one. You can also apply the rule to only the particular status of a TCP session with these two parameters:

- established
- stateless

The established option applies the rule only to sessions that have established the TCP three-way handshake. Check your command-line options; if you have enabled the -z switch, this flow configuration option is not required. The stateless option applies the rule without the stateful inspection feature of Snort applied. The final two flow configuration options apply the rule under different conditions relating to the status of the stream reassembly process:

- no_stream
- only_stream

The no_stream option forces Snort to ignore rebuilt stream sessions. The only_stream option tells Snort to apply the rule to rebuilt sessions. Flow options are specified in the same line:

```
flow:from_server,established;
```

session

The session keyword is used to capture and record session data. The purpose of the session keyword is to monitor user input into a TCP session (such as Web, Telnet, FTP, and so on). You can use the printable option to set session to record only user-viewable data, or use the all option to record all data (including control characters and application communication data). To record all user-input data you would use the following session keyword configuration:

```
session:printable;
```

Session can be computationally expensive, so use it with care.

IP-Related Option Keywords

These keyword options test a packet for various values stored in the IP header. These keyword options are relatively efficient and can be executed quickly.

ttl

The `ttl` keyword option triggers the rule when the exact Time To Live value is discovered. You specify a range using the greater or less than symbols. Simply specify the `ttl` keyword option and the TTL value for which you want to monitor.

Attackers often use a low TTL in a packet to feed garbage data to an IDS. The garbage data breaks up the signature and makes it difficult for the IDS to properly interpret the traffic. To monitor for a TTL value less than 5, you would add the following keyword option:

```
ttl: <5;
```

tos

This is another keyword option that checks the IP header field for a value and triggers the rule if the value is matched. This option monitors the Type of Service (TOS) field. Again, it matches only on the exact value specified. The value can be a range if you use the less than or greater than symbols. To be alerted on a TOS value of 1,000 you would use this keyword option:

```
tos:1000;
```

id

The `id` keyword tests the packet for a specific fragmentation ID. If the exact fragmentation ID is discovered, the alert is triggered. The following would alert on the fragmentation ID of 12345:

```
id:12345;
```

ipopts

The `ipopts` keyword monitors packets for whether a specific IP option is enabled. Eight possible IP options are available. Of the eight, five of them are found frequently in normal traffic. They are:

- `eol`   End of List
- `sec`   IP security
- `nop`   No Operation, Nothing
- `ts`   Time Stamp
- `satid`   Stream ID

The three IP options that are unusual and could be cause for alarm are:

- `rr`   Record Route
- `lsrr`   Loose Source Routing
- `ssrr`   Strict Source Routing

The Record Route option is primarily used by ICMP packets. It is used to record and determine the route that a packet takes as it traverses a network. This could be used by an attacker to map your network. The Loose Source Routing and Strict Source Routing parameters are used by attackers to force a packet to take a chosen route through a network. The attacker can force packets to travel through a device he controls, so that packets can be sniffed or altered en route.

`fragbits`

This keyword is used to test three bits in the IP header that relate to fragmentation. Reserve bit can be checked for a particular value. To check for a specific bit, use the character that corresponds to the particular bit:

- M   More Fragments
- D   Don't Fragment
- R   Reserved Bit

You can also append a character that lets Snort know whether you want to test for the specified bit exclusively. The following characters give you more fine-grained detection capabilities.

- +   Alert when specified bit is discovered, in addition to at least one other.
- -   Alert when any of the specified bits are detected.
- !   Alert if any of the specified bits are not set.

To create a `fragbits` keyword option that would monitor for the Don't Fragment bit in addition to any other bits, you would use the following keyword option:

`fragbits: D+;`

`dsize`

The `dsize` keyword is used to detect a packet payload size. It can be configured to check for a size greater than or less than the chosen size. `Dsize` can be used to detect a particular range of sizes as well.

To check for a size larger than the number specified, use the greater than symbol (>). To check for a size smaller than the number specified, use the less than symbol(<). To specify a range of sizes, separate two numbers with both a greater than and less than symbol (<>). If you wanted to discover packet payloads with a size greater than 500 bytes, you could do so with this option:

`dsize: >500;`

`ip_proto`

The `ip_proto` option applies the rule whenever a specific IP protocol is detected. You can use either the name or the number of the IP protocol. Table 12.1 lists the IP protocols and their corresponding numbers.

Table 12.1 **IP Protocols and Their Corresponding ip_proto Values**

`ip_proto` Value	Corresponding IP Protocol
0	IP
1	ICMP
2	GGP
6	TCP
8	EGP
12	PUP
17	UDP
22	IDP

Anything other than 1, 6, and 17 can be considered abnormal. You can also use the inverse operator (!) to check for the IP protocols not supplied. To monitor for IP protocol 9 you would use the following keyword option:

`ip_proto:9;`

`sameip`

The `sameip` keyword option is a simple option that checks whether the source IP address is the same as the destination IP address. To apply `sameip` to a rule, add this keyword option:

`sameip;`

`fragoffset`

The `fragoffset` keyword is used to detect packets with a particular fragmentation offset value. You can set the offset to any value you want to detect. If you wanted to find the first packet in a fragmented packet session, you could set the `fragoffset` to zero, like so:

`fragoffset: 0;`

Note
You would have to detect the more fragments bit as well, to avoid false positives.

TCP-Related Option Keywords

The TCP option keywords relate to the various fields that make up a TCP packet.

`flags`

The `flags` keyword simply applies the rule to the specified TCP flags. It functions in a similar syntax as the `fragbits` keyword. Table 12.2 details which flags correspond to which `flags` character.

Table 12.2 **TCP Flags and Their Corresponding `flags` Values**

`flags` Keyword Value	Corresponding TCP Flag Value
F	FIN
S	SYN
A	ACK
R	Reset
P	Push
U	Urgent
0	No TCP Flags Set
1	Reserved bit number 1
2	Reserved bit number 2

You can additionally specify the same +, *, and ! characters as the `fragbits` option keyword. To detect the flags in an nmap Xmas scan, you would use the following `flags` keyword:

`flags: FUP;`

> **Note**
>
> Most TCP rules formerly made use of the `flags:` A+ keyword to filter content rules so that only established sessions would be examined. This has been largely replaced by the `flow: established` keyword, which is more accurate and efficient. If you find rules with the `flags:` A+ keyword, you may want to convert them.

`seq`

The `seq` option keyword is used to detect a specific TCP sequence number. To trigger the rule on a `seq` value of `12345678`, you would add this keyword:

`seq: 12345678;`

`ack`

This keyword detects a specific TCP header acknowledge field. To detect a value of zero, you could use this `ack` keyword:

`ack: 0;`

ICMP-Related Option Keywords

These options are similar to the IP and TCP keyword options. They allow monitoring for specific values in the ICMP header.

`itype`

The `itype` keyword checks for a specific integer value that corresponds to the ICMP type. Table 12.3 details the possible integers and their associated names.

Table 12.3 **ICMP Type and Their Corresponding `itype` Values**

`itype` Value	Corresponding ICMP Type Field Name
0	Echo reply
1	Unassigned
2	Unassigned
3	Destination unreachable
4	Source quench
5	Redirect
6	Alternate host address
7	Unassigned
8	Echo
9	Router advertisement
10	Router selection
11	Time Exceeded
12	Parameter problem
13	Timestamp
14	Timestamp reply
15	Information request
16	Information reply
17	Address mask request
18	Address mask reply
19-29	Reserved (for robustness experiment)
30	Traceroute
31	Datagram conversion error
32	Mobile host redirect
33	IPv6 where-are-you
34	IPv6 I-am-here
35	Mobile registration request
36	Mobile registration reply
37-255	Reserved

Any type code in the 19-29 or 37-255 ranges is considered abnormal. To monitor for Traceroute ICMP type codes, you would add this keyword:

`itype: 30;`

`icode`

The `icode` keyword checks for a specific code field in the ICMP header. Certain ICMP type fields have corresponding values for the code field, as shown in Table 12.4.

Table 12.4 **ICMP Types and Corresponding** `icode` **Values**

ICMP Type Field Name	Valid Code Field Possibilities
Destination unreachable	0—Net unreachable
	1—Host unreachable
	2—Protocol unreachable
	3—Port unreachable
	4—Fragmentation needed and DF bit set
	5—Source route failed
	6—Destination network unknown
	7—Destination host unknown
	8—Source host isolated
	9—Communication with destination network is administratively prohibited
	10—Communication with destination host is administratively prohibited
	11—Destination network unreachable for TOS
	12—Destination host unreachable for TOS
Redirect	0—Redirect datagram for the network
	1—Redirect datagram for the host
	2—Redirect datagram for the TOS and network
	3—Redirect datagram for the TOS and host
Alternate host address	0—Alternate address for host
Time Exceeded	0—Time to live exceeded in transit
	1—Fragment reassembly time exceeded
Parameter problem	0—Pointer indicates the error
	1—Missing a required option
	2—Bad length

To detect source route failed ICMP packets, you would set the following keyword:

`icode: 5;`

> **Note**
>
> You must include an `itype: 3;` keyword to alert on source route failed ICMP packets.

`icmp_id`

This keyword option applies to ICMP echo packets. `icmp_id` detects a specific ICMP ID number. A number of poorly written covert communication programs use ICMP but make use of a static ICMP ID. To discover ICMP echo packets with an ICMP ID of 666 (used by some Black Hat DDoS agents), use the following keyword:

`icmp_id: 666;`

`icmp_seq`

This is a similar keyword to `icmp_id`. You can test a packet for a specific ICMP sequence field value. To monitor for packets containing an ICMP sequence field of 0, use this keyword:

`icmp_seq: 0;`

Snort Response Option Keywords

This class of keyword options directs Snort's behavior when the particular rule is matched. You can specify the alerting message, the location to log the alert to, and other response actions.

`msg`

The `msg` keyword is the alert text that will be recorded along with the packet that triggered the rule. This is not meant to be a full description, but rather a brief text description to alert you to what type of rule has been triggered. Encapsulate the message text with double quote (") characters. You can set `msg` to be any message text that will help you recognize the rule. To write the message text "Haligh, Haligh, an awful lie" you would use the following keyword:

`msg: "Haligh, Haligh, an awful lie";`

> **Note**
>
> If you are using Barnyard, the message comes from the `sid-msg.map` file, and not the `msg` keyword.

`logto`

This keyword option logs packets that match the rule to a chosen log file. The rule still posts alerts with the enabled output plugin chosen in `snort.conf`. This option cannot be enabled when Snort is logging in binary (that is, tcpdump) format. To log to a file named `new_rule.log`, you would add this keyword option:

`logto: "new_rule.log";`

`resp`

The `resp` option keyword makes use of the Flexible Response (FlexResp) Snort module.

> **Note**
>
> To use this keyword you must compile Snort with the `FlexResp` option. Do to so, configure Snort with the `--enable-flexresp` switch.

The `resp` keyword causes Snort to "snipesessions," which is the closing of active connections that match a particular rule. You may be familiar with session sniping if you have used another IDS. These will not work if Snort is prevented from sending outgoing packets by a unidirectional sniffing cable or another security feature. Using `resp` to close connections can be dangerous because you can block legitimate traffic if the rule triggers on normal traffic. There are a number of possible configuration options for the resp keyword. Table 12.5 lists the options for `resp` and the corresponding action.

Table 12.5   `resp` **Parameters and Corresponding Snort Actions**

`resp` **Parameter**	**Corresponding Snort Action**
`rst_snd`	Send TCP reset packets to the sending socket.
`rst_rcv`	Send TCP reset packets to the receiving socket.
`rst_all`	Send TCP reset packets to sending and receiving sockets.
`icmp_net`	Send an `ICMP_NET_UNREACH` packet to the sender.
`icmp_host`	Send an `ICMP_HOST_UNREACH` packet to the sender.
`icmp_port`	Send an `ICMP_PORT_UNREACH` packet to the sender.
`icmp_all`	Send `ICMP_NET_UNREACH`, `ICMP_HOST_UNREACH`, `ICMP_PORT_UNREACH` packets to the sender.

Be very careful when creating rules that include the `resp` keyword. It is easy to accidentally cut off connections to legitimate sessions. A standard practice is to create the rule that will be used with the `resp` keyword without the `resp` keyword added. After a representative amount of traffic has been monitored with the rule, and no false positives have been recorded, add the `resp` keyword. To have Snort snipe a TCP session from both the sender and the receiver, use the `resp` keyword like so:

`resp: rst_all;`

`react`

The `react` keyword is similar to the `resp` keyword. It enables a FlexResp action when the rule is triggered. It is primarily used to block or display a warning for inappropriate Web usage attempts. When a user attempts to access an inappropriate resource, Snort issues a TCP reset and blocks the request from occurring. The `react` keyword can be configured to send a visible warning to the sending host as well.

`react` requires the `content-list` keyword to be defined. The message text stored in `msg` will appear as the warning to the sending host, whereas the `content-list` file is used to contain the patterns on which `react` will trigger. You must set `react` as the last keyword in the Rule Option portion of the rule for it to function. The following are configuration parameters for `react`:

- `block`
- `warn`
- `msg`
- `proxy`

The `block` option blocks any patterns that match the `content-list`, and sends a visible notice to the sending host. `warn` issues a warning, but allows the connection to complete. If you include the `msg` option, the message text defined in the `msg` keyword appears as the warning message. `proxy` uses a proxy port to send the warning message. To react to block a particular `content-list` and send the `msg` text to the offending host, use this keyword option:

```
react: block, msg;
```

`tag`

`tag` is used to force Snort to log more than the exact packet that matches a rule. `tag` is useful in gathering recording packets for traffic that is important to incident analysis but does not contain a unique signature that can be implemented in a rule. The `tag` keyword can be used to log either packets in the same session as the one that triggered the rule or packets that originate or are destined for the host that set off the rule. You can specify whether to log a certain number of packets or log for a predetermined length of time. Tag has four possible parameters:

- `type`
- `count`
- `metric`
- `direction`

The `type` parameter is required, and can be set to either `session` or `host`. `session` records packets in the same session, and `host` records packets from the chosen host. `count` is used to specify the number of either time in seconds or packets to record. `metric` identifies whether to use seconds or packets with the `count` parameter. `direction` is used only in conjunction with the `host` parameter; it lets Snort know for which host to log data. `direction` can be set to either `src` or `dest`, which indicate the source and destination hosts, respectively. To log up to 500 packets in the same session after a rule has been triggered, you would use the following `tag` keyword:

```
tag: session, 500, packets;
```

To log packets for 60 seconds from the source host, you would use this keyword:

```
tag: host, 60, seconds, src;
```

Meta Option Keywords

The meta option keywords support extraneous metadata features of Snort rules. You can use them to define the priority and classification of a rule, the external documentation resources, and other metadata-related information.

reference

The `reference` keyword is used to link the rule to an external documentation resource on the Internet. The `reference` codes are interpreted by ACID and allow a hyperlink connection to the rule documentation. You can define references in the `reference.config` file. Table 12.6 lists the default references.

Table 12.6 `reference` **Resource Names and Their Corresponding URLs**

Resource Name	URL Prefix
bugtraq	http://www.securityfocus.com/bid/
cve	http://cve.mitre.org/cgi-bin/cvename.cgi?name=
arachnids	http://www.whitehats.com/info/IDS
mcafee	http://vil.nai.com/vil/dispVirus.asp?virus_k=
url	http://

You can define specific hyperlink references with the `url` option. To include a reference to source FTP port traffic, you could include a reference to ArachNIDS like so:

```
reference: arachnids, 06;
```

sid

The `sid` is used by the Snort output plugins to identify Snort rules. The `sid-msg.map` file contains the `sid` and the corresponding text message to apply to the alert. `sid`s are grouped into the following categories:

- <100 = Reserved for future use
- 100-1000000 = Official Snort rules
- >1000000 = Reserved for custom rules

To include a `SID`, use the keyword with the corresponding integer. To specify a `SID` of `1000001`, you would add the following keyword:

```
sid: 1000001;
```

rev

The `rev` option keyword is used to assign a version or revision number to a rule. It is useful in tracking rules and updating them. Simply assign the appropriate integer to the keyword. To assign version 2 to a rule, use `rev` like so:

```
rev: 2;
```

classtype

The `classtype` should be familiar by now; it is used to assign a classification stored in `classification.config` to a rule. Use the classification name as a parameter to enable the `classtype` option keyword. To assign a `trojan-activity` classtype to a rule, use this keyword:

```
classtype: trojan-activity;
```

priority

The familiar `priority` keyword is used to assign a priority to a rule. Set the integer value for the priority parameter to specify the importance of the rule. To set a priority of 1, use the following keyword:

```
priority: 1;
```

Miscellaneous Option Keywords

The remaining keywords do not fit into any one category, so they are grouped into the miscellaneous category.

rpc

The `rpc` option keyword is used to decode RPC-related information. It can decode the application, procedure, and program version. When all three parameters are matched, the rule is triggered. You can specify any value for the application, procedure, and program parameters by using the asterisk (*). To monitor for RPC getport requests, you could use the following keyword:

```
rpc: 100000,*,3;
```

The `rpc` option keyword is rarely used any longer; more accurate methods of detecting RPC traffic have been created. Check the `rpc.rules` file for examples.

rawbytes

The `rawbytes` keyword influences how Snort detects patterns with the `content` option keyword. It applies the `content` keyword directly to raw Telnet data, before it is normalized by the `telnet_decode` preprocessor. This allows you to detect specific Telnet negotiation codes. To monitor for a Telnet no operation negotiation code, you would add the `rawbytes` keyword like so:

```
rawbytes;
```

To the following content pattern:

```
content: "|FF F1|";
```

Writing Rules

Now that you know the elements of a Snort rule, it is a good idea to walk through a few rule-writing samples. There are essentially three methods to writing Snort rules. The first and easiest method is to modify or add to an existing rule. To tune Snort and make it more efficient, you may have already attempted this process. The second method is to create a new rule by using your knowledge of your network. These are fairly easy to create because they do not require extensive traffic analysis. The third method, creating a new rule by examining network traffic, is the most difficult. This section examines all three.

Modifying an Existing Rule

Let's say you have a single IIS server at your organization, and you would like to modify the rules relating to IIS so that they apply to only this server, instead of every Web server. To start with, you would want to modify the `.htr` chunked encoding rule you found posted at the snort-sigs mailing list:

```
alert tcp $EXTERNAL_NET any -> $HTTP_SERVERS $HTTP_PORTS (msg:"WEB-IIS .htr
chunked encoding"; uricontent:".htr"; classtype:web-application-attack; rev:1;)
```

To apply only to your IIS server:

```
alert tcp $EXTERNAL_NET any -> 192.168.1.1 $HTTP_PORTS
(msg:"WEB-IIS .htr chunked encoding"; uricontent:".htr";
classtype:web-application-attack; rev:2;)
```

This would apply the rule only to the Web server located at 192.168.1.1. Notice that the rev keyword was incremented to show this is a newer revision to the existing rule. After running this rule for a while, you would notice that you were getting a lot of false positives. Further research would show that a lot of the false positives were related to server responses that contain the `.htr` pattern in them. To further refine the rule, you would want to apply the rule only to requests to the server, because this traffic is likely to indicate an attack. For posterity's sake, you may also want to apply the rule only to established TCP sessions, to prevent someone from DoSing Snort with a flood of false positives. You would add the flow option like so:

```
alert tcp $EXTERNAL_NET any -> 192.168.1.1 $HTTP_PORTS
(msg:"WEB-IIS .htr chunked encoding"; flow:to_server,established;
uricontent:".htr"; classtype:web-application-attack; rev:3;)
```

After running the rule for a while, you would notice a dramatic reduction in false positives. Unfortunately, you would still generate a decent number of false positives with the new `.htr` chunked rule. Any time an `.htr` file is requested from the IIS server, the rule is triggered. You can add some additional content matching options to further refine the rule, and consequently alert only on chunked transfer encoding requests for .htr files.

```
alert tcp $EXTERNAL_NET any -> 192.168.1.1 $HTTP_PORTS
(msg:"WEB-IIS .htr Transfer-Encoding\: chunked"; flow:to_server,established;
uricontent:".htr"; content:"Transfer-Encoding\:"; content:"chunked";
classtype:web-application-attack; rev:4;)
```

This finally reduces the false positives. Only chunked transfer encoding requests that relate to the .htr file trigger this rule. You now need to change the msg to reflect the new rule. After a time of noticing no new alerts on this rule, you might become suspicious and want to test whether it is actually triggering. Via Telnet or netcat you can send the proof-of-concept (also known as the exploit) code provided by the security researchers who discovered the vulnerability. Send the following session:

```
POST /EEYE.htr HTTP/1.1
Host: 0day.big5.com
Transfer-Encoding: chunked
20
XXXXXXXXXXXXXXXXXXXXXXXXXXEEYE2002
0
[enter]
[enter]
```

This triggers the alarm. But wait—if you do a simple modification to the case of the content, you can avoid tripping the rule.

```
POST /EEYE.htr HTTP/1.1
Host: 0day.big5.com
TranSfer-Encoding: chunked
20
XXXXXXXXXXXXXXXXXXXXXXXXXXEEYE2002
0
[enter]
[enter]
```

> **Note**
> The s in Transfer-Encoding has been capitalized.

The chunked encoding rule is susceptible to a simple evasion tactic. To remedy this, you need to make the content rules not case-sensitive:

```
alert tcp $EXTERNAL_NET any -> 192.168.1.1 $HTTP_PORTS
(msg:"WEB-IIS .htr Transfer-Encoding\: chunked"; flow:to_server,established;
uricontent:".htr"; nocase; content:"Transfer-Encoding\:"; nocase;
content:"chunked"; nocase; classtype:web-application-attack;
reference:bugtraq,4855; reference:cve,CAN-2002-0364; sid:1806; rev:5;)
```

Adding the `nocase` keyword makes each of the content rules not case-sensitive. Additionally, some external references are added now that they are available. This completes the first method of writing a Snort rule.

Creating a New Rule by Using Network Knowledge

These rules are easy to create. If you wanted to monitor for a specific type of Web content, you could create a rule to match a particular content pattern. To create the rule, you first need to write the rule header. You want to look for any Web server request responses.

HTTP communication is over TCP, so you will use that protocol for the rule. You want to monitor any external address you have defined, so you should use the `$EXTERNAL_NET` variable. You also want the rule to apply only to Web servers, so you use `$HTTP_PORTS` to identify the list of ports that are associated with HTTP connections. Lastly, you want to monitor the entire internal network, so you use `$HOME_NET` for the destination addresses. The HTTP request uses any randomly chosen high-numbered port, so you should set the ports for `$HOME_NET` to any. This translates to the following rule header:

```
alert tcp $EXTERNAL_NET $HTTP_PORTS -> $HOME_NET any
```

The rule option will be the content for which you want to monitor. Imagine that you want to monitor for anyone going to a popular security site that includes exploits and hacking techniques:

```
(msg:"POSSIBLE B-HAT packetstorm content"; content:"packetstorm"; nocase; flow:
to_client; prioirity:2; rev:1; sid: 1000001;)
```

This rule alerts on any content that contains "packetstorm", which is a popular site for hackers and security professionals. The packetstorm domain name changes somewhat frequently, so you do not want to use the current domain name. Someone may access the site via an IP address, so you will alert to any "packetstorm" content. You give the rule a priority of 2, and set it to trigger only when the ACK packet is present in the TCP session.

You can use this methodology to create just about any simple Snort rule with your knowledge of your network.

Creating a New Rule by Using Traffic Analysis

Creating a rule by examining packets is the most difficult, but quite possibly the most rewarding method of rule writing. Traffic analysis is frequently used to create a new rule when a new vulnerability or exploit is being researched. Traffic analysis can also be used to refine or modify existing rules.

The easiest way to perform traffic analysis is to pass the exploit by a sniffer in a controlled environment. If you do not have access to the exploit code yourself, and need to capture the traffic from the Internet, you should place the sniffer behind a firewall with only the required ports open. The idea here is to reduce the amount of traffic you will have to page through to create the rule. Imagine you want to create a rule that monitors for the OpenSSL Slapper worm.

Unfortunately, you do not have a copy of the worm handy, so you will have to place a sniffer behind a firewall and allow only the port that Slapper uses. Slapper exploits a security exposure in OpenSSL, so the best port to open is 443/tcp, the traditional HTTPS port. You know that you should get a response from the server that is something like "no job control in this shell" if you are attacked by Slapper. After some time, you grep through the tcpdump logs and find:

```
16:45:00.58749 worm.host.com.3568 > openssl.webhost.https:
 P 561:605(44) ack 987 win 7660 <nop,nop,timestamp 45618795 157894758> (DF)
0x0000  4500 f8a1 0fd5 01bb 6a10 a9ae b61f 10d1    ES.....j.......
0x0010  0f47 57f6 5445 524d 3d78 7465 726d 3b20    .GW.TERM=xterm;.
0x0020  6578 706f 7274 2054 4552 4d3d 7874 6572    export.TERM=xter
0x0030  6d3b 2065 7865 6320 6261 7368 202d 690a    m;.exec.bash.-i.
0x0040  8018 1dce 0945 0000 0101 080a 035f f2c4    .....E......._..
0x0050  0388 0388 56ad 4000 3106 1369 3ee2 2483    ....V.@.1..i>.$.

16:45:00.68799 openssl.webhost.com.https > worm.host.com.3568:
 . ack 210 win 7542 <nop,nop,timestamp 157894758 45618795> (DF)
0x0000  4500 0034 5bdf 4000 4006 028b 8053 f8a1    E..4[.@.@....S..
0x0010  3ee2 2483 01bb 0fd5 b61f 10d1 6a10 a9ae    >.$.........j...
0x0020  8010 1920 37a1 0000 0101 080a 0f47 580b    ....7........GX.
0x0030  035f f2b0                                   ._..

16:45:00.85714 openssl.webhost.com.https > worm.host.com.3568
 P 1147:1182(35) ack 210 win 7542 <nop,nop,timestamp 157894758 45618795> (DF)
0x0000  4500 0057 5be0 4000 4006 0267 8053 f8a1    E..W[.@.@..g.S..
0x0010  035f f2b0 6261 7368 3a20 6e6f 206a 6f62    ._..bash:.no.job
0x0020  2063 6f6e 7472 6f6c 2069 6e20 7468 6973    .control.in.this
0x0030  2073 6865 6c6c 0a              .shell.
```

The first packet contains a content pattern that is unique to this worm attack. The next two are the server response you used to find the attack. You will use `export TERM=xterm\; exec bash -I` to create the signature.

Start with the rule header. You should be alerted of TCP traffic incoming from any external source, from any port. You want the rule to apply only to your Web servers, and specifically only to the HTTPS port (443).

```
alert tcp $EXTERNAL_NET any -> $HTTP_SERVERS 443
```

To build the rule option, make use of the content string you found, being careful to turn off case sensitivity. You also want to be alerted only to TCP flags with the ACK flag set.

```
(msg:"Slapper attack"; flow: to_server, established; content:"export TERM=xterm\;
exec bash -i"; nocase; priority:1; rev:1)
```

You also give this alert a priority of 1, so that you are alerted of it in real time. The completed rule looks like the following:

```
alert tcp $EXTERNAL_NET any -> $HTTP_SERVERS 443
(msg:"Slapper attack"; flow: to_server, established;

content:"export TERM=xterm\; exec bash -i"; nocase; priority:1; rev:1)
```

This completes the rule for the Slapper worm. Obviously, half the battle of writing the rule is identifying the correct packets that contain the actual attack. When writing a new rule, do not hesitate to use the vast Snort community for help. Most likely someone else has some information, resources, or data to share.

Note

When creating a rule based on observed network traffic, make sure that the content you are triggering on is vital for the actual attack.

Summary

This chapter is an introduction to writing rules in Snort. It describes the Snort rules syntax in great detail, and then offers some concrete examples that make use of the syntax.

The goal in creating effective signatures is to write rules that exclusively match the network traffic you want to discover. To write rules that trigger only on the traffic you intend them to, you must research and discover unique properties of the traffic.

Snort rules have a basic syntax that must be adhered to for the rule to properly match a traffic signature. Violating the Snort rules syntax can cause a rule to not load into the detection engine. The most basic syntactical requirement of a Snort rule is that it be in a single line. A Snort rule is divided into two sections: the rule header and the rule option. The rule header defines the type of alert and which protocols, IP addresses, and IP protocol ports are to be monitored for the signature. The rule header is the portion of the rule up to the first parentheses. The rule option is the actual signature and the assigned priority. The signature portion of the rule option is represented with one or more option keywords. These option keywords are used to build the traffic signature for which you would like the detection engine to monitor.

There are essentially three methods to writing Snort rules. The first and easiest method is to modify or add to an existing rule. To tune Snort and make it more efficient, you may have already attempted this process. The second method is to create a new rule by using your knowledge of your network. These rules are fairly easy to create because they do not require extensive traffic analysis. The third method, creating a new rule by examining network traffic, is the most difficult.

13

Upgrading and Maintaining Snort

A NY BOOK CLAIMING TO BE A COMPLETE guide to a complicated software package should have a chapter on upgrading that software. At some point, you will have to make significant changes to Snort to keep it relevant. You will have to update the ruleset, make changes to configuration options, and eventually upgrade the Snort application itself. These topics are covered in this chapter.

There are several different strategies for upgrading Snort rules and changing configuration settings. The first, and most simple, is to physically sit at the console of the computer that has Snort installed on it. You can make your changes with a text editor, save them, and then restart Snort. Another option is to use SSH to remotely access the machine, make your changes, and then restart Snort. These two methods of upgrading and making changes to configuration files are practical for small Snort installations. If you are running a hybrid server/sensor, or have a distributed setup with one or two sensors, these manual methods are preferable. Making the changes manually across five, ten, or fifty sensors can be extremely difficult and time consuming; it is advisable to use a more automated method with a Snort management application. This is not to say you should not use a management application if you have a small or hybrid installation; you are simply not required to.

A number of applications have sprung up in the past few years that aim to make managing the Snort application an easier and more intuitive process. Most of these applications have a GUI that you can use to upgrade or make configuration changes across a large group of sensors. The two applications that are covered in this chapter are IDS Policy Manager and SnortCenter. IDS Policy Manager is a Windows 2000/XP application that can manage Unix-based Snort installations. SnortCenter is a Web application based on the Snort Webmin plugin. Webmin is an administration tool used to manage various services on Unix machines via a Web browser.

Modifying the ruleset and changing configuration settings are used to make incremental upgrades to a Snort installation. Eventually, you will have to make an upgrade to the Snort binary or another portion of the application. Doing so can be a difficult process. Merging the same configuration settings for an old version of Snort to the latest distribution can be difficult. The syntax of `snort.conf` and the `.config` and `.rules` files often changes from one version of Snort to another, meaning that the old version of `snort.conf` and other configuration files will not load with a new version. A new version of Snort usually includes additional features that you may want or need to take advantage of, so these changes need to be addressed as well.

Choosing a Snort Management Application

The choice you make for the Snort management application is largely dependant on the type of operating system you are most accustomed to and have installed on your Analyst Console.

If you have decided to use Windows 2000 for the Analyst Console, you will likely want to make use of IDS Policy Manager. If the Analyst Console you deployed is Unix-based, you cannot use IDS Policy Manager because it runs only on Windows 2000/XP. You have to use SnortCenter. SnortCenter is Web-based, so it can be used on either Windows or Unix consoles.

IDS Policy Manager

IDS Policy Manager is a Windows 2000/XP application that is used to remotely manage Snort sensors. It is used to change settings to the Snort configuration and rules files. IDS Policy Manager can access most of the Snort configuration parameters, including the following:

- Network variables
- Rule classifications
- Preprocessors
- Output plugins
- Snort command-line switches
- Ruleset settings

These setting can be stored in what is known as a "policy." Different policies can be created for different types of sensors. You can create one policy for internal sensors and one for external. You can create a policy to be used in incident response. Policies are a great way to test new features and rules because you can easily roll back to a working state.

Policies can be created from the official Snort configuration and rules files, from scratch, or from an existing sensor. When downloading or uploading a policy from a sensor, IDS Policy Manager makes use of the SCP package included with Putty. This ensures that authentication information, as well as session data, are encrypted.

Installing

You can get IDS Policy Manager at

`http://www.activeworx.com/downloads/index.htm`

Unzip the archive and run the IDS Policy Manager executable. Start up IDS Policy Manager after you have installed it. The first task is to add your sensors to the Sensor Manager. Click on the Sensor Manager tab. Select the Sensor menu and click Add Sensor.

From here you can add each sensor in your Snort installation. Add the sensor information as it corresponds to the sensors you have installed on your Snort installation. A few points are worth mentioning:

- Make sure to use SCP as the Upload Protocol. Without it you cannot download configuration settings from sensors or encrypt sessions.

- Set the Upload Directory to the location of your Snort configuration files (for example, /etc/snort/conf).

- When selecting a policy, you can use the Official policy. As you proceed through this chapter you will change the policy to reflect what is actually configured on the sensor..

IDS Policy Manager should look like Figure 13.1 when you have all the sensors installed.

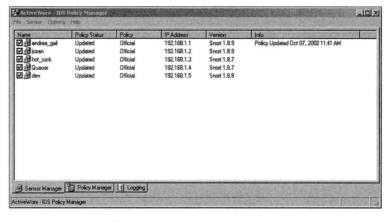

Figure 13.1   The Sensor Manager.

Now you can download the configuration settings for each sensor. Right-click on the sensor and select Download Policy From Sensor to load the configuration settings into IDS Policy manager. If you have several sensors with exactly the same configuration settings, you should download the setting from one of the sensors to avoid duplication.

Note

IDS Policy Manager strips all comments from the configuration files and appends all the .rules files when they are loaded.

After you have the settings downloaded from the sensors, you should add the most current Snort default settings to the Policy Manager. Select the Policy Manager tab and then select the Policy menu. Click on the Add Policy option. Add the correct information to locate an untouched version of the Snort configuration files. Name this policy "default" or something similar.

Configuring

To update the various configuration settings for each sensor, you need to make use of the Policy Manager. The Policy Manager is used to create, modify, and delete policies that can be applied to any number of sensors. You should have loaded all the unique policies into the Policy Manger during the previous installation section in this chapter. This section explains how to configure the various options within IDS Policy Manager, but does not duplicate the documentation pertaining to the function of the Snort configuration options. Refer to Chapter 3, "Dissecting Snort," and Chapter 10, "Tuning and Reducing False Positives," for detailed Snort configuration option explanations.

Double-click on the policy you want to modify. This loads the policy into the Policy Editor. From this window you can make the changes you require to the policy. Select the settings tab to view the familiar Snort configuration settings.

- The Settings submenu enables you to declare or modify existing network variables. You can also customize the classification of rules (mapped to `classification.config`). If the Classifications section is blank, check that the `classification.config` file is located in the same directory that you specified when you added the sensor. If you have placed it in a different location, specify the correct location in the Directory on Sensor text box.

- The Alerting and Logging submenus are where the output plugins are enabled. You enable the corresponding output plugin by clicking on the check box. The Alerting submenu includes configuration for SnortSam, an intrusion prevention application that is covered in Chapter 14, "Advanced Topics."

- The PreProcessors submenu defines the preprocessors to be used for the policy. You can enable and disable any of the preprocessors and their options in this submenu.

- The Option submenu enables you to change or modify the Snort command-line options. You have access to every command-line switch with this submenu—even some of the more obscure and rarely used options. You can also rearrange the rule execution order.

- The final submenu, Custom Actions, allows you to enable, modify, and create rule actions. Here you can define specific rule actions that can be applied to rules. Custom rule actions are used primarily to force a particular Snort rule to use an output plugin different from the rest of the rulset.

After the configuration options have been set, you can move to modifying the ruleset to your liking. Click on the Signatures tab on the left pane to bring up the list of rules. You can merge any `.rules` file to the master ruleset by selecting the Options menu and then Add .Rules File to Policy. Choose the `.rules` file and it will be merged into the ruleset.

Placing a check in the associated check box of the rule category enables the entire set of rules. You can select individual rules in the same manner. If you would like to disable or enable rules that apply to a specific IP address or port, you can do so by selecting Enable/Disable Rules by IP/Port from the Options menu. Here you can apply your knowledge of your network to quickly trim the ruleset. Disabling rules that include ports or IP addresses that you do not wish to monitor is a quick way to reduce the amount of processing power Snort requires.

Note

An empty check box on a ruleset does not necessarily mean the entire ruleset has been deactivated. If even one rule in a set is unchecked, the check for the entire ruleset is removed.

If you select a rule category, the right pane displays the configuration page for the chosen category. From this screen you can modify the Rule Header and Rule Option as you see fit, as shown in Figure 13.2.

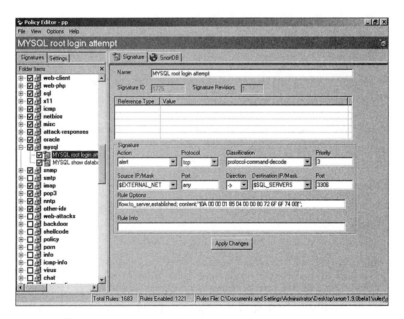

Figure 13.2   Rule modification with IDS Policy Manager.

You can view direct links to the external documentation resources by selecting the corresponding resource tabs. The tabs load the Internet resource into a browser within IDS Policy Manager.

After you have defined your ruleset, you can apply your policy to the sensor or group of sensors. Simply select the Sensor Manager tab and select the Sensor menu. From this menu you can update all sensors or an individual sensor with the various Upload to Sensor options. After you have updated the sensors, you need to restart the Snort daemon manually.

This completes the review of IDS Policy Manager. As you can see, IDS Policy Manager does not add any significantly new functionality to Snort; it merely makes the upgrading and management of Snort configuration files an easier and more automated process.

SnortCenter

SnortCenter is a Web-based management application used to upgrade and maintain Snort configuration settings. It has a similar function as IDS Policy Manager, but uses a PHP/MySQL Web interface instead. SnortCenter has a few additional features that IDS Policy Manger does not have, including the following:

- Snort daemon up or down status indicator
- Remote Snort stop/start/restart functionality
- Access control for SnortCenter users
- Integration with ACID
- Sensor groups

SnortCenter consists of a PHP-based management application and SnortCenter agents. The SnortCenter Management Console can be installed on a Snort Server, whereas the SnortCenter Sensor Agents are installed on the sensors to be managed. SnortCenter leverages the software packages likely installed in a Snort distributed setup. It requires the following packages for the server portion:

- MySQL
- Apache
- PHP
- ADODB
- OpenSSL
- cURL

The only package that is likely to be unfamiliar to you is cURL. Because these software packages have been ported to most operating systems, the SnortCenter Management Console runs on Windows, Linux, and BSD. The SnortCenter Sensor Agent requires the installation of Perl on Unix-based operating systems. The agent can run on Windows-based sensors with the help of some additional precompiled binaries.

Installing SnortCenter

The installation instructions in this chapter assume you have chosen to install ACID. Consequently you should have previously installed MySQL, Apache, PHP, ADODB, and OpenSSL on the machine acting as the Snort server. You can install SnortCenter on either Windows- or Unix-based systems.

The SnortCenter Management Console

The only remaining package to install prior to SnortCenter is cURL. cURL is a command-line tool for transferring files via a URL without user intervention. It is used to manage and control the Snort sensors.

The cURL package is installed on most Linux and BSD distributions by default. You can check to see whether you have the package installed on Red Hat by using the following command:

```
rpm -qa | grep curl
```

This command queries for any package with the `curl` string in it. If you do not have cURL installed, you can download it at

```
http://curl.haxx.se/download.html
```

After downloading, untar, compile, and install the source. After you have cURL installed, download SnortCenter from

```
http://users.pandora.be/larc/download/
```

Download the SnortCenter Management Console for your appropriate operating system. Untar the SnortCenter files into a directory under your Web document root (for example, `/usr/local/apache/htdocs/snortcenter`). After you have copied the files into the SnortCenter directory, you need to configure SnortCenter via the `config.php` file. Open this file for editing and configure the following variables:

- `DBlib_path`   Set this to the location of the ADODB library. If you followed the instructions verbatim in Chapter 6, it should be located at `/usr/local/apache/htdocs/php/adodb`. Make sure not to include a trailing forward slash.
- `curl_path`   Set this variable equal to the location of the cURL binary. By default, cURL is installed in `/usr/local/curl/bin`.
- `DBtype`   Set `DBtype` to the type of database you have installed. Set to `mysql` if you have installed MySQL as the intrusion database.
- `DB_dbname`   This is the name of the SnortCenter database that you will create in the next step. Set to `snortcenter` or a similar name.
- `DB_host`   `DB_host` is the hostname of the Snort server. If the SnortCenter Management Console is installed on the same computer as the database, set this to `localhost`.

- `DB_user` The database user as which SnortCenter will log in. You should create a separate user for the SnortCenter package that has access to only the SnortCenter database. This way an attacker that obtains this authentication information will be limited to the SnortCenter application. This user needs `SELECT`, `INSTERT`, `UPDATE`, and `DELETE` privileges.

- `DB_password` The password for `DB_USER`.

- `DB_port` `DB_port` is the port on which the database is running. If you are using `localhost` for the `DB_host`, you can leave this undefined.

- `User_authentication` This variable sets the user authentication feature for SnortCenter. If set to 1, users of SnortCenter have to log in to the Management Console before working in SnortCenter. If you set this to 0, access to the Web-based console is accessible to anyone who can reach the Snort server.

- `hidden_key_num` Set this variable to a random string of 10 integers or more.

Save your changes and exit `config.php`. The next task is to create the database you specified for the `DB_dbname` variable. Log in to MySQL:

```
/usr/local/mysql/bin/mysql -p secure_password
```

And create the SnortCenter database:

```
create database snortcenter;
```

After you have created the database, bring up the SnortCenter Management Console in a Web browser (that is `https://localhost/snortcenter`). When the page loads, you need to select the Create DB Tables option from the Admin menu, as shown in Figure 13.3.

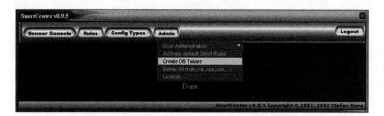

Figure 13.3 Creating tables with SnortCenter.

This creates all the tables necessary for SnortCenter. You can also create them with the `snortcenter_db.mysql` script located in the tarball. This completes the installation of the SnortCenter Management Console. To log in for the first time, you have to use the username `admin` and the password `change`.

The SnortCenter Sensor Agent

To complete the SnortCenter installation, you have to install the SnortCenter Sensor Agents on the sensors you want to manage with SnortCenter. The installation of the agents for Unix environments is covered in this section.

The agents for Unix-based systems require Perl, OpenSSL, and the Perl module `Net::SSLeay`. You should have OpenSSL and Perl installed on the sensor, leaving only the `Net::SSLeay` module to be installed. You can find it on the CPAN Web site at

```
http://search.cpan.org
```

Download and install `Net::SSLeay`. To install it, issue the following commands from the source directory:

```
perl Makefile.PL
make install
```

After you have `Net::SSLeay` installed, you need to create the directories that the SnortCenter Sensor Agent will use. Create the following directories:

```
/usr/local/snortcenter
/usr/local/snortcenter/conf
/usr/local/snortcenter/log
/usr/local/snortcenter/rules
```

Next you need to create an SSL certificate for SnortCenter to use. Create it with the following command:

```
openssl req -new -x509 -days 365 -nodes -out snortcenter.pem
-keyout snortcenter.pem
```

Copy the `snortcenter.pem` file to the `/usr/local/snortcenter/conf` directory. Now you are ready to install the SnortCenter Sensor Agent. Download the appropriate version at

```
http://users.pandora.be/larc/download/
```

Untar and move the files to the `/usr/local/snortcenter/` directory. Run the installation shell script:

```
sh setup.sh
```

The installation script poses a number of questions to you. You have already created the required directories for Snort and SnortCenter; input these when asked. You can use any port for the agent to run on; just make sure to remember which port you chose. Make sure to specify the management NIC's IP address for SnortCenter to listen on. Choose Yes when you come to the enabling SSL option.

You should also take care to remember the login name and password for the agent. You need to enter the authentication information into the Management Console. The final options set the IP address of the Snort Server. This completes the installation of the SnortCenter Sensor Agent. Replicate this process for each sensor in your Snort environment.

Configuring

This section includes how to configure the various options within SnortCenter, but does not duplicate the documentation pertaining to the function of the Snort configuration options. Refer to Chapters 3 and 10 for detailed Snort configuration option descriptions. To update the various configuration settings for the sensors, you must first add them to the SnortCenter Management Console. Log in to the SnortCenter Management Console and select Add Sensor from the Sensor Console menu. Enter the information that corresponds to the Sensor you want to add, as shown in Figure 13.4.

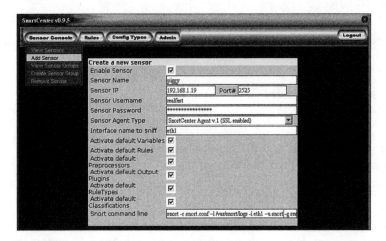

Figure 13.4 Adding a sensor in SnortCenter.

The Sensor Username and Password are the authentication information you chose when running the `setup.sh` shell script. The Snort Command Line is the command line you want to use when SnortCenter starts the Snort daemon. When the sensor is added, its status is displayed on the main page. From here you can start, stop, and restart the sensor. The sensor starts with the Snort command line specified in the sensor properties.

After you have added all the sensors, you can group them into logical groups by using the Create Sensor Group option from the Sensor Console menu. Rules and configuration settings can be applied to individual sensors and sensor groups.

The Snort configuration options are controlled from the Config Types menu. You can modify Network Variables, Preprocessors, Output Plugins, Rule Types, and Rule Classifications via this menu.

You can also enable, disable, modify, and create rules with the Rules menu. The rules list is shown in Figure 13.5.

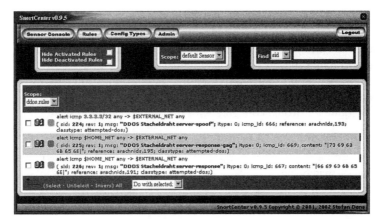

Figure 13.5   The rules list.

You can view categories of rules with the lower Scope drop down box. The upper Scope drop down box applies the ruleset to a particular sensor, group of sensors, or the default sensor configuration.

If the edit icon is clicked next to the rule, the rule editing page is displayed for that particular rule. From here you can change the Rule Header and Rule Option for the selected rule. You can also use the Save As New option to create a new rule. Additionally, the Create Rule option from the Rules menu enables you to create new rules from scratch.

The Import/Update Rules option enables you to insert new rules from the official Snort ruleset at Snort.org or a local file. New rules are deactivated by default; you can add them to a particular sensor or sensor group by activating them in the View Rules page.

Upgrading Snort

The process of upgrading Snort can be quite difficult and confusing the first time through. Historically, a new version of Snort has been released every few months, meaning you are likely to upgrade Snort often. New upgrades to Snort can add functionality to detect new types of malicious traffic, or make detecting malicious traffic easier. Upgrades are also released to combat new IDS evasion techniques and software bugs.

The first step in upgrading the Snort application is to rename the Snort binary. You should rename it to something descriptive that will identify the correct Snort version. You can do so with a command like this:

```
mv snort snort-2.0
```

Now you need to download the new Snort source. Place it in a directory that is different than the current source directory (such as /usr/local/snort-2.1), so that you do not overwrite the source from the previous version.

You many not remember the configuration line you used to build the previous binary, so you should inspect the old configuration files for them. In the old version's compile directory, you will find a file named `config.status`. Open this file, and you should see the options specified in the first few lines.

Move to the new Snort source directory, and use these lines to create the configure command for the new Snort source. For example, if your Snort setup makes use of the FlexResp module, you would configure with the following command:

```
./configure --enable-flexresp
```

Now you can `make` and `make install`. You can test the version of the new binary by using the `-V` switch, like so:

```
snort -V
```

> **Note**
> The V is capitalized.

Now that you have the new binary squared away, you need to discover any changes that have been made to the Snort configuration files. The configuration file that is changed the most often is `snort.conf`. New preprocessors, output plugins, and network variables are loaded in `snort.conf`.

Manually comparing the old and new `snort.conf` files is a tedious process, and is likely to result in mistakes. You can use the `diff` command to automatically find the difference between two files. You can then use the output of the `diff` command to make changes to the new version of `snort.conf`.

The first step is to compare what has changed in the default `snort.conf` files distributed in the source tarball. Compare the new `snort.conf` to a default `snort.conf` from the old version. If you do not have a copy of the old `snort.conf`, download the previous version's tarball from the Snort Web site. Execute this `diff` command to find the difference in the two files:

```
diff ../path/to/old/version/of/snort.conf snort.conf
```

This shows you the changes in the default versions. Make note of each change; if the syntax is incorrect in the `snort.conf` file, Snort may not load or could behave erratically.

Next you need to repeat this `diff` process to discover the settings you changed in the previous version's `snort.conf`. You should reimplement these changes in the `snort.conf` for the new version. Run this `diff` command to find the changes:

```
diff ../path/to/old/version/of/snort.conf old/modified/version/of/snort.conf
```

These two outputs—the changes from the new Snort version's `snort.conf` and the changes you made to the old version's `snort.conf`—make a record of the changes you need to make to have a working `snort.conf` file for the new version of Snort. After you have made the changes, copy the newly created `snort.conf` file over to the new Snort binary directory. Test the new `snort.conf` by using the `-T` switch, like so:

```
snort -T -c snort.conf
```

This should output any errors Snort has in loading the configuration file.

If there are no issues, copy over the configuration files to the Snort binary directory. You should copy the following files:

- `classification.config`
- `gen-msg.map`
- `reference.config`
- `sid-msg.map`
- `*.rules`

You can use this same process for `barnyard.conf` as well.

If changes have been made to the database structure, you may have to make changes to the tables manually. You can use the `diff` command to find the difference between two versions of the `create_mysql` script. If there are significant changes to the database structure, you may be better off creating an entirely new database for the new version of Snort.

Summary

This chapter covers the upgrading of both Snort configuration options and the Snort application itself. Two automated methods of upgrading Snort configuration options were presented. They both involve the use of a third-party application designed to manage Snort sensors. The two applications covered in this chapter are IDS Policy Manager and SnortCenter. IDS Policy Manager is a Windows 2000/XP application that can manage Unix-based Snort installations. SnortCenter is a Web-based management application that installs agents on each sensor.

The choice you make for the Snort management application is largely dependant on the type of operating system you are most accustomed to and have installed on your Analyst Console. IDS Policy Manager is a Windows 2000/XP application that is used to remotely manage Snort sensors. It is used to change settings to the Snort configuration and rules files. IDS Policy Manager can access most of the Snort configuration parameters.

These parameters can be stored in what is known as a *policy*. Different policies can be created for different types of sensors. Policies are managed through the Policy Manager. The Policy Manager is used to create, modify, and delete policies that can be applied to any number of sensors.

SnortCenter is a Web-based management application used to upgrade and maintain Snort configuration settings. It has a similar function as IDS Policy Manager, but uses a

PHP/MySQL Web interface instead. SnortCenter has a few additional features that IDS Policy Manger does not have.

SnortCenter consists of a PHP-based management application and SnortCenter agents. The SnortCenter Management Console can be installed on a Snort Server, whereas the SnortCenter Sensor Agents are installed on the sensors to be managed. SnortCenter involves more installation steps than IDS Policy Manager because it involves deploying agents on each sensor.

The process of upgrading Snort can be quite difficult and confusing the first time through. Historically, a new version of Snort has been released every few months, meaning you are likely to upgrade Snort often. You upgrade Snort by using the `diff` command to discover discrepancies between the new and old `snort.conf` files.

14

Advanced Topics
in Intrusion Prevention

THIS CHAPTER COVERS INTRUSION PREVENTION with Snort. The term "intrusion prevention" has caused quite a stir in the IDS community in the last few years. Some vendors hail intrusion prevention as the next evolutionary step for intrusion detection to take. Others see it as nothing more than a novelty. This chapter does not focus on the debate, but rather outlines the points of both sides and allows you to make your own decision. If you have come this far and deployed a working Snort IDS, you are smarter than the average bear and can make your own decisions.

You have already had a taste of intrusion prevention with the FlexResp module and rules in Chapter 12, "Basic Rule Writing," and the BlackIce plugin in Chapter 9, "Additional Installation Methods." This chapter shows you two intrusion prevention applications that interoperate with Snort—the Snort Inline patch and SnortSam—and demonstrates situations where they are best used.

An intrusion prevention application is similar to an IDS in that both applications aim to distinguish unauthorized activity from normal activity. An intrusion prevention application, like an IDS, has a set of signatures or predefined conditions that, when met, trigger a response. This response itself, however, differs, and is what differentiates an IDS from an intrusion prevention application.

As you know, an IDS is designed to alert a human to potentially unauthorized activity. The underlying concept of an intrusion detection system is that a human must be present in the system to determine when activity is truly unauthorized. An IDS assumes that only a highly trained IDS analyst can make a proper decision on the correct course of action when an intrusion is suspected. Consequently, when unauthorized activity is discovered, the IDS makes every effort to alert a person to potentially unauthorized activity.

A true intrusion prevention application seeks to do away with the human element in intrusion detection. The IDS analyst is an expensive and unreliable component of the entire intrusion detection system. A person can take hours or days to react to an intrusion, often too late to prevent damage from occurring. A far better solution is to automate the response from an IDS to take corrective action. This action can include the dropping or "scrubbing" of packets that match a signature or predefined condition that indicates unauthorized activity. It can also include blocking all traffic with the same source IP address that has triggered the response. Additionally, a HIDS-based intrusion prevention application can disallow specified applications or user accounts from interacting with other applications or operating system functions.

A Warning Concerning Intrusion Prevention

Intrusion prevention seems like a great idea on paper. The organization simply deploys intrusion prevention sensors at critical points throughout network infrastructure. When an attack is perpetrated, the application detects the unauthorized activity and prevents it from occurring at the speed of light. No human interaction is required, no one has to wake up in the middle of the night, and most importantly, the business owners can sleep peacefully at night knowing attacks are automatically prevented.

Unfortunately, in the real world, this is not the case. The key is that the technology that determines whether activity is unauthorized is the same for an IDS and an intrusion prevention application. This means that an intrusion prevention application is just as prone to all the problems of intrusion detection, but with potentially damaging consequences. With intrusion prevention, false positives can render your entire network unreachable.

Unlike an IDS, which simply alerts an IDS analyst when suspicious activity has taken place, the intrusion prevention application takes corrective action with no human intervention. If the alert is a false positive, the intrusion prevention application still takes corrective action. This can include restricting the user from using the application on a HIDS, blocking the IP address of the host that generated the false positive, or scrubbing packets that match a signature. If the traffic generating the false positive contains important data for the organization, it will be lost. If the source IP address is that of a critical business partner, the partner will be prevented from accessing the resource. False positives can have drastic consequences in an intrusion prevention application. Until false positives can be nearly totally eliminated from intrusion detection and intrusion prevention applications, these issues will persist.

Another serious problem with intrusion prevention applications is that they can be used to indirectly attack a network. Any time you have an active response based on predefined situations, an attacker can re-create the exact situations to illicit the response. With Snort, snot and stick attacks will flood the IDS with a hail of false positives. A snot attack could potentially overload Snort, or most likely, harass the IDS analyst and make legitimate attacks difficult to discover in the flood. The same snot attack against an intrusion prevention application can block significant portions of the Internet from reaching the target. It can also overload devices that are used in the prevention response to filter out IP addresses (such as an external screening router or firewall). If the attacker has knowledge of your network, she can make a less noisy and more calculating attack to cut off access to important network connected resources. Because IP addresses are easily spoofed, the attacker can use the intrusion prevention application to block access to any IP address she chooses. The attacker can spoof the address of a DNS server the organization relies upon, and send attacks with packets that include the DNS server's IP address.

For these reasons, an intrusion prevention application can be dangerous. Many people within the IDS community do not look fondly at intrusion prevention applications, as they can create more problems than they prevent. Until the underlying technology that is used to make a distinction between unauthorized and authorized activity is improved upon, intrusion prevention will be relevant only for specific niche situations.

Planning an Intrusion Prevention Strategy

Now that you are aware of some of the latent issues in an intrusion prevention application, you realize that planning the intrusion prevention deployment is an entirely different process than it is for an IDS. The same strategy used to configure Snort would lead to huge problems, as the number of false positives would deny service to many people and applications.

The process of deploying intrusion prevention is lengthier and requires greater attention to detail than installing an IDS. With Snort, a misconfigured option or rule can affect only the performance of the IDS itself. With an intrusion prevention application, a misconfiguration can literally take down your network.

The first step in planning an intrusion prevention strategy at your organization is to define locations and situations where intrusion prevention is appropriate. Because of the potentially dangerous nature of intrusion prevention applications, you should deploy them only in selected situations.

A device used for intrusion prevention can become a single point of failure. Some intrusion prevention applications, specifically gateway IDSs and packet scrubbers, must sit in front of the network to be protected, much like a firewall. When deploying intrusion prevention, you should take into account the new single point of failure and plan a backup strategy. This can be as simple as creating a failover device, or taking extra precautions to ensure the intrusion prevention computer is fully redundant. This can include creating a RAMdisk intrusion prevention device, as described later in this chapter, which does not require a hard drive.

The best way to decide where to place an intrusion prevention system is to consider the priorities of the system to be affected by it. If the chief priority is the availability of the system, and security is not as important, the system is probably a poor candidate for an intrusion prevention system. Conversely, if security of the system is paramount, and a potential reduction in availability is tolerable, the system may be a good candidate for intrusion prevention. The following sections examine some of the specific situations where intrusion prevention is appropriate.

Unpatched Servers

Intrusion prevention applications can deliver the greatest value to networks with servers not up to the required security patch level. Servers can remain unpatched for many different reasons. Software packages critical to the host often don't function with a patch, leaving the server in an unpatched state. Other networked environments are so large that maintaining 100% confidence that all servers are patched is impossible. Some network admins are not security conscious and do not bother to patch servers.

Whatever the reason behind servers remaining unpatched, the important point for this section is that an intrusion prevention application can help. You can create a rule that exactly matches the exploit for the vulnerability present on the potentially affected servers. For the rule action, you can configure a packet scrubber to drop packets that match the exploit signature. In this way, you have protected the unpatchable server.

New Vulnerabilities

There is usually a lag time between when a vulnerability is released and a patch is available. This can create a tense period in which business-critical hosts are vulnerable to an attack. In this time, server admins often have to use a workaround proposed by the vendor or security researcher. The workaround can be extremely unpractical; often the solution is just to turn off the offending service.

An intrusion prevention application can help in this situation, as it would with unpatched servers. You can load a signature that triggers on the exploit for the vulnerability.

Publicly Accessible High-Priority Hosts

Hosts that have extremely high security requirements, such as servers that contain data pertaining to national security, financial institution monetary transfer applications, and online medical record databases, are all good choices for an intrusion prevention system. You may want to enable intrusion prevention to lock out possible attacker IP addresses for a period of time, or scrub packets that match signatures of known attacks.

Intrusion prevention can be useful in these situations, as long as security is a higher priority than availability.

Rules That Never Create a False Positive

Some signatures or rules have a near-zero false positive ratio. The likelihood of such a traffic signature occurring normally is next to zero. An example is the rule that detects packets that have the same IP address specified for the source and destination address. No application would ever create a packet with the same source and destination IP address.

Rules that never have a false positive can be safely dropped. You can configure a packet scrubber to drop these types of attacks, and spend time concentrating on attacks that are orchestrated by more skilled black hats.

There are many other potential candidates for intrusion prevention; these are simply some examples to get you thinking in the right direction.

After you have located points of presence where intrusion prevention is appropriate, you should take a measured approach to installing the intrusion prevention software. The applications detailed in this chapter extend Snort's IDS capabilities by adding new responses when a rule is triggered. When installing intrusion prevention, you should implement the rule that will trigger the prevention action with a benign logging or alerting action first. After running the rule for a time, observe the output and check diligently for false positives. If you find none, then you can enable the intrusion prevention response. Be sure not to modify the rule as you work through this process. Obviously, if you have a shorter time frame than a week, as with the new vulnerability situation described previously, you will have to make do.

Snort Inline Patch

The Snort Inline patch exists as both a separate application, named Hogwash, and a patched version of Snort. Hogwash code has merged into the Snort source tree, where it can take advantage of the considerable accomplishments of the Snort application. The Snort Inline patch can make use of Snort's packet decoding and reassembly features, such as the stream preprocessors, to be a more effective and complete intrusion prevention system.

The Snort Inline patch makes use of the familiar `iptables` and `ip_queue` for packet acquisition and forwarding. You could use `iptables` to create a firewall on the same machine that the Snort Inline patch lives on. Hogwash has its own native code for packet forwarding and acquisition, making it more specialized but not as flexible. This section, covers the Snort Inline patch exclusively. If you want to use the Hogwash code, however, a good proportion of the tutorial here will still apply.

With the Inline patch, Snort can elicit an intrusion prevention response when a rule is triggered. To do this, the Inline Snort host must reside between the source of the attack and the destination, as shown in Figure 14.1. Consequently, all traffic must flow through the Inline Snort computer. Therefore, you have to install two NICs on the machine with the Snort Inline Patch running on it. One will serve the network external to Inline Snort and another will connect to the internal network.

Inline Snort has the same functionality as a normal Snort sensor. You can configure management consoles such as ACID, real-time alerting with syslog-ng, and maintenance programs such as IDS Policy Center, as well as any of the ancillary applications that make Snort more effective for you. Consequently, you can configure Inline Snort to do some intrusion detection work.

> **Note**
> You should not rely on the Inline Snort patch host to function both as a complete IDS and intrusion prevention device. You can easily overload the Snort Inline host if full intrusion detection functionality is added. This can create a bottleneck and adversely affect the hosts you are protecting.

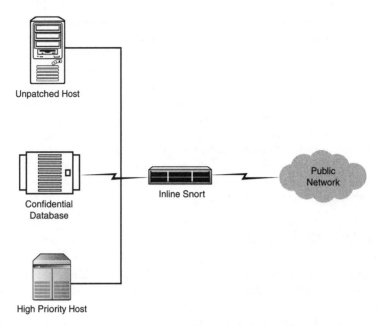

Figure 14.1 An inline Snort network.

Invariably, you will want to generate an alert rather than trigger an intrusion prevention response to some attacks. Certain attacks have too high a false positive rate to always attempt to prevent them, and others you simply would rather be alerted to than prevent. Additionally, you need to test intrusion prevention rules in alert mode before enabling them.

The Snort Inline patch has two intrusion prevention responses, which take the form of the familiar rule action. You can use these rule actions to tell Inline Snort not to allow packets that match a selected rule past the Inline Snort host. The packets are discarded and never passed on. The rule actions can drop the offending packets and generate an alert that a packet was dropped, or silently discard the packets and never generate an alert. These are the `drop` and `sdrop` rule actions, respectively.

Installing Snort Inline Patch

Installing the Snort Inline patch is similar to installing Snort. After you have installed the two NICs, the operating system, and associated applications, you can download the source, compile it, and install it. You can get the Snort Inline Patch at

`http://www.snort.org/dl/contrib/patches/inline/`

Untar the tarball and place it in a source directory. You should build the `configure` command to include all the options you require for the Snort IDS–related functions (such as `—enable-flexresp`). You should also make note of the location of the libipq libraries (IP Queue) and include directories, because you may need them to compile the source. To configure Snort for Inline mode, use the following configure command:

```
./configure <options> --enable-inline
```

If the output complains about the location of the libipq includes or libraries, add these configure lines:

```
./configure --enable-inline —with-libipq-includes=/path/to
/libipq/includes  —with-libipq-libraries=/path/to/libipq
/libraries
```

When Inline Snort is configured, run `make` and `make install` commands.

Configuring

Although the process of configuring the Snort Inline patch is similar to configuring Snort for intrusion detection work, the goal of the configuration process is different. The configuration tasks are familiar. You should set network variables, configure preprocessors, and choose your output plugins. When working your way through the Snort configuration files, keep in mind that the goal of Inline Snort is to prevent malicious traffic from reaching its intended target. Another goal of the configuration process is to ensure that the Inline Snort host does not become a bottleneck.

Network Variables

You are going to have to gaze into the crystal ball when configuring your network variables. Think of what services and hosts you are going to protect with Inline Snort before sitting down and configuring the variables.

If the hosts you want to protect are bound to a particular range or ranges of IP addresses, you should specify them in the $HOME_NET variable. Assigning the `any` value to $HOME_NET should only be done if you are positive that you want Snort Inline to potentially drop traffic for every internal host.

Another option is to define your own variables and then modify the rules to be used in intrusion prevention to reflect the new variable. An example would be to create a variable, $PROTECTED_NET, then use this new variable in all of the rules with `drop` as the action.

You should also consider where trusted external resources exist on your network. You can then define the external trusted hosts with the $EXTNERAL_NET variable and the inverse (!) operator to ensure that traffic will flow unobstructed from these important resources. For example, if you had important business partners regularly connecting to your network from the 192.168.1.0/24 range, you would set $EXTERNAL_NET to be everything but this range with the inverse operator. This could be accomplished with the following line:

```
var $EXTNERAL_NET !192.168.1.0/24
```

The network variables that are used to define service ports and service host locations should be configured with care. These variables are used by rules to define where to apply a rule's signature. For example, if you want to use Snort Inline solely to prevent attacks against an SSL-enabled Web server running on port 443, you would set `HTTP_PORTS` equal to 443 only.

Preprocessors

Following the same strategy used to configure the network variables, you should enable only those preprocessors that are required. Preprocessors such as `frag2`, `stream4`, and `stream4_reassemble` should be enabled in most situations to counter IDS evasion techniques. The other preprocessors should be enabled on an as-needed basis. For instance, if you do not plan on applying intrusion prevention responses to RPC traffic, you should disable the `rpc_decode` preprocessor.

The purpose of disabling the bulk of the unused preprocessors is to conserve resources. Remember, Inline Snort will become a bottleneck if it does not have enough resources to pass packets through in a timely manner.

Output Plugins

Configure the output plugins that you want to use. To keep performance a top priority, you should seriously consider using the Unified plugin in conjunction with Barnyard if you are going to output to a database.

When the output plugins have been configured, you can take on the next task of picking and choosing the rules to implement.

Writing Rules for Inline Snort

Creating rules to be used with the Snort Inline patch is almost identical to creating rules for Snort. The rule syntax remains the same. Inline Snort introduces two new rule actions and a new keyword option. Rules function in the same manner as they do for Snort: when the conditions set by the Rule Header and Rule Option are met, the rule action is executed.

Drop **and** Sdrop

The two new rule actions are `drop` and `sdrop`. They both discard any packet that triggers the rule, not allowing it to pass by Inline Snort. When writing rules, you should test your rules in alert or log mode prior to switching the rule action to `drop`. When you are ready to turn on the intrusion prevention response, simply change the rule action from `alert` to `drop`, as shown in this example:

```
drop tcp $EXTERNAL_NET any -> $HOME_NET 21
(msg:"EXPLOIT FTP passwd appe path"; flags: A+; content: "APPE";
nocase; content: "/passwd";)
```

The `drop` action generates an alert as well, so you will know when a packet or group of packets have been scrubbed. Some drops occur frequently enough that you may not want to be alerted of them. You can then switch the rule action to `sdrop`, or silent drop. An appropriate situation would be anonymous login attempts against an Internet-accessible FTP site. Depending on the size of your network, you could conceivably receive hundreds if not thousands of attempts each day. For this type of scrubbing action, you would want to enable the `sdrop` rule action to silently scrub anonymous attempts, as shown:

```
sdrop tcp $EXTERNAL_NET any -> $HOME_NET 21
(content:"USER"; nocase; content:" anonymous|0D0A|";
nocase; flow:to_server,established;)
```

Replace

The Snort Inline patch introduces a new option keyword as well: `replace`. Replace enables you to modify the matched content in a rule to something else. This is useful when you do not want to discard packets, but would rather neuter them and make them harmless. This is best illustrated with an example such as the following `passwd` request drop rule:

```
drop tcp $EXTERNAL_NET any -> $HOME_NET 80
(msg:"WEB: attempt to request /etc/passwd"; content:"/etc/passwd";)
```

This rule triggers when someone or something attempts to access the `passwd` file from a Web server. Many attacks that allow the hacker to access files outside the document root would contain this signature, because the attacker attempted to download the Unix password file. It may not seem like there could ever be a false positive for this rule.

Suppose, however, that you ran a public message board on a Web server that dealt with Unix administration issues. An unsuspecting user of this message board could post content that included "`/etc/passwd`" in response to a question about the location of the `passwd` file. This would cause the request to be dropped, likely bewildering the unsuspecting user.

To remedy this problem, you could replace the content with something that would allow the user to get her point across, but would cause an attacker's request to fail.

```
alert tcp $EXTERNAL_NET any -> $HOME_NET 80
(msg:"passwd content replaced"; content:"/etc/passwd";
replace:"/etc/ passwd"; )
```

Building the Ruleset

There is no universal ruleset that should be configured for every Inline Snort deployment. You must decide which types of traffic are bothersome enough to be dropped. You can use some general strategies to help you decide which rules to implement. Treat these strategies as guidelines, and remember to always use common sense when configuring the Inline Snort patch to scrub traffic.

Rules for Filtering Incoming Traffic

The most obvious set of rules on which to enable a drop rule action are those for incoming traffic from untrusted sources that matches an attack signature. Incoming traffic to whatever service you are protecting (FTP, DNS, HTTP, and so on) is a good candidate.

Rules for Dropping Abnormal Traffic

Another category of rule on which you may want to consider enabling a drop action is traffic that should never exist on your network. Unusual traffic that should not be present is a sure sign that something is amiss. When configured correctly, this type of intrusion prevention response is the most effective and adds the most value. For example, if you do not allow TFTP traffic under any circumstances, you should drop any traffic that is related to TFTP. The rservices (`rlogin`, `rsh`, and so on) are possible genres of traffic to drop because they are rarely used in normal network situations. Another possibility includes dropping ICMP altogether at network borders. This will scrub ping requests and potential covert channels.

> **Note**
> Always exercise caution when dropping packets of this nature. You should consult with other persons in your organization to ensure you are not dropping packets required for a legitimate resource.

Zero False Positives

Any rule that generates zero false positives—that is, always detects a true attempted attack—is a good candidate for scrubbing. As long as you have enough resources available on the Inline Snort machine to check for additional attack signatures, you can save yourself a lot of intrusion detection work by dropping attacks before they hit a Snort IDS sensor. Again, you should let these rules run for a period of time with an `alert` or `log` action before you convert them to a `drop` action.

Potential rules to test on your network for a zero false positive rate include the following:

- Rules in the `exploit.rules` file. These rules have specific content checks that are unlikely to be seen on the service types they monitor for exploits.

- Buffer overflow attacks dispersed throughout the `.rules` files. These types of attacks have specific content signatures, such as the `exploit.rules` rules, that are reasonably rare.

- Rules that contain signatures for privileged file access attempts. A good number of rules exist for attempted access and retrieval of important files. Files such as the Unix `passwd` file, the Windows `SAM` file, and any other request for a confidential file that should never be transmitted in the clear can be dropped.

SnortSam

SnortSam is an intrusion prevention plugin for Snort. It functions by adding a new response to a Snort rule that allows the rule to trigger a change to a firewall or router. The change is usually to block or disallow traffic from or to a particular IP address for a period of time. SnortSam works with the Checkpoint Firewall-1 and Cisco PIX brands of firewalls. It also works with most Cisco-brand routers.

The idea behind implementing SnortSam is that you would be able to detect the early phases or components of an attack and automatically respond before the attacker could complete the attack. An example is reconnaissance attacks: If Snort detects a zone transfer attempt against a DNS server from an untrusted source, a blocking request could be executed in a matter of seconds, effectively locking the potential attacker out.

Another situation is a multi-part attack. If an attacker is able to successfully spawn a shell with a remote exploit, Snort could be configured to send a block request to SnortSam upon detecting the exploit. The attacker would be unable to make use of the exploited host from the IP address from where the attack originated.

As you can see, there are some problems with this: The attacker could simply switch IP addresses. The attacker could also use attacks that have destructive consequences with a single packet. SnortSam is not perfect, but it is useful for preventing self-propagating malware and script kiddies, freeing up more time for you to concentrate on more skilled adversaries.

SnortSam is composed of two basic components: a plugin and an agent. The purpose of this architecture is to allow firewall rules or ACLs to expire after a preset time period. The agent is responsible for making changes to the routers and firewalls, and can both create and remove firewall rules. It has a time function that enables it to wait for a preset time period before expiring a rule. Other intrusion prevention applications make permanent changes to firewalls and routers, which is not ideal for a number of obvious reasons.

This architecture allows a single sensor to interact with many different firewalls and routers. If you have a sensor that is protecting a large environment with many firewalls, the sensor can then control each firewall based on the rule that is triggered. If one firewall protects Apache Web servers, you would want rules that pertain to malicious Apache-related traffic to trigger blocking requests to the Apache firewall. If another firewall protects Oracle database servers, you would want rules that deal with Oracle exploits to block requests to the Oracle firewall.

The plugin is a standard Snort output plugin that is used to send instructions to an agent when a rule is triggered. The instructions are delivered in an encrypted format. The SnortSam agent decrypts the instructions. If the passphrases or keys match what is expected, the agent stores the offending IP address and the length of time to implement the block. The request is now compared against criteria defined by the IDS analyst. This criteria can include lists of addresses for which blocking requests should never be created (called the white-list) and default time periods to use for block requests. If the request passes the criteria, it is then forwarded on to the firewall or router to implement the block.

When the request is implemented, the agent makes note of the time and date of the successful blocking request. The router then implements the request and waits for the agent to issue a request to expire the request and remove the blocked address. When a predefined time limit has been reached, the agent sends another request to remove the blocked address.

In addition to the white-list, SnortSam has a rollback feature that helps mitigate potential attacks against the SnortSam intrusion prevention application. The rollback feature is a customizable threshold that sets the number of blocks that can be processed in a defined period. When the threshold is exceeded, SnortSam undoes a preset number of the previously blocked addresses. It then waits until the number of block requests drops below the threshold before implementing any new block requests. The rollback feature, combined with the white-list feature, limits the amount of damage an attacker can do by using SnortSam to attack a network.

Installing SnortSam

SnortSam has two installation components. The first is a patch that adds the necessary intrusion prevention response facility to Snort. The second is the actual SnortSam agent that is used to process requests from Snort and make changes to a firewall or router.

You have a few options for applying the patch to Snort. One is to download the SnortSam Snort patch and apply it to the Snort source code. You must then recompile Snort with the patched source. Get the patch from the SnortSam download page for your preferred version of Snort:

```
http://www.snortsam.net/download.html
```

Copy the patch to the Snort source directory (/snort/src) and patch the file with the following command:

```
patch < snort-snortsam-patch
```

This patches the Snort source to include the functionality you need to run SnortSam. Now you can compile and install Snort in the manner of your choice. Refer to Chapter 7, "Building the Sensor," for documentation on compiling and installing Snort if need be.

Another method of obtaining a SnortSam-patched version of Snort is to download the precompiled binary from the SnortSam site. This does not give you the same degree of flexibility as patching and then compiling, but guarantees that you will have a working binary. You can get the binary from the same download page as the SnortSam patch.

After you have the patched Snort ready for action, you can get the SnortSam agent. Before downloading the agent, you must decide where it is going to reside. If you plan on using a Checkpoint Firewall-1 firewall to work in conjunction with SnortSam, you should install the agent on the same host as the firewall. If this is not possible (and most firewall admins try to avoid running extraneous daemons on their firewalls), you can install the agent on a different host logically near the firewall. If you are using a Cisco PIX or a Cisco router, you have to choose a host near the firewall to install the

SnortSam agent. The traffic from the SnortSam agent to the firewall is sent in the clear, so you want to minimize the amount of network infrastructure between the firewall and the SnortSam agent.

After you have decided on a host, you need to ensure that the host is properly hardened and locked down. After doing so, you are ready to install the SnortSam agent. Installing a precompiled SnortSam binary is the easiest way to install SnortSam. Optionally, you could compile SnortSam from the source. Get the binary or source from the SnortSam download page.

Configuring

To complete the installation you need to configure the SnortSam output plugin for Snort, the SnortSam agent, and the firewall(s) to be used in the intrusion prevention setup. All these components need to be working in concert for SnortSam to work.

The best way to configure SnortSam is to work outward from the firewall to Snort. The first step is to choose the firewalls and routers to which SnortSam will be permitted to issue blocking requests. After you have identified the blocking devices, you may have to make some internal configuration changes to enable SnortSam to issue blocking requests to them. The next step is to configure the SnortSam agent. Here you create the white-list that determines which IP addresses are never to be blocked. You also set the remainder of the SnortSam parameters. The final step is to make configuration changes to the SnortSam output plugin.

Prepping the Blocking Devices

You need to make a few configuration changes to the routers or firewalls to be used in conjunction with SnortSam. The changes are different depending on the brand of router or firewall used.

Checkpoint Firewall-1

The configuration changes for a Checkpoint Firewall-1 depend on where you are going to install the SnortSam agent. If you are planning on placing the agent on the same physical machine as the firewall, you do not need to make any changes. If the agent is going to reside on another host, you need to make changes to the OPSEC configuration file. This file is usually located at

```
/fw1/ng/conf/fwopsec.conf
```

You need to change the `sam_server auth_port` line to 0, and add a `sam_server port` line to be set to the value of `18183`. The new lines should look like the following:

```
sam_server   auth_port    0
sam_server       port   18183
```

You must also enable remote requests by changing the `sam_allow_remote_requests` line to yes. The configuration line should look like the following:

```
sam_allow_remote_requests yes
```

Save the file and exit. The Checkpoint Firewall-1 is now properly configured to handle requests from SnortSam.

Cisco PIX

SnortSam changes the ACLs on a PIX by Telneting to the firewall and using the SHUN command to block the offending IP address. You must enable the PIX to accept Telnet connections from the host that has the SnortSam agent running on it.

Cisco Routers

To block requests with a Cisco router, you must enable the router to accept Telnet connections from the SnortSam agent as you would for the Cisco PIX. Additionally, the SnortSam agent requires a copy of the default ACL for the router. This ACL is the base list on the router before SnortSam issues any blocking requests. Make a copy of this ACL and have it ready to be used when you configure SnortSam.

Configuring the SnortSam Agent

The SnortSam agent is configured via a file named `snortsam.conf`. Place this file in the default location (`/etc/snortsam.conf`).

> **Note**
> If you create the file in a different location, make note of it because you will have to specify it when you start the SnortSam process.

To build the `snortsam.conf` file, you simply add keyword/value pairs that correspond to the configuration options you want enabled for SnortSam. What follows is a list of keyword/value pairs you can use to build the `snortsam.conf` file.

`defaultkey`

The `defaultkey` keyword sets the password that the Snort sensors will use to authenticate to the SnortSam agent. You need to specify this password when configuring the output plugin. Leaving this keyword out will set `defaultkey` to a default password, which is not recommended. An example:

`defaultkey strongpassword`

`port`

The `port` keyword sets the port on which the SnortSam agent will listen for incoming block requests. The default of `898` is set if this line is omitted. An example `port` setting is

`port 515`

`accept`

This is a list of IP addresses that are allowed to send blocking requests to the agent. You can specify ranges of IP addresses by using CIDR notation. Additionally, you can specify a password to be used for the Snort sensor instead of the `defaultkey`. If no password is supplied, the sensor must use the default key to authenticate to the agent. List each address or address range on a separate line, as shown:

```
accept 192.168.1.0/24
accept 10.0.0.1,specialpassword
```

dontblock

This keyword is used to build the white-list of addresses that will never be blocked. You can specify a range of addresses by using CIDR notation. Take care to build an accurate list. Some of the potential hosts you should consider include the following:

- Root name servers
- Local and ISP DNS servers
- Addresses of trusted business partners that frequently use services behind the firewall
- Administrative consoles
- Any address that is too important to block

List each address to prevent blocking actions on a single line, like so:

```
dontblock a.root-servers.net
dontblock 192.168.55.0/24
dontblock 10.100.0.17
```

override

The `override` keyword is used to specify a maximum time limit for which to block a specific host.

This is used to limit the length of time an attacker can block an address that may be shared with other non-malicious persons. Some corporations or ISPs use a proxy to hide the IP address of many different internal hosts; this limits the length of time any one person can affect others. You add as many override statements as needed on separate lines. An example is to limit the length of time that proxies for major ISPs can be blocked:

```
override proxy.msn.com 5 mins
override proxy.earthlink.com 5 mins
```

rollbackthreshold

This keyword is used to set the maximum blocking threshold. When this threshold is reached, SnortSam unblocks however many block requests are specified with the `rollbackhosts` keyword/value pair and does not accept new block requests for the length of time specified in `rollbacksleeptime`.

If you do not want to set a threshold, leave this line out of the `snortsam.conf`. To enable `rollbackthreshold`, set a number of blocks and the time period on a single line:

```
rollbackthreshold 10 / 2 mins
```

rollbackhosts

The `rollbackhosts` keyword configures the number of previous requests to unblock. You can turn this feature off by not specifying a `rollbackhosts` line in `snortsam.conf`. Simply append the number request to be unblocked:

```
rollbackhosts 25
```

rollbacksleeptime

This keyword is the length of time SnortSam will wait before processing new block requests after the threshold is reached. Specify the length of time for SnortSam to ignore new blocking requests like so:

```
rollbacksleeptime 30 secs
```

logfile

This is the name of the file to which SnortSam-related events are to be logged. SnortSam logs events related to successful blocks, starting and stopping times, and errors. Append the filename as shown:

```
logfile snortsam.log
```

loglevel

This is the level of verbosity to be logged. There are three levels:

  1—Only log errors.

  2—Log errors and successful block requests.

  3—Log everything, including connection state.

To set logging at level 2, you would add the following keyword/value pair:

```
loglevel 2
```

skipinterval

For performance reasons, SnortSam ignores the same block request for the time period set with `skipinterval`. This prevents SnortSam from becoming overloaded when an attack triggers many blocking requests. Set `skipinterval` like so:

```
skipinterval 30 secs
```

skiphosts

This keyword works with the `skipinterval` keyword to set the previous number of block requests to which skipinterval should be applied. The value for `skiphosts` determines how many different requests to save in memory. You can set it with the following line:

```
skiphosts 20
```

fwsam

This keyword is used to set which Checkpoint firewalls are to receive the block request. If SnortSam is installed locally to the firewall, you can use the local loopback address (127.0.0.1). Specify each firewall and router on a separate line:

```
fwsam 192.168.1.25
fwsam 127.0.0.1
```

fwexec

This line is used to call the Checkpoint Firewall-1 executable to initiate IP address blocks. This keyword can be used only if the SnortSam agent is present on the same devices as the Checkpoint Firewall. Set `fwexec` like so:

```
fwexec /fw/ng/fw
```

opsec

The `opsec` line is used to call an OPSEC plugin for a Checkpoint firewall. Set `opsec` to the name of the OPSEC file:

```
opsec opsec.conf
```

pix

This keyword tells SnortSam to connect to a Cisco PIX firewall. You must have Telnet enabled on the PIX from the location of the SnortSam agent. To enable this keyword, you must supply the IP address of the PIX, the Telnet password, and the enable password. An example follows:

```
pix 10.0.0.55 telnetpass enablepass
```

ciscoacl

This keyword is similar to PIX. It is used to connect to a Cisco router and modify the ACL. You must have the default ACL stored on the host where SnortSam is located in a text file. To use this keyword, you must supply the IP address of the router, the Telnet password, the enable password, and the filename of the router's default ACL.

```
ciscoacl 10.0.0.21 telnetpass enablepass filename.acl
```

email

This keyword specifies an SMTP server and email address to receive every block request. Enabling this keyword can cause an enormous amount of email, depending on how many block requests SnortSam will be generating. It is primarily used in testing and debugging situations. Add the keyword like so:

```
email 192.168.55.55 ids.analyst@somwhere.com
```

This completes the description of the keyword/value pairs that are required to build a `snortsam.conf` file. An example `snortsam.conf` follows:

```
defaultkey x8eiq.28a
accept 192.168.1.0/24

dontblock a.root-servers.net
dontblock b.root-servers.net
dontblock c.root-servers.net
dontblock d.root-servers.net
dontblock 192.168.55.0/24
dontblock 10.100.0.17

rollbackthreshold 10 / 2 mins
rollbacksleeptime 30 secs
logfile snortsam.log
loglevel 2

fwsam 192.168.1.99
pix 10.0.0.55 iez2k.z9 9z.29.a1
```

When the `snortsam.conf` file is completed, move on to configuring the Snort output plugin.

Configuring the SnortSam Output Plugin

Adding the additional output plugin for SnortSam is a straightforward process. Open your `snort.conf` file for editing and scroll down to the output plugins section. From here you want to add an output plugin that matches the IP address, port, and password you configured for the SnortSam agent. You could add an output plugin as follows:

```
output alert_fwsam: 192.168.0.13/x8eiq.28a
```

If you specified a different port with the port keyword/value pair, you would add a output plugin like so:

```
output alert_fwsam: 192.168.0.13:525/x8eiq.28a
```

> **Note**
> Make sure to specify the correct password (that is, x8eiq.28a) for the sensor. If a password has not been assigned to the individual sensor with the `accept` keyword, make sure to use the value assigned to `defaultkey`.

Inserting Blocking Responses into Rules

You add the blocking intrusion prevention response to a rule by inserting a new keyword option, `fwsam`. The syntax of the `fwsam` keyword option is as follows:

```
fwsam: ip_address[block_type],time_period
```

The `ip_address` parameter lets the output plugin know whether to block the source or destination address. The source address is the first address in the Rule Header, the destination is the second. Take the following rule:

```
alert ip $EXTERNAL_NET any -> $HOME_NET $SHELLCODE_PORTS
(msg:"SHELLCODE sparc NOOP";
content:"|801c 4011 801c 4011 801c 4011 801c 4011|";)
```

Setting `ip_address` to `src` would block the incoming address that is assigned to the $EXTERNAL_NET variable. Setting `dst` would block the IP address assigned to $HOME_NET.

The `block_type` tells SnortSam which direction to block traffic. You can set it to block only incoming or outgoing packets with the `in` and `out` parameters. You can block both directions with the `either` parameter, and the specific IP address and port combination with the `this` parameter.

The `time_period` parameter can be set to any length of time. You can specify units of time by appending the desired unit to the value. The allowed units are

- Seconds
- Minutes
- Hours
- Days
- Weeks
- Years

If you set the `time_period` parameter to 0, the block will be permanent.

> **Note**
>
> Use caution when permanently blocking an address, as you could deny service to an important resource or overwhelm the blocking device. Remember, each packet that is processed by the firewall or router has to be compared against the list of rules. If this list grows too large, it could exhaust the blocking device's resources.

In the previous rule example, a signature for Sun Sparc no-ops, you would want to block the IP address that the attack originated from. You would want to block traffic in both directions because the attacker may have been able to plant a tool to initiate communication from the host (such as netcat). Try blocking the address for a day. This gives you enough time to investigate the attack for a potential compromise and react accordingly. The rule would be modified to read as follows:

```
alert ip $EXTERNAL_NET any -> $HOME_NET $SHELLCODE_PORTS
(msg:"SHELLCODE sparc NOOP";
content:"|801c 4011 801c 4011 801c 4011 801c 4011|"; fwsam: either, 1 day)
```

When you have added the `fwsam` keyword to the rules on which you want to enable intrusion prevention responses, you can then start Snort and SnortSam.

Summary

This chapter introduced some advanced concepts in using Snort as an intrusion prevention device. Both the Snort Inline Patch and SnortSam are presented as intrusion prevention options.

An intrusion prevention application is similar to an IDS, in that both applications aim to distinguish unauthorized activity from normal activity. The intrusion prevention application, like an IDS, has a set of signatures or predefined conditions that, when met, trigger a response. This response is what differentiates an IDS from an intrusion prevention application. This action can include the dropping or "scrubbing" of packets that match a signature or predefined condition that indicates unauthorized activity. It can also include blocking all traffic with the same source IP address that has triggered the response. Additionally, a HIDS-based intrusion prevention application could disallow specified applications or user accounts from interacting with other applications or operating system functions.

The process of deploying intrusion prevention is lengthier and requires greater attention to detail than installing an IDS. With Snort, a misconfigured option or rule can affect only the performance of the IDS itself. With an intrusion prevention application, a misconfiguration can literally take down your network.

With the Inline patch, Snort can elicit an intrusion prevention response when a rule is triggered. The Snort Inline patch has two intrusion prevention responses, which take the form of the familiar rule action. When working your way through the Snort configuration files, keep in mind that the goal of Inline Snort is to prevent malicious traffic from reaching its intended target. Another goal of the configuration process is to ensure that the Inline Snort host does not become a bottleneck.

Creating rules to be used with the Snort Inline patch is almost identical to creating rules for Snort. The rule syntax remains the same. Inline Snort introduces two new rule actions and a new keyword option. The two new rule actions are `drop` and `sdrop`. They both discard any packet that triggers the rule, not allowing it to pass by Inline Snort. The Snort Inline patch introduces a new option keyword as well: `replace`. `Replace` enables you to modify the matched content in a rule to something else.

SnortSam is an intrusion prevention plugin for Snort. It functions by adding a new response to a Snort rule that allows the rule to trigger a change to a firewall or router. The change is usually to block or disallow traffic from or to a particular IP address for a period of time. SnortSam works with the Checkpoint Firewall-1 and Cisco PIX brand of firewalls. It also works with most Cisco-brand routers.

The idea behind implementing SnortSam is that you would be able to detect the early phases or components of an attack and automatically respond before the attacker could complete the attack. SnortSam has two installation components. The first is a patch that adds the necessary intrusion prevention response facility to Snort. The second is the actual SnortSam agent that is used to process requests from Snort and make changes to a firewall or router.

Troubleshooting

THIS APPENDIX ADDRESSES SOME OF THE common issues with deploying and running Snort. This chapter follows a "frequently asked questions" format.

Snort Issues

This section introduces some of the most common troubleshooting questions encountered when working with Snort. If you cannot find the answer to your issue here, check the online mailing lists. Here is some introductory troubleshooting advice you can use when working with Snort:

How Do I Run Snort on Mutiple Interfaces?

Snort can be configured to listen on more than one NIC. The problem is that Snort accepts only one interface switch (-i) per command line. There are two methods of running Snort on multiple interfaces: one is to run a separate Snort process for each interface, and the other is to bond the interfaces together by using the bonding feature of the Linux kernel.

Choosing the best method of monitoring several interfaces with Snort depends on factors specific to your environment and priorities. Running multiple Snort processes duplicates significant effort, and can consume an unacceptable number of processor cycles. If you have the resources available to run two or more Snort processes, you should next consider data management issues. Assuming all instances of Snort are configured in the same manner, the same attack could be reported multiple times. This can cause headaches for the IDS admin, especially if real-time alerting has been enabled. The ideal circumstance in which to assign an individual Snort process to each NIC is when you are faced with a different intrusion detection requirement for each interface.

If you assign an individual Snort process to each NIC, you can create a quasi-virtual sensor for each interface. You can load different configuration settings, rules, and output plugins for each individual Snort process, housing several "sensors" on one machine. This situation is the most suitable for individual Snort processes.

On the other hand, if you cannot, or do not want to start an additional Snort process for each interface, and you are running Linux, you can bond the interfaces together. This enables you to specify one bonded interface (such as bond0) for the -i switch when starting Snort.

To do so, edit /etc/modules.conf and append the following line:

```
alias bond0 bonding
```

Now, each time the machine reboots, you need to enter the following commands to bring up the bond interface after you have assigned IP address information to the NICs:

```
ifconfig bond0 up
ifenslave bond0 eth0
ifenslave bond0 eth1
ifenslave bond0 eth2
```

> **Note**
>
> You may want to place these commands in a script and include the script in the system startup.

Continue until you have associated all the interfaces with the inenslave command. Then, when you run Snort, use the bond0 interface as follows:

```
snort <options> -i bond0
```

This is a good way to have Snort listen on specific monitoring interfaces without forcing it to listen on the management interface.

Snort Complains About Missing References During Compilation. What Causes This?

You must have the most current version of libpcap installed. If your distribution includes libpcap, uninstall it by following the directions in Chapter 7, "Building the Sensor," and reinstall the most current version available from tcpdump.org.

Portscan Traffic Is Not Showing Up in ACID or the Intrusion Database. What Is Wrong?

The preprocessor reports portscan data only to the alert facility of an output plugin. Hence, the output facility for the output plugin you have enabled must be set to alert rather than log for portscan events to be posted to the intrusion database.

Why Isn't Snort Logging Packet Payloads?

Snort logs payload information only if the -d switch is added at the command line.

The Setup I Have Specified in the snort.conf File Is Not Being Used by Snort.

First, make sure you have entered the path correctly for the `snort.conf` file. With many possible copies of the `snort.conf` on a system, ensure that your –c switch is pointing to the correct version of `snort.conf`.

It is also possible that you have enabled an option that takes precedence over the –c switch. Two possibilities are the –s and the –A switches. The –s switch is used to log to syslog from the command line. If you want to log to syslog (such as for real-time alerting), you should enable the output plugin in the `snort.conf` file rather than specify it at the command line. The –A is used to force Snort to alert in different manners, such as full or null. Using the –A overrides any `snort.conf` file specified with the –c switch.

> **Note**
> Remember, command-line options override the `snort.conf` file in all cases.

Why Am I Still Receiving Portscan Alerts from Hosts Specified in the `portscan2-ignorehosts` Directive?

The `portscan2-ignorehosts` line ignores portscan traffic, but not out-of-spec or malicious traffic detected by the `portscan2` preprocessor. Out-of-spec traffic, such as a SYN-FIN, Stealth, or Xmas scan, is indicative of a potential attack; these types of traffic are not created by legitimate applications.

If you want to ignore out-of-spec of traffic, you should write a pass rule and switch the rule order (-o) to ignore traffic from a specific host.

When I Start Snort, I Notice Errors Relating to My Rules Files. What Is Causing This?

Note which rule file is generating the warning. Whether it is `local.rules` or another `.rules` file that contains custom rules you wrote, check the syntax to ensure the rule has been written correctly.

If the rule is an official rule included with the Snort distribution, it is most often the case that a variable the rule uses has not been defined. Check to make sure you have the variables used in the rule defined in the network variables section of `snort.conf`.

I Wrote A Pass Rule, but Snort Still Generates Alerts. What Is Wrong?

The default order in which rules are applied is `alert`, `pass`, and finally `log`. This means that an alert will be generated before any pass rule is applied when the default ordering scheme is used. To change the order in which rules are applied to `pass`, `alert`, `log`, you should append the -o switch at the command line when starting Snort.

Where Can I Turn for Additional Help?

Snort has a vibrant and intelligent community that is likely to help with any question. Mailing list archives at sourceforge.net, snort.org, securityfocus.com, and archives.neohapsis.com are good locations to find previously asked and answered questions. Be sure to do a little research to see whether your question has already been answered before asking a question. Remember, some people read and contribute to these lists every day and grow tired of answering the same questions over and over again.

If you want to subscribe directly to the lists, navigate over to sourceforge.net. You can also talk about Snort on the IRC channel, irc.freenode.net, in the #snort channel.

ACID Issues

This section introduces some of the most common troubleshooting questions encountered when working with ACID. If you cannot find the answer to your issue here, check the online at

```
http://www.andrew.cmu.edu/~rdanyliw/snort/snortacid.html.
```

Why Are All the ACID Pages Displaying Raw HTML?

Raw HTML code is indicative that PHP has not been installed correctly. If the PHP application server is unable to parse .php, .phps, .php3, and .php4 files, ACID will not load correctly. Review your PHP installation.

I'm Receiving Errors Pertaining to ADODB. How Do I Check to Make Sure It Is Installed Correctly?

ADODB is used by ACID to provide generic access to most relational databases on the market today. Check the $ADODB_DIR variable in adodb-inc.php to make sure its value is the correct path of the ADODB source.

I Get A Parse Error in `acid_conf.php` on Line XXX When Attempting to Open ACID. How Can I Fix This?

Remember, the acid_conf.php is actually PHP source code that is used to define variables for ACID. Like any source, it has a strict syntax that must be followed for the file to be interpreted correctly. Quickly scan the acid_conf.php file for these common syntactical errors:

- Variables that are set to a path (such as DBlib_path) should never have a trailing blackslash (\) character.
- All variables must begin with the dollar sign ($).
- All variable statements must end with a semicolon (;).
- The file must begin with <? or <?php and end with ?>. Remove any extraneous whitespace.

I Am Trying to Use an Email System Other Than Sendmail to Send Alerts, but Emails Never Arrive.

The email application is controlled through PHP with the `php.ini` file. You must specify the command to execute the mailing application in the `php.ini` if it is something other than Sendmail. Edit the `sendmail_path` in `php.ini` to include the full path of the email application, the executable, and the command-line parameters required to send an email.

IDS Strategy

This section introduces some of the most common troubleshooting questions encountered when working with an IDS in general.

How Can I Detect "Slow" Scans?

Slow portscans, usually perpetrated by a determined attacker specifically targeting your systems, can be difficult to discover. Slow scans that use out-of-spec traffic, such as SYN-FIN scans, are easily detected because they have an identifiable signature. Other scans that do not have a traffic signature per se are more difficult to detect. You have to rely on the configuration settings of the `portscan2` preprocessor. The threshold used to configure `portscan2` to detect a slow scan can generate so many false positives that `portscan2` becomes unusable, presenting a major problem in discovering slow scans.

One way to detect slow scan is to configure a Snort process to monitor a range of IP addresses that have no hosts bound to them. The Snort process should have only the `portscan2` preprocessor enabled, along with the preprocessors designed to normalize traffic. By default, any traffic sent to the selected range can be considered suspect because legitimate traffic should never be sent to it. Now you can configure portscan to detect slow scans. Use `nmap` in "paranoid" mode with the `-T` command-line switch to test your threshold.

Is There Anything I Can Do to Prevent Portscanning Activity?

Although there is nothing you can do to totally prevent reconnaissance attacks, you can make the life of those perpetrating them more difficult. If you notice an abundance of portscanning attempts or other reconnaissance attacks from a particular IP address, you can report the activity to the ISP that provides the address. You can look up information pertaining to IP addresses at samspade.org.

Another method of preventing or slowing down portscanning attempts is to install a tool named LaBrea. LaBrea is named after the famous LaBrea tar pits that ensnared and preserved dinosaurs millions of years ago. The LaBrea tool is similar, in that it ensnares and slows down portscanning attempts. LaBrea functions by acquiring unused IP addresses on a subnet and using them to delay the portscan attempt. LaBrea slows down a portscan by accepting all incoming TCP connections and then issuing a response that tells the attacker's host to wait. It sends a small or zero TCP window size, which advises the attacking host that the target is too busy to complete the TCP request. Each port probe attempt can be caught in this waiting game, which will cause the scan to slow down or stop entirely.

Of course, a skilled attacker can create a tool to circumvent the LaBrea-style portscan prevention measures, but the majority of attacks by script kiddies and worms will be mitigated. You can get LaBrea and detailed documentation at

http://www.hackbusters.net/

I'm Noticing a Lot of ICMP Destination Unreachable Alerts. Is This Something I Should Be Concerned About?

ICMP unreachable packets are used to communicate to a sending host that a particular host or protocol is not available at the target host. There are different possible ICMP unreachable messages stored in the Code field. Refer to Chapter 12, "Basic Rule Writing," for the various codes for ICMP packets.

An ICMP unreachable alert can indicate an attacker attempting to gather information about a system. It can also indicate a malfunctioning or incorrectly configured application. You should investigate ICMP unreachable alerts when possible and configure Snort to ignore hosts that generate too much ICMP unreachable traffic.

B

Rule Documentation

THIS APPENDIX LAYS OUT A BASIC DESCRIPTION for the Snort ruleset contained in the Snort distribution. Descriptions are grouped by rule classification type.

> **Note**
> Remember to take into account the business situation in which a rule will be applied. If the classification in this Appendix does not match your needs, feel free to change it. You can always change the classification for any rule by using the methods outlined in Chapter 11, "Real Time Alerting."

Not Suspicious Traffic

The Not Suspicious Traffic rule classification can be misleading. Rules that are categorized as Not Suspicious can be malicious and indicative of an intrusion. The nature of traffic that is defined as not suspicious is dependent on the situation in which it is discovered. Take the following successful Telnet access attempt rule:

```
alert tcp $TELNET_SERVERS 23 -> $EXTERNAL_NET any
(msg:"TELNET access"; flow:from_server,established;
content:"|FF FD 18 FF FD 1F FF FD 23 FF FD 27 FF FD 24|";
classtype:not-suspicious;)
```

This rule may be not be considered suspicious if Snort is monitoring an internal host that is managed via Telnet. In turn, an alert from this rule would be of great concern if Snort were monitoring hosts behind a firewall that did not allow inbound Telnet access.

Unknown Traffic

An Unknown Traffic alert signifies that a potentially unusual event has been detected, but further investigation is required. Similar to the Not Suspicious Traffic genre of alerts, you should take the context in which these alerts are generated to determine the appropriate action. The following rule generates alerts when a Web server denies access to a requesting party. This familiar alert occurs when a person attempts to access a resource that he is not permitted to access, or any number of other access control violations.

```
alert tcp $EXTERNAL_NET 80 -> $HOME_NET any
(msg:"INFO Connection Closed MSG from Port 80";
content:"Connection closed by foreign host"; nocase;
flow:from_server,established; classtype:unknown;)
```

Potentially Bad Traffic

This category of rule encompasses traffic that is definitely out of the ordinary, and is potentially indicative of a compromised system. Attack response rules fall into this category. Take this directory listing rule for example:

```
alert tcp $HTTP_SERVERS $HTTP_PORTS -> $EXTERNAL_NET any
(msg:"ATTACK RESPONSES http dir listing";
content: "Volume Serial Number"; flow:from_server,established;
classtype:bad-unknown;)
```

Alerts generated by this rule signify that "Volume Serial Number" content has been detected coming from a Web server. This type of content is usually detected when an attacker is able to execute commands and pass the output through a Web server. Attackers can do this by escaping out of the Web server document root and accessing system commands (usually via cmd.exe). Attackers often test to see whether a malicious attack is possible by attempting a directory listing. This rule detects such activity and classifies it as Potentially Bad Traffic. Another example of Potentially Bad Traffic is a TFTP Get signature:

```
alert udp $EXTERNAL_NET any -> $HOME_NET 69
(msg:"TFTP Get"; content:"|00 01|"; offset:0; depth:2;
classtype:bad-unknown; sid:1444; rev:2;)
```

This rule detects a request to download a file from a TFTP server. An attacker often sets up a TFTP server to distribute Trojans, rootkits, sniffers, and other malicious tools to a compromised host. Like the directory listing rule, this signature can indicate a potentially compromised host.

Attempted Information Leak

The Attempted Information Leak rule deals with signatures from potentially damaging information gathering attempts. Information leaks or reconnaissance attacks that are classified as Attempted Information Leaks are not proof positive that an information gathering attempt has been successful. Rather, they are a signal that an attempt has been made—that if the right conditions exist, sensitive information that could aid the attacker in compromising a system has been released.

It is indeed possible for Attempted Information Leaks to trigger on successful information gathering attempts. Take the Netbios null session rule:

```
alert tcp $EXTERNAL_NET any -> $HOME_NET 139
(msg:"NETBIOS NT NULL session"; flow:to_server,established;

content: "|00 00 00 00 57 00 69 00 6E 00 64 00 6F 00 77 00 73 00 20 00 4E
00 54 00 20 00 31 00 33 00 38 00 31|"; classtype:attempted-recon;)
```

This rule triggers when an attacker has attempted to enumerate users and other system information via an anonymous connection. This alert originating at an untrusted source could indicate that sensitive information has been disclosed. Other Attempted Information Leaks are generated by applications that can be identified by a specific signature. One example of such a rule is the CyberCop OS probe, which follows:

```
alert tcp $EXTERNAL_NET any -> $HOME_NET 80
(msg:"SCAN cybercop os probe"; flags: SF12;
dsize: 0; classtype:attempted-recon;)
```

Attempted Denial of Service

The Attempted Denial of Service rule category encompasses all rules that detect DoS attacks. Rules that detect somewhat antiquated but relevant DoS attacks are included in this classification. An echo/chargen attack is an example:

```
alert udp any 19 <> any 7
(msg:"DOS UDP echo+chargen bomb"; classtype:attempted-dos;)
```

The denial of service condition that is detected by this signature is an echo/chargen service infinite loop. In this DoS attack, spoofed packets are used to start a infiniate loop to <rewrite>.

Other Attempted Denial of Service rules detect exceptional or unusual input delivered by an attacker with the intent to disable a system or service. By their nature, exceptional and unusual input conditions are often overlooked by application designers and open opportunities for exploitation. The Microsoft FTP STAT globbing DoS is an example of such an attack. The following rule detects a STAT globbing attempt, which may indicate a DoS attack.

```
alert tcp $EXTERNAL_NET any -> $HOME_NET 21
(msg:"FTP EXPLOIT STAT * dos attempt"; flow:to_server,established;
content:"STAT "; nocase; content:"*"; classtype:attempted-dos;)
```

When an attacker appends an unusual number of file globbing characters (*,?, and so on) to a STAT command on a Microsoft FTP server, unpatched versions of the FTP server will crash.

Other Attempted Denial of Service rules are created to detect distributed denial of service (DDoS) attacks. DDoS attacks utilize a large number of compromised hosts to flood a target host with requests. Some tools that are used to perpetrate a DDoS attack have a specific signature that a Snort rule can detect, which would indicate that a host on your network may be compromised and used in a DDoS attack. An example is a SYN flood originating from the shaft DDoS tool.

```
alert tcp $HOME_NET any <> $EXTERNAL_NET any
(msg:"DDOS shaft synflood"; flags: S; seq: 674711609; classtype:attempted-dos;)
```

As you can see, the shaft programmer was lazy and used the same TCP sequence number for every packet when executing a SYN flood. Therefore simply monitoring for a sequence number of 6747116909 detects it.

Attempted User Privilege Gain

The Attempted User Privilege Gain category of rule monitors for attackers trying to elevate privileges to an unauthorized level. An attacker who has access to a user account can make use of various types of system vulnerabilities to elevate her privileges and access data for which she is not authorized.

An example is the modification of the .rhosts file to allow global access rights, effectively removing access control for specific situations on the affected hosts. This Snort rule detects such Attempted User Privilege Gain activity:

```
alert tcp $EXTERNAL_NET any -> $HOME_NET 514
(msg:"RSERVICES rsh echo + +"; flow:to_server,established;
content: "echo |22|+ +|22|"; classtype:attempted-user;)
```

Attempted User Privilege Gains can occur in applications as well. Databases have traditionally been targets for privilege escalation. Users may have access to one type of data, but may desire confidential data stored in the same database or on the same host. Additionally, privilege gain can be used to take control of the host if the user is able to gain superuser or root-level access to the database. These functions often have access to external programs that can be used to fully compromise and control the target. One rule that monitors for such Attempted User Privilege Gain attacks is the xp_cmdshell rule for Microsoft SQL Servers:

```
alert tcp $EXTERNAL_NET any -> $SQL_SERVERS 1433
(msg:"MS-SQL xp_cmdshell - program execution"; content:
"x|00|p|00|_|00|c|00|m|00|d|00|s|00|h|00|e|00|l|00|l|00|";
nocase; flow:to_server,established; classtype:attempted-user;)
```

Xp_cmdshell can be used to execute system commands from the SQL server. The attacker can use xp_cmdshell to fetch Trojans, distribute confidential data, or perform any other task that can be executed from a Windows command line. This rule detects an xp_cmdshell attempt targeted against a Microsoft SQL Server.

Unsuccessful User Privilege Gain

The Unsuccessful User Privilege Gain rules detect privilege escalation attempts that have failed. This can indicate that an attacker is intentionally attempting to elevate privileges and is failing, and that unsuspecting users are unknowingly aiding in a system compromise.

Failed logon attempts make up the majority of Unsuccessful User Privilege Gain alerts. Determining whether the alert is a false positive requires investigation into the source and situation in which the alert was discovered. A good sign that something malicious is occurring is a large number of unsuccessful authentication attempts. An unusual number of attempts can indicate that an attacker is attempting a brute force method of attack. An example of an Unsuccessful User Privilege Gain rule is the PCAnywhere Failed Login rule, as shown:

```
alert tcp $HOME_NET 5631:5632 -> $EXTERNAL_NET any
(msg:"MISC PCAnywhere Failed Login"; flow:from_server,established;
content:"Invalid login"; depth: 16; classtype:unsuccessful-user;)
```

This rule detects failed login attempts to PCAnywhere, a software package used to remotely control and administer hosts.

In other situations, users can be tricked into passing authentication information or be fooled into executing code that would compromise their computers. These types of attacks, such as the attempted Netscape Browser buffer overflow shown here, can be used to escalate privileges:

```
alert tcp $HOME_NET any -> $EXTERNAL_NET 80
(msg:"EXPLOIT netscape unsucessful overflow";
content: "|33 C9 B1 10 3F E9 06 51 3C FA 47 33 C0 50 F7 D0 50|";
flow:to_server,established; classtype:unsuccessful-user;)
```

This rule triggers when a user accesses a Web page that contains a buffer overflow specific to the Netscape browser. This overflow is not functional, but the malicious Web site owner has no way to tell which type of browser will be accessing the page.

Attempted Administrator Privilege Gain

Much like the Attempted User Privilege Gain category of rule, the Attempted Administrator Privilege Gain classification detects privilege escalation attempts that would result in superuser-, root-, or administrator-level access to a host. Attempted Administrator Privilege Gain alerts are not proof positive that an attacker has administrator-level access; rather they signal that privilege escalation may have occurred.

Attempted Administrator Privilege Gain rules detect attempts to access superuser-level resources as well as exploits that attempt to compromise a host and deliver root-level access to the attacker. An attempted access to the ADMIN$ share on Windows system is a good example of an attempt to access a superuser-level resource:

```
alert tcp $EXTERNAL_NET any -> $HOME_NET 139
(msg:"NETBIOS SMB ADMIN$ access"; flow:to_server,established;
content:"\\ADMIN$|00 41 3a 00|"; classtype:attempted-admin;)
```

If an attacker can access the $ADMIN share he can gain control access to the
c:\winnt\ directory of the host Windows system. This directory contains the OS files
and an abundance of other sensitive data.

Other Attempted Administrator Privilege Gain rules detect an attacker attempting to
make use of an exploit against a known vulnerability. One example is the bftpd SITE
CHOWN overflow rule:

```
alert tcp $EXTERNAL_NET any -> $HOME_NET 21
(msg:"FTP SITE CHOWN overflow"; flow:to_server,established,no_stream;
dsize:>100; content:"SITE CHOWN "; nocase; classtype:attempted-admin;)
```

This rule detects an overly long SITE CHOWN command, which could allow an
attacker to execute unauthorized commands with the superuser's context on the target
system.

Successful Administrator Privilege Gain

An alert from a Successful Administrator Privilege Gain rule indicates that there is a
high probability that an attacker has managed to compromise a host with superuser-level
access. Rules that typically make up this classification include signatures of completed
attacks and suspicious file transfers that contain superuser authentication information.

The rule used to detect when the BSD Telnet daemon exploit finishes is an example
of a Successful Administrator Privilege Gain rule:

```
alert tcp $EXTERNAL_NET any -> $TELNET_SERVERS 23
(msg:"TELNET bsd exploit client finishing"; flow:to_client,established;
dsize:>200; content:"|FF F6 FF F6 FF FB 08 FF F6|"; offset:200; depth:50;
classtype:successful-admin;)
```

An example of a file transfer containing superuser-level authentication information
that is likely to indicate a compromised host is the successful transfer of a passwd file
via TFTP:

```
alert udp any any -> any 69 (msg:"TFTP GET passwd";
content: "|0001|"; offset:0; depth:2; content:"passwd";
nocase; classtype:successful-admin;)
```

The transfer of the Unix passwd file should never occur over a protocol as insecure
as TFTP, which neither requires authentication or supports encryption. An alert from this
rule could indicate that an attacker could gain control of the authentication information
for the root account or other important user accounts.

Index

E

echo command, 239
elements, 28
email, sending alerts, 317
email keyword, 309
enabling preprocessors, 300
encrypted traffic, 211
encrypting syslog-ng, Stunnel, 247-248
equality operator (=), 181
errors. *See also* troubleshooting
    acid_conf.php file, 316
    ADODB, 316
    rules files, 315
ethernet networks, 23
event correlation, 32
exactly operator, 182
exec command, 239
external network connections, 74-76
external security, 8-9
external threats, information resources, 8-9
EXTERNAL_NET variable, 156, 212
$EXTERNAL_NET variables, 299

F

-f unified.snort.file command line, 169
facility command, 65
false negatives, 2, 207
false positives, 2, 207-208
    intrusion prevention, 294
    min_ttl, 216
    rules without, 296-297
    Snort, 39-40
    ttl_limit, 216
    zero, 302
field data alerts, 180
[filename] output file, 63
files
    acid_conf.php, errors, 316
    barnyard.conf, configuring, 167-169
    chat.rules, 221
    classification.config, 236-237
    config.php, 285
    ddos.rules, 221

ftp.rules, 221
.htaccess, 131-133
httpd.conf, 198
icmp-info.rules, 222
info.rules, 222
misc.rules, 222
multimedia.rules, 222
other-ids.rules, 222
p2p.rules, 222
policy.rules, 223
porn.rules, 223
.rules, 221
rules, errors, 315
shellcode.rules, 223
snort.conf, 290-291
    configuring, 155-165
    setup, 315
snortsam.conf, 306
.swatchrc, 239-240
syslog-ng.conf, 243-245
virus.rules, 223
filter directive, 167
filtering traffic, 211-213
FIN flags, 71
firewall configuration
    sensor installation, 144
    server installation, 106
firewalls
    BlackIce, 204
    sensors external to, 74-75
    sensors internal to, 75
first tier architecture, 35-37
flags
    FIN, 71
    SYN, 71
    TCP, 180
flags keyword, 265
flexibility, Snort, 38-39
flow keyword, 260-261
fnord preprocessor, 57-58, 162, 213
frag2 preprocessor, 46, 160, 214-217
    detect_state_problems command, 48
    memcap bytes command, 47
    min_ttl number command, 48
    timeout seconds command, 47
    ttl_limit number command, 48

fragbits keyword, 263
fragmentation
    ARPspoof preprocessor, 56-57
    ASN1_decode preprocessor, 57
    BO preprocessor, 55
    conversation preprocessor, 58-59
    fnord preprocessor, 57-58
    frag2 preprocessor, 46-48
    HTTP_decode preprocessor, 52-54
    portscan2 preprocessor, 59-60
    RPC_decode preprocessor, 54
    SPADE preprocessor, 60-61
    stream4 preprocessor, 49-51
    stream4_reassemble preprocessor, 51-52
    Telnet_decode preprocessor, 55
fragmentation tools, fragroute, 214-217
fragoffset keyword, 264
fragroute tool, 47, 214-217
ftp.rules file, 221
full_whitespace command, 54
fwexec keyword, 309
fwsam keyword, 309-310

G-H

-g /path/to/gen-msg.map command line, 169
gathering security event information, 85-86
gd, installing, 125-126

-h command line, 169
hackers, orchestrating attacks, 4, 10
    access, 18-19
    attack phase, 15
    backdoors, 17-18
    black hats, 12-14
    DoS attacks, 15-16
    IP addresses, 12-14
    planning phase, 11
    post-attack phase, 19
    reconnaissance phase, 11

How can we make this index more useful? Email us at indexes@samspublishing.com